THE PUNDITS

For Penny

THE PUNDITS

British Exploration of Tibet and Central Asia

DEREK WALLER

THE UNIVERSITY PRESS OF KENTUCKY

Publication of this volume was made possible in part
by a grant from the National Endowment for the Humanities.

Copyright © 1990 by The University Press of Kentucky
Paperback edition 2004

The University Press of Kentucky
Scholarly publisher for the Commonwealth,
serving Bellarmine University, Berea College, Centre
College of Kentucky, Eastern Kentucky University,
The Filson Historical Society, Georgetown College,
Kentucky Historical Society, Kentucky State University,
Morehead State University, Murray State University,
Northern Kentucky University, Transylvania University,
University of Kentucky, University of Louisville,
and Western Kentucky University.
All rights reserved.

Editorial and Sales Offices: The University Press of Kentucky
663 South Limestone Street, Lexington, Kentucky 40508-4008
www.kentuckypress.com

Maps in this book were created by Lawrence Brence.
Relief rendering from *The New International Atlas* © 1988
by Rand McNally & Co., R.L. 88-S-194.

The Library of Congress has cataloged the hardcover edition as follows:

Waller, Derek J.
    The Pundits : British exploration of Tibet and Central Asia / Derek Waller.
        p.   cm.
    Includes bibliographical references.
    ISBN 0-8131-1666-X (alk. paper)
    1. Asia, Central—Description and travel. 2. Tibet (China)—Description and travel. I. Title.
DS327.7.W35   1990
958'.03—dc20   90-32802
                                                      CIP

Paper ISBN 0-8131-9100-9

This book is printed on acid-free recycled paper meeting
the requirements of the American National Standard
for Permanence in Paper for Printed Library Materials.

Manufactured in the United States of America.

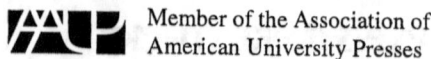

Member of the Association of
American University Presses

Contents

    List of Maps   vi
    Preface   vii
1. The Great Trigonometrical Survey of India   1
2. First Attempts: Abdul Hamid and Nain Singh   33
3. Across the Northwest Frontier: The Mirza, the Havildar, and the Mullah   54
4. To Tibet and Beyond: The Singh Family   99
5. The Forsyth Missions to Yarkand and Kashgar   144
6. Around Everest and Kanchenjunga: Hari Ram and Rinzing Namgyal   169
7. "A Hardy Son of Soft Bengal"   193
8. The Tsangpo-Brahmaputra Controversy: Lala, Nem Singh, and Kintup   214
9. Questions of Secrecy   248
10. Conclusion   267
    Notes   274
    Bibliography   304
    Note on Map Sources   316
    Index   317
    Illustrations follow page 136

Maps

1. Abdul Hamid, 1863-64; Nain Singh, 1865-66   36
2. The Mirza, 1868-69; The Havildar, 1870, 1873-75   68
3. The Mullah, 1873-74, 1875-76, 1878   96
4. Nain, Kalian, and Mani Singh, 1867; Kalian Singh, 1868; Kishen Singh, 1871-72; Nain Singh, 1874-75   106
5. Kishen Singh, 1878-82   128
6. Forsyth Mission, 1873-74; Abdul Subhan, 1874; M.S., 1878-81   152
7. Hari Ram, 1871-72, 1873, 1885-86   180
8. Sarat Chandra Das and Ugyen Gyatso, 1879   198
9. Lala, 1875-76; Nem Singh and Kintup, 1878-79; Kintup, 1880-84; Rinzing Namgyal and Phurba, 1885-86   218

Preface

I first became aware of the activities of the pundits in the course of relatively casual reading about the history and politics of Tibet. I discovered that many authors had referred, but only rather briefly, to their exploits. This book will, I hope, go some way toward assigning to these Indian explorers, and to the British officers of the Great Trigonometrical Survey of India, their rightful place in the history of the exploration of Tibet and Central Asia.

A number of libraries and archives have been vital in supplying material for this book. I should like to give particular thanks to the staff of the India Office Library and Records; the Jean and Alexander Heard Library of Vanderbilt University; the Library and Archives of the Royal Geographical Society; and the British Library. I am also pleased to acknowledge assistance from the library of the University of Leeds, the archives of the Royal Society, Cambridge University Library, and the Public Records Office.

The staff of the National Archives of India in New Delhi were helpful in allowing me to see many volumes in the Dehra Dun series of the Survey of India Records. Unfortunately, the government of India does not permit inspection of all the volumes in this series (or, at least, it did not when I visited the archives in 1981).

The fifth and final volume of Colonel R.H. Phillimore's *Historical Records of the Survey of India, 1844-1861* (Dehra Dun, 1968) is a difficult book to come by. The work was apparently never actually issued, and only a few copies, which were sent out in advance of publication, are known to be extant. I must therefore express my gratitude to the Royal Engineers Corps Library at Brompton Barracks, Chatham, who kindly made a copy of volume five available to me.

A number of people were generous in their comments on various sections of the manuscript. For their assistance, I am indebted to Gary Alder (who also provided me with copies of some documents), Felicity Browne, Scott Colley, Faith Evans, Peter Hopkirk, and Nicholas Rhodes. In addition to commenting on the manuscript, Nicholas and Deki Rhodes also provided a great deal of information concerning Rinzing Namgyal and Ugyen Gyatso and gave me illustrative material on these two explorers, some of which is reproduced in the text. I also thank Henry Brownrigg of London, owner of the surveying instrument inscribed to Nain Singh, for allowing it to be photographed.

A grant enabling me to travel to New Delhi was given by the University Research Council of Vanderbilt University, and financial assistance toward publication was provided by the Graduate School of the University. I am more than happy to acknowledge both awards.

I am also indebted in other ways to Howard Boorman, the late Forrestt Miller, Bert Pullen, David Snellgrove, and Hugh Tinker. Special thanks to Tommye Corlew, who uncomplainingly deciphered my handwriting, typed, retyped, and typed again.

ONE
The Great Trigonometrical Survey of India

On a September day in 1863, a Moslem named Abdul Hamid entered the Central Asian city of Yarkand. Disguised as a merchant, Hamid was actually an employee of the Survey of India, carrying concealed instruments to enable him to map the geography of the area. Hamid did not live to provide a firsthand account of his travels. Nevertheless, he was the advance guard of an elite group of Indian trans-Himalayan explorers—recruited, trained, and directed by the officers of the Great Trigonometrical Survey of India—who were to traverse much of Tibet and Central Asia during the next thirty years.

In the public documents of the Survey of India, these men came to be called "pundits" or "native explorers," but in the closed files of the government of British India, they were given their true designation as spies or secret agents. The use of these agents was sanctioned in the 1860s only after the closing of the borders of Tibet to foreigners, the deaths of several European explorers in Central Asia, the unwillingness and inability of the Chinese authorities to make provision for British travelers, and decades of reluctance by the government of India to allow technically qualified Indians to survey beyond the frontier.

As they moved northward within the Indian subcontinent, the British demanded precise frontiers and sought orderly political and economic relationships with their neighbors. The British were also becoming increasingly aware of and concerned by their ignorance of the geographical, political, and military complexion of the territories beyond the mountain frontiers of the Indian empire. This was particularly true in the case of Tibet. Tibet was certainly the highest, and arguably the most remote and inaccessible, country in the world. The deserts of Turkestan spread to the north, and on the south and west stretched the vast ranges of the Himalayan chain. These could be crossed, but with difficulty, as even the passes were at altitudes in excess of 16,000 feet. To the east, Tibet could be entered from China but only by crossing serried ridges of mountains, running in a north-south direction. Very little was known of the country's geography, not even the exact position of its capital, Lhasa. There was speculation as to the route of the Tsangpo, its major river, and whether the Tsangpo flowed into India as the Brahmaputra or the Irrawaddy. The true sources of the Tsangpo and Indus rivers were still unknown. The best available map was one made on the basis of measurements taken by two Tibetan lamas—trained as surveyors by Jesuits in Peking—and drawn up in 1717.

The British were, however, by no means completely ignorant about Tibet. "They . . . make handsome cups out of the heads of their [dead] parents, so that when drinking out of them they may have them in mind in the midst of their merrymaking. This was told me by one who had seen it."[1] So wrote Friar William of Rubruck in the narrative of his mission to the Mongols in the mid-thirteenth century, thus providing to the Western world one of the first intriguing glimpses of life in Tibet.

The following century, another Franciscan, Friar Odoric of Pordenone, journeyed to Peking and then returned to Europe through Central Asia. Although it is unlikely that he visited Lhasa as he claimed, he did meet people who had been there, and he returned home in 1330 with the first substantial knowledge of Tibet. It was to be almost three hundred years before European visitors were actually to enter Tibet and return with a more reliable description.[2]

The Portuguese had set up a base at Goa on the Indian coast in 1510, which was followed later in the sixteenth century by a Jesuit mission to the Moghul court at Agra, near Delhi. It was probably there that the Jesuit father Antonio de Andrade learned of the journeys of two travelers in the lands to the north. The first of these was a Portuguese merchant named Diogo de Almeida who visited Ladakh around 1600, and when he arrived in Goa in 1603, he reported a Christian community apparently surviving there.[3] The second journey was that made by a fellow Jesuit, Benedict Goes, who started out from Agra in 1602 in search of lost Christian communities in Cathay, a country thought by many at that time to be separate from China. Goes passed through Kabul and Badakhshan and crossed the Pamir to Chinese Turkestan, before dying in China in 1607.[4] His Armenian traveling companion succeeded in making his way to Peking, giving details of Goes' adventures to the Catholic mission there.

Goes had solved one problem by showing that China and Cathay were one and the same. But reports of Christian rituals being practiced in Tibet tantalized the curiosity and imagination of Andrade, who set off from Agra in 1624 in the company of Manuel Marques, a lay brother of the mission. The two crossed the Mana pass over the Himalayas into the western Tibetan province of Guge and were well received at its capital, Tsaparang. There they stayed for three weeks before returning to Agra the same year.[5] The following year Andrade, Marques, and another father were back in Tsaparang building a permanent mission. More Jesuits followed, and excursions were made to other parts of western Tibet, including the town of Rudok. The Tsaparang mission flourished in a small way, but eventually the religious practices of the Jesuits aroused the wrath of the lamas, who incited the population against them. The mission lost its leader in 1630 when Andrade was recalled to Goa, where he died in 1634. When the friendly king of Guge was overthrown from Ladakh, a Father Francisco Azevedo was sent, without success, to seek help from the king of Ladakh. Azevedo did, however, provide some of the first insights into life in the Ladakhi capital of Leh.[6] The Tsaparang mission was eventually closed in 1635, and an attempt to reopen it in 1640 failed. In its ten years of life, it was never able to acquire more than one hundred converts. Andrade, however, wrote a letter detailing some of his experiences in Tibet, which was published in Portuguese as a small book in Lisbon in 1626 and was subsequently published in other European languages.[7]

While at Tsaparang, Andrade had become aware of the kingdom of Utsang to the southeast and of its capital Shigatse. He urged that a mission be established there. In 1626, the Portuguese Jesuit fathers John Cabral and Stephen Cacella (who had been part of the Tsaparang mission) set out for Shigatse. After an arduous journey via Bhutan (a country which they were the first Europeans to enter), they were warmly received in Shigatse and provided with a church. Cabral returned to India in 1628 through Nepal, and Cacella followed him early in 1629. Cacella soon set out to return to Shigatse, this time accompanied by Father Manuel Diaz. Alas, Diaz succumbed on the way. Cacella reached Shigatse, but died there in March 1630, shortly after his arrival. Father Cabral returned alone to man the mission, arriving in Shigatse in June 1631. Although he was well treated there and had good contact with the lamas at the great Tashilhunpo monastery nearby, no contact was permitted with the Tsaparang mission. Eventually the Church authorities decided, because of difficulties of communication, against the continued existence of the Shigatse mission, and by 1632 Cabral was back in India.[8] With the closure of the Tsaparang mission three years later, missionary work in Tibet ceased and was not to be resumed until the next century.

This did not mean, however, that Tibet was completely unvisited by Europeans. In 1661, two more Jesuits entered Tibet and reached Lhasa, the first Europeans to do so. They were the Austrian John Grueber and the Belgian Albert d'Orville. The two traveled not from India, but from Peking via Sining and Koko Nor. Their objective was to reach India by the overland route, the usual sea routes now being controlled by the Dutch. The two fathers resided briefly in Lhasa in October 1661, before proceeding on through Kathmandu to Agra. There, in the spring of the following year, d'Orville died. Grueber continued on to Rome, and although he never returned to Tibet, he was the first to provide Europe with an eyewitness description of Lhasa (including a drawing of the Potala palace) and a brief account of Tibetan life, as published by the German scholar Athanasius Kircher in 1667.[9] Armenians and Muscovites were also well known as trading in Tibet at that time, and there was a resident community of Ladakhi Moslems and Nepalese in Lhasa.

After the departure of Grueber and d'Orville, no more priests were dispatched to Tibet until early in the following century. By that time, jurisdiction over missionary work in Tibet had been placed in the hands of the Capuchins, who maintained a small presence in Lhasa from 1707 to 1711.[10] Seemingly unaware of these developments, the Jesuits were marshaling their own resources to reestablish themselves north of the Himalayas in Ladakh and try to make contact with any remaining converts at Tsaparang. Although this idea was first put forward in about 1704,[11] it was not until 1713 that the man selected to accomplish this goal, the Italian Jesuit Ippolito Desideri, arrived in India from Genoa. At Agra, he met up with his superior, the Portuguese Father Manuel Freyre. They left for Tibet in 1714.

The two fathers traveled first to Srinagar in Kashmir, where they spent the winter, and then continued on to Leh in Ladakh. The journey to Leh was awful. Desideri wrote the following year in a letter from Tibet that "much snow had fallen on the path, which winds between mountains as far as Leh, or Ladak, the fortress where the King resides, which are the very picture of desolation, horror and death itself. They are piled one atop of another, and so close as scarcely to leave room for the torrents which course impetuously from their heights, and dash with such deafening noise against the rocks as to appal the stoutest traveller . . . I assure you that I shudder now at the bare remembrance of these dreadful episodes in our journey."[12]

Desideri believed that there were just two Tibets, "Little Tibet," or Baltistan, and "Great Tibet," or Ladakh. It was only in Leh that he and Freyre learned of the existence of a "third Tibet" to the south and east of Ladakh. Desideri was in favor of remaining in Leh laboring "towards the salvation of men's souls," but was overruled by Freyre, who insisted that they continue on to Lhasa. Freyre, who wanted to leave all the Tibets as rapidly as possible, chose this route as the easiest passage back to India. He was unwilling to return by the way they had come and unable to take the shorter route through Garhwal because of reports of brigands. The two continued, "against my wish," says Desideri, reaching the capital on 18 March 1716.[13] On their way, they became the first Europeans to see the holy Mount Kailas. They also passed through Gartok but made no attempt to make the short detour to Tsaparang, as they were ignorant of its location.[14] That proceeding to Lhasa might provoke a problem with the Capuchins there did not concern Freyre, for having arrived there, he remained for only a few weeks before leaving for India.[15] In any case, as late as 1713, the Jesuit order was still unaware that Tibet had been assigned to the Capuchins.[16]

Desideri remained, the only European in Lhasa. But not for long, as a group of three Capuchin monks appeared in October to reopen their monastery. Their arrival immediately triggered a jurisdictional dispute with the Jesuits. The matter was referred to Rome, and the decision was made in 1718 in favor of the Capuchins. Communications being what they were, however, Desideri was able to reside in Lhasa for five important years, in the course of which he witnessed the imposition of Chinese authority over Tibet in 1720.

At the time of the establishment of the Qing (or Manchu) dynasty in China in 1644, Lhasa was ruled by Mongols from the Koko Nor area. They built up the Dalai Lama as a religious power, and it was the Dalai Lama who also began to assume secular authority following the death of the Mongol leader in 1655. His policies were generally in accordance with those of the Qing, particularly the policy of keeping a rein on the hostile Dzungarian Mongols of the Ili region. But with the demise of the Dalai Lama in 1682, a complex dispute arose around the question of his successor, intertwined with the possibility of a Mongol reunification under Tibetan auspices threatening the power of the Qing emperor. In 1717 the Dzungarian Mongols invaded Tibet. At first welcoming the invaders, the population soon turned against them and sought assistance from the Chinese in expelling them. The Emperor Kangxi was only too happy to oblige and sent an army to Tibet, which was roundly defeated by the Mongols in 1718. A second, larger Chinese force was more successful and occupied Lhasa in 1720. The Chinese army was warmly received as the savior from the Mongols and the restorer of the new Dalai Lama to his rightful position. The foundation of Chinese suzerainty over Tibet had been laid in a masterful manner, and with the cooperation of the Tibetans themselves.[17]

The three Capuchin monks who arrived in Lhasa in 1716 to reopen their mission included Orazio della Penna and Domenico da Fano. Dogged by the hostility of the lamas and by poor health, the Capuchin mission made few converts. It closed again in 1733, was reestablished in 1741, and closed for good when the remaining monks were expelled by the Chinese in 1745.

One foreign traveler to Tibet at the time of the Capuchins was a Dutch merchant-adventurer named Samuel Van der Putte. In the course of making a return journey from India to China, he passed through Lhasa twice, in 1718 and again in 1730, staying with the Capuchins on both occasions. Regrettably, he left little in the way of a record of his travels; all his records were burned, at his own request, as he lay dying in Batavia (modern Jakarta).[18]

The Catholic missionaries, however, had by the mid-eighteenth century built up a fairly substantial body of information on Tibet. Some of this appeared in the work of the French geographer Jean Baptiste du Halde (1674-1743), who published the first edition of his geography of China in Paris in 1735.[19] An English-language version appeared the following year, published in London.[20] The account of Tibet in du Halde's work was very general, and much of it dealt with the map of Tibet printed in the atlas produced by d'Anville in 1737 and issued as a complement to du Halde's geography.[21] French Jesuit missionaries in Peking, acting on instructions from the Emperor Kangxi, had completed the map twenty years earlier, from material provided to them by lamas whom they had trained to survey Tibet. This map remained the best available until improved on by the work of the pundits of the Survey of India in the latter half of the next century.

Less than a decade after d'Anville's map appeared, Thomas Astley began to publish his monumental *Voyages and Travels,* the fourth volume of which contained a valuable description of Tibet, including information on its geography, economy, religion, and government, derived from the work of earlier travelers.[22] This description also reproduced a number of the drawings made by Grueber, including his picture of the Potala.[23]

The contribution by Grueber gave details of the route he and d'Orville followed to and from Lhasa and touched on some of the more exotic customs he perceived among the Tibetans. "They have a most cruel custom in these kingdoms; for when they judge their sick people to be past hopes of recovery, they carry them into the fields, and casting them into deep ditches full of dead corpses, there leave them to perish, and their bodies, when dead, to be devoured by birds and beasts of prey, esteeming it an honour to have living creatures for their tombs."[24] There are substantial citations in the footnotes which referenced the material available on Tibet at the time. Astley also included some account of the travels of the Jesuit and Capuchin missionaries, from Andrade to della Penna.[25]

The next compendium of material to appear on Tibet was the *Alphabetum Tibetanum,* authored by Giorgi, published in Rome in 1762, and compiled from Capuchin reports dispatched from Lhasa.[26] Although a large quarto-sized work of some 900 pages, containing a mass of information, it was not translated from the Latin, and a leading English geographer pointed out that much of the material "is overlaid by a confusing and superfluous mass of erudition and puerile etymologies."[27]

It was the Jesuit Ippolito Desideri who provided "the first accurate general description of Tibet, in all its particulars—the flora, fauna, products of the soil, the inhabitants and their special customs ... made possible by his perfect knowledge of the Tibetan language."[28] Unfortunately, his 633-page manuscript was not discovered until 1875[29]; the bulk of it was published (in Italian) only 1904[30]; and it was not until 1931 that a reasonably complete version appeared in English.[31] Meanwhile, persons interested in Desideri's view of Tibet had to make do with those few of his letters which were available in published form.[32]

Although direct European contact with Tibet came to a halt for almost thirty years with the departure of the last Capuchins, a considerable amount of data on the country, its geography, trade, and customs was now available to those interested enough to search for it. The British, however, had played no role in the acquisition of this material. But with British authority becoming more extensive in India in the latter half of the eighteenth century, it was inevitable that this would change. Clive's victory over the Moghul forces at the battle of Plassey in 1757 soon established British paramountcy in Bengal, over territory extending to the foothills of the Himalayas. There the Tibetans exercised influence beyond their own territorial borders extending from the peoples of Ladakh in the west, through Nepal to Sikkim, Bhutan and Assam, all linked to Tibet by ties of politics, trade, and religion.[33]

The Jesuits and the Capuchins were, above all, missionaries, not geographers or surveyors. And unlike the Jesuits and the Capuchins, the British were interested in trade, not in the propagation of religion. The East India Company viewed trade with Tibet both as desirable for itself, particularly with respect to Tibetan exports of gold and silver, and also as a back door to the lucrative markets of China proper, bypassing the officially sanctioned entry point of Canton.

Unfortunately, this interest on the part of the East India Company coincided with the closing of many of Tibet's doors to the outside world. This occurred partly as a result of the increasing imposition of Chinese authority and partly because of the overthrow, by 1769, of the traditional Newar rulers by the Gurkhas and the establishment of a Hindu kingdom in Nepal. Racial and religious bonds between Tibet and Nepal were broken, and the traditional trade routes through the Nepalese passes between India and Tibet were largely closed. In addition, the Gurkhas did not look kindly upon the British, who had rendered military assistance to the Newars. As a result, the East India Company began to look for alternative routes through Bhutan or Assam which could open Tibet to trade and which did not pass through Nepal.

Warren Hastings had been appointed governor-general of Bengal in 1772. In the same year a crisis in the relations between Bhutan and the small state of Cooch Behar on its southern border resulted in the sending of a British military expedition against Bhutan. The Gurkhas, who may have had designs on Bhutan themselves, encouraged the Tashi Lama of Tibet to write to Hastings on behalf of Bhutan, a state traditionally dependent on Tibet. Hastings, who by 1774 had been elevated to the position of governor-general of India, seized the opportunity to initiate a dialogue with this important Tibetan leader. The Panchen, or Tashi Lama as he was known at the time, derived his name from his position as head of the great monastery of Tashilhunpo, near Shigatse, about 150 miles southwest of Lhasa. The Tashi Lama was second in religious and political importance only to the Dalai Lama in Lhasa. When the Dalai Lama was a minor, deferring to a regent, the Tashi Lama had sufficient prestige to be able to take such an independent initiative as addressing a letter to Warren Hastings.

Hastings responded to the communication with lenient treatment of the Bhutanese and by selecting a twenty-eight-year-old Scot, George Bogle, to represent the East India Company on a mission to Tibet. Bogle, accompanied by Alexander Hamilton, a company physician, left for Tashilhunpo in May 1774. He carried with him a copy of d'Anville's map.[34]

Bogle's objectives were to open trade and communication between British India and Tibet. He was also required to gather basic intelligence on roads and communication between Tibet and its neighbors and relations between Tibet and other states. His mission, although one requiring tact and diplomacy, was primarily commercial.

Proceeding through Bhutan and the Tibetan town of Gyantse, Bogle and Hamilton finally met the Tashi Lama in November 1774. Bogle and the Tashi Lama got along well and became close friends, although Bogle was not permitted to visit Lhasa, by order of the regent. Bogle stayed in Tibet until April 1775. The Tashi Lama agreed to Bogle's proposals concerning trade between the company and Tibet, but pointed out the suspicions about British intentions harbored by the regent and the Chinese authorities in Lhasa.

The thin link between Britain and Tibet depended very much on the authority and personality of the Tashi Lama, and it was upon him that Hastings pinned his hopes for more stability in the area around Bhutan, increased trade through Bhutan to Tibet, and the possibility of intercession with the emperor in Peking to generate an overall improvement in Anglo-Chinese trade.

Because of the delicacy of the situation involving Tashilhunpo, Lhasa, and Bengal, it was not until 1779 that Hastings readied Bogle for a second mission. Bogle then learned that the Tashi Lama had left for China. His journey was first postponed and then canceled when news arrived that the Tashi Lama had died of smallpox in Peking in 1780. Bogle himself died of cholera in Calcutta the following year, aged thirty-four.

Bogle was the first Englishman to penetrate the Himalayas to Tibet. His report showed that Tibet exported gold, salt, yak tails, and woolen cloth. Fine wool for "cashmere" shawls was sent to Kashmir. It was also known that Tibet exported borax and imported large quantities of Chinese tea, although these were not mentioned in the report. Bogle also discussed Tibetan imports of iron, fruit, spices, silk, rice, coral, and broadcloth. The bulk of Tibetan trade was with China, but there was also considerable commercial activity to the south, through traditional trade routes to Nepal, India, Bhutan, and Assam.[35]

Bogle's narrative of his travels was not published for a century. He was apparently negotiating with a publisher when he died.[36] It was not until 1876 that Clements Markham, of the Geographical Department of the India Office, acquired the papers from the Bogle family and produced the book, *Narratives of the Mission of George Bogle to Tibet, and of the Journey of Thomas Manning to Lhasa*. Markham did not mention that Bogle married a Tibetan, possibly a sister of the Tashi Lama, and that they had two daughters.[37]

Despite the deaths of Bogle and the Tashi Lama, Hastings pressed on, selecting Samuel Turner, a relative of his and a lieutenant in the army of the East India Company, as his next emissary. Turner left India in 1783 and returned in 1784 after a friendly visit to Tashilhunpo, where he met the regent to the infant reincarnation of the Tashi Lama.[38] Trade with Tibet did increase as a result of the Turner mission, but only briefly, as external political events resulted in Tibet's doors firmly closing to Europeans.

Nepal invaded Tibet in 1788 in search of the treasure housed by wealthy monasteries. Unable to oppose them, the Tibetans sued for peace and promised to pay an indemnity. The Gurkhas then withdrew, but not before Tashilhunpo had appealed for help to Lord Cornwallis, who had replaced Hastings as governor-general in 1785. Cornwallis declined, promising only that he would not assist the Gurkhas. The Gurkhas invaded again in 1791, on the grounds that Tibet had not fulfilled the agreement over the indemnity. Shigatse was captured and Tashilhunpo was sacked. A strong Chinese army then entered Tibet and defeated the troops withdrawing to Nepal. Now it was the turn of the Gurkhas to request aid from the British. Cornwallis again refused, though he offered to provide mediation, which aroused the suspicions of the Tibetans and angered the Gurkhas. Cornwallis had succeeded only in alienating all three parties—Tibetan, Chinese, and Gurkha. A large Chinese army now occupied the most populous part of Tibet, and Britain was not to regain its influence there until the twentieth century. The Chinese Emperor Qian Long closed the frontiers of Tibet to the outside world, thus imposing on Tibet an exclusionary policy similar to that already enforced for China proper, one which kept nearly all foreigners away by restricting trade only to the port of Canton. The Tibetans agreed. They had been angered by the lack of British assistance against the Gurkhas and were alarmed by the spread of British power along the foothills of the Himalayas. The Chinese also insinuated to the Tibetans that Britain had actually helped the Gurkhas and, fearing for their own position, encouraged the Tibetans in their suspicions of the outside world, suggesting that the Europeans might wish to replace Buddhism with Christianity. This exclusionary policy continued to be in effect throughout the nineteenth century. Apart from the eccentric British traveler Thomas Manning, no Englishman (and few other Europeans) reached the Tibetan capital until the twentieth century and the Younghusband military expedition of 1904. Manning, who wandered into Lhasa in 1811, was the first Englishman ever to see the city. He was the last for almost a hundred years. However, Manning returned from Tibet in 1812 with little substantial information, and few were aware of his journey until his narrative was published by Markham in 1876.[39] The only other Europeans who succeeded in seeing Lhasa during the nineteenth century were two French Lazarist priests, Evariste Huc and Joseph Gabet, who arrived there from Peking in 1846. They remained in Lhasa for several weeks before being expelled by the Chinese authorities and returning to China.

The closing of the borders stimulated British interest in Tibet. As the nineteenth century progressed, curiosity increased with the occupation of territory along the Tibetan border, acquired as a result of the deteriorating relations with Nepal. With the Chinese firmly in control of Tibet and closing its borders to Bengal, the East India Company looked initially to revive the trade routes to Tibet through Nepal. This was despite the failure of the mission of Captain William Kirkpatrick, who had been sent to mediate between the Gurkhas and the Tibetans in 1792. A second mission under Captain Knox was dispatched in 1801. Knox became the first British Resident in Kathmandu and, on behalf of Britain, signed a treaty with Nepal shortly after his arrival. However, as a result of internal political developments in Nepal, Knox withdrew in 1803, and the treaty was dissolved. The continued forays by the Gurkhas into areas of British interest and protection ultimately led to the Anglo-Nepalese War of 1814-1816. The British were victorious and, by the Treaty of Segauli, were given possession of territory to the west of Nepal in Kumaon and Garhwal, thus giving British India a common frontier with Tibet for the first time. Relations between Britain and Nepal, however, remained cool until a change of regime in Kathmandu in 1846. Treaties in 1817 and 1861 with Sikkim, another Himalayan state on the frontier of Tibet, gave Britain influence in that area. Sikkim was also a major trading route from Bengal to Lhasa. Further to the east, Britain acquired the province of Assam, after victory in the first Anglo-Burmese War in 1826. This opened the possibility of alternative routes to Lhasa and southwest China. In the extreme western part of Tibet, British interest in *pashm*, used to make fine cashmere wool, led to the construction of the Hindustan-Tibet road betwen 1850 and 1858. Designed primarily to improve trade, the road went from the plains of India through Simla, the summer capital, before passing through Bashahr and terminating at Shipki on the Tibetan border.

From 1816, British interests in developing trade to the north of the Himalayan chain were concentrated on western Tibet. This area stretched from Nepal in the southeast to the Karakorum mountains in the northwest. To the southeast was British territory in Kumaon and Garhwal. Adjacent to them were a number of British protected states, such as Bashahr, and beyond them the kingdom of Ladakh, itself next to British territory.[40]

The East India Company hoped that the distance of Lhasa from Gartok, western Tibet's major trade mart, would mean a comparable diminution of political control and that the Gartok area, which depended far more on trade with other states than did Lhasa, would be more open to overtures of a commercial nature. In this regard, the shawl wool *(pashm)* trade was of particular interest. The travels of William Moorcroft in western Tibet in 1812 had encouraged the company's thinking along these lines.

Moorcroft was a veterinary surgeon and superintendent of a stud farm in Bengal for the East India Company. An adventurous traveler, he journeyed in disguise with Captain Hyder Young Hearsey across the Garhwal Himalayas into western Tibet. He was the first Englishman in the area, and he visited the sacred Lakes Manasarowar and Rakas Tal and reached the capital of Gartok. Moorcroft's objective was to purchase specimens of Tibetan horses and to acquire information about the shawl wool trade. Although the company realized the value of the shawl wool trade in the local economies, it was not sufficiently interested to provide Moorcroft with official backing. He made further travels a few years later, residing at Leh in Ladakh for two years before dying in 1825 in northern Afghanistan, on his way to Bokhara.[41] His journey to western Tibet demonstrated that the central authorities were by no means unaware of what was going on in the outlying regions of the country; for permitting Moorcroft to enter their territory, the chief administrator was recalled to Lhasa for punishment.

Other attempts by Englishmen to enter Tibet proved far less successful, regardless of whether they were traveling in an official or a private capacity. Local officials in western Tibet generally proved to be as hostile as their counterparts closer to Lhasa. The officials usually had good intelligence of the arrival of a Western visitor and intercepted him, politely insisting that he must turn back and refusing to provide him with any supplies for progress into Tibet.

Examples of such treatment were numerous. G.W. Traill, the commissioner for Kumaon, attempted in 1819 to enter into discussions about trade with officials on the Tibetan side of the border. He was unable to do so. At around the same time, the brothers Alexander, James, and Patrick Gerard explored the Himalayas on a number of occasions, between 1817 and 1821. Alexander was a surveyor with the Bengal native infantry, as was Patrick, who made meteorological observations on their expedition. James, a surgeon, accompanied them. Between them, they produced highly accurate data on the peaks and passes along the frontier of western Tibet. In 1821, Alexander Gerard wrote to the authorities at Gartok, requesting permission to visit Lake Manasarowar. The request was denied, although he managed to reach the Tibetan border and acquire much useful information on the Indian side of the Himalayas.[42]

No more success in penetrating Tibet was had by Captain William Webb, surveyor of Kumaon. In 1816, Webb tried to visit Lake Manasarowar but was turned back at the border of Tibet. "The Tartar chief who opposed his passage was exceedingly civil, but said that his orders were positive; that in future none would be allowed to cross that mountain from the southward side of India; and that the Deba or governor of Ghertop [Gartok] had been removed from his government and ordered to Lassa, for having permitted two Englishmen to visit the lake: these, it appears, were Captain Hearsay [sic] and Mr. Moorcroft."[43] Webb tried again in 1819, following in Traill's unsuccessful footsteps. Traveling in disguise to the Kumaon-Tibet border, he did have some discussions with the Chinese officials there about opening a trade mart. But in the end, no progress was made.[44]

The French botanist Victor Jacquemont fared no better in 1830, when he crossed the border briefly once or twice before being forced to retreat.

After the conclusion of the first Anglo-Sikh War, a treaty was signed in March 1846, by which the Sikhs ceded Jammu, Kashmir, and Ladakh to Britain. Because he had remained neutral during the conflict, the Dogra Raja of Jammu, Gulab Singh, was made ruler of this new state. Part of the separate treaty specified that commissioners should be sent from both sides to determine the boundary between Ladakh and western Tibet. This was important, because doubts about the precise location of the boundary might one day, the British thought, result in further aggression against western Tibet by Gulab Singh, who in 1841 had already attacked and briefly occupied the area up to Lake Manasarowar. If this occurred, it would again disrupt the economies of British protected states such as Bashahr.[45] In July 1846, the British appointed as their commissioners Captain Alexander Cunningham and Mr. P.A. Vans Agnew. In addition to demarcating the boundaries, they were also charged with the task of inquiry into the state of trade with Tibet. The governor-general, Lord Hardinge, wrote letters to Lhasa, both via Gartok and via Hong Kong and Peking, requesting that Tibetan and Chinese commissioners be sent to conduct the joint demarcation. But even if the letters were delivered, which is doubtful, no Chinese or Tibetan officials arrived to join Cunningham and Vans Agnew in Ladakh.

In 1847, the British appointed a second boundary commission, again commanded by Alexander Cunningham, who was joined by Henry Strachey and Dr. Thomas Thomson. Strachey was instructed to enter western Tibet and, if possible, visit Lhasa.[46] The British were not, however, permitted to enter Tibet; no Chinese or Tibetan commissioners arrived; and Gulab Singh was uncooperative. After defining the boundary by themselves, the British commissioners retired, and the government gave up the idea of a joint demarcation.

A few individuals were able to trespass briefly into forbidden territory. Henry Strachey (and his brother Richard) had had more success in penetrating Tibet in an unofficial capacity. Henry had made an unauthorized visit to Lakes Manasarowar and Rakas Tal in 1846,[47] one which was repeated by his brother Richard, in the company of J.E. Winterbottom,[48] a botanist, in 1848. The following year, the two brothers briefly entered Tibet after ascending the Niti pass in Garhwal.[49] Three German brothers, Adolph, Hermann, and Robert Schlagintweit, made a monumental scientific study of the Himalayan region between 1854 and 1858 and at one point penetrated into western Tibet.[50] A year later, in 1856, two British sportsmen succeeded in slipping across the border to visit Lakes Manasarowar and Rakas Tal.[51]

Chinese Central Asia

Chinese (or Eastern) Turkestan, an area of about 400,000 square miles, is now known as the Xinjiang Uygur Autonomous Region. The Tian Shan range, which runs northeast from its intersection with the Altai, bisects Chinese Turkestan. On the far side of the Tian Shan lies the Dzungarian desert. On the west the boundary is formed by the Pamir, from which the Kunlun and Karakorum ranges stretch eastward, defining the southern limits and the border with India. Passes crossing these mountains are few, and the Takla Makan, which meets the Gobi Desert in the east, is a major obstacle to travelers arriving from that direction.

The desire to undercut Russian trade with Tibet had been one motive for building the Hindustan-Tibet road. In addition to commercial relations with Tibet, the Russians also had unofficial religious ties through Mongols who were Russian citizens. But fear of Russian influence in Tibet, although it existed in the 1850s and 1860s, did not become a major factor until the end of the century. Of more pressing concern was Russian influence in Chinese Turkestan. This was a product of Russian expansion into Central Asia during the 1850s and 1860s. Trading privileges had been obtained in 1851 and extended by the 1860 Treaty of Peking. As the Russian presence was moving east, the British were pushing northward. Both empires attempted to exert influence over Chinese Turkestan, particularly in the three cities of Kashgar, Yarkand, and Khotan. Situated on the fringe of the great Takla Makan desert, they are watered by the rivers which flow from the mountain chains abutting the area on three sides.

At the time, the positions of Yarkand and Khotan were not known with certainty. Marco Polo had passed through Yarkand in the late thirteenth century, followed in 1603 by the Jesuit traveler Benedict Goes, seeking Cathay. Mir Izzet Ullah had been sent there via Ladakh to glean information on caravan routes by the explorer William Moorcroft in 1812.[52] An American named Alexander Gardiner possibly went to Yarkand in the 1820s, but left no description.[53] The German explorer Adolph Schlagintweit was certainly there in 1857, but was soon murdered near Kashgar. All these accounts, together with some Chinese sources, did not add up to a great deal at a time when a good knowledge of the physical geography of the area, including villages, crops, and mountain passes, was clearly a pressing need with the Russian Empire expanding inexorably toward the frontiers of British India. The possibility of a land invasion of India had first been raised by Napoleon and Czar Alexander in the early nineteenth century. With Russian expansion into Central Asia, the fear of this possibility increased as the century progressed.

As the British consolidated their hold over the Indian subcontinent, so they became increasingly concerned by their ignorance of the lands beyond the mountain ranges to the north and northwest. This concern was felt particularly strongly by the surveyor-officers of the Great Trigonometrical Survey, an institution which had its origins in India in the last part of the eighteenth century.

Up to that time, the mapping of India had been primarily a matter of making route-surveys, using a perambulator—a wheel with a cyclometer attached to count the revolutions—and a compass, with latitude and longitude checked by observations of the stars. It was from these route surveys, and other information available, that James Rennell, the first surveyor-general of India, produced his general map of "Hindoostan" in 1782. Although useful, Rennell's map was inadequate, in part because mapping was not being carried out on the basis of a sustained national plan, and partly because of inaccuracies derived from the astronomical bearings.

To remedy this situation, surveyer William L. Lambton proposed, in a letter to the Madras government in February 1800, to cover southern India, from Coromandel to the Malabar coast, with a network of triangular measurements "with a view to determine the exact positions of all the great objects that appeared best calculated to become permanent geographical marks, to be hereafter guides for facilitating a general survey of the Peninsula."[54]

Work began at the end of 1800, and the Great Trigonometrical Survey of India, as it eventually came to be known, continued its work for over eight decades, until 1883, when the principal triangulation of the entire subcontinent was finished. During this time, operations were never completely suspended at any point, not even during the Mutiny.

Describing his work in 1803, Lambton wrote that "the trigonometrical part of the survey is the foundation from which all distances and situations of places are deduced; a true delineation of the river valleys, ranges of mountains, with some noted points near the ghauts [gorges] and passes, will also be a foundation for more minute topographical surveys such as are immediately wanted for military purposes."[55]

The first step in this process was to measure a baseline as accurately as possible, then to take a bearing on a distant point from each end of the baseline, and by trigonometry, calculate the position of the distant point and the lengths of the other two sides of the triangle, both of which could now be used as baselines for a further series of triangles. Later surveyors would add topographical details to the area within the triangle.

This system proved to be of much greater accuracy than the older reliance on astronomical data and route surveys; it showed, for example, that the breadth of the Indian peninsula at the latitude of Madras was more than forty miles in error, measured astronomically, when compared with the more accurate trigonometrical data.

The lines of triangles eventually covered immense distances. For example, the line of triangulation (or arc, as it was called, reflecting the curvature of the earth) from Cape Comorin at the extreme southern tip of the Indian peninsula to the Karakorum mountain range in the north would stretch on the American continent from the Gulf of Mexico to Hudson Bay.

Reflecting its national orientation, the survey was officially titled the Great Trigonometrical Survey of India in 1818. Since its sphere of operations had now passed beyond the boundaries of the Madras presidency, the GTS was placed under the control of the government of India. Lambton was made superintendent of the GTS, and a young captain of artillery, George Everest, was appointed his Chief Assistant.

Meanwhile, the territory of British India also continued to expand. Both the conclusion of the Nepal War in 1816 and the occupation of Assam a decade later opened up new areas for exploration and survey. The consolidation of British power in Assam on the northeast frontier also stimulated debate over the true source of the Brahmaputra River, and whether it flowed from the Tsangpo River of Tibet, a controversy which was only to be resolved years later by one of the pundits of the Survey of India.

The GTS was placed under the orders of the surveyor general of India only in 1823. The then surveyor general, Valentine Blacker, firmly backed the GTS, at a time when some were calling its northern extension into question, saying that it was "the only permanent foundation of Indian Geography."[56] In the same year, Lambton, still tirelessly involved in the work of the GTS, died of tuberculosis at the advanced (for India) age of 70, while on his way to establish a new survey headquarters in Nagpur. George Everest was appointed superintendent of the GTS to succeed him and then became surveyor-general of India in 1830, continuing the two posts in one man.

Under Everest, by 1837 the principal arc of triangulation had been carried as far north as Dehra Dun (the headquarters of the Survey of India) near the foothills of the Himalayas. In 1841, Everest completed the principal arc, some 1,500 miles in length, forty years after its commencement. Like Lambton, exhausted by the rigors of the work and the climate, Everest, suffering from malaria, was forced to leave India to recuperate in the Cape of Good Hope between 1820 and 1822, and again in England between 1825 and 1830. This latter leave was particularly beneficial to the Survey; for Everest, while on leave, provided the Survey with better, more accurate, and lighter instruments, which were employed when he returned to India as surveyor general in 1830.

Attacks on survey parties by robbers were common, as was a lack of cooperation from local inhabitants and from the British Resident or political agent. Above all, the surveyors had to combat the effects of the climate on their health. Because of the climate and the difficult terrain, hundreds of employees of the Survey lost their lives or their health in the service of "the map." The toll was particularly high in malaria-infested regions such as the terai, south of Nepal, but the effects of climate and loneliness were felt in most other parts of India, particularly during the rainy season. One English surveyor, left alone out on field survey during the rainy season with no European companion, burnt off all his toes and several fingers in the flame of a candle, "together with diverse other particulars of a similar or even more lamentable nature" having been overcome by a fit of religious mania.[57]

This was an extreme case, no doubt, but all were affected to some degree. Everest himself wrote in 1824, just before his furlough in England that "this illness . . . within the last few months has arrived at a crisis by the formation of an abscess at my hip, and another at my neck, from both of which fragments of decayed bone have repeatedly been extracted, sundry incisions and other surgical operations of rather an unpleasant kind having been also performed."[58]

The surveying parties generally operated during the rainy season, despite its adverse effect on health, because the hazy atmosphere during the dry weather made it difficult to measure the angle to a distant point. In the opaque air, poles and flags could not be seen. Everest solved this problem by introducing the use of luminous signal lamps at night and heliotropes (a mirror device) by day. Now the relatively healthy cold season from November to February and the hot, dry period lasting until June became the preferred time for surveying. Everest used an oil lamp which, shining through the aperture of an inverted bowl to keep the wind out, could be seen on a clear night for over forty miles.

The surveyors of the GTS, when working in remote parts, were expected not only to provide precise maps, but also collect information on the peoples of the area, the nature of their livelihood, the available crops, and other details, military and commercial, which might be useful to the government of India. Surveyors who had worked for years in distant places thereby became experienced intelligence agents on behalf of British rule in India, and the GTS continued to be administered by the Military Department of the government of India.

At the head of this organization was Lieutenant Andrew Scott Waugh, who was appointed surveyor-general and superintendent of the GTS in December 1843, on the retirement of Everest. Waugh was an engineer, like most of his successors and contemporaries. Under his administration, the world's highest mountain was first located and measured in 1856, and in 1860 he proposed that it be named "Everest" after his predecessor.[59]

By the mid-nineteenth century the GTS, systematically mapping the whole of India, had reached the Himalayan chain forming the northern boundary of the subcontinent and separating India from Tibet and China. Political problems made further surveying difficult, if not impossible. The Himalayan state of Nepal ran along much of the border. Nepal was out of bounds to surveyors, by virtue of the treaty signed in 1816, which did not allow for penetration of the Nepal Himalayas. Kashmir, however, was a different matter. Lying northwest of Nepal, Kashmir had come under the control of the Sikhs in 1819. Following the death of the Sikh ruler Ranjit Singh in 1839, war broke out between the Sikhs and the British, and after the defeat of the Sikhs in the first Sikh War in 1846, the Punjab was annexed by Britain. Kashmir was handed over to Gulab Singh, the ruler of the neighboring state of Jammu.

Waugh was particularly interested in the mapping of the Himalayas. He had therefore prevailed upon Gulab Singh, as a friend of the British, to permit surveys of his territory. During his term of office, Waugh had carried the triangulation of India westward to the Indus, and he was responsible for surveying most of what is now Pakistan. But his most important survey was that of Kashmir in the western Himalayas. It was to be carried out between 1855 and 1865 by a Captain Montgomerie of the Royal Engineers.

Thomas George Montgomerie was born on 23 April 1830, the fourth son of a colonel in the Ayrshire Yeomanry. After graduating at the head of his class and winning the medal for the most distinguished cadet from the East India Company's school at Addiscombe, he was gazetted second lieutenant in the Bengal Engineers. He arrived in India at the age of 21. In May 1852, after working with the Fifth Company of the Sappers and Miners on the Hindustan-Tibet road, he applied to be appointed to the GTS, saying that he had "read the usual engineer course of mathematics, including spherical trigonometry, differential and integral calculus, and the rudiments of astronomy."[60] His application was accepted by Waugh, and he joined the GTS in November. For the next two years, he was active in the field, observing triangles and assisting in the measurement of the Chach baseline near Attock. He must have come to the personal attention of the surveyor-general during this time, for in September 1856, Waugh announced his intention of placing the young Montgomerie, now promoted to first lieutenant, in charge of the Kashmir survey.[61] Photographs of Montgomerie give the impression of diffidence, but his career shows him to have been a man capable of exercising his authority over both British and Indian subordinates.

The Kashmir party was officially formed on 1 January 1855, with William Johnson as Montgomerie's second in command. Johnson had already had experience in surveying at high altitudes.

The triangulation of the territories of the maharaja of Jammu and Kashmir began in the spring of 1855, with the network of triangles carried over the fifteen-thousand-foot peaks of the Pir Panjal range. Conditions were difficult: trig points had to be based on rock, and the surveying party was happy when they had to dig down through "only" eleven feet of snow to find it; static electricity made the men's hair and clothing crackle and spark; and snow blindness was a problem even with improvised eye protectors made of fir twigs and horse hair. Despite the hardships, Montgomerie wrote enthusiastically of seeing "the bright point of light shining from the apex of a noble snowy cone with that intense light peculiar to a well served heliotrope."[62] By July, measurements had been worked across the Pir Panjal, and the party arrived at Srinagar in the Kashmir valley.

Work began again in the Kashmir valley the following spring, after a winter spent mapping at Dehra Dun. Montgomerie meanwhile made a preliminary reconnaissance of Ladakh, from which he caught his first glimpse of the Karakorum range, separating India from Chinese Turkestan. It was at this time that Montgomerie observed K^2 (no. 2 in the Karakorum range) which, at 28,250 feet, came to be recognized as the world's second highest mountain.

The Indian Mutiny of 1857 and the death of Gulab Singh that August created worrying times for Montgomerie. It transpired, however, that Rambir Singh, who succeeded his father, was equally desirous of maintaining good relations with the British. Montgomerie himself felt it necessary to stay close to the maharaja, although the Kashmir Survey continued throughout the Mutiny. When Montgomerie found that "drafts on the [East India] Company's treasuries were looked upon as so much waste paper,"[63] the maharaja was kind enough to lend him money. The only local military action was the apprehension of a group of mutineers who had escaped from Peshawar. Montgomerie later received high praise from Colonel Waugh for the "tact, delicacy and ability, with which [he] maintained amicable relations with the court, a difficult one to deal with."[64]

In 1858, the triangulation moved north toward Skardo, the capital of Baltistan or "Little Tibet," whose territory stretched to the Karakorums. Montgomerie himself returned to Ladakh, mapping the upper reaches of the Indus River. Having surveyed Baltistan and Ladakh between 1858 and

1861, Montgomerie's parties were now occupied on the frontiers, fixing points across the border in Tibet and Chinese Turkestan and along the Karakorum and Kunlun ranges.

"Year by year," Montgomerie reported, "as the Survey has advanced, the physical difficulties have increased; the average height of the stations has latterly been from 17,000 to 20,000 feet above the sea."[65] But in November 1864, Montgomerie was able to declare the completion of the survey of the maharaja's territories. An area of about 7,700 square miles had been surveyed, including 1,400 square miles of glaciers, and at heights which no man had reached before without the aid of a balloon. Montgomerie had proved himself a strong administrator, with an excellent ability to get along with both local rulers and his own assistants. His efforts had already won high praise from many quarters. He spent the winter of 1858-59 in Dehra Dun creating a map from the surveying observations, and he sent the finished product off to Calcutta in May 1859. This map, covering most of Kashmir and Jammu south of the great Himalayan range, embraced an area of over 8,000 square miles and included more than 4,600 villages. On receiving it, the deputy surveyor-general, Henry Thuillier, said that "all the beauties of such an elaborate and highly finished production are not to be appreciated by a single inspection."[66] Thuillier personally took the map to Lord Canning, the governor-general. Canning was unstinting in his praise, and in a letter to Sir Roderick Murchison, president of the Royal Geographical Society, he lauded Montgomerie's courage and tact during the Mutiny, and stated of the map that "to my unlearned eye it is as fine an example of topographical drawing as I have ever seen."[67] Canning also sent a letter to Waugh, referring to the map and its author's efforts in the highest terms. The governor-general further noted that he had sent the map to the secretary of state for India and said that he hoped the RGS would honor Montgomerie. The secretary of state in turn passed the map over to the RGS, which exhibited it at a meeting in London in December 1859 and described it as "beautiful . . . good proof of the knowledge and skill employed in the survey."[68]

On the conclusion of the Kashmir Survey, Montgomerie returned to England for his first furlough since he arrived in India. While in London, the RGS awarded him its prestigious Founder's Gold Medal in May 1865. Montgomerie thus followed in the footsteps of Waugh, who had been awarded a gold medal by the RGS in 1857. In his presentation address, Murchison praised Montgomerie for his accurate scientific observations from stations, "one of which was five thousand feet higher than the summit of Mont Blanc."[69] Montgomerie couched his reply in modest terms,

The Great Trigonometrical Survey

referring to others who had helped him, but who had not themselves been similarly honored.

At the age of thirty-five, Montgomerie's future in India was assured. But he was not to be remembered in history only for his mapping of Kashmir. Although this was a significant achievement, it was eclipsed by Montgomerie's initiative and enterprise in the use of native explorers for the trans-Himalayan exploration of Tibet and Central Asia.

The Pundits

It was indisputably dangerous for Europeans to leave the protection of British-administered territory. The legendary William Moorcroft had been killed after leaving Bokhara in 1825, and the German explorer Adolph Schlagintweit had been murdered near Kashgar in 1857. Others had met a similar fate. Major James Walker (later General Walker, superintendent of the GTS) wrote while on survey near Peshawar, close to areas inhabited by the Afridis, that "to go into their country excepting by force is never possible for a European, and is at all times dangerous for a native."[70] The same was true of other areas in East and West Turkestan, regions often unvisited by European travelers since the time of Marco Polo.

The government of India was anxious to avoid conflict between its citizens and peoples across the border, where hostile activities against British citizens could be neither defended nor avenged. For this reason the instructions given to Montgomerie at the commencement of the Kashmir survey, although they had stated that the survey should "obtain the means of rectifying our imperfect geographical knowledge of the regions beyond British influence," had also included the admonition that the survey was not "to risk the safety of the party nor to entangle Government in political complications."[71] Similarly, while triangulating east from Leh in Ladakh, the surveyors had been warned that "you must be careful to prevent all collision with the Chinese Tartars on the common boundary."[72]

Those who ignored these instructions had earned the marked displeasure of the government. William Johnson, Montgomerie's assistant on the Kashmir survey, had been granted permission to survey in the border areas of Ladakh in 1865. On reach ng Leh, he received and accepted an invitation from the khan of Khotan to visit that city (Ilchi). He made his way there, observing and sketching, and stayed for over two weeks before returning to Leh through uncharted territory by way of the Karakorum pass. He was the first European visitor to Khotan for centuries. Although the government was pleased to see Johnson's report of his remarkable journey, he was subjected to severe censure. The government noted that had he "been detained at Khotan, or murdered on the way, he would have involved the Government in all the odium arising out of an unredressed injury to one of its British servants."[73] Johnson resigned from the Survey the following year. His report was well received by the Royal Geographical Society, which elected him a Fellow and then in 1875 awarded him a gold watch, which Montgomerie accepted on his behalf.[74]

Since they were generally unable to cross the frontiers themselves, the British had employed Indians as explorers from time to time since the eighteenth century. Montgomerie was no doubt aware of this. The first recorded example was in 1774, when a sepoy officer collected information on the territory between Bengal and the Deccan. Later in the century, either *munshis* (native secretaries, often Moslems) or *pundits* (learned Hindus) were used to obtain geographical details and make route surveys both of central India and of the extreme northwest in Chitral and the Hindu Kush.[75]

In 1807, Charles Reynolds, the surveyor-general of Bombay, had produced a "Map of Hindustaun." This map was designed primarily to describe territories outside the control of the East India Company, and it relied for much of its material on Indian explorers sent out to gather data.[76]

Better-educated Indians were taught to use a compass and measure distances by using a perambulator. John Hodgson (in charge of a survey in northwest India) sent a Brahman posing as a physician ("with medicines for those who are so unfortunate as to become his patients") up into Ladakh and western Tibet in 1813. The Brahman returned with some useful information, and Hodgson considered sending him to Kashgar "to get some idea of the distance and route to the nearest part of the Russian Dominions." The government of India, however, discouraged this practice by refusing to provide funds for native explorers. The government did not want Indians to be taught surveying techniques or to acquire geographical information about the country, especially the sensitive northern border areas. The use of Indian explorers therefore languished, except for their occasional use by enterprising individuals, for half a century, until the need to obtain geographical intelligence beyond the borders required a reconsideration of the policy.[77]

One such enterprising individual was William Moorcroft, who had traveled to western Tibet in 1812. At the same time he sent "an intelligent native friend," Mir Izzet Ullah, to explore Central Asia and reconnoiter the area with a view to developing its trade potential with India.[78] Mir Izzet Ullah crossed the Karakorum pass and visited Yarkand and Kashgar before halting at Bokhara and returning in 1813 by way of Kabul.[79]

Moorcroft was the first European traveler to use Indians to measure distance by means of a measured pace, a technique later adopted by the GTS. In a journal detailing his explorations of 1812-13, Moorcroft wrote that "Harkh Dev Pandit was directed to stride the whole of the road at paces equal to 4 feet each." This occasioned a comment from the editor of the journal that "the Pandit's measure of the road would probably have been more correct, had he been directed to step his usual and natural paces, the length of which might have been easily determined with precision by a small trial."[80]

Moorcroft later took pains to show that no Indian was in fact crossing the Himalayas with giant strides. In a letter from Leh, penned at the start of his second journey in 1820, he explained: "the measurement of the Road distance was made by an intelligent Servant, who had no other employment . . . so that barring the occasional irregularity of a step consequent on fatigue, this measurement may be presumed to be as accurate as possible without a perambulator, the use of which was not practicable . . . In my last journey the measures counted by his right foot alone enumerating each double step, which was found to average 4 feet, as one step. [sic] This circumstance, not sufficiently explained in a note in my last Journal, has led to the misconception of his having stepped 4 feet at a single pace."[81]

Over a decade later, Claude Wade, Political Agent in Ludhiana on the Sikh frontier from 1823 to 1840, wrote to the surveyor-general in 1836, concerning the countries east and north of the Indus above Attock. He observed that "since the time of the late Mr. Moorcroft, nothing has been done to improve our knowledge."[82] Wade urged the employment of "an enterprising European officer" to remedy the situation. It is not likely that this request was granted. Wade, however, actively employed his own agents to ferret out geographical and political data concerning the Punjab and its Sikh government. As he states in his autobiography, "these enquiries, which could then only be conducted with great secrecy and precaution, by intelligent natives specially despatched by me to Lahore and Amritsir . . . gave me a complete knowledge of the country and its production and inhabitants, which was not then to be acquired from any other source."[83]

Wade was probably acting on his own, as the government of India continued officially to discourage the use of "natives" for geographical reconnaissance purposes. However, by the 1830s, particularly under the governor-generalship of Lord William Bentinck (1828-35), Indians were admitted to positions in the public service, including the Survey of India. One such surveyor, Muhommad Ali, educated at the Engineer Institute of Bombay, was disguised as a pilgrim going to Mecca and traveled with Alexander Burnes on his famous journey to Bokhara in 1832.[84]

Nevertheless, many British officials took a rather jaundiced view of the capabilities of Indians. Although Indians had been hired because of a shortage of Europeans, Waugh noted that "the introduction of the native surveyors . . . is experimental. They have not, it is believed, the same coup d'oeil and power of drawing from nature that Europeans have." But he concluded that if the Indian surveyors were to prove successful, "it will tend to economy."[85]

The Indians proved to be quite satisfactory. With the government becoming increasingly concerned about the expansion of Russia in Central Asia and the potential threat this posed to India, "the jewel in the Imperial crown," the British soon found other uses to which the local inhabitants might be put.

A case in point was that of Abdul Mejid. Mejid was a *mullah*, or Muslim learned in law and religion. He had been brought up in Kabul and became a merchant traveling widely in Central Asia. In 1860, on the orders of the governor-general, Earl Canning, he was dispatched from Peshawar. His mission was to carry a letter and presents (which included music boxes, watches, and rifles) to the ruler of Kokand, a city about one hundred miles southeast of Tashkent. There he was to estimate the degree of Russian presence in the area. Mejid left for Kokand via Kabul and the Pamir. His mission was successful, and he returned to Peshawar the following year with an interesting report of his travels, details of the political and military situation in Kokand, and the extent of Russian influence.[86] The government of India was pleased with the success of the enterprise and directed that Mejid be given a "suitable substantial acknowledgement."[87] Mejid also made geographical history by undertaking the first recorded passage of the Pamir from south to north.[88] For this he was subsequently awarded a gold watch (value £26.5s) by the Royal Geographical Society in London. Accepting the watch for Mejid in his absence, Lord Strangford pointed out that "to us as geographers it is a great advantage to have the means of exploring countries inaccessible to Europeans, in the cooperation of these meritorious native travellers."[89]

Meanwhile, Montgomerie continued to grapple with the problem of surveying the territories beyond his domain. He was stimulated by the success of Abdul Mejid. As he commented to a meeting of the Asiatic Society in Calcutta, Mejid had shown what might be done, given the support of the government. Mejid, Montgomerie observed, "if he had been able he could have taken latitude observations and made a rough route survey without any danger."[90] If the Jesuits in China were able to use Chinese in the service of geography, then, he concluded, surely the British could "get at least as good work out of some of the natives of Hindostan."[91]

In March 1861, Montgomerie submitted a report to the Punjab government in which he expressed the hope that the conflict between Britain and China would eventually result in increased trade between India and Chinese Turkestan, and that the GTS would "succeed hereafter in fixing the geographical positions of some of the great cities of Central Asia."[92]

During the progress of the Kashmir survey, Montgomerie had already given considerable thought to the methods by which geographical information might be acquired concerning those regions of Tibet and Central Asia which were blank on his maps. He had been able to glean some details from reconnaissances made into areas which were sparsely inhabited. "In this way," he wrote, "the country was surveyed for several marches beyond the Karakorum Pass," and another quick survey was carried ten marches into western Tibet. Although more extended surveys in this direction might be possible, noted Montgomerie, it was clear that further advances across the Karakorum pass in the direction of Yarkand would bring the surveyors "within the range of the Khirgiz hordes who infest that road."[93]

It was obvious to Montgomerie that normal surveying procedures were not applicable in these regions both because of the very uncertain welcome that the local population might extend toward Europeans, and because of the views of the government of India concerning such explorations. Indian travelers, though, were a different matter. While on operations with the Kashmir Survey in Ladakh, Montgomerie had noticed that many Indians were able to cross the frontier freely between Ladakh and Yarkand. Montgomerie therefore conceived his momentous idea of forming a group of native travelers who would be trained to carry out simple surveying operations, using instruments concealed among their possessions, and who would cross the Indian frontiers disguised as pilgrims or traders. These native explorers were to become famous as "the pundits."

The first available evidence showing that Montgomerie was moving to request official approval for his idea came in a memorandum he wrote to Major Walker, superintendent of the GTS. Dated 20 August 1861 from Camp Little Tibet, the letter was written in response to a request from the surveyor-general for information on the status of the exploration of Chinese Turkestan. Montgomerie responded that "I estimate the unexplored Chinese territory that is accessible from British India at about 1,400,000 square miles . . . We have a general idea of about 400,000 square miles of this, but are entirely ignorant of the remaining 1,000,000 square miles." He then observed the lack of any coherent system for trans-Himalayan exploration, with each explorer essentially starting afresh, and no orderly accumulation of data or assignment of geographical tasks. "The present," concluded Montgomerie, "appears to be a capital opportunity for putting Indian explorers on a more permanent footing that would keep up its traditions and transmit the experience gained and the thread of the work in regular succession."[94]

In April 1862, Montgomerie presented a paper on the geography of Chinese Turkestan to a meeting of the Asiatic Society of Bengal. During this meeting he gave the assembled members the benefit of his idea of training "natives of Hindostan" to take latitude observations and make route surveys in Central Asia and elsewhere. Montgomerie spoke of testing their work by first sending them into areas already explored by Europeans, so that the accuracy of their results could be verified. He then concluded by asking the Council of the Society to consider his proposals, and said that he was willing "to draw up a project" if the Council wished.[95]

To gain approval for his ideas, Montgomerie mobilized support from his superiors. In March 1861, Waugh retired as surveyor-general, and Henry Thuillier was appointed as his successor. At this time, the posts of surveyor-general and superintendent of the GTS were separated, with Thuillier appointing Major James Walker of the Bombay Engineers, aged 34, as head of the GTS. The positions were to remain separate until Walker himself became surveyor-general in 1878.

In 1860, both Walker and Montgomerie had been candidates for the prestigious post of astronomical assistant, an honorary title awarded to an officer with outstanding qualifications. Walker, four years older than Montgomerie, won the title on Waugh's recommendation because of his seniority in rank and survey experience. Waugh, in recommending Walker, nevertheless described Montgomerie as "an officer of great policy and judgment . . . the success which has attended his labours proves that he possesses great energy, zeal, and ability as well as capabilities for extensive command."[96] Montgomerie and Walker were also the leading contenders for the superintendency of the GTS, which again went to Walker because of his greater practical experience. Montgomerie had to be content with being appointed astronomical assistant, the title being relinquished by Walker.

Montgomerie was able to win support from both Walker and Thuillier for his proposal to train Indians as trans-Himalayan explorers. Like his predecessor, Andrew Waugh, Thuillier was equally aware of the need for information on areas across the Indian boundaries. At the conclusion of the Kashmir Survey, he had written to the Royal Geographical Society bemoaning the fact that Montgomerie's surveyors would have to halt their operations at the Nepalese frontier because of the "inherent jealousy of the Nepalese."[97] Sir Robert Montgomery, lieutenant-governor of the Punjab, also backed Montgomerie.[98]

Major Walker had had good results in the past with native surveyors, one of whom had traveled with the Schlagintweits in 1855, "into the snowy ranges to the north of Kashmir."[99] As superintendent of the GTS, he was known to be in favor of an "active" or "forward" policy. Indeed, he preferred the hostile actions of the tribes on the northwest frontier, which resulted in retaliatory expeditions by British forces and the consequent gathering of geographical information, to the "passive obstruction of the inhabitants of Chinese Tibet," which provided no such excuses.[100] At a meeting of the Asiatic Society in 1863, it was Walker who read out a letter from Montgomerie. The letter gave more details of Montgomerie's plans. It was written at "Camp Ladakh" and dated 28 July 1862.[101] In the letter, Montgomerie proposed the use of "Mahomedans" from the northwest frontier of India to explore Central Asia. Other races would be employed in Tibet. Each explorer would be trained to use a sextant and an "artificial horizon." Since the sextant was primarily an instrument for use at sea, measuring the elevation of the sun or stars above the sea horizon, an artificial horizon, either a dish of mercury or a darkened glass, was needed on land, where there was no visible sea horizon. Both mercury and the dark-glass artificial horizons were employed by the pundits. They were also to be equipped with a boiling-point thermometer to determine heights, a pocket compass with a clinometer to measure the slope of the roads, and a chronometer watch. With these instruments, they could observe for latitude and height (and a rough guess at longitude could be made). They could also make a survey of the route taken and write an account of the major places visited. When he was dispatched the following year, the first pundit actually carried with him a selection of instruments that mirrored very closely those listed in Montgomerie's proposal.

In order to ascertain the distances marked, Montgomerie had observed his first pundit and obtained an estimate of his normal walking speed. On his journey, the pundit read his compass to determine the bearing of the road along which he was traveling and then used his watch to measure the time elapsed to reach the next stage.[102] Knowing the speed with which the pundit walked, Montgomerie was therefore able to produce a rough route-survey of his journey. Use of the sextant to determine latitude acted as a check on the accuracy of the route survey. The boiling-point thermometer gave the altitudes of places visited.

These arrangements were refined for later pundits as Montgomerie's system was developed. Instead of estimating their normal walking speed, Montgomerie had the pundits trained to walk a measured pace (regardless of the terrain), with two thousand paces equaling one mile. In order to assist the counting of his paces, each pundit was given what would have seemed, to the casual observer, a traditional Buddhist rosary of 108 beads. Closer inspection, however, would have revealed that the rosary manufactured by the Trigonometrical Survey had only 100 beads, with every tenth bead slightly larger than the rest. If a small bead was the equivalent of one hundred paces, then every large bead represented one thousand paces; and knowing the length of each pace, it was a simple matter to calculate the distance traveled. Observations of the number of paces and compass bearings had, in the case of Montgomerie's first pundit, been written onto the pages of a small book. For greater secrecy, later explorers were given a Tibetan prayer-wheel with a revolving barrel, which was customarily twirled in the air by pilgrims and travelers. The barrel contained Buddhist prayers, and each revolution sent the prayers to heaven. The prayer wheels of Montgomerie's pundits, however, were used to store observations of bearings and distance made on the march, hidden there from the eyes of prying frontier officials. Later expeditions took larger and more accurate sextants and an aneroid barometer for calculating height above sea level. The aneroid barometer measured altitude by measuring atmospheric pressure, which itself varies with altitude above sea level.

The surveys made by the pundits were not, strictly speaking, maps. They were "route maps," that is, an accurate (often remarkably accurate) survey of the route traversed, which could be followed by later explorers. The pundits also kept a record of the terrain over which they passed and of the country to either side of their routes. In addition, they often acquired information about the people of the area, their customs, economy, and military and political resources.

Latitude, the distance from the equator, was measured by using the sextant to measure the altitude of either the sun by day or the stars by night. Estimating longitude was more of a problem, since it required knowledge of the distance between the meridian of the observer (a meridian being the shortest line drawn over the surface of the earth between the two poles) and the fixed prime meridian at Greenwich. The procedure was to measure the angle of the sun or a fixed star and calculate the difference in time between the local time of the observer and time at Greenwich. Since the earth rotates 360 degrees in twenty-four hours, each hour of difference is the equivalent of fifteen degrees of longitude. A comparison with Greenwich would then place the observer a certain number of miles east or west of the prime meridian. The problem was having an accurate measurement of Greenwich time while on the march. The pundits often carried chronometers, but these could be affected by the joltings of rough travel and by changing temperatures in the mountains. Small errors in time could easily be transformed into major errors of longitude on the map, since four seconds of time (at the equator) is the equivalent of one mile. For his first explorer, who was not provided with a chronometer, Montgomerie was able to make a good estimate of the longitude of Yarkand, using the route survey alone, because the explorer traveled almost entirely in a north-south direction, so that his longitude did not vary greatly from its known starting point.[103]

Considerable attention was paid by Montgomerie and his successors to ensuring that the pundits would not be able to falsify their data. They were not taught how to calculate latitude or longitude from their observations or how to map out a route survey. The first pundit was tested by sending him over a route already surveyed by the GTS, withholding from the pundit the results of the earlier survey.[104]

Montgomerie admitted there might be difficulties in recruiting reliable natives "with sufficient nerve." They also had to be capable of learning to use survey instruments. But he referred to one man, formerly employed by Major Walker on the Peshawar Survey, who he thought would be suitable. He also named others who, he estimated, could be trained in the use of instruments at GTS Headquarters in a period of about eight months. Montgomerie proposed the city of Yarkand in Chinese Turkestan as the target for the first journey. The exploring party could leave from Kashmir in May of 1863 and return in November crossing the Karakorum pass, up to which point their observations could be checked against those of the Kashmir Survey. Later expeditions might cross the northwest frontier beyond Kabul, or even venture toward Lhasa.

Major Walker expressed to the Asiatic Society his own strong opinion in favor of these plans. So did the president of the society, who spoke of geographical exploration beyond the British frontier as being "lamentably limited," and suggested that in addition to Central Asia and Tibet, the northeast frontier around Assam and the valley of the Brahmaputra would also be suitable areas for exploration, owing to the hostility there of the hill peoples to Europeans.

Montgomerie's proposals were officially passed to the government of India by a letter of 8 May 1862, together with a request for Rs. 1,000 to provide for their training. It was proposed that the explorer recruits should receive a monthly salary of sixteen to twenty rupees.[105] Approval was eventually received, but not until 1863.

It was probably the failure of two British-led expeditions that attempted to enter Tibet that moved the government of India to approve the training of Indian spies for exploration purposes. One expedition, from China, got close to the Tibetan border before turning back. The other, from India, was never able to start.

The China party traveling up the Yangtse was made up of Lieutenant-Colonel H.A. Sarel of the 17th Lancers, Captain Thomas W. Blakiston, a noncommissioned officer with four Sikhs of the 11th Punjab Infantry, a Dr. Barton, and a missionary who could speak Chinese.[106] It left Shanghai on 11 February 1861 and was the first expedition to travel under the provision of Article 9 of the Treaty of Tientsin (1858) as ratified in 1860 by China and Britain. Article 9 stated that "British subjects are hereby authorized to travel for their pleasure or for purposes of trade, to all parts of the Interior, under Passports, which will be issued by their Consuls and countersigned by the Local Authorities."[107] It was the hope of Sarel and his men to cross Tibet from east to west, keeping to the north of the Himalayas, and emerging on the northwest frontier of India.

The Sarel expedition was therefore the first test of the new treaty rights, which the British hoped would gain them legal access to Tibet. Accordingly, the members of the expedition carried passports signed by Thomas Taylor Meadows, HBM Consul in Shanghai, and duly countersigned by the local Chinese authorities.[108] Each passport stated that the holder was desirous of proceeding to India via Tibet. The diplomatic and geographical significance of the expedition had not been lost on the British authorities, even though it was a privately organized venture, ostensibly traveling for purposes of exploration and sport. A flurry of letters traveled between military headquarters in Shanghai, Hong Kong, Calcutta, and London during the spring and summer of 1861. The commander of forces, Hong Kong, said the mission was "of great interest" and that it was "in accordance with the wishes of H.M. Government that it should proceed."[109] The adjutant-general of the Army, in Calcutta, requested that the governor-general help "these enterprising officers."[110] Accordingly, the government of India sent a letter to Major Ramsay, British Resident in Nepal, asking him to look out for the expedition and render them all necessary assistance.[111] Ramsay contacted Montgomerie, giving him details, and Montgomerie responded that Sarel should reach Lhasa in August.[112]

Alas, by that time the expedition, foiled by rebellions in Szechuan and by the unwillingness on the part of any Chinese to accompany them overland through disturbed areas, had already turned around and headed back the way it had come.[113] The failure of the Sarel expedition was to have an adverse effect on another expedition to penetrate Tibet. This was the attempt of Major Smyth to enter Tibet from India.

Major Edmund Smyth, education officer in Kumaon, was widely traveled on the Indian side of the Himalayas. He was anxious to continue his exploration across the Himalayas into Tibet and had been organizing a substantial expedition since 1860. The Survey of India supplied some equipment and proposed that a trained surveyor travel with Smyth.[114] Smyth intended that the expedition members should assemble at Almorah (in Kumaon) in March 1862 and leave in April for Lake Pangong on the Ladakh-Tibet frontier.[115]

With the return of Sarel and Blakiston down the Yangtse, however, the Smyth expedition was halted in its tracks, and in October 1861 the Indian government informed a disappointed Smyth that "the expedition to Central Asia is not to be proceeded with."[116]

Smyth did not give up. In 1862 he applied to be allowed to try to reach Lhasa without a passport.[117] His application was unsuccessful. The government in Calcutta was nevertheless supportive of Smyth's attempts to enter the western part of Tibet, away from Lhasa. Smyth proposed a four- to six-week trip to a town 120 miles south of Gartok, starting in September 1863. He said that he would take with him "two large magic lanterns for exhibiting dissolving views . . . in order to induce the Authorities to allow me to enter the country."[118] The government, determined not to allow a border conflict to occur, warned Smyth not to force his way into Tibet "against the wishes of the authorities."[119]

Alas, Western magic did not unlock the doors to Tibet. The local Tibetan authorities, although friendly, refused to allow Smyth to proceed beyond the border, saying that the two principal officials from whom he would need to obtain permission were in Gartok. A passport from Peking, however, Smyth was told, would do the trick. A request for a passport was made by the Indian government, acting on Smyth's behalf, to Frederick Bruce, the British ambassador in Peking. The ambassador responded that "there is no prospect at present of obtaining such a document."[120] Bruce said that he had "seen a curious letter from the chief Tibetan authority to the Chinese Government" railing against Catholic missionaries trying to cross the frontier and complaining of the harm done by the French Lazarist priests Huc and Gabet, who had spent six weeks in Lhasa in 1846. In this letter, Bruce continued, the Tibetans had shown themselves to be well aware of British desires to explore Tibet. They feared that this exploration was for missionary motives, and so they urged the Chinese to refuse passports to the British and said that even with passports the safety of travelers could not be guaranteed. Bruce commented that it was in China's interest to accede to this request. China gained from her connection with Tibet by virtue of the authority it gave her over the Mongol tribes who recognized the religious supremacy of the Dalai Lama.[121] Under these circumstances, the Chinese, already weakened by foreign and domestic problems and in danger of losing control over territories on the periphery of their Empire, were unwilling to violate the religious susceptibilities of the Tibetan lamas, which could have provoked a revolt. Furthermore, to issue passports just to have them ignored by the Tibetans was only to advertise Chinese weakness in the area. This had happened in the case of two Catholic missionaries in 1862.[122]

It was thus to the advantage of the Tibetans to exclude the British. Apart from the religious motives for so doing, Tibet at the time suffered only the formality of Chinese suzerainty over their country. But if the Chinese saw their interests in the area threatened, they might be tempted to make their presence more of a reality.

Tibet and China therefore each had its own private reasons for wishing to exclude foreigners from Tibet. In public, each laid the blame on the intransigence of the other. Whatever the real reasons, public or private, the result was that the British found themselves unable to use the Treaty of Tientsin to gain legal entry into Tibet. The government of British India therefore decided to reach its goals by clandestine means. The use of native explorers was approved, and by the summer of 1863, Montgomerie's first agent was on his way. His destination was the city of Yarkand in Chinese Central Asia.

TWO
First Attempts: Abdul Hamid and Nain Singh

The journey of Abdul Hamid to Yarkand was an "experimental expedition" initiated by Montgomerie with the assistance of the lieutenant-governor of the Punjab and with the Punjab government paying the cost.[1] Montgomerie selected Yarkand in Chinese Turkestan as the target because "our knowledge of that city [is] particularly vague" and because he believed that its position was erroneously marked on contemporary maps.[2]

The locations of many of the cities of Central Asia, as recorded on the maps of the time, were derived from measurements taken by the pupils of the French Jesuit missionaries in China during the eighteenth century. While these measurements were reasonably reliable for China proper, Montgomerie believed that they were quite inaccurate for the frontier areas of the Chinese empire. Using data derived from information collected in India, Montgomerie had made his own estimations of the latitude and longitude of Yarkand, arriving at figures at considerable variance not only with those of the Jesuits, but also with more recent observations provided by the Schlagintweit brothers. The mission of Abdul Hamid was designed to check the accuracy of Montgomerie's estimate of the position of Yarkand and to test the utility of Indians to explore the inhospitable and unknown regions beyond the borders of British territory.

The area in which Yarkand was situated had been plagued by constant violent uprisings by the Moslems against the Chinese. This made it a dangerous place for Europeans. But the city did have the advantage of being only fifteen marches from the northern frontier of India. Furthermore, Abdul Hamid (or Mahomed-i-Hameed, as Montgomerie called him) seemed an ideal candidate. Hamid was not only a Moslem, like the majority of the population of Yarkand, but had also worked in the north of India and knew part of the route. He was described as a *munshi*, a term used to describe a teacher of native languages or, more generally, any educated Indian. Hamid was initially identified as a possible explorer by Sir Robert Montgomery, the lieutenant-governor of the Punjab, who sent him off to the Survey of India.[3]

With the assistance of Douglas Forsyth, then Secretary to the Punjab government (and destined to lead a mission to Yarkand himself some years later), Hamid was brought to Montgomerie's base camp in Kashmir in May 1863. Time was short, as Montgomerie wanted him to start that summer so as to return early the following year. Luckily, Hamid already knew the basics of route surveying and could use a prismatic compass and read a vernier, a rather difficult device employing a movable scale for the accurate measurement of barometric readings. During his month at the base camp, Hamid was taught how to take observations for latitude with a pocket sextant and to measure the temperature of the air and of boiling water. By June 12, he had, according to Montgomerie, "acquired tolerable proficiency" and so left for Leh, the capital of Ladakh, with a survey party which was going in that direction. In addition to his pocket sextant and its accompanying dark-glass artificial horizon, prismatic and pocket compasses, and two thermometers ("all of the smallest size procurable"), the *munshi* was also equipped with two "plain silver watches," a copper jug and oil lamp to boil water for the thermometer, a small tin lantern so as to be able to read the sextant at night, two books in which to record his observations, and some spare paper.[4]

Hamid, in addition to his instruments, also had with him a spiked staff common to travelers in the area. His, however, had a dual purpose in that the head of the staff was larger than usual and flat. By resting a compass on it, bearings could be taken without attracting attention.[5] The art of concealing surveying equipment so that it would not be conspicuous was to be further refined for later explorers.

Hamid and the survey party reached Leh on July 4. Montgomerie then tested the route survey the *munshi* had made to Leh from Kashmir. This proved satisfactory, and the decision was made to send him on to Yarkand. But difficulties then developed. The original plan was for Hamid to leave for Yarkand in the company of a guide named Mahomed Amin, who had been in the service of Adolph Schlagintweit and had traveled widely in Central Asia. Amin had been sent to Leh by the Punjab government, but on arrival refused to go to Yarkand, saying that he had been forbidden to enter the city. Inquiries made by the GTS in Ladakh showed Amin to be of doubtful character, and it was decided that Hamid should have nothing to do with him. Instead, the explorer was instructed to join a *kafila*, or caravan, of Ladakhi merchants heading for Yarkand, along one of the most difficult trade routes known to man, across the Karakorum and Kunlun ranges.[6] After hiring two servants and a pony and purchasing merchandise to lend credence to his disguise as a trader, Hamid left Leh on 24 August 1863 (Map 1).

His task was to make a route survey from the British frontier to Yarkand and to fix the position of that city. Route surveys customarily included details of the country traversed, such as hills, mountains, and ridges, together with information on the crops of the area, if any, details of rivers and lakes, observations of towns and villages and their populations, and a close description of the road traveled.[7] Hamid took observations daily to ascertain his position, and timed his marches so as to estimate the distances covered.

The seventh day from Leh brought the caravan before the Karakorum pass (18,290 feet), the *munshi* suffering intermittently from headaches brought on by the high altitude. The party rested for two days and then left for the desolate heights of the Karakorum range. They saw no habitation for nineteen days, and many ponies in the caravan died for lack of food before the *kafila* emerged from the mountains on 20 September. (Following the same route about forty years later, a British traveler counted the remains of five thousand horses, with the vultures "so gorged they could hardly move."[8]) Once on level ground, Hamid was able to make better time. He discovered some nephrite, a form of jade found in a wide belt across Central Asia, on the bed of the Karakash River. The party reached Yarkand ten days after leaving the mountains, and the *munshi*, perhaps overemphasizing the contrast with the Karakorums, commented enthusiastically on the fertility of the city, watered by the runoff of melting snow and ice from the mountains and distributed by irrigation canals.

Montgomerie pointed out that the *munshi*'s journey gave some idea of the immensity of the Himalayan ranges, about four hundred miles wide at their narrowest point. For twenty-five days the "road" never fell below fifteen thousand feet. Hamid took nineteen days to travel from the last village south of the Karakorum range to the first village on its northern flank, while by comparison, said Montgomerie, a good walker could do the same for the Alps in a single summer's day.[9]

Hamid made a complete route survey from Leh to Yarkand, taking bearings every hour or so. He stayed in Yarkand through the winter, taking observations secretly at night to determine the position and climate of the city and its height above sea level.

Yarkand was ruled by a Moslem governor in charge of day-to-day administration, who was responsible to a Chinese official. Chinese troops provided the garrison force. Through an old friend, Awaz Ali, Hamid became closely acquainted with the governor, and it was no doubt from this friendship that he was able to produce an account of Yarkand, its Chinese administration, and the various political factions in the area. He also drew up a general map of the region, which indicated the major cities and showed

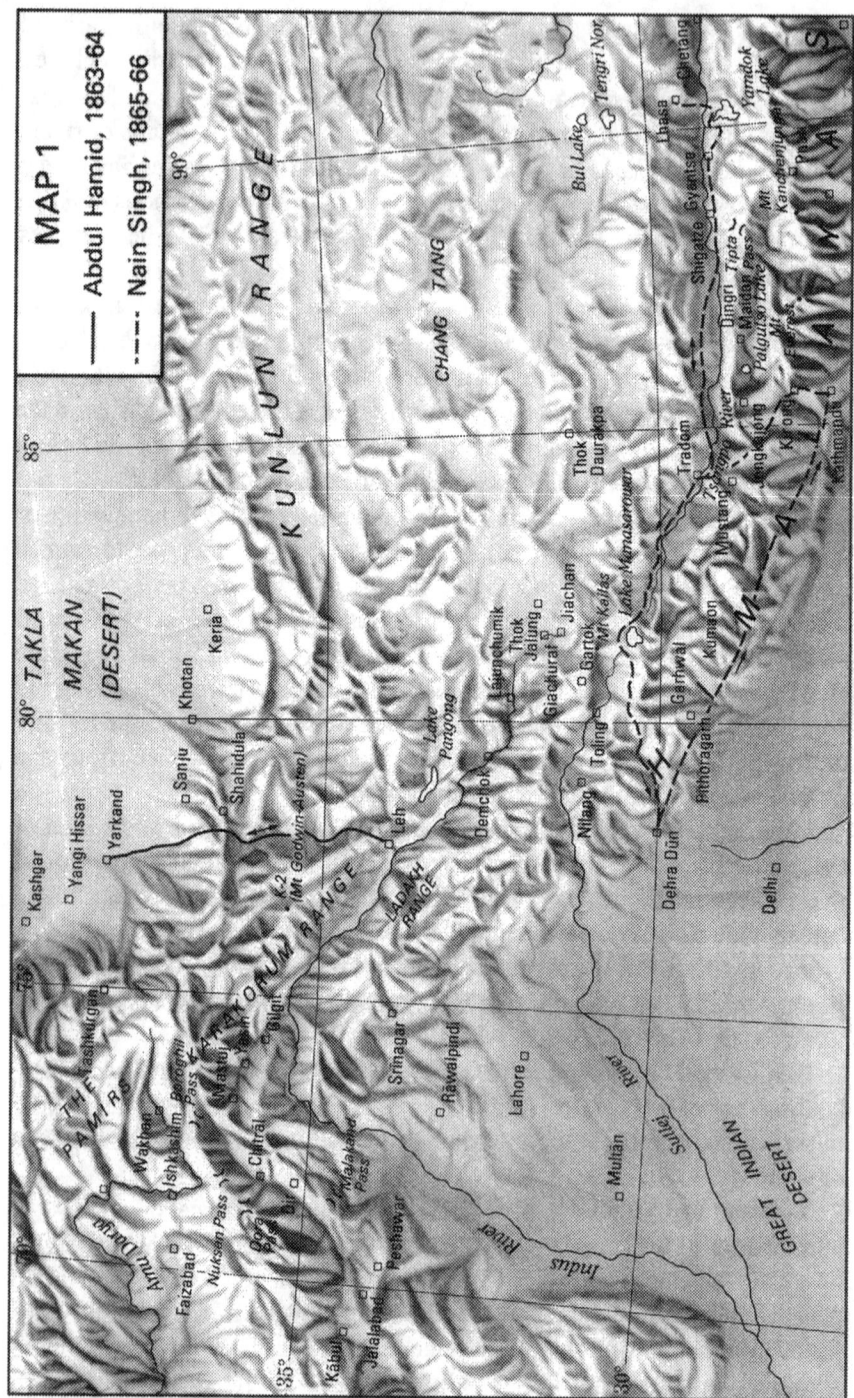

the extent of Russian influence. While in Yarkand, Hamid was under the political protection of the Kashmiri *Aksakal* (or Consul) "who sheltered him from the evil reports of designing Kashmiri merchants."[10] Possibly the established merchants, in their ignorance of Hamid's real identity, feared his making inroads into their trade.

The winter was severe, the thermometer recording 0° F at one point. Snow fell in January. Toward the end of March, Hamid was warned by the governor that Chinese officials were becoming suspicious of his activities. Hamid and Awaz Ali promptly joined another caravan returning to Leh and were safely conducted by the *Aksakal* back to the Karakorum pass. They survived the passage through the most dangerous section of the journey, but then both the unfortunate *munshi* and his friend, now in British protected territory, became ill and died. This occurred close to a GTS encampment headed by William Johnson, who investigated and was told by the members of the caravan that the two men had succumbed after eating poisonous wild rhubarb, abundant in the area. Johnson was suspicious of the circumstances but could prove nothing.

Johnson was, however, able to recover all of the *munshi*'s instruments, papers and books, and these were forwarded to Montgomerie, reaching him in early 1865. Montgomerie deeply regretted the death of Abdul Hamid and said of him that "he was an honest and patient observer, and had he lived, his exertions would, I am sure, have been handsomely rewarded by the Punjab government."[11] It was also a loss that Hamid was not present to elaborate upon his observations.

Nevertheless, Montgomerie's plan was vindicated, and Abdul Hamid can be considered the first of the Indian Survey's trans-Himalayan explorers.[12]

By careful checking of the written data, Montgomerie said that the position of Yarkand had now "been determined within narrow limits."[13] On the basis of Hamid's observations, Montgomerie concluded that Yarkand lay at latitude 38° 21' and longitude 77° 31'. This is close to the present-day figures, as given by the *Times Atlas,* of 38° 27' and 77° 16', and closer than the positions put forward by either the Jesuits or the Schlagintweits. Hamid had also collected useful geographical and political information about the city and much of Chinese Turkestan.

Shortly after receiving Hamid's papers, Montgomerie passed the political information over to the Punjab government. When Colonel Walker, superintendent of the GTS, returned from leave, Montgomerie departed for England on 20 February 1865, taking the geographical data with him. He had been on survey duty continuously since 1852 and was suffering from "low jungle fever."[14] Soon after arriving in England, he married the daughter of a former senior officer of the Bengal Artillery and settled down to write up his report.[15]

Montgomerie was invited to deliver his paper, titled "On the Geographical Position of Yarkand and Other Places in Central Asia," to the Royal Geographical Society's meeting in London on 14 May 1866. Geographers had already been impressed by his survey of Kashmir, for which he had won a gold medal from the RGS, and his reputation was further enhanced by his presentation. The president of the RGS, Sir Roderick Murchison, stated at the meeting that the paper was "of the very highest importance to geographers." Sir Andrew Waugh, the former surveyor-general of India, corroborated Montgomerie's interpretations of the *munshi*'s observations and basked in the glory reflected from his old pupil.

Sir Henry Rawlinson pointed out at the meeting that Hamid's survey of Yarkand in the south, when combined with Russian mapping of the Tian Shan to the north, meant that only a strip of territory about three hundred miles in width separating the two now needed to be mapped. "When that was done," he concluded, "Central Asia would be brought into the category of known geography."[16] This was an exaggeration. But Montgomerie's triumph undoubtedly was, as Sir Henry Yule later wrote, "the first step toward placing the geography of the great basin of Eastern Turkistan on a satisfactory footing."[17]

More ambitious plans were already under way. Even while Abdul Hamid was on his ill-fated journey to Yarkand, Montgomerie had received approval from the government of India to recruit and train two more Indian explorers. Before he left for England, they had already been dispatched to Lhasa, the capital of "forbidden" Tibet.

The selection of the two recruits had commenced during 1862 and 1863, when Montgomerie contacted Major Smyth of the Education Department in Kumaon and asked him to recommend likely candidates.[18] The approach to Smyth was a wise decision from two points of view. Kumaon, lying to the west of Nepal, was an administrative division of British India which had been annexed from Nepal by treaty of 1816 following the successful conclusion of the Gurkha War. A mountainous area enclosing steep valleys, a thirty-mile stretch of its northern border embraced some eighty peaks over twenty thousand feet. Most important, Kumaon was the first British territory to have a common border with Tibet, as its northern frontier bordered the southwestern part of Tibet known as Nari or Ari (from a Sanskrit name for the region). In the remote northern part of Kumaon, at altitudes of ten thousand to thirteen thousand feet, lived the Bhotia people, whose name was derived from a Tibetan term for their country. The Bhotias, of Tibetan origin themselves, and of similar customs and language, were an intelligent, enterprising, and hardy race, able to carry heavy loads at high altitudes. But what was more important for the purposes of the Survey of India was that the Bhotias earned their living in the summer months by trading with Tibet. They had a monopoly on trade between Kumaon and Western Tibet and traveled freely across the border, exchanging flour, rice, and English manufactured goods for Tibetan wool, salt, gold-dust, ponies, and borax. If they were willing to be recruited and capable of being trained, they seemed to be the best choice for the exploration of Tibet.[19]

Major Smyth, as Inspector of Education, was well placed to be able to identify likely prospects. He was an ardent climber, hunter, and traveler, who had crossed over the frontier into Tibet on many occasions.[20] Between 1860 and 1864, he made several attempts to proceed with an expedition to Tibet, but met with repeated rebuffs.[21] It was in connection with this expedition that Smyth was in correspondence with Montgomerie. Perhaps because he was unable to reach Lhasa himself, Smyth was more than willing to help recruit those whose explorations the government would sanction. He therefore recommended two Bhotias from Milam, a village situated over eleven thousand feet above sea level, northeast of Nanda Devi and nestling in a forested valley less than twenty miles from the Tibetan frontier. The Bhotias of Milam were used to traversing difficult routes. Their valley was entered by a huge gorge, some twelve miles in length, the path through which was often just a series of steps hewn from the edges of a precipice.[22] The village was inhabited only from June to November, as the climate forced the residents nearer the plains during the winter months. The two recruits, amenable to Smyth's proposals, were sent off to the headquarters of the GTS in Dehra Dun in early 1863, for training there and in the neighboring Engineering College at Roorkee.[23]

Walker supervised their initial training, and when he left to go on leave in November 1863, this process was brought to completion by Montgomerie.[24]

The Bhotias selected from the village of Milam were Mani Singh and his cousin, Nain Singh.[25] They were the sons of the two Singh brothers who had helped William Moorcroft and his companion Captain Hearsey while they were detained in western Tibet in 1812. To what degree the two were instrumental in freeing Moorcroft and Hearsey is unclear. Certainly Moorcroft traded his coral beads for sheep and shawl-wool goats (to the advantage of the Singhs, he allowed), and the Singhs offered a loan of one thousand rupees (which was refused) in the belief that the travelers' problems were due to a shortage of funds. Moorcroft and his companion did provide the Singhs with a number of testimonials, which later passed into the hands of another of their sons, Kishen Singh, himself subsequently an explorer of the Trigonometrical Survey.

Neither Nain nor Mani was new to exploration. Both had traveled in Western Tibet in the service of Richard and Henry Strachey and, together with another family member named Dolpa Singh, had accompanied the brothers Schlagintweit during 1855-1857. Mani came from a wealthy family in the Johar district of Kumaon, in which the village of Milam was situated. He was the "Patwarie," or chief native official, of the district. Henry Strachey, in expressing his gratitude for information provided about routes, said that he was "indebted chiefly to the Jwari Bhotias (particularly to the family of the Patwari of Milam)," who "far surpass the others in intelligence."[26] Mani Singh had been hired by the Schlagintweit brothers, and had made the arrangements for them to go to Tibet. He accompanied them into Tibet, and traveled with them to Chinese Turkestan.[27] Adolph Schlagintweit described Mani as "clever, intelligent, honest, [and] trustworthy," with a good knowledge of several surveying instruments. Schlagintweit said that he had discussed with Mani a plan to go to Lhasa and explore eastern Tibet, and he recommended that Mani should be accompanied by Nain Singh, "a very sharp young fellow who has learned with us to read instruments, a little map making and a little English writing."[28]

Nain Singh traveled with the brothers Hermann and Robert to Ladakh in 1856. They described him as "a well disposed and intelligent native," who was interested in observing, and learned to use surveying instruments so that he could read off the numbers and write down the results in English. The plan for Nain and Mani Singh to go to Lhasa never materialized. The Schlagintweits even proposed to take Nain back with them to Europe, but "like all hill men, he was too much attached to his native mountains to bring himself to leave them, and he unexpectedly went away from us at Raulpindi [sic], leaving behind a long letter of apologies."[29]

When Mani and Nain Singh left Kumaon for Dehra Dun in February 1863, they carried with them their letter of recommendation from Adolph Schlagintweit, and a covering letter from one of Major Smyth's colleagues, which said that the two were "intelligent and anxious to learn," although Mani, by comparison with his cousin, was described as "not so active or bright."

This latter communication also gives some idea of one motive behind the willingness of the Singhs, and other Indians, to volunteer for arduous and dangerous assignments. "Manee," the letter noted, "is anxious to obtain some permanent government employ a little better paid than what he gets as a Patwaree."[30]

Mani became known as "the Patwar" or GM, the latter pseudonym derived from the reversal of the first and last sounded consonants of his name.[31] Even though he was senior to Nain Singh, and more experienced, Mani proved to be rather a weak reed. He was, as Smyth put it, "too well off in his own country to take to the rough life of exploration."[32] Nain Singh, however, eventually rose to be the most famous of all the Indian explorers, and his code name, "the Pundit" (or "schoolmaster"), which was employed like the "GM" of his cousin to preserve anonymity, later became the general term used to embrace all the Indian explorers of the GTS. At the time he was sent for training to Dehra Dun he was about thirty-three years old and had been the schoolmaster in the village of Milam since 1858. He belonged to the Kshatriya (or warrior) caste[33] and could read and write Tibetan.[34]

The Pundit was the younger son of a small *zamindar* (landlord), from whom he inherited a few fields. Part of his time he cultivated his fields, and part of his time was spent in trading with Tibet. It was his knowledge of Tibet which first brought him to the attention of British officials in Kumaon, who, impressed by his abilities and enterprise, then appointed him as master of a "good vernacular school" in Kumaon, where he remained until recruited by Major Smyth.[35]

Walker had sent orders from his camp to Dehra Dun, outlining the kind of instruction the Singhs were to receive. This was to depend on their abilities, which might perhaps measure up to learning the full use of a sextant or perhaps only to partial use of the instrument, so as to take observations for latitude. Possibly just the taking of compass bearings and walking with a measured pace might be all that they could be trained for. Not that Walker's view implied any lack of intelligence on the part of the Singhs—rather, he believed that "their fingers are probably too old and stiff for the delicate manipulation of tangent screws."[36] In any event, Nain Singh proved himself quite competent to make full use of the sextant.

The two Singhs were first taught how to take bearings with a prismatic compass. Then they were drilled on the parade ground to walk with a measured pace of 31-½ inches, with two thousand paces adding up to almost a mile. Finally, they were instructed in the use of the sextant to take meridian altitudes and so determine latitude and were taught how to recognize the larger stars. By knowing the distance traveled, by taking compass bearings and using the sextant, and by checking against astronomical observations, a good route survey could be obtained. The Singhs were also shown how to use a boiling-point thermometer to measure their altitude above sea level, and to keep accurate notes of their measurements. However, in order that they might not be tempted to falsify data, they were not supplied with astronomical tables, nor were they instructed in the methods of calculating the route survey from the observations taken. This was done by Montgomerie and others only after the explorers had returned.

The explorers also took with them a Tibetan prayer wheel and a rosary, each adapted for survey use. The drum of the prayer wheel was detachable and contained not prayers, but long strips of paper on which to record paces marched and sextant observations made. The prayer wheels also had the advantage, it was discovered, of not being subject to examination by officials at the frontier, and so later versions were fitted with a compass.

The Buddhist rosary of the explorers was used to count paces. Carried hidden in the folds of the left sleeve, it was made up of 100 beads manufactured from red composition to simulate coral, with every tenth bead being larger than the rest and made from a dark, corrugated seed. In this manner, with the rosary and prayer wheel, distances were measured and recorded in secrecy. Other equipment included two large sextants, two box sextants, prismatic and pocket compasses (with Persian or Hindi rather than English numerals), thermometers to measure the temperatures of both air and boiling water, a pocket chronometer, and a watch.

The use of the large sextant with its six-inch radius presented problems, and on his journey to Lhasa and back the Pundit was able to observe latitudes with it at only thirty-one different places. The difficulty stemmed from the fact that the Pundit needed to take observations of the night stars while remaining unobserved by anyone else in the party with which he might be traveling. Mercury, carried in a coconut, was used to provide an artificial horizon (considered preferable to the dark-glass artificial horizon carried by Abdul Hamid), and a reserve was held in cowrie shells sealed with wax. The Pundit had a wooden bowl with a spout of the kind frequently used by Bhotias for eating and drinking. The mercury was poured into this bowl, the deep sides of which protected it from the wind. Reading the measurement from the sextant at night was no easy task. Initially the Pundit used a bull's-eye lantern, but was forced to sell this to curious Tibetan officials, and from then on he tried to use an oil wick. But when the wind was strong the light blew out, and the sextant had to be laid aside to be read by daylight.[37]

By this time, tests of the Singhs' work were showing that the cousins had assimilated their training. These tests involved sending them into areas for which maps existed in manuscript form, but had not been published. Their observations were then checked against these maps.

Abdul Hamid and Nain Singh 43

At last the two Pundits were ready to proceed (Map 1). In December 1863, the Military Department of the government approved the request of the GTS that the trans-Himalayan explorers be provided with three years' salary in advance "as they will be working in distant and unknown countries beyond the reach of communication."[38] They themselves, according to Montgomerie, had proposed a visit to Lhasa and had suggested that they should head northeast from Milam, crossing the Tibetan border to reach Lake Manasarowar in Western Tibet.[39] Montgomerie then directed that they should make a route survey of the road that ran from Gartok southeast to Manasarowar, continuing almost due east some 800 miles to Lhasa. It was known from native reports that this road existed, as it was a major trading route between Ladakh and Lhasa. The Jesuit priests Desideri and Freyre had traversed it in 1715-16, but their account had not been published. Since the road was thought to follow the Tsangpo, the great river of Tibet, for much of the way, geographical data as to the course of the Tsangpo would also be acquired. At the time only one point on the river had been defined with any certainty, which was near Shigatse, southwest of Lhasa, when Samuel Turner was there in 1783. The Pundits were also instructed to determine the position of Lhasa, hitherto a matter of conjecture based largely on native information gathered by Turner in Shigatse seventy years earlier. Finally, the Pundits were to return to Lake Manasarowar by a more northerly route.[40]

The Tsangpo River valley could be considered a distinct geographical area of Tibet, lying between the main Himalayan range to the south and the Kailas range to the north.[41] On the far side of the Kailas range lay the Chang Tang, or "northern plain," a high arid plateau characterized by strong winds, brackish lakes, and extreme cold—a combination sufficient to deter most life, although yaks and wild asses fed on the sparse vegetation. Nomadic herdsmen were found in the southern extremities of the Chang Tang; otherwise the only people were a few collectors of salt and borax. The Chang Tang began in the northwest corner of Tibet between the Karakorum and Kunlun ranges and expanded east and southeast to cover most of the northern part of the country (approximately half the total area) as far east as Lhasa. To the east of the capital city of Lhasa were the fertile valley systems of the Yangtse, Mekong, and Salween Rivers. The bulk of the population, then as now, lived in these valleys and in the valley of the Tsangpo and its tributaries, particularly around Lhasa and the two other major towns of Shigatse and Gyantse.

Much of the country was at extremely high altitudes, which had earned for Tibet the name (shared with the Pamir) of "roof of the world." The

Chang Tang was generally over 15,000 feet, and the Tsangpo River valley lay between 10,000 and 12,000 feet above sea level.

The route of the two pundits was to follow the valley of the Tsangpo, a geological depression between two mountain ranges, further deepened by the eroding effects of the river. Lake Manasarowar, close to Mount Kailas, was to be their Tibetan starting point. This area was sacred to Hindus and Buddhists alike, Kailas being considered by the former as the home of the god Shiva and by the Buddhists as the center of the universe. The Sutlej River had its source near Lake Manasarowar, and the sources of three other major rivers, the Indus, Tsangpo-Brahmaputra, and the Karnali (a major tributary of the Ganges) were close by. The climate in the valley was more temperate than that of the Chang Tang, and the rainfall was greater, though because it was concentrated at limited times of the year, vegetation was generally not abundant.

In March 1864, after a year's training, the pair left Dehra Dun and returned to Milam, their home village. The official account, as published by the Survey of India, noted only that they attempted to proceed from Kumaon via Lake Manasarowar but "did not find it practicable."[42] They were apparently delayed because one of their chronometers stopped working, and they believed it was impossible to continue with only a watch. The chronometer was sent to Roorkee for repair. Two sources confirm that the two did make an attempt to cross the border but were recognized and forced to turn back.[43] Why they should have been refused entry to Tibet is unclear, bearing in mind that Milam had an established trading relationship with Gartok. The fact that the bulk of the population was at the Gartok Trade Fair, while they were perhaps taking a pass further to the east in the direction of Manasarowar, may have excited suspicion. In any event, the two Pundits returned to Montgomerie in Dehra Dun in December 1864. At this juncture, because the season for traveling to Manasarowar had ended with the advent of winter and as it seemed foolish to wait and then make a second attempt having already been turned back once, the Singhs suggested to Montgomerie that they try to reach Lhasa through Nepal.

The reason behind this proposal lay with a meeting they had had in Kumaon with a party of Bhotias who had returned from the Tibetan districts just across the border to the north. Several Chinese officials from these districts had recently been arrested and sent to Lhasa, and when the belongings of these officials were seized, some property of the Bhotia traders was inadvertently confiscated at the same time. The traders appealed to Colonel Ramsay, formerly British Resident in Nepal and now the British Commissioner in Kumaon, asking him to send an agent to Lhasa to retrieve the property on their behalf. Ramsay promptly appointed Nain and Mani Singh to act as their *mooktiyars* (intermediaries) and also provided them with a letter of introduction to the British Resident in Nepal.[44] Montgomerie agreed that to have the Pundits act as agents for the Bhotia traders would provide a most plausible excuse for their journey to Lhasa. Furthermore, the Nepalese maintained contact with Lhasa, and traders frequently crossed the border. Montgomerie accordingly directed that the Pundits should first go to Kathmandu, the capital of Nepal, and then travel due north to meet the Gartok-Lhasa road at about its halfway point. The Singhs set off again on 8 January 1865 and reached Kathmandu on March 7, making a route survey as they progressed.[45] They were now very much on their own, in another country miles distant from Survey headquarters in Dehra Dun. Montgomerie himself had departed for leave in England in February, still worrying that he had sent his explorers off carrying instruments too large and likely to arouse suspicion.[46]

On arrival in Kathmandu, the pair inquired as to which pass might be free of snow so early in the year. Finding that the most direct route was still impassable, they soon left together with four servants for Kirong, a border town of three to four thousand people. They were dressed as Bashahris, traditionally a people allowed to travel unquestioned to Lhasa, and claimed that the purpose of their journey was to obtain recovery of the Bhotia property, buy horses, and to make a pilgrimage. Alas, this attempt was a failure. As soon as they reached Kirong, they were stopped by Chinese officials. The Chinese were suspicious since they knew that the Singhs' route was an unusual one for Bashahris, who would not normally be traveling to Lhasa via Nepal. Their luggage was searched, but luckily without discovery of the survey instruments hidden in secret compartments. The Pundits then planned to make personal representation to the Kirong governor but fortunately discovered before doing so that the governor had known Mani personally and would therefore be quick to uncover his deception. Both Pundits and their servants were forced to retreat back to Kathmandu, where they arrived on 10 April. This was a great disappointment to the two explorers, and it seemed as though their mission was to be frustrated before they had even set foot in Tibet. Nain Singh tried, but could find no one he could accompany to Lhasa. Friends urged him to abandon the attempt. But he wrote in his diary that "suffering from anxiety, and losing nearly all hope of ever accomplishing my design, I determined to overcome my despondence and make one effort more."[47]

Searching the city, the cousins eventually found a Bhotia merchant who was about to depart for Lhasa. However, as his planned route was through

Kirong, the Pundits agreed to separate, with only Nain Singh accompanying the merchant. Mani, forced to make alternative arrangements because he would have been recognized by the governor, left for Tibet by a more devious route. Mani failed in his mission, however, later claiming ill health and unsafe roads. Montgomerie thought a more likely reason was "want of determination." Mani did make a route survey of northwest Nepal and eventually returned to his home in Milam.[48]

Nain Singh was now on his own. He persevered with the merchant, lending him one hundred rupees on promise of repayment in Lhasa. The merchant kept delaying his departure, so eventually the Pundit left (3 June) with a servant, the merchant agreeing to catch up with him later. Because he was afraid that the border officials might recognize him, the Pundit this time assumed the disguise of a Ladakhi going to buy horses. He wore the appropriate clothes, and a pigtail. They halted some days later at an agreed place, but the merchant never appeared. Nain Singh promptly visited the merchant's family and was able to persuade the merchant's brother to act as a guarantor to allow him to pass beyond Kirong to visit relatives. However, Nain Singh agreed that under penalty of death he would not proceed to Lhasa, at least within the year. Having signed and sealed a declaration to this effect, the Pundit crossed the border into Tibet. On the road he encountered a caravan of Bashahri merchants with two hundred yaks heading for Lake Manasarowar by way of Tradom monastery on the Gartok-Lhasa road. Nain Singh declared that he was a Bashahri himself and found that he was welcome to join them. He claimed that he was visiting the monastery at Tradom in order to worship there, before proceeding to Manasarowar to catch up with a cargo of medicinal plants he had sent ahead by another route. Crossing the Himalayas and cutting through the No La (Pass) at 16,600 feet, Nain Singh caught his first glimpse of the great Tsangpo River of Tibet. The Tsangpo immediately inspired respect as he watched three men drown when their flimsy coracle, a wood-framed boat covered with leather, was swamped. The Pundit crossed the river safely by ferry on 6 September to reach Tradom on the northern bank. The caravan continued west, but Nain Singh pretended to be ill and remained in Tradom. Inquiring about the river from the people he met on his travels, he found that they were unanimous in saying that the Tsangpo, after flowing from west to east, turned south into India where it became the Brahmaputra. This indeed was the case, but was not conclusively proved to be so for several decades—and after much controversy—because of the difficulties of exploration in the rough and dangerous terrain of Assam in northeast India through which the river ran.

At the time of the Pundit's journey, no European had traveled the Gartok-Lhasa Road since Desideri, and none was to see it again until the twentieth century.[49] The Pundit measured the altitude of Tradom at about 14,200 feet above sea level. From Tradom to Lhasa, the road followed the Tsangpo River or one of its tributaries quite closely, occasionally crossing from one bank to the other. Since the river was not fordable, boats were used to ferry passengers across. For those who could not afford the fare, there were several iron suspension bridges. Neither method of crossing was without danger. The bridges were constructed of two iron chains, each up to three hundred feet long, and constructed of links three-fourths of an inch thick, from which rope netting hung. One hundred and fifty years earlier, Desideri had commented on these iron bridges, saying that he only used them when "forced by dire necessity."[50] Nain Singh agreed that they were very dangerous and that people preferred the boats, even though while the Pundit navigated across the river at 13,500 feet above sea level, his boat was almost sunk by large waves.

Never falling below ten thousand feet, and rising above sixteen thousand feet on several occasions, the road, more a desolate track, was swept by very high winds. Although not paved in any way, it was nevertheless well maintained, cleared of stones, with staging posts which provided accommodation for up to 150 to 200 people and supplies of fresh horses and yaks. The road was also a vital communication link, messengers on horseback traveling the eight hundred miles from Lhasa to Gartok in as little as twenty days.

The Pundit noted that these messengers generally looked "haggard and worn" since they halted only to eat and to change horses. Their coats were sealed in order to ensure the secrecy of the letters they carried. Nain Singh said he saw several of them arrive in Lhasa from Gartok, "their faces . . . cracked, their eyes blood-shot and sunken, and their bodies eaten by lice into large raws, the latter they attributed to not being allowed to take off their clothes."

The distance from Tradom to Lhasa was about five hundred miles, which the Pundit covered in thirty-seven marches. For security he joined a Ladakhi caravan of some twelve men and seventy yaks, part of the regular exchange of trading caravans between Tibet and Kashmir. He left Tradom on 3 October and reached Lhasa on 10 January 1866, an average daily march covering ten to fifteen miles. For two weeks after leaving Tradom, the area through which the caravan passed was devoid of population; but on reaching Ralung on 19 October, willow trees appeared and there was some cultivation, which increased as they approached Lhasa. The Pundit's report does not comment on the grandeur or immensity of the Himalayas, as the main range would have been hidden from him by smaller mountains lining the river valley.

Nain Singh and his fellow travelers usually started off at dawn, following the piles of stones marking the route. The Pundit also found these cairns useful for taking compass bearings. He and his servant would walk at some distance from the rest of the party, pretending to be immersed in religious devotions, and this ploy generally proved sufficient to prevent others from interrupting him in the counting of his paces. The caravan customarily halted at around 2:00-3:00 P.M., at a staging post if possible. If not, tents were used, and sometimes the Pundit had to sleep in the open air, exposed to the cutting wind. Nain Singh continually counted his paces (although many of the party went by boat), took observations with his sextant and thermometers, and recorded information about the terrain and the climate.

A few marches before reaching Shigatse, the road bore south away from the river, and the gray gravel gave way to a more grassy cultivated terrain, with increasing numbers of houses and people closer to the town. The caravan arrived in Shigatse on 29 October and halted there for almost two months. No European had seen this town since Turner, in 1783.

The Pundit described Shigatse as being three-quarters of a mile long and half a mile wide, surrounded by fertile soil, with a population of nine thousand and garrisoned by a force of one hundred Chinese and four hundred Tibetan soldiers.

After resting, the Ladakhis went to pay their respects to the Panchen Lama in the great Tashilhunpo monastery nearby. Approaching the monastery, with its gilded spires and 3,300 priests, the Pundit worried that the Panchen, who was believed to be able to discern all secrets, might penetrate his disguise. Nain Singh would have preferred not to go with the Ladakhis, but thought it impolite to decline. Once inside the monastery, he was relieved to find that the Panchen was only an eleven-year-old boy. The audience was brief and formal. Each visitor bowed his bared head and offered a piece of silk. Then after the Panchen had placed his hands on each head, the visitors sat and were asked three questions: "Is your King well?"; "Is your country prospering?"; and "Are you in good health?" Presumably the guests responded affirmatively, after which the Panchen placed a strip of silk around their necks and gave them a cup of tea.

While waiting in Shigatse, the Nepalese agent with whom Mani Singh was supposed to be traveling arrived in the town. Nain Singh was disappointed not to find his cousin among the party. Low on funds, he was forced to supplement his dwindling resources by teaching Nepalese shopkeepers a Hindu method of arithmetic.

The Ladakhis left on 22 December, the Pundit with them. The road at this point turned to the south of the Tsangpo and led to Gyantse, a city about the same size as Shigatse, which they reached on 25 December. Gyantse had also been visited by Bogle, Turner, and Manning, and its fort was to be occupied by the British in 1903. After a few days the caravan left and followed the route taken by Manning to Lhasa through the Karo pass and to the west of Yamdok Lake. Here they were attacked by robbers. While Nain Singh was able to escape unharmed by urging his horse to a gallop, this does raise the question of how he could have been pacing his distance if he were on horseback. Montgomerie asked the Pundit about this on his return and was told that this stretch, and a few others which were also covered on horseback or by boat, were measured on foot during the return journey. Internal checks on the measurements seemed to verify this.

Finally, on 10 January 1866, the Pundit entered the fabled city of Lhasa, where he rented two rooms in a caravansary belonging to the Tashilhunpo monastery. From one of the rooms he was able to take observations with his sextant. He familiarized himself with the city, and his description of it was the first to be made since that of the Lazarists Huc and Gabet in 1846. His report, which provided details of Lhasa's geography, economy, and religion, and of the Chinese military presence, corroborated that of the French priests.[51]

The city, he said, was circular with a circumference of two and a half miles, standing on a generally level plain, and surrounded by mountains. The population, which totaled about fifteen thousand according to an 1854 census which the Pundit learned of, lived in mud dwellings, although the rich might have houses of brick and stone. The city was garrisoned by a force of one thousand Tibetan and five hundred Chinese soldiers. Although Tibet could accurately be described as "forbidden" as far as the British were concerned, Nain Singh was able to recount the cosmopolitanism of Lhasa as a trading center for merchants from China, Bhutan, Sikkim, Nepal, Ladakh, Kashmir, and elsewhere. From China came silk, carpets, and tea. Kham, in eastern Tibet, supplied musk perfume; rice was imported from Bhutan; tobacco from Sikkim; cloth, saddles, precious stones, and Indian manufactured goods from Darjeeling; and saffron from Ladakh and Kashmir. Merchants generally came in December and left in the spring before rain made the rivers impassable.

Like Huc and Gabet, the Pundit visited the Sera monastery three miles outside the city and commented on its golden spires and gem-studded idols. As in Shigatse, he felt obliged to join the Ladakhis in pilgrimage, but this time to the Dalai Lama, resident in the Potala, magnificent on its hill on the outskirts of Lhasa. For a second time, Nain Singh was fearful that his true motives might be discovered. However, the lama was again only a boy aged about thirteen, seated on a throne six feet high. The audience was once more brief and formal. Montgomerie later wrote that "the Pundit's ancestors were Buddhists, and hence you can easily imagine his feelings when ushered into the great Lama's presence, with his prayer-wheel stuffed with Survey notes and an English compass in his sleeve. Fortunately, he was not very closely examined; and, finding that his thoughts were not divined, he regained his nerve, and managed to take the dimensions of the Great Lama's residence and fort as he returned from the audience."[52]

Nain Singh was right to be particularly concerned about his possession of mapping equipment. In 1846, the Tibetan authorities had been very alarmed by the maps of Tibet and elsewhere belonging to Fathers Huc and Gabet, fearing that they had constructed them on the basis of their travels. It was only with the help of the Chinese that the two priests were able to convince the Tibetans that the maps were printed in France and not drawn by them personally. The Tibetan regent, perusing their copy of Mercator's map of the world, asked to be shown where Lhasa was in relation to Calcutta. " 'The Pelings [English] of Calcutta are very near our frontier,' he said, making a grimace and shaking his head. 'No matter,' he added, 'here are the Himalaya mountains.' "[53]

His funds exhausted by his long stay in Lhasa, the Pundit again supported himself by teaching Hindu accounting methods. But then he had a nasty shock when two Muslims of Kashmiri descent quickly spotted that he was not a Bashahri. But they agreed to keep his secret, and the Pundit was even able to borrow money from them by leaving his Survey watch as security. Another unsettling incident occurred when the Pundit caught sight of the Kirong governor in the street. Since he had agreed to forfeit his life if he proceeded to Lhasa, his alarm can be imagined. Justice in Lhasa was swift, and the Pundit had already seen one man beheaded. He quickly rented another room and remained in it as much as possible.

Luckily, the Ladakhi merchant with whom the Pundit had traveled to Lhasa and with whom he had struck up a friendship was now about to leave for home, and readily agreed to take care of Nain Singh on the return journey. The Pundit had been in Lhasa for over three months. They left Lhasa on 21 April and, taking the same route, arrived back at the Tradom monastery on 1 June, after an uneventful journey.

Instead of returning to Kathmandu, the Pundit left Tradom the following day, continuing with the caravan westward along the Lhasa Road towards Gartok. The party journeyed at an altitude of between 14,000 and 16,000 feet, passing only a few nomads with their flocks of sheep and yaks. Nain

Singh continued his route survey along the road, traveling on the north bank of the Tsangpo, and reached Lake Manasarowar on 16 June. Here he met a friend from Kumaon who settled his accumulated debts with the Ladakhis—all the debt, that is, except the watch pawned in Lhasa and now in their hands. Nain Singh said he would send money to Gartok to redeem it.

The Pundit now parted from the Ladakhi caravan and headed for British territory and home, leaving his servant with his friend from Kumaon as security for the loan. After some difficulties because of snow on the passes, he crossed the Himalayas after a lengthy detour and returned to Milam. He then dispatched two men to pay his debt and return with his servant. He also met up with his cousin, whom he instructed to go to Gartok and redeem the watch, completing the route survey he himself had not been able to do. All these missions were safely accomplished, and Nain and Mani Singh arrived at GTS headquarters in Dehra Dun on 27 October 1866. It was almost 17 months since the Pundit had set out on his epic journey from Kathmandu to Lhasa.

According to some accounts, the travelers presented themselves to Captain Montgomerie.[54] This could not have occurred, however, as Montgomerie did not return to India from England until early 1867, rejoining the Survey on 1 May.[55] They probably reported in the first instance to Colonel Walker, superintendent of the GTS. When he returned, Montgomerie was appointed in charge of the Survey in Kumaon and Garhwal. Nevertheless, until he was forced to leave India in 1873 for medical reasons, Montgomerie continued to interview returning trans-Himalayan explorers, prepare maps from their observations, write up their reports, supervise the training of new recruits, and decide on the time and direction of their dispatch.

The results of Nain Singh's travels, as outlined by Montgomerie, were as follows: a large number of observations including thirty-one observations for latitude, allowing the calculation of the positions, heights and climates of Lhasa[56] and other important towns; an elaborate route survey of over twelve hundred miles covering the whole of the great road from Lhasa to Gartok as well as the route from Kathmandu to Tradom; and the defining of most of the course of the Tsangpo/Brahmaputra from its source near Lake Manasarowar to the point where it was joined by its tributary from Lhasa. In addition, valuable data were supplied on the Nepal valley.

By perusing the Pundit's observations for internal consistency, and by checking them against those made by Samuel Turner, Montgomerie was able to conclude that the Pundit was a "most excellent and trustworthy observer," whose work was "well done" with "highly creditable" results.

The Pundit also collected a considerable amount of miscellaneous information of a political, religious, and economic nature. His description of Lhasa agreed closely with that of Huc and Gabet. Since his rented rooms were only twenty paces away from the Jokang, one of the holiest places in the city, the Pundit was able to observe the many religious ceremonies of the Tibetan New Year.[57] Although more of Montgomerie's emissaries subsequently reached Lhasa, Nain Singh's description of the city was never improved upon by them.

Montgomerie must have been overjoyed at the successful return of Nain Singh and the acquisition of so much valuable information. The way was now clear for the training of further explorers to map the rest of Tibet and other parts of Central Asia.

Montgomerie was also anxious to share his discoveries with the Royal Geographical Society, for this journey of "his" agent could only enhance his own standing in the world of exploration. As soon as the report was written, a copy of it was sent to the RGS in London by Colonel Walker. Montgomerie then wrote to the president of the RGS, Sir Roderick Murchison, summarizing his results and giving due credit to the work of his explorer. He was clearly on good personal terms with Nain Singh and added that "I wish I could present the Pundit to you in person. I am sure he would make a good impression anywhere."[58]

Montgomerie's report, which was susequently printed in the journal of the RGS, was read to the Society in Montgomerie's absence on 23 March 1868. The luminaries of the Society heaped praise on both Montgomerie and Nain Singh, and the exploit was described as a combination of "native enterprise directed by English intelligence."[59] Later that year Nain Singh received the first of the many honors to be bestowed upon him, when the Council of the RGS awarded him a gold watch, valued at thirty guineas.[60] The only carping note came in a letter from Consul M.C. Morrison in Peking, who frowned on these clandestine surveys and urged travelers to apply openly for passports from the Chinese authorities to visit Tibet. Morrison seemed to have been unaware that these requests would have met with short shrift from the Chinese.

The success of Nain Singh's mission to Lhasa encouraged Montgomerie to request a further Rs. 5,000 from the Home Department of the government of India for the purpose of organizing additional expeditions. His request was forwarded, with the commendation of the Home Department, to the Foreign Department, which responded on 23 August 1867 that the "Governor-General in Council cordially approves of the proposal to employ Asiatics in the exploration of the Trans-Himalayan Regions, and directs that it be intimated to each explorer who may be sent out by the Trigonometrical Survey that any important political intelligence he may bring back will receive a separate pecuniary acknowledgement, according to its value, from the Foreign Secretary."[61] Montgomerie, his need for topographical data married to the government's desire for political intelligence, was on his way, and the stage was set for the continued expansion of his explorations.

THREE
Across the Northwest Frontier: The Mirza, the Havildar, and the Mullah

Throughout the nineteenth century, like two juggernauts, czarist Russia and British India lurched toward each other across Asia.[1] In 1800, vast distances separated the two, but by the close of the century only a thin strip of Afghan territory, extending up to the Chinese border, prevented Russia and India from sharing a common frontier. In the intervening years the "Great Game," a struggle for political and military supremacy in Southwest Asia, was played out in Afghanistan and Persia, through the deserts of Turkestan, and over the peaks and passes of the Pamir and the Hindu Kush.

In 1809, the frontier of British India lay on the south bank of the Sutlej and was far from attaining its natural limits among the mountain ranges to the north and northwest. The Russian border extended from the northeastern tip of the Caspian Sea along the Ural River to Orenburg, and then eastward. Nevertheless, for the British, this was the most important and the longest frontier (excepting that between Canada and the United States) in the Empire, and one on which no firm boundaries had been established by India, Afghanistan, or Persia.

Historically, India had been the recipient of many invasions across its northwest frontier, that area which starts at the tangled junction of the Pamir and Karakorum ranges and follows the line of the Hindu Kush southwest to the Indian Ocean. Alexander the Great had crossed the Hindu Kush through Swat to Peshawar. The Mongols of Genghis Khan followed in the thirteenth century, and in turn were succeeded by Tamerlane, Babur (the first of the Moghul emperors), and the Afghans and Persians in the eighteenth century.

British thoughts as to the vulnerability of this frontier were first raised by Napoleon when he and Czar Alexander, after their rapprochement at Tilsit in 1807, considered the possibility of a land invasion of India via Persia. Although Napoleon's invasion never materialized, and although the Russians never actually adopted a scheme to occupy India, nevertheless, after the fall of Napoleon, Russia became the bogeyman for British policymakers. The British realized that their navy, serving as the guardian of imperial possessions, would be of little use against a land invasion, and

London consequently viewed with alarm each Russian advance into Central Asia. Similarly, from the perspective of St. Petersburg, British conquests in India, with their inexorable progress north, combined with subsequent occupations of Afghanistan, were also viewed with great suspicion as being part of a plan to counter rightful Russian political and commercial interests in Central Asia.

The southward movement of the Russian empire, which had slowed in the latter half of the eighteenth century, resumed in the nineteenth. The 1813 treaty signed after the Russo-Persian War had the effect of turning the Caspian Sea into an area of Russian influence. Further concessions were extracted from Persia following another conflict between 1826 and 1828. The British treaty with Persia was shown to be ineffective in the absence of an ability to apply military pressure. Russia was now ominously close to Afghanistan, and in 1838, a British army occupied Kabul and Kandahar in an attempt to place a pliant Afghan ruler on the throne.

These forward moves by the British, plus their own desire to restrain attacks on Russian trading caravans, provided the government in St. Petersburg with reason enough to restart its advance into Central Asia against the three great khanates of Khiva, Kokand, and Bokhara. The first military force was sent against Khiva in 1839, but was defeated by the terrain, the climate, and problems of supply. A second expedition, a year later, was halted in 1842 on signing a treaty with Khiva.

By 1847 the czar's forces had advanced to the mouth of the Jaxartes (Sir Darya) River on the Aral Sea. By 1853 they had control of close to three hundred miles of the river, encroaching into the Oxus-Jaxartes basin, and thus bringing Russia into contact with the territory of the khan of Kokand. A lull ensued while Russia was occupied with the Crimean War, but in 1860 the khan attacked a Russian position, and the Russians, who needed new supplies of cotton to make up for the deficiency caused by the American Civil War, and perceiving British weakness after the Indian Mutiny of 1857, responded by capturing the city of Tashkent in 1865, and forming the province of Turkestan from territory lying between the Aral Sea and Lake Issyk Kul. The Russians were now within range of the three khanates. Crossing the Jaxartes, Russian forces reached the border of Bokhara, and Samarkand (within the territory of the khan of Bokhara) was annexed in 1868. Khiva fell in 1873, and Kokand was annexed in 1876. Russian conquests in the area were completed by 1884 after the Tekke Turkomans were defeated, and the Russians occupied the great oasis of Merv, only one hundred miles north of the Persian-Afghan border.

The British were also on the move, advancing in the northwest of India in pursuit of defensible frontiers for the Empire. Following the death of the

Sikh leader Ranjit Singh in 1839, the Sikh kingdom fell into disorder. Two wars against the British ensued in the 1840s, after which Britain annexed outright the Sikh kingdom of the Punjab in 1849. Sind had been annexed in 1843. Britain had now crossed the Indus, and the boundary of the Indian Empire in the northwest had reached its natural limits on the Hindu Kush.

Exactly where to draw this boundary remained a problem throughout the nineteenth century. It was not practicable to stop in the foothills of the Hindu Kush, because of raids by fanatical Pathans from the hills. Nor was it militarily or economically feasible to extend the frontier beyond the mountains to the Kabul-Kandahar line, the so-called "scientific frontier." Ultimately, the eastern parts of the Pathan hill territory were defined as being within the British border, with the other Pathans being declared part of Afghanistan. This was enshrined in the 1893 Durand Line, named after its negotiator, Sir Mortimer Durand, foreign secretary of the Indian government. These frontier districts of the Punjab, lying between the Indus and Afghanistan, were eventually formed into the separate North-West Frontier Province in 1901.

Although the Pathans were a nuisance, and outrages committed by them had continually to be avenged by punitive campaigns, they were, when all was said and done, only a nuisance. The real threat to the plains of Hindustan came not from warring hill tribes, but from the great European land power behind the mountains. Against the tribal peoples the British could deploy artillery and, given time, reinforcements by sea. But to defend the plains against a modern army, the British ideally wanted to control the passes through the Hindu Kush by occupying Kabul, Kandahar, and Badakhshan, as the Moghul emperors had done. Since this was not possible in the circumstances of the time, Britain sought, in the latter half of the nineteenth century, to defend its northwest Indian frontier, always a cause of anxiety, by creating in Afghanistan a friendly buffer state for protection against the advance of the Russian empire.

As early as 1809, Britain had sent Mountstuart Elphinstone as an emissary to the Afghan capital of Kabul to build a defensive alliance and so counter the possibility of a French invasion of India. But with the departure of Napoleon, Russia became the prime threat, and British efforts were directed toward denying Russia the right of access to India across the territory of its Afghan neighbor.

In 1836 Persia made ominous moves toward the Afghan city of Herat, which, lying on the western flank of the Hindu Kush, is often considered the key to India, since it guards the routes to India both via Kabul and the Khyber Pass, and via Kandahar and Quetta. Persia had an ancient claim to the city, and had long wanted to recover it. But given Persian defeat in

Central Asia at the hands of the Russians, a Persian victory would have meant an extension of Russian influence into Afghanistan. The Afghans appealed to Britain for assistance, and a political mission was dispatched to Kabul under Alexander Burnes. The Afghan ruling house was Pathan, and its plea for help from Britain against Persia was complicated by a further request for aid to regain the Pathan city of Peshawar, occupied by the Sikhs earlier in the century. British aims, in addition to forestalling Russian influence in the area, were to install a more compliant ruler on the Afghan throne. The Burnes mission failed in its endeavors, and the result was the first Afghan War of 1838-42. Although Britain was unable to place its choice of ruler over Afghanistan, the Persians, too, were foiled in their attempts to take Herat, following the dispatch of a British expedition to the Persian Gulf. Herat was the center of a further flurry of political and military activity when, in 1856, the Persians seized the city, only to be forced to withdraw, and to agree not to interfere in Afghanistan again, after a British declaration of war.

While the British occupied Kabul in 1839, the Russians mounted their first (and unsuccessful) attack against the khan of Khiva. The British were now less concerned about Russian-backed attempts on the part of Persia to recover Afghanistan, and more worried about Russian acquisitions of territory across the northern border of Afghanistan along the Oxus River (Amu Darya).

In 1869, a strong Afghan ruler emerged and expanded his rule, as emir of Kabul, along the Oxus to Badakhshan and Wakhan in the Pamir. In the same year, the British and the Russians started negotiations over the demarcation of the boundary between Russia and Afghanistan. In 1873 a preliminary agreement was reached, with the encouragement of Lord Mayo, who was pursuing a policy of nonintervention beyond the frontier. The upper Oxus was to form the boundary, and both Badakhshan and Wakhan were to be included in Afghanistan. Afghanistan, Russia agreed, was outside its sphere of influence. But, decades were to pass before this frontier would be defined along its entire length, and innumerable problems arose because of the lack of knowledge of the geography of the area.

Agreement on the Oxus boundary did not prevent further conflict along the northwest frontier. Russian advances in Central Asia and intrigues in Afghanistan resulted in the second Afghan War of 1878-80, as a result of which the emir of Kabul agreed to allow Afghan foreign relations to be determined by Britain. The Russian annexation of Merv in 1884 and the subsequent movement toward Herat stimulated British efforts at precise definition of the frontier. The Russo-Afghan Boundary Commission, in which Britain participated, delimited part of the frontier, and this line was extended up to the Chinese frontier in 1893 by the Durand Agreement. By the 1895 Anglo-Russian Convention, the Wakhan strip was established as part of Afghanistan running up to the Chinese border in the Pamir, thus ensuring that the territories of the two empires, British and Russian, would never touch.

British fear of a Russian invasion of India during the nineteenth century was based partly on reality, partly on illusion. The passes to the north, crossing the Kunlun and the Karakorum ranges to Ladakh, or farther west at the convoluted knot where these ranges join the Pamir and the Hindu Kush, were far too difficult to cross in force, and too easily defended. Similarly, although the passes through the Hindu Kush were easier, the generally difficult terrain and the substantial distances to the north of the passes over which massive Russian forces and supplies would have to be transported, made this an unlikely route of attack. But not all was illusion. The passes to the north and northwest had never proved a barrier to pilgrims or traders. Small bands of armed men could certainly stage diversionary attacks, or instigate native uprisings against the British among the hill tribes. These attacks, small though they might be, would require the diversion of substantial military and political resources, while the main thrust of a Russian invasion could be through southern Afghanistan across Baluchistan and Sind.

Those invasion routes to the north and northwest, although impracticable, were not known to be so at the time, and even if no one in St. Petersburg seriously considered trying to occupy India, nevertheless, perceptions of vulnerability and fear of a Russian attack, if only a feint to cover real aims in Europe, colored British frontier policy. It was not until the century was far advanced that the viceroy sent a military expedition "to determine to what extent India is vulnerable through the Hindu Kush range." The surveys of this expedition of 1885-86, commanded by Colonel Lockhart, concluded that the Russians could penetrate the Hindu Kush range only with raiding parties.

British ignorance of the geography of the Hindu Kush was matched by ignorance of the Oxus River, vital to Britain as a long part of the Afghan-Russian frontier. The diplomatic negotiations initiated between London and St. Petersburg in 1869 had culminated in 1873 in the Gorchakof-Granville Agreement, which established the general principle that the Oxus should be the Russo-Afghan boundary. Specifically, it was agreed that the Oxus should be the frontier, from its Pamir source to a place named Khojah Saleh (or Khwaja Sahar), a distance of nearly seven hundred miles, and that from there the boundary should diverge from the river southwest to the Persian frontier.[2] Numerous problems were to arise in demarcating the actual frontier, in direct proportion to Anglo-Russian geographical ignorance of the area. For example, Wood's journey of 1838 had given rise to the belief that Lake Zorkul (Victoria) in the Pamir was the true source of the Oxus. This proved to be incorrect, but the fact that the source defined a boundary point rendered the question a matter of political debate. In addition, Khwaja Sahar, which marked the western extremity of the Oxus as a frontier, and which had been defined as a "post" by Alexander Burnes in his exploration of the area in 1832, could not be located. It was only much later that Khwaja Sahar was found to have been the site of a long-defunct ferry, the post itself having been washed away by floods.[3]

Montgomerie returned to India early in 1867, having been promoted to the rank of major and appointed the official "in charge, trans-Himalayan exploring parties." He was soon writing up the report of Nain Singh's journey to Lhasa and planning further exploits for his explorers. In his letter to the Royal Geographical Society, written early the following year, he stated that "I am trying to extend the exploration northward into that great blank between the Himalayas, Russia and China proper."[4]

In addition, he was made deputy superintendent of the Great Trigonometrical Survey under Walker, and acting superintendent, between May 1868 and January 1869, of the Topographical Survey while General Thuillier, the surveyor-general, was in England on official business. He was also given the task of surveying the Himalayan districts of Kumaon and Garhwal.

Nevertheless, despite all these responsibilities, Montgomerie was able to mount no fewer than four expeditions by the pundits during the next two years.[5] Of these four expeditions, the one that was specifically directed toward filling in the "great blank" was made by an explorer named Mirza Shuja, known to the survey as "the Mirza," who crossed the Hindu Kush to Kashgar, passing through Afghanistan via Kabul and across the Pamir. This was largely unexplored territory, lying between British India and the Russian Empire, about which geographical and ethnographical knowledge was becoming more and more vital as the two empires extended their frontiers and narrowed the gap between them.

At the time that the Mirza began his travels to the area in 1868, Anglo-Russian negotiations concerning the Oxus as the northern boundary of Afghanistan were just about to start. It might, therefore, be thought that the Mirza was sent on his expedition as a result of a directive from London or from the government of India, requesting further information on the unexplored territory between the Oxus and the northwest frontier of India. No such directive seems to exist, however. The Survey of India apparently acted as an independent entity, anxious to fill in the unexplored areas on its maps, with the initiatives coming not from London or Calcutta, but from Survey Headquarters in Dehra Dun.

Montgomerie's report on the travels of the Mirza refers only to his own plan for the exploration of areas beyond the frontiers, and to the way this plan was applied in the case of the Mirza, "when the exploration of the Upper Oxus and Pamir Steppe was proposed."[6] In all probability, Montgomerie decided on the plan by himself, in consultation with General Walker. The GTS did not take the view that information was needed on trans-frontier regions to defend British interests against Russian advances—quite the reverse. Walker made his request for further funds for exploration on the basis that he would in the future no longer be able to receive geographical information from St. Petersburg because Russian military advances would be halted by Afghanistan and the Hindu Kush.[7]

The Pamir

The Pamir, or "Bam-i-dunya" (Roof of the World) as the Arabs called them, are the central knot linking the mountain ranges of the Hindu Kush, rising in Afghanistan from the southwest, to the Kunlun, Karakorum, and Himalayan ranges, which emerge from the east and southeast; they separate Chinese Turkestan from Tibet, and Tibet from India. Joining the Pamir in the north is the north-south Sarikol chain of mountains, which is the watershed dividing Russian Turkestan on the west from the rivers which flow to the east, supplying the Chinese cities lying on the edges of the Takla Makan desert.

The Pamir is a series of wide, elevated valleys, running from west to east at an average altitude of 12,000 to 14,000 feet, and divided by snow-covered peaks. Of glacial origin, the valleys are treeless and strewn with boulders. Harsh winds sweep them in the spring and summer, and the passes are closed for at least half the year by ice and snow. There are no permanent human inhabitants of these unsheltered and inhospitable depressions, but in the summer months when the grass grows and the flowers bloom, nomadic Kirghiz tribesmen graze their flocks of yaks and horses. The famous wild sheep of Marco Polo, *Ovis poli*, with their curved horns, can also be found.

To arrive at the upper reaches of the Oxus and traverse the Pamir to Kashgar, the traveler has first to cross the northwest frontier of India and pass through the territory of the Pathans. The Pathans are Moslems, factionalized into numerous tribal groups, and as the Mirza noted, "a very lawless race, and much addicted to high-way robbery." Much of their time was spent in endless vendettas, usually involving money, land, or women, against other families or clans. Because their mountain retreats possessed cultivable land inadequate to support the population, the Pathans constantly attacked passing caravans and repeatedly sallied forth to raid the population of the Punjab plain.

Pathan territory was mostly unexplored at the time of the Mirza's travels, and the area was largely unadministered by the British, although a semblance of control was maintained by a mixture of bribery, threats, and coercion in the form of punitive expeditions. Even a decade after the Mirza's explorations, the then viceroy, Lord Lytton, could write that "I believe that our northwest frontier presents at this moment a spectacle unique in the world; at least I know of no other spot where, after 25 years of peaceful occupation, a great civilized power has obtained so little influence over its semi-savage neighbors, and acquired so little knowledge of them, that the country within a day's ride of its most important garrison is an absolute *terra incognita,* and that there is absolutely no security for British life a mile or two beyond our border."

As an example of what could happen to an Englishman in this region, and the embarrassment that could be caused to the government, one can cite the case of George Hayward, who aimed to explore the Pamir and the source of the Oxus on behalf of the RGS. Hayward's route to the Pamir was from the east, from Kashmir via Gilgit. The viceroy, Lord Mayo (himself assassinated by a Pathan fanatic in 1872), reporting to the Royal Geographical Society in a letter of 27 September 1869, said that he had refused Hayward's requests for money, mules, and arms, and for an order to the maharaja of Kashmir to provide him with supplies. Observing that Hayward would probably leave for the Pamir anyway (which he did), the viceroy noted that he was doing so "against my wishes and without any authority from me." He continued, "the real truth is that our relations with the peoples and tribes beyond our frontiers are at this moment so exceedingly delicate that I am opposed to the appearance of any European among them at present . . . nothing could be more disastrous in the present state of things than that Mr. Hayward having started with a free pass given by the Rajah of Cashmere under our orders, and with Govt. mules and arms, should be either turned back, robbed or murdered. Any one of these three disasters are most likely to happen."[8] Once again, the Survey of India went its own way in such matters, for at the same time that the government was trying to stop him, Hayward was in close touch with Montgomerie, who was giving him all the assistance he could.[9]

But Lord Mayo was right. Hayward was murdered in Gilgit on 18 July 1870. The task of burying Hayward's body was given to Frederick Drew, a geologist employed by the maharaja of Kashmir. In a document headed

"Note of an Examination of Mr. Hayward's Body," Drew writes that "the corpse was brought into Gilgit on the evening of the 26 October 1870. This was more than three months after the murder; it was quite unrecognizable except by the brown colour of the hair [Drew interjects here that "all the men in his service had black hair"] of which a little was left, and of the beard, and perhaps by the form of the hands and feet which those with me said they could recognize anywhere for an Englishman's."[10] Why "the form of the hands and feet" were obviously those of an Englishman is not clear. With Hayward dead over three months, skin color could not have been a factor. Perhaps the fact that he wore shoes, while his servants most likely did not, might, by lack of calluses, identify his feet as those of a foreigner, but this does not explain his hands. What is clear is that it was most dangerous for a European to venture far beyond the frontier, that any attempt to adopt a local disguise was not likely to succeed, and that the unpleasant consequences of discovery could be fatal to the traveler and embarrassing to the Indian government. The employment of Indian explorers such as the Mirza, however, did not suffer from such grave objections.

The Forerunners

Although a number of Chinese Buddhist pilgrims crossed the Pamir between the fourth and seventh centuries A.D., the first detailed record was provided by the redoubtable Marco Polo, who traversed the area in 1274 on his way to China and the court of Kublai Khan. Over three centuries then elapsed before the Jesuit Benedict Goes undertook his missionary journey in 1602-03 from Peshawar to Kabul by way of Kafiristan, and then across the Pamir to Yarkand in Chinese Turkestan. Marco Polo was the only European to precede Goes across the Pamir, and Goes, traveling with the annual caravan from Lahore, probably followed the route of his predecessor. It was to be over two centuries after Goes before the next adventurous European, and the first Englishman, visited the Pamir.[11]

John Wood, a lieutenant in the Indian Navy, had traveled with Alexander Burnes when the latter was appointed commercial agent at Kabul in 1836. While Burnes himself remained in Kabul, Wood set off for Badakhshan in 1837, and following the routes of Marco Polo and Benedict Goes, reached Wakhan in 1838, where he explored the upper Oxus River to what he claimed was its source at Lake Zorkul in the Pamir.

Among Indian travelers, Abdul Mejid had crossed the Pamir from south to north in 1860, although his journeys were of diplomatic rather than geographical significance. Mahomed Amin, the guide of the murdered Adolph Schlagintweit, had also supplied the government of India with details of some itineraries, including a north-to-south route across the Pamir, but it was unclear how accurate this information was.

Indians employed as British intelligence agents had also penetrated into Central Asia. Pundit Munphool, who worked in the secretariat of the Punjab government, had volunteered in 1865 to visit Central Asia and collect information on Russian political and military progress in the area. He left in 1865 with three companions, and he returned the following year. All four traveled in disguise and used assumed names. Pundit Munphool and one of the party traveled around Badakhshan, while the other two went on to Bokhara. Both teams submitted reports to the governor on their return.[12]

There is some overlap between the work of these men and that of Montgomerie's native explorers, but the distinction must be made between Pundit Munphool and his assistants, none of whom was a trained surveyor, and employees of the Trigonometrical Survey, such as the Mirza, whose main task was to provide geographical data on which to base maps of unexplored areas.

Afghanistan proper, with its major cities and roads between them, was much better plotted on British maps, the information being drawn from the Elphinstone mission to Kabul in 1809, and the journey of Burnes across Afghanistan on his way to Bokhara in 1832. Burnes, after he was stationed in Kabul in 1836, had produced, with Wood and others, a number of maps of different parts of the country. Eldred Pottinger, leaving after the siege of Herat in 1839, had sketched the country while traveling to Kabul through Kohistan, north of the city. Above all, the first Afghan War of 1838-42, and its two attendant British invasions, had resulted in a surge of topographical and other information on Afghanistan.

But with the exception of Afghanistan, there was still a dearth of hard data on the region. Most of the area of the remote and lonely Pamir, situated at the apex of three empires, British, Russian, and Chinese, was still unvisited. Furthermore, in the case of the earlier travelers, there was great difficulty in deciphering the actual routes taken and in identifying the names of places seen.

The Mirza

In his search for a suitable Indian to explore the upper Oxus and the Pamir, Montgomerie employed the same principles that had guided him in his selection of Nain Singh, namely that what was needed was a man who had traveled through or traded in the area to be visited, who was of the same religion as the local inhabitants (Moslem), and who spoke the native language (Pushtu or Persian). It was by no means easy to find a competent, literate, and trustworthy man, capable of being trained in surveying techniques, who would fulfill these demands. Montgomerie was perhaps overconfident when he told the Asiatic Society in Calcutta in 1862 that "I do not think it would be very difficult to get one or two more [Indian explorers] from Peshawar or elsewhere, who might be trained to the work in a few months." Not that there was any shortage of volunteers. A search of the Peshawar bazaars, and a request for assistance from British officers stationed on the frontier, produced many applicants who believed that they were "well fitted for the task." But, continued Montgomerie, "a very little inquiry however reduces the number of likely men nearly down to zero; many cannot write, others are too old, most have no ideas beyond those of trade, and nearly every one has special ideas as to what pay and rewards they are to get, and generally have special stipulations to make; all however apparently thinking nothing of the risks and exposure involved."[13] Risks there certainly were, even for Indians, when traveling through the warlike peoples of the northwest frontier. The first attempt on the part of Walker and Montgomerie to penetrate this area in the 1860s had come to grief with the murder of their explorer, whom Walker described as "a Pathan of the Native Sappers and Miners—a very intelligent man indeed, and one who promised exceedingly well."[14] After undergoing training for a year, he was dispatched from Peshawar towards Chitral. Unfortunately, the GTS were not aware of a Pathan blood feud in his family, which caught up with him six weeks later.

"For mountain regions inhabited by a treacherous Mohammedan population," said Walker, "men of great physique, great courage and considerable intelligence, are required; and Pathans, as a rule, have lots of pluck and nerve, but ninety-nine out of a hundred do not know how to read and write. It is, therefore, particularly difficult to make a beginning with them."[15] However, although Walker thought that many Pathans had lots of courage, he did not always have the same degree of confidence in their trustworthiness, for he went on to recount that a Pathan being trained by Nain Singh had stolen the gold watch which had been presented to the pundit by the RGS. The theft could not be proven conclusively, so the Pathan was simply dismissed from the survey, after which, says Walker, "the last thing heard of him was, that he had attached himself to the unfortunate Mr. Hayward; and it was believed that he was murdered with Mr. Hayward; but if not, it was not improbable that he had a hand in the murder of that gentleman."

Montgomerie finally thought he had secured a likely candidate, a silversmith who traveled regularly from Peshawar via Kabul to Yarkand, making ornaments from precious metals. But before a definite proposal could be made, the silversmith left on his travels. At this point, Montgomerie abandoned his search and decided to try out a man who was already known to him and who "was qualified in some respects." This was Mirza Shuja, or Sajjad, who was to be called simply "the Mirza."

The Mirza's father was a Turkish trader based in Meshed, but his mother was from Persia, where the Mirza himself was born. Traveling with his father to the Afghan city of Herat, the Mirza had in some way come to the notice of Lieutenant Eldred Pottinger, the British officer who helped organize the defense of the city against the Persians in 1837-38. This would put the Mirza's year of birth as unlikely to be much later than 1822, but even this would make him 45 years old and a middle-aged man at the time of his first journey on behalf of the survey in 1867. When Pottinger left Herat, he took the Mirza with him to Kabul. Here the Mirza met Captain Colin Mackenzie, a friend of Pottinger, who taught him English. He also learned to speak Pushtu, as well as Persian.

The next that is heard of the Mirza is over a decade later, when he was working as a *munshi* for General (then Lieutenant) Walker. Walker was making a military survey of the Peshawar area following the close of the second Sikh War in 1849. By September 1850, he had moved as far north as he could go without risking his life. His map indicates this line, beyond which "further proceedings were stopped by the hostility of the natives."[16] For this reason, and because of a shortage of manpower, authority was given to Walker to hire two Indian surveyors. Since none were available, four *munshis* were tried out. One of the four was the Mirza, who passed his tests successfully, and "rendered valuable assistance." However, noted Walker, "he was incapable of field sketching or computing."[17] The Mirza remained with the Peshawar survey for three years and was employed in public works around the city until 1855, when he rejoined Walker, who recommended him to the surveyor-general for a formal appointment with the great Trigonometrical Survey, saying that "his mathematical attainments are not enough to enable him to take a share in the computations. . . . He would probably be better placed in the Kashmir series . . . reconnoitering the countries beyond the boundary. He is . . . well born and respectable and may seek information among Mussulman tribes who would not suffer the approach of Europeans."[18] The Kashmir Survey, however, had only just begun that spring, and Montgomerie was unable to use his talents. Later in the year, the situation changed and Waugh asked Walker if the Mirza could be spared to help Montgomerie.[19] Walker responded that he felt it best that the Mirza stay where he was, for further training. While surveyors could locate the mountain peaks in Swat and Gilgit, "the map showing these peaks will be rendered more interesting and valuable if the principal villages in the valleys can be shown." Walker said that the Mirza could accomplish this by exploring the valleys with a compass.[20] So the Mirza remained with Walker, who was instructed by the surveyor-general to teach him the principles involved in measuring latitude and longitude, distances, angles, and temperatures, so that he might be able to explore beyond the frontier at a later date.[21]

At this time, it was still proposed that any Indian explorer would have to be capable not only of making observations, but also of undertaking the calculations necessary to reduce the figures to a map. It was Montgomerie who separated the two stages, with the explorer taught how to take observations, but not how to reduce them. This lessened the amount of time needed for training, did not force the elimination of those like the Mirza, who had no head for figures, and made it difficult (though not impossible) for the explorers to falsify figures or attempt to prove that they had been to places they had not in fact reached.

The Mirza stayed with Walker for a further two years, learning the basic techniques of surveying. He demonstrated his leadership abilities with the local population on a part of the hilly frontier southwest of Peshawar by going among a wild tribe who "bore a noted character for thieving," and persuading them to permit survey parties across their territory.

Remaining with Walker until October 1857, the Mirza was given six months' leave to go to Kabul "to recover some money, with which a merchant of Peshawar has absconded."[22] He failed to rejoin the Survey at the end of this leave, and wrote to Walker in May the following year explaining that he was unable to return because he was teaching English to the sons of Dost Mohammad, the then ruler of Afghanistan.[23] He remained in Kabul for a decade, continuing in the service of the new emir of Afghanistan, Sher Ali, the third son of Dost Mohammad, after the latter died in 1863. When Sher Ali was temporarily forced to leave Kabul because of the rivalry of his brother, the Mirza was unemployed, and so made his way back to India. While resident in Kabul, he had kept his connections with the British by providing intelligence to Major Pollock, the commissioner of Peshawar. The Mirza's return from Kabul coincided with a request from Montgomerie to Pollock for "men to explore beyond the North West frontier."[24]

If the Mirza had returned to India promptly after his 1857 leave, it is probable that he, and not Abdul Hamid, would have been the first of Montgomerie's explorers. In his 1862 proposal, Montgomerie had said that "at present I know of but one man fitted for such work" and identified him as the Mirza. As it happened, however, the Mirza was rehired in 1867 and brought to GTS headquarters at Dehra Dun. There it was decided that his surveying knowledge was very rusty, so he was sent on the "training course" at Roorkee, and then posted to Peshawar.

The Mirza left Peshawar in the autumn of 1867 (Map 2). His objective was to reach Kashgar, exploring the upper Oxus and the Pamir, and the routes from the Pamir to the cities of Kashgar and Yarkand. He was disguised as a merchant and traveled with a number of baggage animals. Probably the top of his head was shaved, with the hair at the back and sides flowing to his shoulders. He would have worn a turban and cap, a long white Peshawar *loongi,* and boots.

Almost immediately, a hitch developed. Sir Robert Montgomery had been replaced as lieutenant-governor of the Punjab in January 1865 by Sir Donald Macleod. Walker, as was to become customary with him, had not informed Macleod of developments, even though the Mirza was to journey through this territory. This only came to Macleod's attention when Montgomerie asked for an introduction for the Mirza to "our Agent at Kokand." Macleod complained to the Foreign Department that Montgomerie must not be aware "how completely without the knowledge or consent of the Kokand or Russian authorities these persons are employed by us, and what exceeding jealousy and hostility would at once be engendered by the discovery of this fact."[25]

The viceroy, Sir John Lawrence, was an exponent of the school favoring "masterly inactivity," or noninterference in affairs beyond the frontier. He did not support the views of those who urged a "forward policy" to oppose Russia in Persia and Afghanistan. Accordingly, he temporized, responding to Macleod in a letter of 12 December 1867: "I have told Muir [Sir William Muir, Secretary to the government of India] to send you officially the papers connected with the deputation of natives from the Trigonometrical Department into Central Asia for your opinion. You should have been referred to in the first instance, but the impression on my mind was that you were in accord with General Walker on the subject. I have no wish myself to allow it, if you think it should not be done."[26]

At the same time, Lawrence wrote to Walker, asking him to halt the expedition until the views of the lieutenant-governor were known. Walker responded that "it had not occurred to him" to get the opinion of the Punjab government, since they had, in the past, supported Montgomerie with funds to send Abdul Hamid to Yarkand, and had sent Abdul Mejid and others off on their own initiative. In any case, said Walker, the Mirza had already left British territory and was "beyond recall."

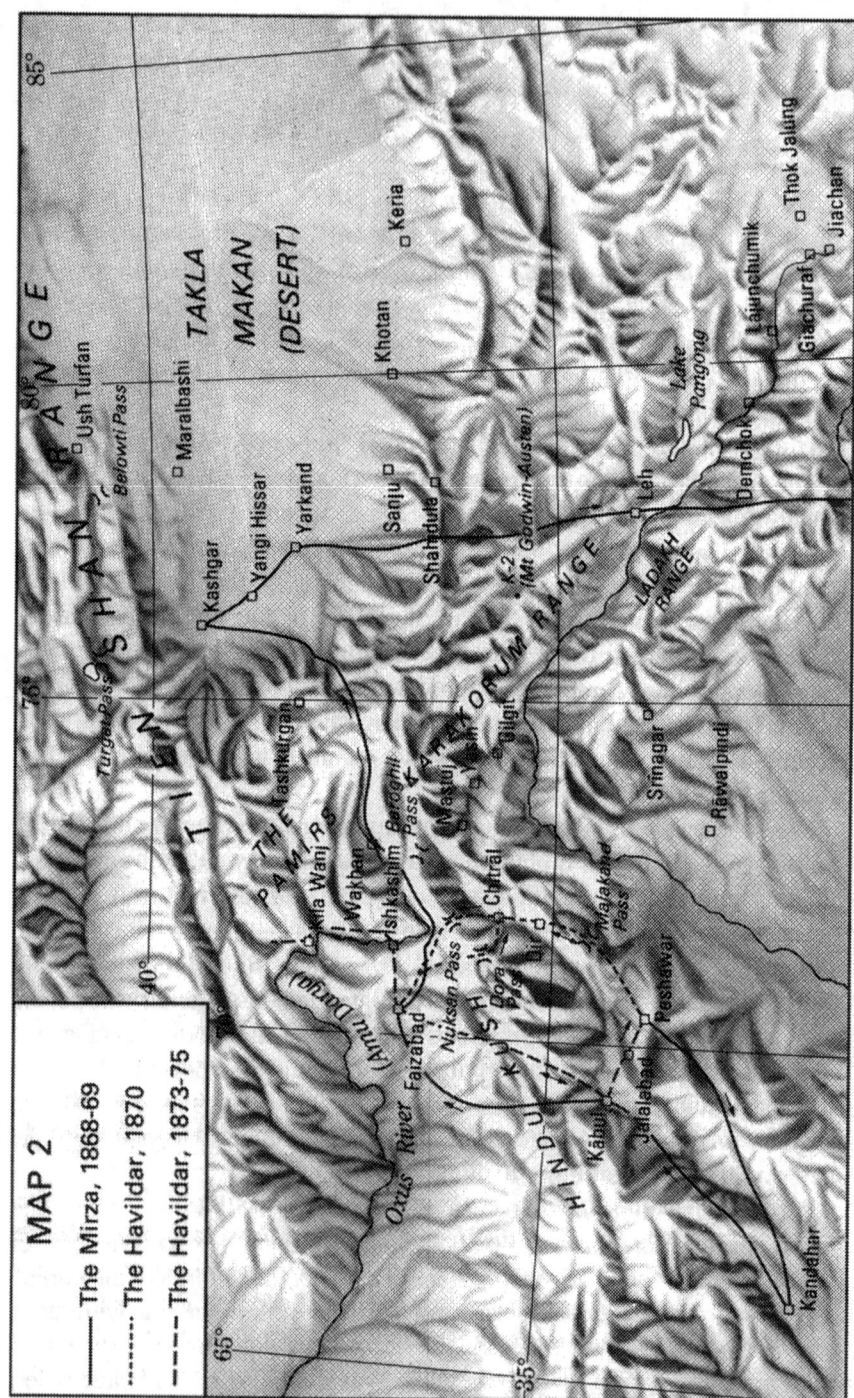

The matter was eventually smoothed over. Macleod said he had no wish for the Mirza to be recalled, but he suggested that future explorers, before approaching British agents in Kokand or elsewhere, be provided with a cover story—if traveling as traders, they could carry with them "recommendations" from merchants in Kokand and the Punjab to agents in the areas to be visited.

The viceroy agreed with Macleod's suggestions and told Walker that they should be "rigidly attended to," and that henceforth, no explorers should be sent out without "special sanction."[27]

There the matter rested, not to rise again in the case of the Mirza, who did not, in fact, reach Kokand. But it illustrates Walker's disregard for bureaucratic niceties. This was later to become a major problem when substantial disagreement arose between the government and the Survey of India over how much information regarding trans-Himalayan exploration should be made available to the public.

Meanwhile, the Mirza was having problems of his own. Montgomerie had instructed him to proceed initially to Badakhshan by the most direct route, north through Chitral. But winter was settling on the Hindu Kush, and the passes were blocked by snow. The Mirza made no fewer than four unsuccessful attempts to break out of the mountains which surrounded Peshawar and cross into Afghanistan, moving further south on each occasion, but was foiled time and again by the weather, the hostility of the people, and the unsettled state of Afghanistan at the time. On his fourth attempt, he sold his baggage animals at Dera Ghazi Khan on the Indus, and took the steamer down the river to Sukkur, where he tried to penetrate the Bolan pass. Not succeeding, he made one last attempt, heading northwest from Sukkur across the Indus plains to Kalat, via the Mula pass. This was a march of almost two hundred fifty miles. The Mula pass itself is one hundred miles in length, following the Mula stream. The Mirza crossed and recrossed the stream, winding his way through narrow defiles with sheer rocks towering on either side of him to emerge from time to time into valleys of tamarisk jungle. Crossing the top of the pass at 5,250 feet, the Mirza descended into Kalat. Here he recognized a man from Kandahar, from whom he bought donkeys, and who agreed (for a price) to take him to the city. The two arrived there in May 1868.

With civil war raging in Afghanistan, the Mirza was naturally anxious to move north to Kabul, and then to proceed on his mission as soon as possible. He had an initial fright when some baggage and documents he had sent ahead were captured, and he was denounced as a spy. But he managed to talk himself out of the situation, and joined Sher Ali's army marching to Kabul, where he arrived safely at the end of June. The Mirza was welcome at the court of Sher Ali, as he had been in his service for several years. He also met Sher Ali's son, Yakub Khan, who was briefly to be ruler in 1879.[28] Even after Sher Ali had taken control of Kabul, the Mirza found that the city was in a very disturbed state, with the people so suspicious that he could not put together his arrangements for servants and provisions for his onward journey to Badakhshan. Accordingly, he left Kabul for an outlying village, and he made his plans there. Even so, this took time, and he was unable to leave until 10 October 1868. With the arrival of winter, this was to make his journey more arduous.

While in Kabul, the Mirza met Pundit Munphool. Munphool, who had been handsomely rewarded with the payment of Rs. 5000 for his journey to Badakhshan, was jealous of the other explorers of Central Asia.[29] The Mirza alleged that Munphool was trying to hinder his travels. The British authorities sent for Munphool, who denied the charges. Montgomerie would never have employed Munphool, because of his lack of surveying knowledge. The Indian Government had already toyed with, but dismissed, the idea of making him consul at Bokhara, because he was a Hindu. He was eventually recommended for the award of the Star of India.[30]

Kabul, situated some seven thousand feet above sea level, has been described as the key to northern India. Surrounded by mountains, it controls the passes to the north through the Hindu Kush, and those in the west from Kandahar. The Mirza reported that the city "was in anything but a flourishing state." In fact, he said it was generally in a "filthy condition, not pleasant either to the nose or to the eye."[31] This reinforces the remarks of an earlier English traveler to the country, who said "the climate is fine: and if dirt killed people, where would the Afghans be?"[32] The city, in fact, seems not to have recovered from its destruction at the hands of the British army of occupation in 1842. Before that time, it was more picturesque and prosperous. One contemporary account described Kabul as

> well-built and handsome and one mass of bazaars. Every street has a double row of houses of different heights, flat-roofed, and composed of mud in wooden frames. Here and there a larch porch of carved wood intervenes, giving entrance to the court-yard of the residence of the nobles, in the centre of which is a raised platform of mud, planted with fruit-trees, and spread with carpets. A fountain plays near . . . The houses overhang the narrow streets; their windows have no glass, but consist of lattice-work wooden shutters . . . richly carved . . . The shop windows are open to the sun, and the immense display of merchandise, fruits, game, armour, and cutlery defies description.[33]

But things had changed, and the Mirza was glad to be gone. His route took him northwest over the Hindu Kush to Bamian, through Kulm-Tashkurgan and into Badakhshan. Now moving in a generally easterly direction, he joined the Oxus at Ishkashim and followed the river upstream as far as Kila Punja in Wakhan. Bamian, his first major halt, was about eighty miles northwest of Kabul, on the main trading route to Turkestan. The Mirza, hampered by the midwinter snows, had to cross passes at twelve thousand feet and bribe frontier guards, in order to reach the valley in which Bamian sits. Bamian had a long history—Genghis Khan had sacked it in the thirteenth century, and others followed. The valley through which the Mirza rode was lined with cliffs. Buddhist figures were carved in the rock, and cave dwellings could be seen.

His next stop was Kulm-Tashkurgan, 150 miles farther due north. Tashkurgan (or "stone fort") was the old city, Kulm the new. Kulm was the major trading mart of northern Afghanistan, where caravans from India met *kafilas* going to Central Asia. Mir Izzet Ullah, traveling on behalf of Moorcroft, had said that the city had about eight thousand houses. Later visitors reported that Tashkurgan, approached from the west, appeared to be a garden city, composed entirely of apricot and other trees, surrounded by mud walls. It possessed a long bazaar which the Mirza must have seen, covered over by matting, with a dome-shaped building at the center decorated with china saucers set into the walls. But the bazaar was the only public, lively spot. As for the rest of Tashkurgan, one European later wrote that "I know of nothing more dreary and monotonous than an Eastern town. Except in the actual street devoted to the bazaar, there is no sign of life—everything is shut up and hidden behind those interminable mud-walls, and were it not for a few men sitting solemnly and silently here and there at the various corners, one might be in a city of the dead."[34]

Close by Kulm-Tashkurgan, the party was attacked by bandits, who wounded two and absconded with much of the goods and some animals. But once inside the city, the Mirza climbed to the top of the fort that dominated the town, for his first glimpse of the Oxus, about twenty miles north.

At Tashkurgan, the Mirza was joined by a traveler who was wearing European dress, and who was considered to be a European by the other members of the caravan. The Mirza was initially inclined to agree, and almost told the stranger the true story of his mission. However, the "European" spoke such perfect Persian (the Mirza's native tongue) that the Mirza decided that he must be someone sent to make inquiries about him. He, therefore, kept to his story of being a trader bound for Kashgar, and eventually the stranger departed.

The weather, now that it was December, began to deteriorate badly. Snow hampered the progress of the caravan and the Mirza's servants grew mutinous and threatened to leave him. But eventually they reached Faizabad, the central town of Badakhshan. Here the *serai*s (lodgings) were full of slave girls from Chital, who were to be traded for horses.

Halting in Faizabad, the Mirza presented himself at the court of the mir of Badakhshan. The mir did not make a good impression, and the Mirza described him as "about forty years of age . . . decidedly Tarter features, with small eyes and a scanty beard. He is given to drinking, and allows his petty officials to do very much as they like; he is consequently unpopular."[35]

Nevertheless, the Mir was of assistance, recommending the best route to Chinese Turkestan, and telling the Mirza that the Kirghis bandits had left the Pamir for the winter. But problems persisted. His men were reluctant to leave Faizabad bcause of the cold, and one of them had the Mirza denounced as an infidel, spying on the country for the English. Once again the Mirza had to talk himself out of a tricky situation and shut the man up with a bribe.

The small party left Faizabad on 24 December 1868, on foot, as the road was too bad for riding. The Oxus was reached for the first time in early January. This was at Ishkashim, where a fort marked the start of the Wakhan. Here the road degenerated into a rough path, running up and down a series of ridges. Staying on the south bank, the Mirza could see that the Oxus was frozen solid and could easily be crossed if necessary. For this reason, and because the Kirghiz were forced to move their flocks off the Pamir to find fresh grazing land in the winter, this time of the year was the preferred season for caravans on the route from Badakhshan to Turkestan, despite the weather. When the Oxus thawed, it became difficult to ford.

On the march, the Mirza passed Alif Beg, the former ruler of Sarikol, going in the opposite direction. Sarikol professed allegiance to Yarkand and paid a nominal tribute every year in return for its military protection of the road to Badakhshan. This allegiance had not been demonstrated for some years, and the new leader of Yarkand and Kashgar, the Atalik Ghazi, had been too preoccupied to lay claim to it. But in 1868, the Atalik demanded that the eldest son of the former Sarikol ruler come to him with tribute. Unknown to the Atalik, the eldest son, "having some defect of speech and weakness of intellect," had been passed over in favor of the second son, Alif Beg, who, instead of going himself, sent his retarded elder brother. In 1868, the Atalik, on meeting the brother, sent troops to enforce his summons, and Alif Beg fled to seek asylum in Wakhan.[36] The Mirza said that Alif Beg, who had poisoned his wives and his mother for fear of their falling into the hands of the Atalik, "appeared to be much dejected by his misfortunes."[37]

The two stone-and-mud forts at Kila Punja marked the place just upstream of which the Oxus divided, the northern branch climbing to Zorkul (Wood's Lake) about 80 miles distant, and the southern branch about 120 miles to the Pamir Kul Lake. The Mirza had no specific instructions as to which branch to take, and accordingly took the southern route because it seemed to be the larger of the two. This might only have appeared to be the case, since the source of the northern tributary was at a higher altitude, and would, therefore, have been smaller and frozen when the Mirza observed it. However, since Wood had explored the northern route, it was fortunate that the Mirza took the southern tributary, since the two reports combined provided Montgomerie with details of the drainage of virtually the whole of the upper Oxus River.

Before leaving Kila Punja, the Mirza had to regale the mir of Wakhan and his retinue with the power of the Feringees (British) in India and to show them that the power of the Russians was not as great. All were astonished at tales of the steam engine, but were not inclined to believe the Mirza's story of the telegraph, even though he lengthened to half an hour the time it took to send a message two hundred miles.

More difficult was getting provisions to carry the party across the Pamir, together with a guide and fresh horses. It proved to be necessary to bribe every official in sight, practically forcing the Mirza into destitution, and just when he thought he was finally on his way, a request arrived for a "present" from the mir himself. Since the Mirza did not wish to part with the valuable items he would need in Kashgar, he divested himself of his white *loongi* and sent it off to the mir, together with some tea. With this gift, the party was finally able to get away on 8 January 1869, the baggage now carried on the backs of hardy Punja ponies.

As far as Punja, the Mirza had followed the route of Wood, with whose observations the Mirza's were subsequently found to be in close agreement. But trekking along the southern branch of the Oxus, through the cold and snow, the Mirza's party was very much in uncharted terrain.

The most difficult part of the journey to Kashgar, in Chinese Turkestan, now lay ahead, a twelve-day march from Kila Punja, through the Wakhan valley, and across the Pamir, with no villages or food available for eight marches beyond the last village in the Wakhan. For supplies the Mirza bought and killed some sheep, relying on the intense cold to preserve the meat. Other provisions included flour, dried fruit, and sugar candy.

Through the Wakhan valley, the road was just a narrow path, crossing and recrossing the frozen Oxus. In summer it would have been impassable. The valley seemed prosperous, the hardy people producing wool for export from sheep, goats, and yaks. The party was able to shelter each night in one of the flat-roofed stone and mud houses, each warmed by a large stove sunk in the center of the floor. The family and guests slept on raised platforms around the sides of the room. At the last village, Patur, a guide was found to lead them over the Pamir, and they set off through a snowstorm, trudging along beside the Oxus, the ground covered by a dense growth of small willow trees. The wind grew more piercing as the path ran along the bottom of a stupendous ravine. There was no grazing here, and only the sight of white falcons, highly prized in Badakhshan and Bokhara.

Conditions continued to deteriorate. After a long march there was little shelter from the biting wind, the heavy snowfall extinguished the fires they built each night, and at the altitude of thirteen thousand feet both men and animals suffered from shortness of breath. The Mirza and his men were now clad in woolen *choga*s and sheepskin coats, fur hats, two pairs of woolen stockings, and boots filled with wool. Even so, all suffered from the combination of cold and wind. Snow blindness was common, breath froze on mustaches, and the wool in the boots absorbed moisture through the thin leather soles and then froze. In the mornings, says the Mirza, "the men literally rose out of a bed of snow."

Passing to the north of the Pamir Kul Lake, one of the sources of the Oxus, the Mirza must have had to draw on all his resources. Disheartened by the climate, the men became mutinous "and began to murmur, when told to light a fire and make the usual preparations." The Mirza was forced to beat one particularly impertinent servant, and with this the incipient revolt collapsed. Even throughout these trying days, the objective of the mission was not forgotten. A route survey was made continually, with compass bearings taken, and distances measured by pacing. The Mirza had two or three of his men, with himself, relieving one another for the pacing, dropping a bead from the string every one hundred paces, and a larger bead at every tenth to represent a thousand paces. In addition, astronomical observations for latitude were made by sextant at important points. Since the area was Muslim rather than Buddhist, no prayer wheel was used.

The party was now traveling through the sweeping valleys of the Pamir. In summer lush with sweet grass like an English meadow, the Pamir, which Marco Polo described as "the best pasturage in the world," were transformed into a white wasteland by winter. Over two centuries earlier, Benedict Goes had also had difficulties crossing the Pamir in midwinter. Five of his horses had died from the cold and thin air, against which the only "remedies" were garlic, onions, and dried apples, eaten by the men, and in the case of the garlic applied to the mouths of the animals.

After one particularly unpleasant night in the snow, the Mirza set off at first light. By full daylight he saw that they had at last reached the Pamir watershed. To the west, the waters flowed to the Aral Sea; to the east, into Chinese Turkestan. The scene, according to the Mirza, was the most desolate he had ever seen, a snow-swept landscape without any sign of life. At this point, some of the men demanded that they be allowed to return home to the Wakhan. The Mirza paid them off, and the remainder of the diminished party headed east. As the altitude decreased, deer and other game could be seen, the snow lessened, there was grass for the ponies, and the stunted willow trees reappeared, replacing the small prickly shrubs whose woody roots had provided the only fuel on the Pamir. On the twelfth day they reached Tashkurgan, the former chief of which the Mirza had passed earlier, fleeing from the troops of the Atalik Ghazi of Kashgar.

Tashkurgan (to be distinguished from Kulm-Tashkurgan) lay in the Sarikol valley. This elevated valley, the Mirza reported, was eleven thousand feet above sea level, thirty to forty miles long, and twelve to eighteen miles wide, well watered and producing wheat and corn. Just a few days before the Mirza's arrival, nearly all the original inhabitants had been forced to leave on the orders of the Atalik, and had moved to Yarkand or Kashgar. The Kirghiz had moved in, in their place. The whole valley was dotted with small square forts and dominated by the ruins of a large stone fort, about a mile long and four hundred yards across, inside the ruins of which unroofed houses were clustered. It was here, on the evening of his arrival, that the Mirza was invited to meet the new governor of Sarikol, a brother of the Atalik Ghazi. After stumbling about along narrow passages, the Mirza was ushered into a small dark room. Eventually the governor, who appeared to be about sixty years old, entered with lights. After tea and hard wheat-flour cakes, the governor interrogated the Mirza as to the reasons for his journey to Kashgar and demanded to have all his merchandise brought to the fort and opened. The Mirza was greatly alarmed at this order, for it meant the discovery of his concealed surveying instruments. But with gifts to the governor, which the Mirza described as being specimens of the goods he was carrying, and by claiming friendship with the Atalik's chief of artillery, whom he had known in the past, the Mirza was able to persuade the governor not to press his demands. The governor's suspicions were not entirely allayed, however, for he forced the Mirza to accept an escort of a Kirghiz chief to accompany the party to Kashgar. The party and escort left Sarikol on January 27, on the last stage of their journey. Even though the

Mirza was now under virtual open arrest, he was able to persist in taking his observations, in part because the Kirghiz chief insisted on riding well ahead of the rest of the group.[38]

Here the Mirza was pioneering new ground for geographical exploration. At his annual address to the Royal Geographical Society, made in the same year as the Mirza's travels, the president, Sir Roderick Murchison, had said that "between Yarkand and the plateau of Pamir . . . our maps had nothing to show implying human occupancy beyond one or two names resting on questionable authority, and representing one knew not what."[39] Sir Roderick was referring here to the itineraries given to George Hayward by Mahomed Amin. Marco Polo had probably followed this route, as had a cousin of the emperor Baber. It was not, therefore, "entirely new ground," as Montgomerie described it in his report. But the Mirza was the first to provide information based on astronomical observations and scientific measurements.

It took the Mirza a week to reach Yangi Shar, the new city of Kashgar, about five miles south of old Kashgar. Kirghiz nomads were plentiful along the route, settled temporarily to live off supplies left by the local population fleeing from the Atalik Ghazi. At one encampment, the Mirza was ushered into a portable tent constructed of felt over a wooden frame, and offered the opportunity of joining in the evening meal. This consisted of a whole boiled sheep, placed on a grubby cloth in the middle of the tent, from which each man hacked pieces with his knife. The Mirza, reflecting that he never knew where his next meal was coming from, reluctantly joined in.

The most formidable part of the journey to Kashgar was the crossing of the Chichiklik-Davan pass, clambering eleven miles through the snow along a path "fit only for goats," and then struggling for twenty miles on hands and knees down the steep descent on the other side. The Mirza noted that "some high peaks were visible to the north-west." Among these must have been Muztagh Ata, at over twenty-four thousand feet, the highest mountain in the Muztagh range.

Several horses died on the pass, and the Mirza only just managed to stop another mutiny from breaking out among his men. But the humor of the men improved on entering a lush valley with flowing water and easy slopes covered with fruit trees. The only uncomfortable moment came when one of the Kirghiz spotted the Mirza taking a compass bearing and rode up to ask him what he had in his hand. Ever resourceful and quick-witted, the Mirza substituted a cheap compass that pointed to Mecca for the prismatic compass he had been using. The Kirghiz chief had never seen such an instrument before, and was delighted when the Mirza made him a present of it.

Soon the mountains lay behind them, and they found themselves in flat fertile country where villages nestled in large orchards of fruit trees and mulberry groves. About thirty-five miles short of Kashgar, they passed through the small town of Yangi Hissar. From then on the road was well populated and dotted with shops selling a variety of inexpensive refreshments, including hot tea, sour milk, boiled fowls, and fresh bread.

Kashgar itself was actually three cities, two living, one dead. To the south was Yangi Shahr ("new city"), with massive mud walls surrounded by a ditch. Built in 1838, it was separated by the river from Kuhna Shahr ("old city") five miles to the north. Kuhna Shahr was smaller, with fortified clay walls, and just beyond it lay the ruins of ancient Kashgar (Aski Shahr), destroyed in 1514.

Strategically located, Kashgar had long been a center of economic and political importance. Through it passed first Buddhism and then the religion of Islam in the tenth century A.D. To it came traders from India, through Khotan and Yarkand, from Samarkand in the west, from China via Aksu, and, like the Mirza, from Persia or Afghanistan along the trade routes of the upper Oxus.

Kashgar had been visited by Marco Polo, but the Venetian gave few details of the city. But the next European in the area was one of the Schlagintweit brothers, Adolph, who was murdered outside the city in 1857 (his murderer was later executed by Yakub Beg, the Atalik Ghazi).[40]

Geographically, Kashgaria, bordering on Tibet and India, makes up the southern half of Chinese Turkestan, a region divided from west to east by the Tian Shan, or "heavenly mountains." Like Afghanistan and Tibet, Chinese Turkestan had no outlet to the sea. Together with Afghanistan, it acted as a Central Asian buffer zone between British and Russian interests. Together with Tibet, it was the least Chinese part of China, populated mostly by Uighurs, Moslem by religion, few of whom could speak Chinese. China first exercised control over the area in the second century B.C. From the fifteenth century onwards, the development of seaborne commerce replaced much of the trade along the Silk Road crossing Chinese Turkestan, and the area lost some of its strategic importance. In the nineteenth century, Chinese rule was waning; local officials (often exiled there as a punishment) were of poor quality, and Chinese resources and attention were concentrated on the massive Taiping rebellion in China proper and on the impact of the West. The advances made by Russia in Central Asia gave the Russians military and commercial privileges in Kashgaria. In 1860, they acquired the right to open a consulate in Kashgar.

Kashgaria had been Islamic since the tenth century, and Moslem revolts against their Chinese overlords were frequent. In 1862, the Tungani Moslem uprising against the Chinese broke out in the neighboring province of Gansu. The uprising spread to Kashgaria, where it was encouraged by Kokandi merchants seeking trading privileges. This was the opportunity seized by a military adventurer from Kokand named Yakub Beg, who gained control of the area in 1864 when the Chinese leaders, their garrison having held out for a year, blew themselves up, "after spitting towards Pekin."[41]

In his thirteen years of rule, Yakub Beg, who soon restyled himself the Atalik Ghazi (or "father like") set up an autocratic Islamic regime with Kashgar as its capital, and proceeded to open up diplomatic relations with other countries, including Britain, Russia, and the Ottoman Empire, signing commercial treaties with London and St. Petersburg.

Yakub Beg was a minor military despot with some talent for administration who has been described by one authority as "a dancing-boy turned brigand."[42] Nevertheless, he was able for a few years to play an international role. Britain sent two missions to his capital, hoping for strategic and commercial benefits. The Russians were alarmed by his rise to power, for he had fought against them in 1853, and they saw him as friendly to the British, who might use him to extend their influence north and perhaps even to drive a wedge between European Russia and Siberia. For this reason, the Russians occupied the Ili valley in the Tian Shan in 1871 (although they gave most of it back in 1883). Because of their weakness, the Chinese were forced to cede some 350,000 square miles of Turkestan to Russia by treaty in 1864.

When the Chinese regained their strength, they counterattacked in order to halt Russian and British penetration of their frontier area. The Atalik found no help forthcoming from Britain or Russia, and his army was defeated by the Chinese in 1877. He himself died in May of that year, and Kashgar was retaken in December. In 1884, the Chinese, by Imperial Decree, created from Chinese Turkestan the province of Xinjiang, or "New Dominion."

But in 1869, when the Mirza was exploring the area for the British, the Atalik was at the height of his power. The new city of Kashgar, said the Mirza, was built on a slope between two branches of the Kazul River, which joined just east of the town, and which could be crossed by two bridges in the summer and anywhere on the ice during winter. The city was surrounded by a high wall of sun-dried mud bricks, with watchtowers at regular intervals and three wood and iron gates. The flat-roofed houses within the walls were built of the same bricks, and housed a mixed population of Turks, Tunganis, Badakhshanis, Kashmiris, Afghans, and others. All were Moslem, however, and every street had its mosque in which the population prayed five times a day.

The population had numbered about sixteen thousand, but many had emigrated with the rise to power of Yakub Beg. The Mirza described the inhabitants as good-humored, but profligate, crafty, and inhospitable, echoing Marco Polo's comment that they were "close fisted." Women were seldom seen outside the house, for in public they were forced to conform to Yakub Beg's demand to wear the *burkha,* which covered them head to toe. This, said the Mirza, "the women particularly dislike."

The climate apparently was healthy—dry and cold in the winter, although stormy in the spring. This was the time that the Mirza was in Kashgar, and he noted that the sun was always obscured by a haze for three or four hours every morning. This was fine loess dust, raised by the wind. When well irrigated, the loess allowed the abundant cultivation of a variety of crops, including wheat, rice, cotton, peas, radishes, pomegranates, melons, plums, and grapes. With the expulsion of the Chinese, however, tea was in short supply, which alerted Montgomerie to the possibility of trading Indian tea with Kashgar.

The Mirza's stay in Kashgar did not begin auspiciously. Immediately on arrival he was taken to meet Nubbi Buksh, the jemadar (lieutenant) in the service of Yakub Beg. The jemadar was a remarkable man, having risen to a position of considerable power after starting life as a gunner in the Sikh army. Unemployed in 1855, he had been recommended by the Mirza for a job in Kokand, after which he had risen rapidly to become the Atalik's chief of artillery. The Mirza, therefore, presumed on this acquaintance, but the jemadar was hostile, not wanting others to know of his lowly origins, and initially refused to admit he knew the Mirza. Eventually, he was forced to recognize this, but then accused the Mirza of not being a merchant at all, and wanted to know what the real object of his journey was.

The hostility and suspicion of the jemadar dogged the Mirza during his four months in Kashgar. The morning after his arrival, he was brought to meet the Atalik Ghazi. The Atalik was friendlier than expected to the Mirza, who described him as being "of the middle size, dark complexion, and . . . about fifty years of age." He was uneducated and unable to read or write, except for the Koran, which he had learned to read at the age of forty-five and apparently studied every morning. For political advice, he relied upon the governor of Yarkand, an educated man. Most of the Atalik's associates were quite uneducated, and none of them could keep accounts, so the government had simply dispensed with keeping accounts altogether. The Atalik was a devout Moslem, forbidding wine, opium, and smoking, and ordering everyone to pray five times a day. A generous man, he fed several thousand people daily after prayers. The Mirza collected details of the Atalik's armed forces, and concluded that he was a good soldier.

Montgomerie, however, could see no evidence for this, and described him more accurately as a "bold intriguer." On the negative side, the Mirza said that the Atalik was a suspicious man and had a violent temper. Officials were paid irregularly, and they in turn oppressed the common people, who frequently voted with their feet and took off on pilgrimages to Mecca, either emigrating for good or hoping to be treated better on their return.

Under the wary eye of the jemadar, the Mirza and his men were housed in poor quarters. The Mirza was questioned by the Atalik and others several times, but stuck to his story of being a merchant. One day a servant brought him a compass and a sextant, and asked to be shown how to use them. Feigning ignorance, the Mirza declined, fearing a trap. Nevertheless, under great difficulty, he managed to take observations of the night stars and bribed his guards so as to be able to slip away on three occasions to the old city of Kashgar. Befriending a merchant from Tashkent, he even acquired military information about the nearest Russian fort, nine days' march away from Kashgar.

Almost as soon as he arrived in the city, the Atalik's officials had asked him if he knew about the two English officers who had recently entered Kashgaria. The two were George Hayward, sponsored by the RGS to explore the Pamir (and destined to be murdered on his next expedition there), and Robert Shaw, a tea planter more interested in the commercial possibilities of Turkestan. Shaw, the uncle of Francis Younghusband (who was to head the British occupation of Lhasa in 1904) later became the joint commercial and political agent at Leh.[43] Each wanted to be the first European in modern times to visit Yarkand and Kashgar (and return alive) and it was quite by chance that their expeditions met in Ladakh. Intense rivals, colleagues only by coincidence, they made their separate ways to Kashgar. Shaw was the first to reach the city, arriving there on 4 January 1869, and Hayward followed on 5 March. The Mirza, arriving on 3 February, was therefore ahead of Hayward but after Shaw. The Mirza promptly risked approaching Shaw on 11 February, sending a message in English with his servant, saying that he had been sent to explore, asking for the loan of a watch for astronomical observations, and wanting to know the date. Believing that the Mirza might be an agent provocateur, Shaw refused these requests.[44] This rebuff explains why the Mirza apparently made no attempt to communicate with Hayward when he turned up the next month.

All three men were in detention. Neither Hayward nor Shaw was allowed to visit the old city of Kashgar. The Atalik probably believed that all three were spies. As Shaw commented, "by some magic the explorer is supposed to carry off a plan of the roads, and by those roads a European army follows." After describing this as the "nightmare of central Asiatic rulers,"

Shaw went on to say that "of course there is some truth in this view."[45] Eventually, hoping perhaps to enlist British help in stemming Russian influence, the Atalik allowed them to depart. Shaw left for Yarkand on 9 April, and Hayward, his dreams of heading for the Pamir dashed, followed on 13 April. The Mirza was in despair when they went, fearing that he would be imprisoned at Kashgar forever. In desperation, he threatened to appeal over the head of the jemadar to the Atalik himself, with whom he got on well. This had the desired effect: the jemadar asked the Atalik for permission, the Mirza and his men were provided with passports with the Atalik's seal, and the Mirza was made a gift of a robe and sixty rupees of gold dust so that he could buy a horse. Much relieved, they rode out of Kashgar on 7 June.

The Mirza and his party headed southeast along the road to Yarkand. There they joined a *kafila* of three hundred people, mostly pilgrims on their way to Mecca, and crossed into Ladakh over the Karakorum pass. The only unpleasant event on the journey came when one of the Mirza's men developed an attraction for a Yarkandi woman. According to the Mirza, the man was in a "demented state" and threatened to expose the Mirza if he was not allowed to stay and marry the woman. The Mirza persuaded him to continue by letting him think that if he stayed behind, he would be carried off to the Atalik as a Hindustani slave. A little money also changed hands.

Leh was reached in August 1869, and from there the Mirza made his way through Kashmir and back to the headquarters of the GTS at Dehra Dun. He had been gone for almost two years.

The expedition was a major achievement. The Mirza could have died of exposure along the upper Oxus or on the desolate Pamir. He could have been robbed or killed by bandits. Many times he was threatened with exposure as a spy of the British (which he was). Twice he was denounced as an infidel (which he wasn't) and nearly stoned to death by fanatical Moslems. Shaw heard a rumor that he had been imprisoned in Kashgar with a wooden log tied to his leg. Apparently unharmed, the Mirza managed to surmount all the obstacles and complete his grueling journey by sheer force of character, quick-wittedness, and physical presence. Speaking of the political confusion in Afghanistan, and the unsettled state of Kashgaria, Montgomerie concluded that "the discretion of the Mirza seems to be established by the fact of his having made his way through such difficult countries when in such a disturbed state."

What had the Mirza accomplished? He had, first of all, produced a route survey of 2,179 miles, the most important section being the 1,042 miles from Kabul via Kashgar to Yarkand, 350 miles of which was very little known. Since the Mirza started and finished his observations at known points, Kabul and Yarkand, Montgomerie was able to test the precision of his pacing. He was surprised to find that it was remarkably accurate, given the mountainous terrain, the snow on the ground, and the condition of open arrest under which the Mirza had to travel at times.

Just as the Mirza confirmed much of the work done by Montgomerie's first explorer, Abdul Hamid, so his own observations were verified by later travelers. Gordon, accompanying the Forsyth Mission in the reverse direction to the Mirza from Kashgar to Badakhshan, said of him that "he worked under great difficulties, and . . . on the whole, we proved his information to be extremely accurate."[46]

The relative positions of Yarkand and Kashgar were now altered as a result of the new information, which helped explain why Marco Polo went first to Kashgar and then to Yarkand, the route from Badakhshan to Yarkand being less direct than at first assumed. The route survey accounted for the geography of eighteen thousand square miles of previously unexplored country. The position of Yarkand, first defined by Montgomerie's explorer Abdul Hamid, was confirmed by the Mirza and ratified by the RGS, who proved Shaw's measurements to be in error.[47]

Despite this, it was not easy to convince the luminaries of the geographical establishment that the measurements of a "native" could be trusted. Writing only a short while after the RGS had established the veracity of the Mirza's data, Colonel Henry Yule wrote that "had we not been prepared for his results by the labour of Mohamed Hamid [Abdul Hamid], corroborated by Messrs. Shaw and Hayward, which showed how erroneous were the longitudes heretofore assigned to the great cities of Eastern Turkestan, there can be little doubt that the accuracy of the Mirza's work would have been subject to general misgiving."[48]

Yule indicated that he himself was not without misgivings concerning the Mirza. Finding it "satisfactory" that the Mirza's work was generally in accordance with that of Wood, he observed that the two did not agree quite as closely as Montgomerie claimed, and that in fact there was a difference of 10' in their longitudes at and between Kunduz and Faizabad. "I have no doubt," pronounced Yule, "that the preference is to be given to Wood."[49] Yule's automatic preference for Wood led him astray in at least one instance. While the precise measurement of longitude which was assigned by Wood to Faizabad is unknown, the Mirza's figure of 70° 36' is only 4' from the *Times* Atlas's 70° 40', and if Wood differs from the Mirza by 10' (as he does, according to Yule), then the Mirza must have had the more accurate measure.

Yule is on less shaky ground when he is critical of the Mirza's heights, taken by boiling-point thermometer. Wood is considerably nearer the mark.

Nor was Yule ungenerous to the Mirza in his overall assessment of the man, saying that "justice cannot be done to his work without attention to the hardships and difficulties under which his observations were made on those high lands in the depth of winter, superadded to the absolute necessity of secrecy in accomplishing them."[50]

The Mirza's observations at Kashgar corrected those made by the early French Jesuits, and those of the Schlagintweits. Was the Mirza the first to locate Kashgar accurately on the map, or was he preceded by Robert Shaw or George Hayward? Colonel Trotter, Montgomerie's successor, said that Hayward was the first to take astronomical observations at Kashgar, but Trotter must be mistaken, for the Mirza arrived in the city a month before Hayward, and started his observations immediately.[51] Montgomerie did admit that Hayward was the first to publish his results.[52] Shaw actually beat them both to Kashgar. However, the Mirza had also made three excursions to the old city, and his measurement of its position was the only one provided to the British that had been made from an actual visit. With the conclusion of the Mirza's travels, said Montgomerie, "the positions assigned to the chief places in Eastern Turkestan may now be considered to be accurate enough for all general geographical purposes."[53]

In addition, Montgomerie stated that "the Mirza's route gives us another determination of the great watershed which separates Eastern Turkestan from the basins of the Indus and the Oxus," and showed that the Pamir were a continuation of the Himalayan chain, with the watershed running along the crest of the Pamir plateau.[54] These data on the hydrography of the Pamir were much desired by geographers of the day. In conjunction with other recently acquired survey data, the Mirza had helped nearly double the presumed distance between Faizabad and Kashgar, explaining what had perplexed many geographers—why it took so long for Marco Polo, Benedict Goes, and others to journey from west to east Turkestan.[55] Over and above the purely geographical information, however, the Mirza also provided very useful political and military intelligence on Afghanistan. Traveling with the emir's army advancing from Kandahar to Kabul, he supplied the British with accounts of military actions, accounts which, Montgomerie said, "at the time were rather valuable, as it was difficult to get any other information."[56] The same was true for northern Afghanistan, between Kabul and the Oxus, and on Chinese Turkestan. Information was also provided on routes from Kashgar to the Russian frontier. Implying that the Mirza, unlike Shaw or Hayward, could get on the inside of things, Montgomerie wrote: "The Mirza is a very intelligent man, and has as a native, an Asiatic, got a very considerable insight into the state of affairs in Eastern Turkestan."[57]

Montgomerie now had the task of reducing the Mirza's observations and constructing a map from them. This perhaps took his mind off the loss of his son, who had died in the hill station of Mussoorie just a few days after he was born on 11 September 1869.

When Montgomerie's paper on the Mirza's explorations was read to the RGS on 24 April 1871, both he and the Mirza received great praise. In their absence, the president of the RGS, Sir Henry Rawlinson, praised Montgomerie's "system of educating natives of India for geographical exploration." Sir Andrew Waugh referred to Montgomerie as "our Gold Medallist" and lauded him for bringing order out of chaos in the geography of Kashgaria. The Mirza too was given full credit for his "pluck and endurance . . . as well as for the professional skill he displayed." From today's perspective, the only discomforting note came from General Walker, superintendent of the GTS, who spoke of the difficulty of accurately determining longitude, being "far beyond what can be expected of the native explorers." Longitude, he continued, could be derived from their observations in a rough and ready manner, "but, considering the class of men employed, it is the best—in fact, the only one—that could possibly be attempted."[58]

Montgomerie was soon to be described by the viceroy of India as "the first living authority on the topography of the districts lying on, or immediately beyond our NW Frontier."[59]

As for the Mirza, Montgomerie sent him and his son-in-law on a second expedition, to Bokhara, in 1872-73. They passed Herat and reached Maimana safely. But beyond there, somewhere on the road to Bokhara, both were murdered by their guides while asleep.[60]

The Havildar

The Mirza, it will be remembered, had been foiled by the winter snows from pursuing his original route, due north from Peshawar to Badakhshan via Chitral. But one year after the Mirza's return, in August 1870, Montgomerie had ready a trained explorer called "the Havildar" who was dispatched from Peshawar in time to take advantage of the brief summer period during which the passes over the Hindu Kush would be open. The Havildar took his alias from his rank, since he was a havildar, or sepoy noncommissioned officer in the Bengal Sappers and Miners. He was Moslem, a Pathan, and was recommended to Montgomerie by Major Pollock, the commissioner of Peshawar. Pollock himself had obtained the services of the Havildar from Lieutenant-Colonel Frederick Maunsell, commandant of the Sappers and Miners, the same officer who had previously supplied Montgomerie with the first Pathan explorer. The Havildar, whose real name was Hyder Shah, came from Kohat, a town south of Peshawar.[61]

Montgomerie was seeking geographical data on the large area lying between Afghanistan and what he described as "Little Tibet," or Baltistan, to the northwest of Kashmir (Map 2). Bounded on the north by the Hindu Kush range, and on the south and southeast by the Indus River and its tributary the Kabul, this large region included Kafiristan, Chitral, Swat, and Yasin. Despite the rough terrain and the violent nature of the inhabitants, a fair amount of information had already been gleaned about this northwest frontier region. Two employees of the India government, Abdul Mejid and Pundit Munphool, had traversed parts of it in 1860 and 1865, respectively. Neither was a trained observer or surveyor, however. The main sources of knowledge were men of the region who came down to Peshawar to trade. Many of these men were mines of information about the valleys in which they lived, but being uneducated, they were unable to describe their locations relative to their neighbors in parallel valleys, separated from them as they were by the steep ridges characteristic of the area. Thus, Montgomerie had detailed knowledge of isolated parts only, and believed that a route survey through the heart of the region would enable him to pull all his information together, and so produce a serviceable map. After the first Pathan, killed in Swat, a second who was dismissed for the theft of Nain Singh's gold watch, and then the Mirza, this was Montgomerie's fourth attempt to penetrate the districts south of the Hindu Kush. This time he was to be successful.

Beyond the Hindu Kush, Montgomerie was also interested in learning more about the Oxus region of Badakhshan, through which the Mirza had passed, and of the territory lying to the north of the Oxus.

The Havildar's instructions were to march north through Swat and Dir to Chitral, and then to head northwest across the Hindu Kush into Badakhshan. At its capital, Faizabad, he would cross the route of the Mirza, which would provide Montgomerie with a check on the accuracy of his route survey. He was then to continue north, crossing the Oxus, and after surveying its upper reaches, head for his ultimate destination of Kokand.

On 12 August 1870, the Havildar, accompanied by his assistant (who, as "the Mullah," was subsequently to become an accomplished explorer himself) and a number of servants, left Peshawar and within three days was out of British territory, crossing the Malakand Pass, and arriving in Alladand, the small town which represented the capital of Swat. Before reaching the Malakand Pass, the party had to pass through the tribal territory of the fierce Yusufzai. Two decades earlier, Major Walker had tried to extend a survey into this area, but was shot at each time he approached it, and was forced to retire.[62]

The Swat valley extends northeast from the junction of the Swat and Panjkora rivers for about seventy miles, the sides of the valley reaching nineteen thousand feet in height, and its breadth ranging from ten miles to only a few hundred yards. The population were Pathans and Sunni Moslems. The "capital" of Alladand, so called because it was the current residence of the khan of Swat, was a town of about three hundred poorly constructed mud and stone houses. The khan, reported the Havildar, was such a poor ruler that the people were constantly intriguing to replace him with his predecessor. For the British, Swat had military significance in that it lay on the most direct route to Chitral, and on the passes over the Hindu Kush. It was not visited by a British surveyor until thirteen years after the Havildar's visit, when William McNair traversed the valley in 1883 on his way to Kafiristan.

The morning following their arrival in Alladand, after paying a tax imposed by the khan on their goods, the party ferried over the Swat River on rafts, crossed a low range of mountains, and marched down to the Panjkora River. Here they narrowly avoided being looted by brigands. Each night was spent in a different village, the Havildar fending off questions about his journey by saying that he was going to Chitral to buy falcons—highly prized on the plains of the Punjab. Observations of the stars were taken when possible. The ascent over the mountains into Dir was made in rain, although the party was sheltered to some degree by the dense pine forests on the northern slopes. The capital of Dir, a small town of about four hundred houses, and of the same name, was entered on 23 August. Dir was a little over halfway from Peshawar to Chitral. The British later formed Dir, Swat, and Chitral into a single unit called the Malakand Agency. Dir itself was important because of its location across the primary route from Chitral to Peshawar. For the Havildar, however, there was a more immediate problem, for the road to Chitral from Dir, a distance of about thirty-five miles as the crow flies, was known to be infested by Kafir brigands.

Kafiristan, the home of these non-Moslem people, who worshiped tribal and household gods, lay to the west, a mountainous area of irregular valleys between Chitral and Afghanistan. Mountstuart Elphinstone, who led the mission to Kabul in 1808, had dispatched a native into Kafiristan and obtained an account of the district. Other secondhand reports had followed, describing a people of fair complexion, in legend (though not in fact) descended from soldiers of Alexander the Great, left there on his invasion of India. No Englishman was to explore this inaccessible region until the Lockhart mission of 1885. MacNair, disguised as a native doctor, wrote an article detailing his travels in Kafiristan in 1883, but actually only briefly penetrated the border, after following much the same route as the Havildar.[63] Violently hostile to their Moslem neighbors, who because of their religious hatred attacked the Kafirs for their land and as a source of slaves, the Kafirs in turn wreaked havoc on caravans of traders passing on the boundaries of their territory.

For protection, travelers generally halted at Dir (if going north) until a large number of them, up to two hundred, had gathered together, forming a force which offered some protection against marauders. No number was completely safe, though, as the hundreds of memorial cairns and flags by the roadside testified. The route indeed was one long graveyard. Unfortunately for the Havildar, a large party had recently left Dir for Chitral, meaning that special arrangements would have to be made. The Havildar therefore asked the local chief for an armed escort of twenty-five men, which was provided after the gift of a gold-laced scarf was proffered. On 31 August, after a six-day march, and sustaining nocturnal small arms fire from the predatory Kafirs, they succeeded in reaching Chitral unharmed.

Chitral, about fifty miles southeast of the Hindu Kush watershed, was the capital of the area of the same name. Virtually unexplored at the time of the Havildar's travels, it later became famous in 1895 when British forces were besieged there. The siege was lifted by two relief columns, one of which took the same route as the Havildar.[64] Situated between Gilgit on the east, and Kafiristan and Afghanistan to the west, the Chitralis, a Moslem, but non-Pathan, people, lived in an area about the size of Wales (or Massachusetts). Sir George Robertson, who was present at the siege of Chitral, described the country as a harsh and poor land. It was, he said, "bigness combined with desolation; vast silent mountains cloaked in eternal snow, with glacier-born torrents, cruel precipices and pastureless hillsides where the ibex and the markhor find a precarious subsistence."[65] "Food," continued Robertson, "is so scarce that a fat man has never yet been seen in the country; even the upper classes look underfed, and the most effective form of bribes is a full meal."[66]

The day before reaching Chitral, the Havildar heard his first report of the death of George Hayward, who had been killed not far off, in Yasin, some six weeks earlier. His murderer, a local petty chief of Yasin by the name of Mir Walli, had arrived in Chitral three days prior to the Havildar, and was the guest of the shah of Chitral, Aman-i-Mulk. Rumor had it that the shah of Chitral, although professing anger at Mir Walli for the killing of Hayward, had in fact conspired in the murder with him. The Havildar reported that the two appeared to be close friends, and that the shah not only took his share of the spoils looted from Hayward's camp, but also carried one of

Hayward's rifles. It was therefore with considerable apprehension that the Havildar obeyed a summons to a durbar from Aman-i-Mulk. At the meeting, the Havildar found himself seated between the shah and Hayward's executioner, Mir Walli. Later, he confessed confidentially to Montgomerie that he did not believe he would leave the durbar alive, and that he clutched a loaded revolver the whole time, concealed in his pocket, determined that if any move was made upon him, he would shoot the two chiefs first.[67] But the Havildar remained outwardly calm, and was able to satisfy his questioners by saying that he was on his way to Bokhara to recover money owed to him by some of his countrymen resident there.

At this point Aman-i-Mulk told the Havildar that the road to Bokhara was closed at the Oxus, on the orders of the shah of Badakhshan, acting on behalf of Sher Ali, emir of Kabul. Supposedly Sher Ali's nephew, a rival for the throne, was under Russian protection in Bokhara. When three men traveling from Kabul to Bokhara were discovered to be in possession of letters from parties in Kabul, intriguing with the nephew, Sher Ali ordered the three to be "blown away from guns," and promptly closed the border. This was the first intimation—later proved correct—that the Havildar would not be able to complete his full mission to Kokand.

Nevertheless, he decided to press on for Badakhshan, in order to see for himself. Leaving Chitral on 5 September, the Havildar reached Faizabad twenty days later, after an arduous journey. The difficulty lay with the Nuksan pass, which, at seventeen thousand feet, provided one of the main links over the Hindu Kush between Chitral and Badakhshan. The Havildar had never before been in mountain snow which, combined with the steepness of the ascent, made for slow progress, watching out for Kafirs all the time. Montgomerie reported that, having reached the ascent of the pass, the travelers had to cross huge fields of snow and ice, "the road for a distance of 400 or 500 paces being literally cut through the ice to a depth of from 6 to as much as 12 feet."[68] The Havildar provided Montgomerie with the first evidence of the existence of glaciers in the Hindu Kush. No doubt the Army quartermaster-general's Intelligence Department was also interested to hear details of this important pass. The height of a pass was always a consideration, but the details of the ascent and descent, whether steep or gentle, and its suitability for pack animals or carts were at least of equal concern.

Ascending the pass, the party began to suffer from altitude sickness and chewed raw onions in the belief that this would provide relief. On the northern side of the Hindu Kush, the wind dropped and conditions improved. Apples grew in profusion and a small coin bought fifty of them. Soon the Havildar came to Zebak, a village through which the Mirza had passed the year before, on his way over the Oxus. The two route surveys of the Mirza and the Havildar were now connected.

In Faizabad, the truth of what they had been told in Chitral was confirmed—that the road north across the Oxus was closed. The Havildar therefore remained in Faizabad for a little over a month, collecting some interesting information on the political situation there, and on Russian activity to the north, before starting the return journey.

After leaving Zebak, they travelled with a caravan accompanying the murderous Mir Walli, who had been in Zebak for a meeting between the Chitral and Badakhshan chiefs. The Havildar noted with some satisfaction that Mir Walli's leg had been broken by the kick of a horse and that he was in considerable pain because the bone had not been allowed to set. It was now November and the Nuksan pass was closed by snow, so the group decided to head for the Dorah pass about twenty-five miles to the west. Although less steep and at a slightly lower altitude than the Nuksan, this pass was usually avoided because it carried the road into Kafiristan. With the caravan and Mir Walli's armed escort, however, it seemed worth the risk.

Kafirs were successfully avoided, but the weather almost saw the end of the party. The Havildar reported that with the desertion of his servants, plus the snow, cold, and high winds, and the omnipresent threat of the Kafirs, he experienced "the height of misery." The Dorah pass, he said, was worse than the Nuksan. However, this was probably due to the snow, for after ascending the Dorah pass in the summer of 1883, MacNair reported that it was the easiest of all the passes leading from Chitral across the mountains.

After some uncomfortable moments in Chitral, where the shah, having heard rumors that the Havildar was employed by the British, was in consequence very cold to him, the explorer and his party proceeded back the way they had come in the summer. The Havildar was able to note that when they left, Mir Walli was still in agony from his broken leg and the bone could be heard grating when he moved. Montgomerie commented with relish that he was likely to become permanently lame, "which may yet perhaps assist in bringing him to justice and to the fate he so richly deserves."[69]

The party reached Peshawar safely on 13 December, after an absence of four months, and then the Havildar proceeded on to Dehra Dun to present Montgomerie with his results.

The Havildar's observations proved to be very accurate, and in agreement with those of the Mirza, where the two routes overlapped. For the first time the British had a continuous route survey of 286 miles from Peshawar to the Hindu Kush. The position of Chitral and other important places had been fixed, which, together with observations of mountain peaks taken both by the Havildar and from frontier stations, would allow the construction of a good map of the area.

The Havildar's finding that Chitral was only a little over 7,000 feet in height was surprising, bearing in mind its proximity to the Hindu Kush range with peaks in the 22,000- to 28,000-foot bracket. But it confirmed the measurement taken by Hayward that Yasin, about the same distance from the mountain range, was at 7,700 feet.

By combining the route survey with the positions of mountain peaks measured trigonometrically, Montgomerie proclaimed that the Havildar "may be said to have put into my hands the key of the geography of the whole of the unknown region which was desirable to explore, with the exception of Kafiristan proper."[70]

Finally, the explorations of the Havildar also enabled Montgomerie to make use of the observations made by his first Pathan explorer, who traveled up to the sources of the Swat River and was killed in Swat in 1869. The papers of the murdered man had been recovered but could not be taken advantage of because they lacked the closing point of the survey. This missing link was supplied by the Havildar.[71]

The president of the RGS, Sir Henry Rawlinson, described the Havildar as a "most remarkable man," praising him in his annual address to the Society as a "bold, energetic, and well trained officer, . . . [with] a combination of boldness and discretion which is very rare in an Asiatic."[72] Montgomerie noted how the Havildar was able to escape being discovered, and perhaps executed or sold into slavery, by putting on a bold front, thus giving the impression of resources he did not in fact have. He was clearly a man who possessed considerable self-control in a tight spot.

Colonel Walker was present at the RGS meeting in London in May 1872, at which Montgomerie's paper on the travels of the Havildar was read. Neither Montgomerie nor the Havildar was able to attend. Colonel Walker expressed the view that it was the last that anyone, unfortunately, would hear of the Havildar, because "after receiving a good reward, these men liked to go to their homes, and live in peace for the rest of their lives."[73] One could hardly blame them. But Walker was wrong. Montgomerie, who had become acting superintendent of the GTS when Walker left for leave in England in December 1870, had already sent the Havildar off on a second journey to explore the route from Kabul to Bokhara via Balkh and Karshi.

No account of this mission to Bokhara was ever compiled. Years later, soon after the Havildar's third and final expedition, Montgomerie, now retired from service in India, was told by Walker that the Havildar had been falsifying his data. Montgomerie replied to Walker that "I had some doubts as to his observations at Bokhara, which I could make nothing of." This would explain why, although the Havildar succeeded in reaching Bokhara (or at least said he did), no account of this excursion was ever published. Why did the Havildar "cook the books"? According to Montgomerie, "it is the Pathan blood coming out. It is very annoying, for otherwise the man is very satisfactory."[74] The Havildar apparently preferred the risk of being found out and dismissed from the Survey to the peril of being unmasked as an agent of the British, and so concocted data to show that he had observed in areas that he had not in fact visited.

Despite not being able to make sense of the Havildar's observations on his second journey, Montgomerie nevertheless dispatched him on a third mission in 1873, later described by Kenneth Mason as the Havildar's "most important contribution to geography."[75] But since Mason seems to have been unaware of the correspondence between Walker and Montgomerie concerning the veracity of the Havildar, doubts must be cast upon this assertion. Even Henry Trotter, who wrote up the report of this, the Havildar's last journey, said of his account that it was "somewhat meagre," although having analyzed it, he came to the conclusion that it was "trustworthy."[76]

What we can be certain of is that this was one of Montgomerie's last operations. It was he who selected the route of the Havildar, although even before the party left in the late summer of 1873, Montgomerie himself had already gone on leave back to England. He never returned to India.

The Havildar departed from Peshawar on 19 September 1873 in a group of six, there being in addition to himself two servants, plus a corporal in the Sappers, and his nephew (both of whom had accompanied him before), and his assistant, "the Mullha," who journeyed with them only as far as Jalalabad before parting from the group to set off on his own expedition, also prearranged by Montgomerie (Map 2).

The Havildar's instructions were to proceed through territory previously unexplored, to map the upper reaches of the Oxus River. He disguised himself as a cloth merchant, and pretended to be a servant, passing off the corporal as the headman of the party. Heading due north from Kabul, the Havildar and his entourage crossed the Hindu Kush main range by the Sarolang pass, the same pass that Benedict Goes probably took in the early seventeenth century, and the one that Lieutenant John Wood of the Indian Navy unsuccessfully tried to negotiate on his journey to the Oxus in 1837. On 19 November the Havildar reached Faizabad in Badakhshan, thus linking his survey both with that of the Mirza and with his own earlier route of 1870. Claiming that the road north across the Oxus was completely blocked with snow, the group remained in Faizabad until late April of 1874. Captain Trotter, who wrote up the Havildar's report, was clearly unhappy with this explanation of the delay. However, during his stay there, the Havildar was able to collect information on the political economy of Badakhshan, some of which was later to cause problems for Trotter, Montgomerie's successor.

When the snow abated, the group departed and soon crossed the Oxus, at Samti, on a raft of inflated skins. They were now in the territory of the khanate of Bokhara. The Havildar had been instructed by Montgomerie to stay as close to the Oxus as possible, but decided to keep to the frequented roads inland, in order to avoid suspicion and preserve his disguise as a merchant. The party was shortly moving up the valley of the Oxus, that is, traveling south toward Shignan, on the right bank where the Oxus made its great swing to the north. The road here was very difficult, in some cases being only a series of iron pegs driven into the rocky cliffs, the traveler holding on to them while resting his feet on rope suspended from the pegs, the Oxus meanwhile tearing through the narrow defile below.

Unfortunately, the Havildar was stopped before arriving at Shignan, and was forced to turn back. He was therefore unable to continue his survey south to Ishkashim, where the Oxus began its bend north, which would have again linked his work with that of the Mirza, thus giving the British a virtually complete map of the upper reaches of the river.

Retracing his route, the Havildar decided to make one more attempt to reach Shignan, by returning to Faizabad, and then traveling southeast to Ishkashim, and this time following the Oxus north into Shignan instead of approaching from the opposite direction. Regrettably, after marching thirty-five miles along the Oxus, the Havildar was halted at the border village of Shignan and had to retrace his steps.

His journey was not at an end, however. Following instructions, he returned to Faizabad and again crossed the Oxus at Samti and surveyed the area to the north of the river, this time heading west for about a hundred miles before recrossing the Oxus and reaching the town of Kulm-Tash-kurgan. From there he took the easier route over the Hindu Kush to Kabul, and then on to Peshawar, arriving on 11 January 1875.

This, the last journey of the Havildar, was a most significant achievement. His route across the Hindu Kush from the Sarolang pass to Badakhshan had never been previously surveyed. The information he provided about the geography of the great northern bend of the Oxus furnished the locations and other details of towns of which only the names had previously been known. This information also served to clarify rather vague details of the region supplied earlier by Abdul Mejid. The Havildar also found the solution to what Trotter called "one of the great problems of modern geography," namely the positive identification that the Surkhob and Vakhsh rivers were one and the same, and that this tributary of the Oxus in fact joined the river eighty miles farther downstream than had always been supposed.

It was unfortunate that the Havildar was halted, while heading south, on the border of Shignan. Unknown to him, some two months earlier another native surveyor, Abdul Subhan, or "the Munshi," dispatched by Trotter, had followed the Oxus downstream, traveling north, and had reached a point only one good day's march from the Havildar, of whose mission he was himself ignorant. Had the Havildar been able to proceed, the survey of this section of the Oxus would have been completed. As it was, a gap of about twenty-five miles remained.

The Havildar's survey of the upper Oxus was of potential value because of the Anglo-Russian agreement, made the year he commenced his expedition, that the river's upper reaches should form the frontier between Russia and Afghanistan. So little was known of this territory that it became a complex matter before the boundary was delimited in 1885. In the 1873 understanding Britain and Russia had agreed that Afghan territory included all that territory under the control of Sher Ali, emir of Kabul. But this was not the same as taking the Oxus as the frontier, for there were close ethnic and historical ties between the Afghans south of the Oxus and Bokhara to the north, closer in many ways than their ties to Kabul. Furthermore, Bokhara, as well as Shignan and Roshan, all had tenuous claim to territory on the left bank of the river. Diplomacy eventually solved these problems, aided by better maps, and demarcation teams on the ground. There was also considerable activity on the part of the government in St. Petersburg. At the time the Havildar concluded his survey, a party of Russian surveyors reached and fixed the position of two towns visited by the Havildar. When their results reached India, one of the first connections was established between British and Russian surveys in Central Asia.

The two towns were Kolab and Kubadian, now part of Soviet Tadzhikistan, and named Kulyab and im Nasir Khisrav.[77] The Havildar's determination of the positions of these places compares well if his measurements are placed against those of the Russians (of 1875), and the correct locations as defined by the *Times* atlas. In the case of Kulyab, the Russians are closer to the *Times* with respect to the measurement of latitude, but are about equally at variance with the Havildar on longitude. For Kubadian, the Havildar's figures for both latitude and longitude are much the more accurate.

This indicates that Trotter's confidence in the Havildar's work was not misplaced, in spite of Walker's views that the explorer had falsified his material in the past. Even so, this is virtually the last that is heard of the

Havildar. Whether he was dismissed by Walker, or pensioned off and returned home, is not known. It is even possible that he was sent on yet another mission, for he died of cholera in the Afghan city of Jalalabad in 1879. His transgressions forgiven, or forgotten, the anonymous writer of his obituary for the RGS acclaimed him as a native explorer second only to Nain Singh.[78]

The Mullah

On his last journey, the Havildar had been accompanied by "the Mullah," who was now about to embark on his first independent exploration. The Mullah (or "learned man") was in reality named Ata Mahomed,[79] and was the brother of Montgomerie's first Pathan recruit, killed in Swat in 1869. Educated at the Nawab's College in Rampur, he was fluent in Arabic and succeeded at Montgomerie's request in recovering the papers and possessions of his murdered brother, after which he acted as assistant to the Havildar, who provided him with on-the-job training while they journeyed together.[80]

Separating at Jalalabad from the main party led by the Havildar on 28 September 1873, the Mullah, accompanied only by one servant and a pony laden with cloth, muslin, and silk, set off in a northeasterly direction (Map 3).

The Mullah's objective was to map the course of the Kunar (or Chitral) River, an objective which he accomplished except for a stretch of twenty-five miles. While this was not without its achievements and adventures, the later journeys of the Mullah exploring the wild gorges of the upper Indus River were to be of far greater significance.

On his first excursion beyond the frontier, the Mullah in part followed the same route through Dir and Chitral as the Havildar had in 1870. Crossing the Hindu Kush by the Baroghil pass, the Mullah then reached a point in the Wakhan already surveyed by the returning members of the Forsyth mission to Yarkand.[81] Because of this, Captain Trotter, who was the surveyor on the Yarkand mission, and who wrote up the Mullah's report, was able to check his observations thoroughly. Trotter concluded that "his survey is more carefully executed than that of any of the Mahometan explorers before employed by the Great Trigonometrical Survey. His route from Jalalabad to Sarhadd shows 183 bearings with prismatic compass, or one in every two miles—a very good performance indeed, considering that the country is thickly inhabited, and that throughout the whole of it, the discovery of his employment would probably have entailed short shrift and sudden death."[82]

The travels of the Mullah, which lasted over a year, took him as far as Yarkand, before he returned to India, crossing the Karakorum into Ladakh. The most useful part of the route was the first section as far as the Wakhan, which surveyed 380 miles, and corrected the positions of some places supplied by the Havildar.

After a respite of over a year, the next task of the Mullah was to survey the course of the Indus River from where it entered the plains of India at Amb (about fifty miles northwest of present-day Islamabad) to its confluence with the River Gilgit. This was only 150 miles in a straight line drawn on the map, but on foot a journey of 220 miles across difficult and dangerous terrain. Most of the 2,000-mile course of the Indus, from its rise near Lake Manasarowar in Tibet, and its course westward through Tibet and Ladakh, had been surveyed years before (in part by the pundits of the Singh family),[83] and its route from Amb to the sea was also well charted. But only a dotted line on the map showed its hypothetical course between Gilgit and the plains through the rugged mountainous regions of Kohistan and Hazara. Here the river cut its way through mountain ranges rarely less than 15,000 feet high, passing by the great Nanga Parbat at 26,660 feet, in a series of precipitous gorges.

The heights of the mountain peaks had been measured from a distance by trigonometrical stations. Such information as there was about the country itself had been put together from bits and pieces provided by native travelers, for no European had ever actually penetrated the area.

The primary reason for this was that the hill tribes inhabiting the territory adjacent to the valley of the Indus were all naturally suspicious not only of outsiders, but also of each other. One consequence was that most of the local people never traveled outside their own valley, leaving trade to a few specially designated individuals. The Mullah was one such person and was therefore an ideal candidate for the Survey of India.

On this occasion, the Mullah was to be working in concert with another man from the area, a Maulvi named Saiyad Amir from the village of Seo.[84] The two met in Peshawar in late 1875 and agreed to travel disguised as traders. The Maulvi left first, in December, carrying some goods, and the Mullah, accompanied by two servants, followed on 13 February 1876.

The Mullah met up with Saiyad Amir in the latter's home village of Seo on the Indus on 21 March. After an eight-day rest, the Mullah proceeded up the Indus. He was alone except for coolies carrying his goods. Turning east to follow the course of the river, the Mullah passed Nanga Parbat (which he

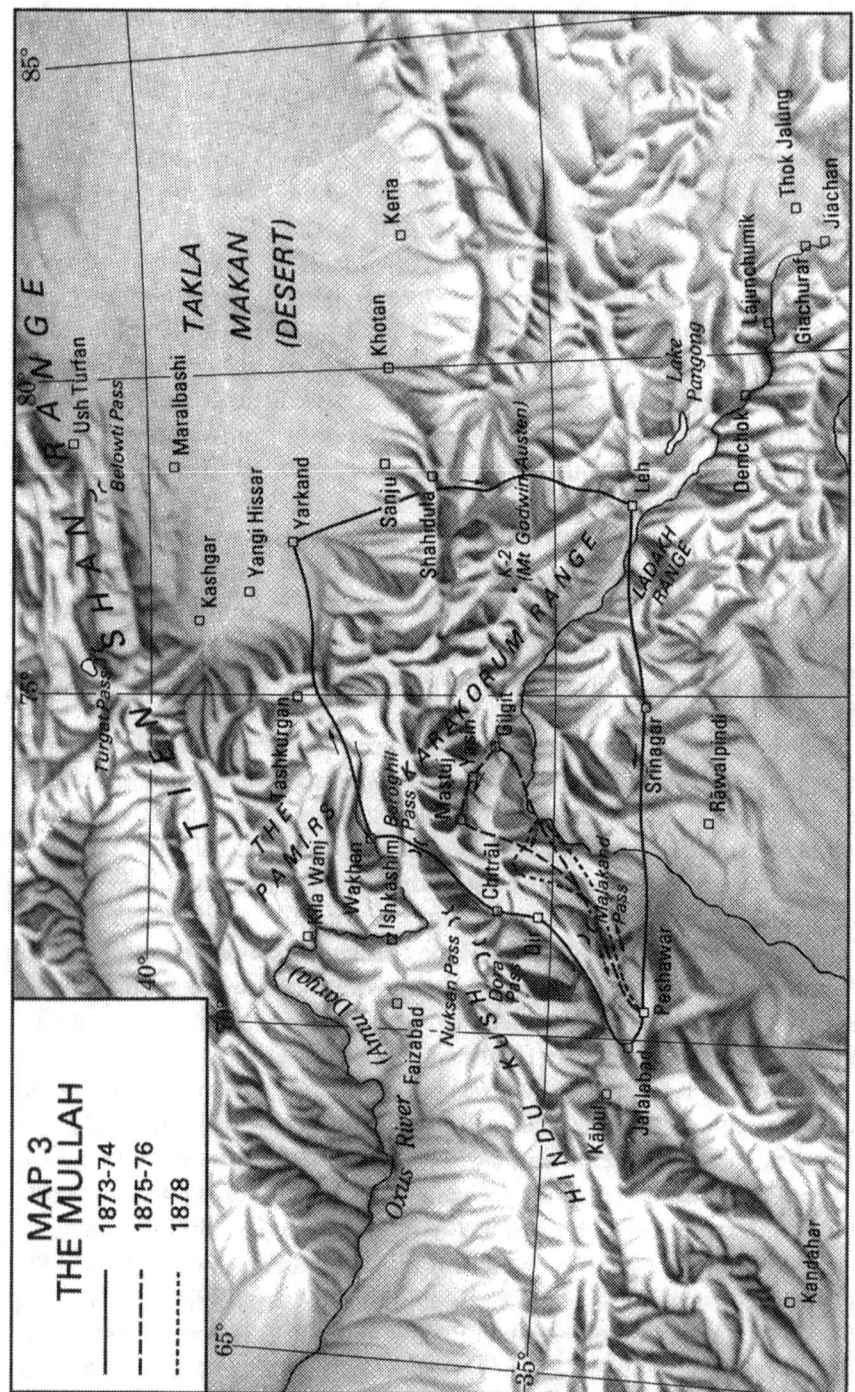

refers to only indirectly as "a high snowy ridge with . . . peaks") and shortly thereafter closed his survey.[85]

His next task was to survey the route from Yasin to Mastuj. To reach Yasin he had to head northwest and pass through Gilgit. Here he did not count his paces or take bearings, because the area had already been surveyed by the late Captain Hayward, murdered in Yasin in 1870.

The Mullah stayed for two weeks in Gilgit, establishing his bona fides as a trader. He then continued and reached Yasin safely on 27 June. From Yasin, the road to Mastuj ran off to the west, and the Mullah restarted his survey. The road was very treacherous in parts, the worst part being "where the traveller has to proceed with one foot on a log of wood thrown across a chasm, and the other on a narrow ledge of rock only a few inches broad on the face of a perpendicular scarp."[86] The Mullah closed his survey at Mastuj, which he had already visited in 1873. From here he traversed other relatively unknown parts of Kohistan, before returning to British territory near Peshawar on 21 October 1876.

Some details of this exploration of the Mullah were subsequently published by J.T. Walker, the surveyor-general of India, in his report on the operations of the Survey of India for the year 1876-77.[87]

The Mullah, the *General Report* said, had "added much to our knowledge of the geography of the interesting regions lying beyond our northern Trans-Indus Frontier." For example, a route which had been thought to run straight in one direction was found to turn back on itself. Even more than thirty years later, it could still be authoritatively stated of the Mullah's explorations in 1876 that "the little that is known of the course of the Indus between Bunji and Attock has been derived from [his] observations."[88]

These explorations of 1876 had skirted east and north of the valley of the River Swat. The acquisition of knowledge about this area was considered vital to an understanding of the geography of the region. Accordingly, in 1878 the Mullah was dispatched on his last exploration.[89] He received his orders in 1877, probably from Colonel Tanner, but then went to his home for a year, to let suspicions about his being an agent for the British die down.[90] He eventually started out from Peshawar on 23 April 1878, in the guise of a trader seeking to purchase timber.[91]

The Mullah was only a short way into his expedition when he found himself crossing the Swat River and listening to a story, told by one of the ferrymen, of a man, a Pathan from Peshawar like himself, who had been murdered by his companion while washing at the same spot on the bank where the Mullah had been standing. The Mullah realized immediately that the murdered man must have been his brother, who had been sent off on his first exploration by Montgomerie in 1869. Despite what he might have taken as an inauspicious omen, the Mullah pressed on.[92]

He eventually returned safely to Peshawar on 30 August, after surviving a journey full of "perils and privation steadily faced and patiently surmounted,"[93] which included attacks by robbers, very bad weather, avalanches, dysentery, and fever. Nevertheless, the Mullah, in a survey which was linked at several points to his explorations in 1876, acquired much useful information on the Swat valley and adjacent areas, which was not to be more fully surveyed until the uprising there of 1895-97.

The Mullah was later described by the surveyor-general as "the most painstaking and reliable of any of the Mussulman explorers that have been employed by this Department."[94]

The last reference to the Mullah is a note in the financial accounts of the survey for 1888, recording expenses for his "secret and confidential explorations across the frontier" into Afghanistan.[95]

But the use of Indian pundits on the northwest frontier waned well before this time, as the area was increasingly penetrated by British surveyors and military expeditions.[96] The regions to the north of the Oxus were similarly explored by their Russian counterparts, and geographical information on these parts of Central Asia was, to a degree, shared by the two governments.

From the early 1870s onward, the Survey of India diverted the major effort on the part of its clandestine probes to the opening up of Tibet, that "great closed land," and its border areas.

FOUR
To Tibet and Beyond: The Singh Family

Western Tibet is that part of Tibet to the west of the 81° line of longitude passing through Lake Manasarowar, and to the south of the 35° line of latitude, which runs to the north of Lake Pangong. It is bounded by Ladakh on the northwest and Nepal on the southeast.[1]

Lakes Manasarowar and Rakas Tal are in the extreme southwestern corner of Western Tibet, only forty miles north of the Nepalese border. With their attendant Mount Kailas, they are sacred to both Buddhists and Hindus. Mount Kailas is believed to be the home of Siva and center of the world. Pilgrims obtain merit by circumnavigating the mountain, a distance of twenty-eight miles, taking three to four days. But the most devout do so by stretching themselves full length on the ground, marking the spot reached by their outstretched fingers, and prostating themselves again from that point. This procedure takes about three weeks.

Lake Pangong (actually a series of four interconnected lakes) is on the frontiers of Tibet and Ladakh, the border almost bisecting it. It was once a freshwater lake, but by the nineteenth century the water level had sunk below the outlet and the lake was saline. Both Lakes Pangong and Manasarowar are part of an extensive lake system stretching east across Tibet to Lhasa, many of them, like Lake Pangong, being salt or alkaline and without external drainage.

Although Mount Kailas, with its snow-capped, temple-shaped dome, dominates the surrounding territory at 22,028 feet, it is not the tallest mountain of southwestern Tibet, that honor going to the highest peak of the massive Gurla Mandhata conglomeration, to the south of Lake Manasarowar, which reaches 25,355 feet.

To the southeast of the Mount Kailas region runs the Tsangpo-Brahmaputra river of southern Tibet. Elsewhere, southwestern Tibet merges into the desolation of the Chang Tang or northern plain, a high plateau sparsely inhabited by nomads, whose barren terrain is relieved only by brackish lakes and hardy tussocks of furze. Nevertheless, it supports an abundant variety of animal life.

Western Tibet is rimmed on the south and west by the Himalayas, which run along the border to meet the Karakorum range in Ladakh. Further to the north stretch the Kunlun mountains, separating Chinese Turkestan from the Tibetan plateau.

The area was known to the Indians as Hundes, and to the Tibetans as Ngari-korsum (the three districts of Ngari) comprising Guge, Purang (near the Nepal border) and Rudok.

Generally situated at altitudes of more than thirteen thousand feet, the bulk of the population is settled in the deep valleys carved out of the plateau by the rivers Indus and Sutlej (and their tributaries), both of which have their sources close to Lake Manasarowar. In these cultivated river valleys where barley and vegetables are grown, the population density is estimated to average about ten people per square kilometer, while in the even more lightly inhabited highland plateaus of the area, there is only an average of one nomad per square kilometer.[2]

Sheep, goats, and yaks graze on the course grass. Wild yaks and antelopes are found in large numbers in spite of the barrenness and desolation of the general area, with its thin vegetation, low rainfall, and paucity of drinkable water. Except in the valleys, there are no trees or shrubs (in fact no vegetation over a foot high) to break the perpetual wind from the south or west that blows during the day, gusting up to 35 miles per hour over a dreary landscape strewn with large stones. The stones make traveling difficult, hindering the progress of the yaks and sheep which, in the absence of any wheeled vehicles, provide transport for goods and people.

The temperature is subject to violent fluctuations—very hot under a clear summer sky, but dropping quickly and steeply at night, or as clouds appear. Indeed, the air is so thin that "a bare headed man with his feet in the shade can get sunstroke and frostbite simultaneously."[3] Provisioning for nineteenth-century travelers was difficult, as there was little wood with which to cook food, and yak dung, which provided the only readily available fuel, imparted an unpleasant taste.

Nevertheless, climates vary widely in the area, and thriving communities existed in the cultivated valleys. Western Tibet was famous, for example, for its apricots.[4] The reports of the pundits tended to exaggerate the bleakness of the region, as they were frequently forced to avoid populated areas for fear of discovery.

Gartok was the main town and capital of western Tibet. The title of "capital" did not imply a teeming metropolis, for the town, about eighty miles northwest of Lake Manasarowar, hemmed by mountains to the north and west, was really a cold and windy village composed of only a fort and a few houses, most of the people living in tents. At an altitude of nearly fifteen thousand feet, Gartok was only the summer capital, host to the Bhotias, Ladakhis, and travelers from China and Turkestan during the August and September trade fair. In the winter months it was deserted, its inhabitants moving to Gargunsa, two or three days' journey northwest down the tributary of the Indus. Subordinate to the Garpon (administrator) in Gartok was the district seat of Rudok, a small town 120 miles (or eight to ten days' march) to the northwest, off the southwestern branch of Lake Pangong.

Other clusters of population included Tsaparang-Chabrang, and Toling (or Totling), both close to the passes over the Himalayas. Tsaparang had been the ancient capital of the kingdom of Guge, the conquest of which by Ladakh led to the closing of the Catholic mission in Tsaparang in 1635. Reincorporated into Tibet in the latter part of the century, it was again briefly overrun from Ladakh, by the Dogras, in 1841. At some point, the site was rebuilt nearby as the modern village of Chabrang, which had a number of stone and clay houses, roofed with wood from the poplar trees that grew on the banks of the nearby Sutlej.[5] Toling, also on the Sutlej, was the site of a famous monastery, and a royal temple of Guge, built around 1020. In 1867, the Toling monastery, with about fifty or sixty monks, allowed the pundits to spend the night there. Toling was also the location of the only bridge in Tibet across the Sutlej.

Gartok was a center of the wool trade, particularly for *pashm,* the soft underwool of the goat, imported by Ladakhi traders to be made up into the famous cashmere shawls. Tibet also exported horses, salt, borax, and, to a limited extent, gold. Imports consisted primarily of European silk, cloth and cotton goods, dried fruit, grain, sugar, and saffron. The major trade arteries ran west, into Ladakh, but there were also routes across the Himalayas to Kulu, Spiti, Lahul, Bashahr, and Garhwal.

At the time of the exploration of Western Tibet organized by Montgomerie in the 1860s, most of the border states were not yet British Indian territory.

Kashmir and Jammu had been conquered in 1819 by the Sikh ruler Ranjit Singh. He appointed the Dogra chieftain Gulab Singh as governor of Jammu in 1822. In 1834, Gulab Singh's military commander Zorawar Singh invaded and conquered Ladakh, which became a dependent territory of the Sikh government of the Punjab. But after Zorawar invaded Western Tibet in 1841, his forces were cut to pieces by a Tibetan army and he himself was killed in battle.

Worse was to follow. Following defeat in the first Anglo-Sikh war, the son of Ranjit Singh was forced to cede Kashmir to Britain by the treaty of

Lahore in 1846. One week later, by the Treaty of Amritsar, Gulab Singh was rewarded for his neutrality and willingness to act as an intermediary by being recognized by Britain as Maharaja of Jammu and Kashmir. This area included Ladakh, but excluded Lahul and Spiti, over which Britain maintained direct control, primarily because an important route for the shawl wool trade ran through Spiti from Gartok.[6]

Kulu, a small area of about six thousand square miles to the south of Ladakh, included Lahul and Spiti. Wool was carried from Gartok, through Spiti to Rampur, the capital of the hill state of Bashahr. Bashahr itself, a British-protected state, lay between Lahul and Spiti to the north, and Garhwal to the south. Most of the goods crossing the Himalayas into Western Tibet were carried either by the Bashahris, or by the Bhotias of Garhwal. Another important route through Bashahr led from Simla (later the British summer capital), through Rampur, which lay on the Sutlej, and then over the 15,400-foot Shipki pass to Toling. Traversing the Tibetan border from Ladakh in the northwest to Nepal in the south, the last Himalayan state was that of Kumaon and Garhwal, acquired by Britain following the victory over the Gurkhas in the Anglo-Nepalese War of 1814-16. This acquisition gave British territory a common frontier with Tibet for the first time.

The first European to cross the Himalayas, the Catholic missionary Andrade, did so via the Mana pass in Garhwal in 1624, and again the following year, setting up a small mission in Tsaparang. The Jesuit priests and Desideri and Freyre, on their way to Lhasa, had been the first Europeans to see the Ladakhi capital of Leh, in 1715, before continuing their journey via Gartok and Lake Manasarowar.

It was over the Niti pass (also in Garhwal) that the first Briton crossed the Himalayas into Western Tibet, in 1812. William Moorcroft, accompanied by Hyder Young Hearsey, visited Lake Manasarowar and believed he was the first European ever to see it, not being aware of the previous journey of Desideri and Freyre. He was, however, the next European to follow them, almost two hundred years later. Moorcroft penetrated as far as Gartok in his attempt to open up the shawl-wool trade.[7]

After the successful conclusion of the war with Nepal, a number of Englishmen tried to visit or establish commercial relations with Western Tibet, but they were usually able to get no further than a few miles from the border before being stopped and turned back by Tibetan border guards.[8] With the advent of the 1840s, some travelers did manage to make more substantial probes into the area.[9] The commissioner at Bareilly, Robert Drummond, even had the temerity to launch a boat on the sacred Lake Manasorawar. It was later rumored that the local official in charge had been decapitated for allowing the spirits to be disturbed in this manner.[10]

Nevertheless, despite the information provided by these explorers and sportsmen, Western Tibet was still very much virgin territory to the geographers and administrators of the 1860s.

Even the boundaries of Western Tibet were unclear, although the British had tried, in places, to remedy this. Under Article 2 of the Treaty of Amritsar, Gulab Singh had agreed to allow the British to survey his territory. He also agreed to appoint commissioners who, together with the British, would define his eastern boundary. This boundary was primarily that between Ladakh and Tibet but also included the boundary between Lahul and Spiti on the south and Ladakh on the north, and where the two joined the Tibetan frontier. Britain's view was that an unsettled boundary—a common cause of disputes in the area—was to be avoided if at all possible, in order to lessen the likelihood of another Dogra attack on Tibet, which in turn would both harm Anglo-Chinese relations and disrupt the trade of the Indian hill peoples with Tibet. Specifically, a border clash had the potential to injure the trade in *pashm*.

British desires, however, whether to capture the wool trade or demarcate the boundary, went largely unrequited in the face of the intransigence and procrastination of both the Tibetans and the Chinese. In 1846, the British appointed Vans Agnew and Captain Alexander Cunningham as their boundary commissioners.

The two commissioners did some survey work in Spiti and Lahul, but were prevented from reaching the Ladakh-Tibet border by a combination of bad weather and a rebellion in Kashmir. Attempts to engage the interest of the Chinese and the Tibetans continued, and in 1847 new boundary commissioners were appointed. In the event, no Chinese or Tibetan commissioners appeared, thus ending the first attempts to demarcate a frontier between the British and Chinese empires.

The survey of Kashmir and Ladakh was continued, and in 1864, Montgomerie was able to declare that all of Ladakh "at present accessible to Europeans" had been surveyed, including the Indus "up to, and slightly beyond, the Chinese boundary."[11] Before going on leave in 1865, Montgomerie had even requested that William Johnson be permitted to survey east of Lake Pangong, where, said Montgomerie, he thought that about sixteen thousand square miles could "be sketched without interruption."[12] It is not clear why Montgomerie took this view, bearing in mind that others, such as Godwin-Austen in 1863, had been halted by Tibetan officials when they had attempted to do just this. In any case,

Johnson was diverted from this task by the famous invitation he received to visit Khotan.

Explorations by the Pundits in 1867

In the late nineteenth century, the Mana pass, at over eighteen thousand feet, provided a major link between British Garhwal and Western Tibet. The route through the Mana valley up to the pass was described in 1907 by the great mountaineer Thomas Longstaff as being desolate and very difficult, "the upper half of the track [lying] over an absolute chaos of unstable rocks of all shapes and sizes."[13] Nevertheless, it was over the Mana pass that three pundits of the Singh family crossed into Tibet on 28 July 1867.[14]

Montgomerie was always critical of previous explorations, each of which had proceeded independently of the other, the travelers providing pieces of information but never in such a manner as to be able to fit the puzzle together and so draw up a coherent map. Before leaving for furlough in England in 1865, Montgomerie had already decided that the next mission of Nain and Mani Singh would be to fill in a number of missing links in the map of western Tibet.

In his journeys of 1865-66, Nain Singh had surveyed the route east from Lake Manasarowar to Lhasa and had connected the lake with survey points in British Kumaon. His cousin Mani had traversed two separate routes from Kumaon to Gartok, the capital of western Tibet. What was lacking was an accurate picture of the territory lying from the west of Gartok to the Ladakhi border. If this gap of about one hundred miles could be filled, an important link would be completed in the construction of a map of Tibet.

Another task of the mission was to investigate details of the headwaters of the Indus, one of the great rivers of northern India, and the Sutlej, one of its major tributaries. The pundits were to confirm the existence of a large branch of the Indus River which had been reported to surveyors in Ladakh by the local inhabitants. Secondly, they were to explore the upper reaches of the Sutlej, and finally to explore east of Gartok, "to gain some knowledge of the vast *terra incognita* lying between the desert of Gobi and Lhasa."[15] This last objective also aimed at clarifying the mystery of the gold and salt mines to the east of Gartok, about which Mani Singh had heard while visiting the town.

Since Mani Singh seemed to lack mental stamina, having failed to enter Tibet, Montgomerie decided to supplement the party with a third member of the family, Kalian Singh, the brother of Nain.[16] Like the other members of his family, Kalian, or G.K., was a Bhotia from the village of Milam in Kumaon.

According to the *Times* correspondent, writing only in 1869 when the mission had long since concluded and been made public, Montgomerie had applied for passports for his pundits from the Chinese through Sir Rutherford Alcock, British minister-plenipotentiary in Peking from 1865 to 1871. Alcock, said the *Times* correspondent, "could do nothing for the Pundits, or at any rate he did nothing."[17] The mission therefore proceeded in secret.

It began from Mussoorie on 2 May 1867 (Map 4). Preparation had been made that spring, after giving Nain and Mani Singh time to recuperate from their previous exploits, which had ended but a few months earlier, in October 1866. Montgomerie officially rejoined the Survey from leave in England only on 1 May 1867, but no doubt he was present in an unofficial capacity to brief the trio prior to their departure. After they were gone, Montgomerie took charge of the survey of Kumaon and Garhwal.

Heading east and then north, the three pundits marched up through the foothills of the Himalayas, passing through Badrinath (a place sacred to Hindus, as it is considered the source of the Ganges) about three weeks later, and reaching the village of Mana some miles short of the pass, on 3 June. If not obscured by cloud, Mount Kamet would have been clearly visible to the east. At Mana, they halted, pending the formal opening of the pass by the Tibetan authorities. Before this could be done, the Tibetans annually ascertained whether there was any epidemic of disease or outbreak of famine in India that might affect them. Montgomerie sarcastically commented that this "inquiry seems to be carried out with all that assumption of lofty superiority for which Chinese officials are famous. Looking down from their elevated plateaus they decide as to whether Hindustan is a fit country to have intercourse with."[18]

The *Times* went even further, referring to the "amusing impudence" with which, according to its correspondent, "they [the Tibetan officials] gravely inquire and decide every year whether Her Majesty's Eastern Empire is worthy of their patronage or lofty recognition."[19] However, since smallpox had in the past been introduced into Tibet from India, with devastating effects on the inhabitants, the Tibetans may be considered to have taken a natural precaution before throwing the passes open to travelers.

While delayed at Mana, the pundits made good use of their enforced idleness by hiring three men, all of whom claimed to know the routes to the Tibetan goldfields. These three in turn acquired servants and purchased asses for carriage of the goods they were taking into Tibet, ostensibly for purposes of trade. Armed with weapons borrowed in Badrinath in order to

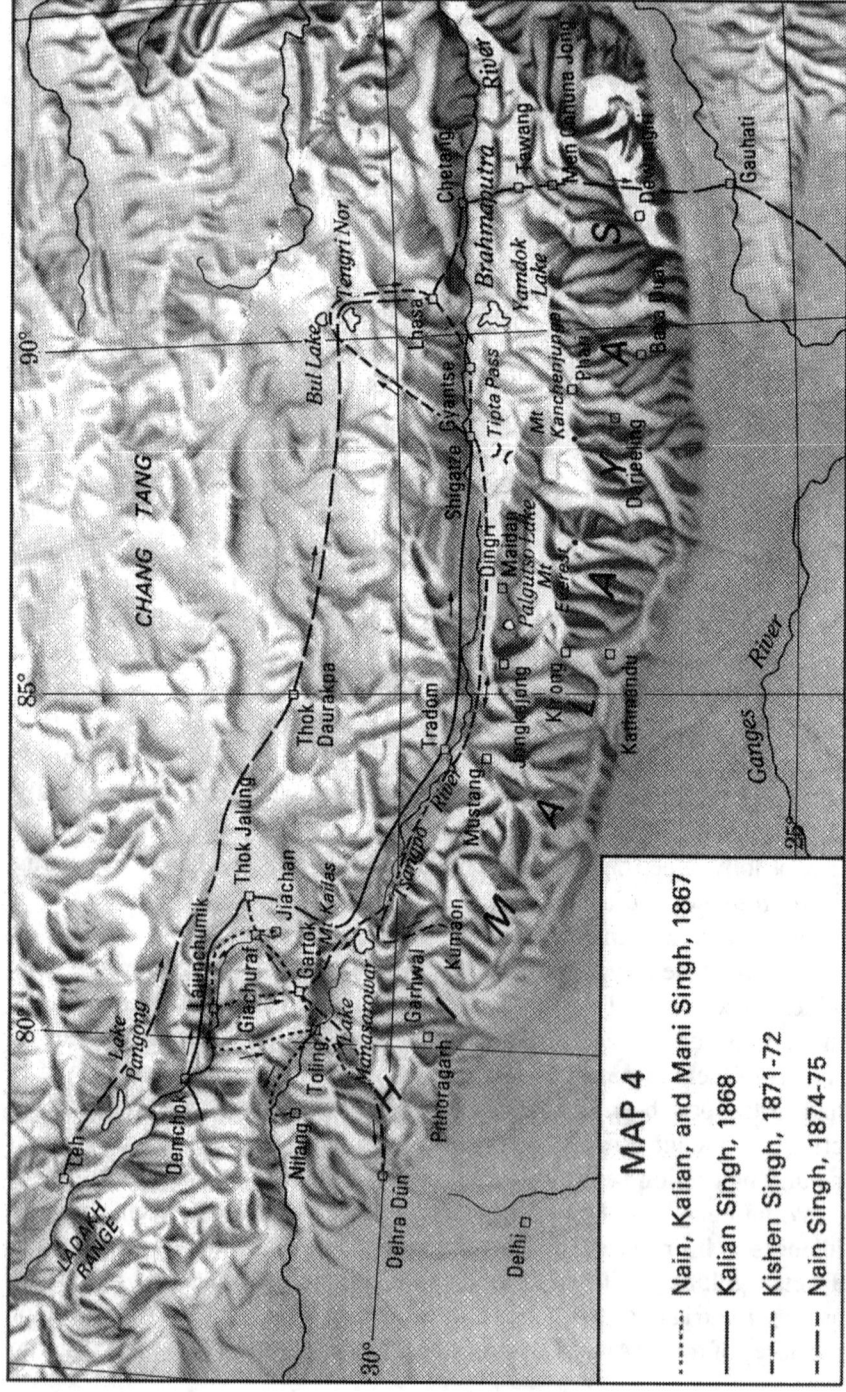

MAP 4

.... Nain, Kalian, and Mani Singh, 1867
———— Kalian Singh, 1868
– – – – Kishen Singh, 1871-72
— — — Nain Singh, 1874-75

deter robbers, the complete party, now composed of eleven men, twelve asses, and one pony, crossed the Mana over the Himalayas on 28 July. By 6 August they had reached Toling on the Sutlej, passing close by Tsaparang, where Andrade had established the first Catholic mission in Tibet. Of Toling, the pundit noted only that he stayed for a night or two at the monastery, with some fifty to sixty monks, although later European travelers noted that the town had brightly colored temples and was perched on a precipice overlooking the Sutlej.[20]

On leaving Toling, the party crossed the Sutlej by a remarkable wooden cantilever bridge, reinforced by two iron chains. The pundit gave the dimensions of the bridge as seventy-six feet in length, seven feet wide, and forty feet above the water. The chains were formed of links of iron, each link on the shape of a figure eight, about a foot long and a square inch in cross-section. Local folklore said that the bridge was built by Alexander the Great. Later photographs show what appears a very rickety structure, but the bridge was still there to be used forty years later by Rawling and Hedin, and the latter reported that it did not even tremble when his horses crossed it.[21] According to the pundit, the iron was preserved by the dry climate and an annual lubrication with butter.

Once over the bridge, the party soon ran into trouble. Heading in a northeasterly direction, they bypassed Gartok in order to avoid arousing the suspicions of the officials there and found themselves on the desolate waste of the Antelope Plain, dotted with lakes of brackish water. The problem arose when the pundits descended down from the plain to the banks of the Indus, reaching Giachuraf camp in mid-August. Once they had crossed the Sutlej, the party had adopted the clothes worn by Bashahri traders, claiming to be in Tibet to sell coral in exchange for shawl-wool. The disguise of a Bashahri had served Nain Singh well on his previous expedition, because the Bashahri were the only Indian hill people allowed to trade freely over all Tibet. On this occasion, however, their disguise was quickly penetrated by the Tibetans at Giachuraf, who pointed out that they could not have come from Bashahr, since all the routes were closed because of an outbreak of smallpox. The direction in which Nain Singh and his party was heading might also have given cause for alarm. They were only thirty miles from the goldfields and well past Gartok, the main mart for the trade in wool, and where merchants were most likely to go.[22]

It was only by dint of repeated protestations and bribes that some of the party were allowed to proceed. Mani Singh, whose nerves had been shaken by the fear of discovery, was left behind as a guarantee of good faith. Nain and Kalian Singh, with some servants, left Giachuraf on 22 August, but

Kalian was soon dispatched on a separate expedition, and Nain Singh continued alone. He reached the fabled gold mine of Thok Jalung on 26 August.

The tradition of Tibetan goldfields may be traced back as far as the Greek historian Herodotus, who referred to "great ants, in size somewhat less than dogs, but bigger than foxes" who dug for gold in a land to the north of India.[23] That this land was Tibet is unlikely—Herodotus is very unreliable in his descriptions of India, and although some believe he could have been referring to the area explored by Nain Singh,[24] there is no confirmatory evidence. Others are inclined to place Herodotus' "great ants" in the Indus valley of Ladakh[25] or near Yarkand.[26]

One authority cites a tenth-century Arabic document as the first positive identification of gold in Tibet.[27] This was followed by reports from the Jesuit and Capuchin missionaries of the eighteenth century. The East India Company learned more details about Tibetan gold from the missions to that country of George Bogle in 1774 and Samuel Turner in 1783.

Gold was exported in the eighteenth century to China and Ladakh, and to Bengal. However, the conquest of what is now Nepal by the Hindu Gurkhas cut into the trade with Bengal, and by the nineteenth century shawl-wool had become a much more important export item to Ladakh than gold. The bulk of Tibetan gold therefore went to Peking, although some gold dust continued to find its way to Leh and into Kumaon.

Peking's control over the goldfields of Western Tibet had been increased in the aftermath of the Dogra invasion of 1842. The number of miners was regulated, and Tibetan civilian and military supervisors were installed, partly to protect the gold, and partly to have the miners available to defend Gartok in case of an emergency.[28] Although the location of the goldfields had remained of some interest to the East India Company into the nineteenth century, it was the discoveries and descriptions of Nain Singh that rekindled this interest.

The mines of Thok Jalung ("thok" is Tibetan for gold or goldfield), which Nain Singh approached in 1867, were very new, having probably been worked, so Montgomerie reported, for only eight or nine years. As the pundit descended the pass leading to Thok Jalung, he saw the diggings lying ahead of him on an otherwise empty plain of reddish-brown earth and could hear the sound of cheery singing from the miners and their families. The "mine" was more of a trench, about a mile in length, twenty-five feet deep, and varying in width from ten to two hundred paces. A stream ran along the bottom of the trench, and the men sluiced earth, excavated by long-handled spades, with water from the stream, which carried the soil away leaving the heavier gold behind.

The pundit introduced himself to the chief of the goldfield, a middle-aged man from Lhasa, possibly a lama, who was wearing a red robe and a brown felt hat with a broad turned up brim. Nain Singh proffered a gift of Indian tobacco. The chief was affable, but astute. He was familiar with the order prohibiting Bashahris from entering Tibet that year, and it took all the pundit's power of persuasion, plus the sale of his coral to the chief's wife at a disadvantageous price, to get permission to stay at the camp for five days. The coral had been kept in a substantial wooden box, which also housed the large sextant in a secret compartment. The pundit admitted that he was in a "great fright" when the chief, impressed by the good workmanship of the box (needed, according to Montgomerie, "in order to make the secret compartment fit properly"), examined the box carefully, luckily without finding the sextant.[29] Nain Singh explained his possession of such a fine box by saying he had bought it at a *sahib*'s auction.

The chief, like the miners, lived in a tent made of yak hair pitched in a hole seven to eight feet below the surface of the ground. This was done to provide protection against the freezing winds that swept the plain, making conditions worse than at Nome or in the Klondike region.[30] At an elevation of over sixteen thousand feet, the pundit reported he had never been so cold before. It was probably the highest place in the world inhabited all year round. The tents, dug into the ground, plus the furs worn in winter could conceivably have provided the basis for the legend of Herodotus' "gold digging ants."

Although the pundit was able to ascertain some details of the price of the gold, he did not venture any estimates of annual production, saying only that "the yield of gold seems to be large." The Thok Jalung field, he heard, was just one of many which stretched from Lhasa into Western Tibet, running to the north of the Tsangpo watershed.

It was thirty-nine years after Nain Singh's visit before the first European saw Thok Jalung, and he apparently came away with no better information as to their production, for British authorities could still write that "the output of the Tibetan fields however, is quite unknown, a circumstance to which the many stories of their fabulous wealth are no doubt to be attributed."[31]

Retracing his steps to Giachuraf, Nain Singh was reunited with Kalian, who had been earlier sent on his separate expedition up the river on which Giachuraf stood. Although the existence of this river, which joined the Indus in Tibet about forty miles from the Ladakh border, had been locally reported and marked on maps, it had never been observed by a European or a trained explorer. The pundits had now shown that the "eastern branch of the Indus" did indeed exist, and by tracing the river to where it joined what had been thought to be the main branch of the Indus, flowing from Gartok, they were able, by comparing the respective sizes of the two branches, to show that the eastern branch was in fact the main stream of the Indus River. The tributary was then called the Gartang River.

The Gartang was wider than the Indus, but the latter had a depth of four to six feet by comparison with only one to two feet for the Gartang. Kalian had tried to follow the Indus upstream to determine its source. Tracing the Indus through a broad, flat valley, he had marched south toward Mount Kailas, although he was unable to take a bearing, as the peak itself was obscured by cloud and rain.

Kalian reached Jiachan, which he was told was only three or four marches from the source of the river. Unfortunately, here his servant was attacked by armed robbers, and although the pundit (described by Montgomerie as a "tall, powerful man") drove them off, swinging one robber round by his pigtail in the process, it was decided that the bandits might bring reinforcements, and so the two turned back toward Giachuraf. The last few miles to the actual source of the Indus were finally traversed by Sven Hedin, but not until forty years later, in 1907.

At Giachuraf, Kalian rejoined Nain and Mani, and the full party headed down the Indus to its junction with the Gartang, through a broad valley with its banks lined with low jungle. From the junction, Nain Singh sent Kalian further down the Indus, into Ladakh, so that their surveys could be connected to that of Ladakh, while he and Mani proceeded up the lesser branch to Gartok. Nain Singh did not delay in Gartok, as he discovered that a rumor was abroad that he was in the pay of the British. Hurriedly, the party left and marched to Toling, crossing back over the Sutlej by the same cantilever bridge. Here, as agreed, they waited for Kalian Singh, who had carried the survey of the Indus as far as Demchok.[32] Kalian had then turned south, crossed a high pass, and reached the Sutlej, carrying his survey of the area back up to Toling, where he rejoined the rest of the party on 29 September.

The three pundits separated again at this point, with Kalian and Mani Singh sent on a long detour, descending the Sutlej to Shipki, on the border of Bashahr, and then crossing the Himalayas to reach Nilang on the Ganges, while Nain Singh retraced his steps directly to Badrinath. The three then again joined up and returned to British territory at the beginning of November 1867.

The expedition had lasted six months, and for the final three the pundits had been continuously at elevations greater than thirteen thousand feet. Significant results were achieved, although they were not as extensive as those derived from the Singhs' previous venture into Tibet. The explorers had paced a route survey of 850 miles, taking 80 measurements for altitude and 190 latitude observations at some 75 different points. All this added up to a considerable amount of new geographical data covering an area of about eighteen thousand square miles in western Tibet.

Highlights of this new information included the tracing of the courses of the Sutlej and the Indus. The Sutlej was mapped from Toling down to Indian territory, which portion had never been surveyed before. In the case of the Indus, it was now shown that the eastern branch of the river, about which information was very hazy, was in fact the main stream, and this main stream had been traced almost to its source. The other branch was also mapped for a considerable portion of its length.

The position of the town of Gartok had now been confirmed.[33] Originally determined by Mani Singh in 1866, its position was now verified by a second set of measurements. Furthermore, by carrying the route survey down the Indus to Demchok, both Gartok and other parts of Western Tibet were now linked to the regular survey of eastern Ladakh begun by the boundary commissioners of 1846-47 and completed by Godwin-Austen and others in 1864.

Nain Singh himself had carried the route survey across the Indus to the east, reaching the goldfields of Thok Jalung, and providing the only firsthand account that the British had of Tibetan gold-mining processes as well as information from travelers about other goldfields and salt mines in the area, extending all the way to Lhasa, probably following the depression to the north of the Tsangpo. Tibetan techniques of mining appeared to be so crude that only the very richest ground could be worked, with much of the gold left unextracted. This provided one explanation for the reduced production of the Thok Jalung "mines" by the turn of the century. Other possible explanations include high Chinese taxes and "want of enterprise characteristic of all things Tibetan" stemming from a fear of disturbing the spirits of the earth.[34]

Nevertheless, the Indian government believed that Tibet was rich in gold and that the Russians had designs on it,[35] although commercial interests in Britain do not seem to have investigated the possibilities of gold mines in Tibet until the late nineteenth century.[36]

Nain Singh, the leader of the expedition, was highly praised by Montgomerie, who also noted that the third pundit, Kalian Singh, had proved "a very valuable addition." Mani Singh, however, whose nerves seemed not to have improved, was said only to have been "useful in various ways."

This was the first systematic survey of Western Tibet, and Montgomerie was determined to build upon it. While in Thok Jalung, at the furthermost extension of his travels, Nain Singh had heard of the lands to the east, sparsely populated by nomads "addicted to highway robbery." Nevertheless, Montgomerie wrote to the RGS, this was the area into which he hoped to conduct further explorations.[37]

1868: Kalian Singh

It was characteristic of Montgomery to pick up on scraps of information gleaned by his explorers and to integrate them into his "grand plan." This plan was based on a proposed series of explorations to map a continuous line beyond the frontier of British India, starting from Sind in the West, progressing through Baluchistan and Kabul to the Oxus and across the Pamir. From there the line continued to the Karakorums, through Ladakh to the Indus and then from Lake Manasarowar following the Tsangpo to Shigatse, and on to Lhasa. About five thousand miles long, this line was basically complete by 1868. The only large unmapped section lay east of Lhasa towards Assam. But Montgomerie did not stop at this point. He energetically proceeded to explore the territory behind this line.[38] One of the most difficult areas for this exploration was the vast and thinly inhabited region that lay to the east of Western Tibet, stretching from Rudok and the goldfields of Thok Jalung for over a thousand miles across the Chang Tang and the mountain ranges of the Kunlun and Nan Shan toward the end of the Great Wall of China.

The mission of Kalian Singh in 1868 was designed to be a first step in this direction (Map 4). Specifically, he was directed to explore beyond the eastern watershed of the upper Indus, starting from Rudok and going beyond Thok Jalung (visited the previous year) to investigate reports of a road running east through more goldfields to Lake Namtso (Tengri Nor). After that, Kalian Singh was to try to continue along this road to Lhasa and, if that did not prove possible, then to proceed south through Selipuk to the Tradom monastery on the Tsangpo. There he could link up with the survey made by his brother, Nain Singh, in 1865.[39]

Preparations for Kalian Singh's expedition to Tibet were made "early in 1868" and got under way in April. He adopted the disguise that had served him well the last time, that of a trader from Bashahr, and together with a party of genuine Bashahris, "whom he had induced to accompany him," he made his way from Spiti through Ladakh to Demchok, a village which he had reached from the opposite direction the previous year. Here he measured the dimensions and rate of flow of the Indus River before proceeding to Rudok, the district capital.

Montgomerie was anxious to have a precise determination of the position of Rudok, for although Henry Strachey in 1847 and Godwin-Austen in 1863 had both come within twelve miles of the town, no European in modern times (with one possible exception) had actually been there.[40] The exception was referred to in a letter, where Montgomerie wrote of "a tradition that an officer, a well-known sportsman, did get to the place some years ago, but for reasons of his own he has not thought fit to divulge his experiences in print. He appears to have approached the district on a shooting expedition and though the Tartars turned out he got the better of them and finally concluded a treaty between himself and the great Garpon which the latter ratified over prunes and brandy. The officer is said to retain the privilege of shooting over certain parts of that country, but whether by the further contributions of prunes and brandy is more than my informant could say."[41]

This anonymous sportsman had not, however, provided either the location or a description of Rudok. Montgomerie says that Kalian Singh took observations for latitude and height while he was there (although they are not given in the report) and that the town consisted of a stone fort, situated on top of a 250-foot rocky hill. This single hill rose from a flat landscape. Four monasteries housing a total of 150 monks were situated close to the fort, and some 150 houses were scattered around the base of the hill. Later travelers described this setting as "picturesque" and added that the monasteries were painted red and that the houses were whitewashed. Rudok, situated on a road connecting with both Lhasa and Leh, was over thirteen thousand feet above sea level. This road through Rudok was an alternative to the more southerly route via Gartok and Mount Kailas, following the Tsangpo. Caravans from Kashgar, after crossing the Karakorum, would pause at Rudok before continuing into Ladakh. The town was also well known for its ponies.[42]

Kalian and his party left Rudok on July 22, initially backtracking their steps before heading east. The ground was a dazzling white, like the soda plains of the Aksai Chin plateau to the north, and was capable of inflaming the eyes in the same manner as snow blindness. Kalian was now marching into the Chang Tang, a cold, windy, and barren plateau situated at over fifteen thousand feet above sea level. In his report, Montgomerie speculates that the Chang Tang extended to the east "nearly up to the end of the great wall of China near the city of Sewchoo."[43] However, although the Chang Tang is immense, covering almost half of Tibet, it does not approach "Sewchoo" (or Suchow, now called Jiayuguan) and is in fact separated from it by mountain chains and the Tsaidam basin. Because the Chang Tang rarely received more than one inch of rainfall per year, it was inhabited only by nomads who nevertheless carried on a thriving trade in wool, salt, borax, and yak tails.[44]

Robbery was another economic activity of the nomads. An encampment of 150 tents was looted while Kalian Singh was there. The Jongpen, or local administrator, stopped the robbers by getting each tent to contribute about five pounds of tea or one or two rupees as blackmail. Thinking that he could be robbed again, Kalian sent most of his goods off with one of his men, ordering him to take the road along the Tsangpo to Lhasa, where they would meet.

Kalian and his remaining goods and men then continued east, past salt and brackish lakes and abandoned goldfields, until he reached the Thok Jalung gold mine, visited by Nain Singh the year before. Traveling now at an altitude of fifteen thousand to sixteen thousand feet above sea level, they reached Kinglo, near a large lake (Nganglaring Tso). The northern route to Lhasa continued from here in an easterly direction, and it was this road that Montgomerie had told Kalian Singh to follow. The local ruler, however, would not permit this, and so the party headed in the direction of Montgomerie's secondary objective, which was to proceed from the Selipuk monastery (called Shellifuk by Montgomerie) to Lake Manasarowar. This the pundit did, although there is no evidence he actually saw the lake or the monastery at Selipuk, which remained unmapped until Sven Hedin went there forty years later. The report of Kalian does not record him as meeting any people on the way to Manasarowar, although birds and animals were present in great abundance. These included wild yaks, antelopes, goats, wild sheep, wolves, foxes, hares, marmots, geese, ducks, storks, eagles, and vultures. The pundit and his party reached Manasarowar safely, and the pundit made a traverse of the lake, taking bearings of the mountains around it, while he waited for the caravan from Ladakh which he hoped to join on its way to Lhasa. The caravan did arrive, but for some reason he was not able to accompany it; he made his way independently along the road to Lhasa, reaching Shigatse before he was stopped. This testifies to the efficiency of the Tibetan intelligence system, for the halt was ordered by mounted couriers sent by the Garpon at Gartok, over five hundred miles distant.

The man whom the pundit had earlier separated from the main mission had been more successful. He had succeeded in joining the caravan from Ladakh and reached the Tradom monastery before he, too, was halted by the couriers of the Garpon. It seemed as though the man would be returned to

Gartok for punishment, but he told the Ladakhi merchant that he was carrying goods for Nain Singh. The merchant remembered Nain Singh warmly and persuaded the guards to release the man, who was allowed to cross the Himalayas into Nepal, taking a route running south past the shrine at Muktinath.[45]

Montgomerie comments that this was very unusual, for the Tibetan authorities always returned suspect travelers by the road on which they entered the country, lest they acquire new information. He says that they may have been deceived by the looks of the man, a Ladakhi from the Zanskar region, who appeared "humble and rather stupid." Montgomerie says that in fact "in spite of his appearance, [he had] a shrewd idea of distances and points of the compass."[46]

This mission of Kalian Singh, while not as momentous as some, did pioneer new ground and add some links to Montgomerie's chain of explorations. Kalian's survey had been connected to earlier explorations of Demchok and Thok Jalung, territory to the east and southeast of which had now been partly mapped for the first time. Many details had been added about the mineral deposits in Tibet, particularly gold, salt, and borax. Kalian also took bearings along the road from Manasarowar to Shigatse, which Montgomerie said would "no doubt add considerably to our knowledge of the mountains on either side of that route."[47] The fact that the pundit's Zanskari servant was allowed to take a new route out of Tibet to Nepal and then to India provided Montgomerie not only with data on a new line of rough bearings across the Himalayas but also the ability to link this with the observations made by Mani Singh three years earlier.[48]

Montgomerie said that future explorations would attempt to cross the Aksai Chin and then explore further east "towards the end of the great wall of China." But he confessed he was not optimistic, for "the jealousy of the Chino-Tibetan officials renders success very doubtful."[49]

Montgomerie's lack of optimism did not stop him from attempting to expand the area of his operations. In 1871 another exploration commenced, designed to build on the results of Kalian Singh's mission to the goldfields of western Tibet. This was the first major operation of the explorer Kishen Singh who, under the aliases of "A.K." and "Krishna,"[50] was to build a reputation for himself to rival that of his cousin, the Pundit Nain Singh.[51] He came from the same village of Milam in Kumaon and was apparently recruited and brought to Dehra Dun in 1867. After training by Nain Singh, he made a trial exploration in 1869. Kishen Singh was probably in his late twenties when he left for Tibet in 1871.[52]

The party under his leadership left Kumaon in the summer of 1871 and headed in the direction of Lake Manasarowar (Map 4). The group consisted of Kishen Singh himself, described as a "semi-Tibetan, a young man who had been thoroughly trained for the work," and four assistants.[53] The official instructions to the expedition were to explore "some portion of the unknown regions north of the Tibetan watershed of the upper Brahmaputra."[54] Nain Singh had traveled along the Brahmaputra to Lhasa, as had Kalian Singh as far as Shigatse. But no explorer had succeeded in penetrating very far to the north of the river, where most Tibetan territory lay. Montgomerie refers to "many failures" before Kishen Singh's successful expedition of 1871-72, which would explain the lapse of three years in prosecuting the exploration of Tibet since Kalian's exploration of the Thok Jalung gold mines in 1868. Montgomerie was also perhaps preoccupied with the work of crossing the northwest frontier, carried out by the Mirza and the Havildar.[55]

Kishen Singh and his entourage had to detour off the main route almost to the Nepalese border in order to avoid mounted robbers and eventually reached Shigatse on 24 November 1871. This was to be their starting point as they headed north across the Tsangpo-Brahmaputra. Their time was occupied in Shigatse in buying fifty sheep as beasts of burden. The ground, they were told, was too stony for yaks. After crossing the Tsangpo by raft, they traveled in a northeasterly direction toward the Tengri Nor, a sacred lake. At first, the party encountered a number of monasteries, but as the altitude increased, there were only nomad encampments. While still in the inhabited part, Kishen Singh exchanged his silver Indian rupees for gold. The gold was then inserted into several hollow walking sticks which he had brought with him. The road was a well-traveled one, used by pilgrims going to Tengri Nor and by traders in borax and salt. Before passing over the mountain range to the north of the Tsangpo, they saw several geysers, some hurling near-boiling water sixty feet into the air. In the intense cold ("the mercury of his thermometer did not rise out of the bulb till after 9 or 10 in the morning") the hot water froze almost immediately on falling, producing great cones of ice.

On 13 January 1872, the party got their first glimpse of the Tengri Nor. At over fifteen thousand feet above sea level, it was frozen solid in spite of its salinity. Kishen Singh decided to make a complete circumnavigation of the lake. This took him over two weeks, and he determined that it was about fifty miles long and between sixteen and twenty-five miles across. Two rivers flowed into it, he reported, but it had no exit.

After resting for three days, the party again set off north, coming soon to the Bul (or Borax) Lake. Borax was much in demand by the Tibetans as a spice for tea and meat, or for washing clothes. They had intended to continue north, crossing Tibet and entering China, perhaps getting as far as the city of Sining at the end of the Great Wall. Alas, disaster struck when over sixty armed men robbed them, leaving them only the minimum amount of supplies plus the instruments which, the robbers said, would arouse suspicions if the authorities ever caught up with them. The gold-filled walking sticks disappeared with the bandits. There was nothing for it but to head for Lhasa and hope to reach inhabited territory before their meager supply of food ran out. After almost dying of starvation, they reached Lhasa on 9 March, after following a similar route into the city to that of the Fathers Huc and Gabet in 1846.

Even in the midst of these hardships, Kishen Singh continued faithfully to count his paces, although he admits that he became so weak that his stride grew shorter.

They had hoped to borrow money in Lhasa so as to be able to continue with their original plan to get to Sining. But this proved to be impossible, and so Kishen Singh pawned his aneroid barometer with a trader whom he accompanied to Gartok. The recipient believed it was a very large watch. From there he returned to Dehra Dun, reaching GTS Headquarters in the summer of 1872, "after a long and difficult journey."

This expedition was not as successful as it might have been. Nevertheless, all the participants returned safely and with some achievements. An initial penetration of a vast and remote area had been accomplished. A route survey of over 320 miles was made, which, together with observations for latitude and height, enabled Montgomerie to fill in some twelve thousand square miles of geography in what had been a virtually blank map. For this, he was commended by the Indian government and the secretary of state.[56] Kishen Singh had proved the existence of "a great snowy range" running north of the Tsangpo, indicating once again the immensity of the Himalayan system. A northern tributary of the upper Tsangpo had been explored, and data had been gathered on the roads, lakes, and peoples of the area. As regards the road from Lhasa to Sining, Montgomerie said that "even the slight amount of information gained respecting it is encouraging," and he vowed to make a further attempt to send an explorer along it, so as to link the trans-Himalayan explorations of the Survey of India with the surveys carried out by the French Jesuit missionaries.[57] Montgomerie noted that Kishen Singh had "shown a large amount of skill, observation and determination," and he accurately observed that "A.K." would further distinguish himself.

Nain Singh's Last Exploration

The Singh family had made very substantial contributions to the exploration of Tibet between 1865 and 1872. The journeys of Nain, Mani, and

Kalian had crisscrossed much of the southwestern corner of the country, while Nain had mapped southern Tibet along the Tsangpo and north of the river to Lhasa. Kishen had carried a route survey north of Lhasa for over a hundred miles to Tengri Nor and the Bul Lake. But most of Tibet still remained unvisited and unmapped. Between Tengri Nor and the Nganglaring Tso of Kalian Singh stretched over four hundred miles of virgin territory, quite unvisited, as were the further reaches of northern Tibet. In 1874 came the opportunity to penetrate this area, to map fresh territory, and to provide a new link between Lhasa and the surveys already conducted in southwestern Tibet.

Nain Singh, together with Kishen and Kalian Singh, had been attached to the second Forsyth Mission to Yarkand, which left India in 1873.[58] For reasons beyond his control, Nain Singh had not been able to break much new ground while attached to the Mission. But when the Mission returned to Leh in the summer of 1874, Captain Trotter, who had succeeded Montgomerie on the latter's departure from India in 1873, dispatched Nain Singh by a northerly route across Tibet to Lhasa.[59] The exploration was undertaken on the instructions of General Walker, superintendent of the GTS. It was initially intended that the Pundit should be accompanied by Kishen Singh, but Kishen was suffering from exposure, incurred on a journey from Khotan.

There is evidence that Nain Singh was worn out after nearly two decades of the rigors of traveling under difficult and dangerous circumstances. In a letter to General Walker discussing the pundit's participation in the second Forsyth Mission, Montgomerie wrote that "I do not think he was greatly taken with the idea of going North and East of Ladak, though he would not have minded anything to the South East." Montgomerie continued: "he may make one grand push if he fully understands that it is likely to be his last, and that he will get some position given him, or a pension. He does not at all fancy having much more of actual exploration."[60] According to Trotter, "on the return of the mission to Ladakh, being anxious to have an opportunity of gathering fresh laurels, he [Nain Singh] volunteered to proceed on a fresh exploration."[61] This was to be his last "grand push," and he may have volunteered with the promise of a pension or other inducement, particularly since the journey involved the relatively level plains of Tibet rather than the rugged passes over the Karakorum and the Kunlun.

The objectives of this last journey were to survey a route from Leh to Lhasa by a much more northerly path than the one he had taken in 1865. From Lhasa he was to try to join the caravan to Peking, which the Survey of India had heard left from Lhasa every three years. Should this not prove possible, his instructions were to return to India by an unexplored route, either down the course of the Tsangpo Brahmaputra,[62] or through the Himalayan kingdom of Bhutan.[63]

This was the pundit's third clandestine penetration of Tibet. Officials on the frontier would have been on the lookout for him. He had also been in Leh on numerous prior occasions and was known to be in the service of the Indian government. Accordingly, more elaborate precautions than usual were needed in order to ensure his safe passage in disguise across the border. The frontier crossing was the key to everything. Once into Tibet, Nain Singh would be relatively safe, since he would be passing through thinly populated areas.

The deception involved a rather complex scheme in which William Johnson (famous for his visit to Khotan in 1864), now wazir of Ladakh in the service of the maharaja of Kashmir, was to conspire with the headman of the village of Tankse, near the Tibetan border. The headman was to collect a number of sheep for the Pundit, giving the impression to the Ladakhis that the sheep were to be used as baggage animals to carry the Pundit's merchandise on the road to Yarkand. This was quite plausible. The sheep were indeed to be used as baggage animals, and Tankse was on the Changchenmo route to Chinese Turkestan. The Pundit, however, was not going to Chinese Turkestan, but to Tibet.

Another problem which Trotter had to address was the question of how to provide security for the funds the Pundit would need to reach Lhasa and then continue to Peking and home to India. For the first stage of the journey, as far as Lhasa, the pundit carried sufficient cash with him. But to carry more, even in the form of merchandise, through areas infested by robbers was to Trotter's mind to risk the life of his explorer. As it happened, the triennial Lopchak mission from Ladakh to Lhasa was about to leave Leh. Nain Singh had traveled with this caravan before, and Johnson got the Lopchak to agree to take money to Lhasa for Nain Singh, who would collect it personally when he arrived. Since the caravan was a large one and traveled along a well-known road, it was felt that this arrangement would provide ample security.

For the final section of his journey, from Peking back to Calcutta by sea, Trotter provided the Pundit with a letter of introduction to the British Minister in Peking. The minister was to arrange transportation for the Pundit once the letter was presented.

Nain Singh's party included four attendants. One of these was his servant Chumbel, two were Tibetans who had also accompanied him in the past, and the fourth was a local man, loaned by the headman of Tankse. They set out from Leh on 15 July 1874, Nain Singh leaving behind the impression that he was returning to Yarkand.[64]

Nine days later they reached the last village before the Tibetan border, and under cover of darkness the pundit and his companions dressed in the priests' robes which had been tailored secretly for them in Leh. At first they did follow the Changchenmo road north, but after two days turned east. Slow progress was made, the pace determined by the speed of the sheep. Crossing the "frontier" was something of an anticlimax, just one hut with a small guard, which they passed without incident. The party was now in Tibet, on the north bank of Lake Pangong, and proceeding in a generally southeast direction, parallel to the Tsangpo but at distances varying from one hundred to two hundred miles north of the course of the river. The villager from Tankse had gone ahead of them and by using his good offices had obtained from the local officials the permission needed to proceed into the heart of Tibet. The pundit continued past Lake Pangong and was able to fix the location of its eastern extremity. Godwin-Austen and others had mapped the western parts of this elongated lake, but the easternmost point, well into Tibet, had now been located for the first time.[65]

Nain Singh's route now took him on to the great lacustrine plain of central Tibet. Most of the lakes were salt, but some were fresh water and the travelers were able to fill their waterskins, made of sheep stomachs. For the first ten days the road was not far to the north of the route taken by Kalian Singh while on his way from Rudok to the gold mines of Thok Jalung.

For security, Nain Singh had secreted his Indian rupees in a number of hiding places, the main one being in a worn pad on the back of an old donkey. This animal was dubbed the "Government Treasurer." Occasionally, they would deliberately camp well off the road, to avoid robbers whose favorite trick was to cut the tent ropes at night and plunder the camp while the sleepers were trying to extricate themselves.

The altitude was, on average, a little over fourteen thousand feet. A few shepherds were seen, but the paucity of human population was more than made up for by an abundance of animal life.

About one-third of the way between Lake Pangong and Tengri Nor, Nain Singh entered an area inhabited by Khampas, who said that they had migrated there from Kham (north and east of Lhasa) twenty-five years earlier. Accomplished horsemen and sportsmen, they tended herds of horses, sheep, and goats. They also had a bad reputation for plundering caravans. However, because one of his servants had befriended one of the Khampas in Ladakh some years before, the pundit was able to join a small group of them going in the same direction, and which afforded some protection for a while. Then, taking a devious route to minimize the risk of being robbed, they arrived in the gold-mining area of central Tibet.[66]

The pundit's account of the mines of the Thok Daurakpa area led Trotter to downgrade the importance which had been attached to the Tibetan goldfields as a result of his earlier report of 1867.[67] The mining area through which Nain Singh was now passing did produce gold of a higher quality than that found in Thok Jalung to the west. But the gold of Thok Daurakpa was embedded in rock, rather than soil, and the water for washing the pulverized rock had to be carted in skins on the backs of donkeys from a stream over a mile away. The amount of gold produced was so small that the local shepherds were wealthier than the gold diggers. Furthermore, said the Pundit, he believed that only two other mines in northern Tibet were being worked, and both were even smaller than Thok Daurakpa.

Pausing for just one day at the gold mines, Nain Singh and his companions, now halfway to Tengri Nor, continued across the Chang Tang. Their altitude was now sixteen thousand feet, but the sun was warm, grass grew underfoot, and herds of antelope grazed nearby. On his route from Lake Pangong, the pundit had been marching parallel to a snowy range lying just to the south, a chain of mountains now known as the Nain Singh Range.[68] The extension of this range continued up to a point south of Tengri Nor.

Nain Singh struck the northwest corner of Tengri Nor (the easternmost point of which is about eighty miles due north of Lhasa), after a journey of sixty-four marches from Noh, near Lake Pangong. He had mapped a chain of lakes across central Tibet, none of which had been seen before. Only Tengri Nor itself had been visited before by a trans-Himalayan explorer, in 1872, when Kishen Singh made a complete tour around it.

Nain Singh followed the path of Kishen Singh along the northern shore of Tengri Nor for fifty miles and then, like his predecessor, turned to the south in the direction of Lhasa. After some ten to twenty miles, he struck off by a different and less direct route to the Tibetan capital.

The pundit and his party entered Lhasa on 18 November 1874. They had started from Leh on 15 July, averaging less than ten miles per day over the 1,095 miles from Leh to Lhasa. But the sheep purchased in Ladakh, although slow movers, had more than proved their worth. Of the twenty-six that started out on the journey, four or five covered the entire distance. Others were eaten or had been taken sick. All carried twenty to twenty-five pounds of baggage on their backs and foraged for whatever food they could get.

Nain Singh was anticipating small luxuries such as fresh vegetables, beer, and a more comfortable accommodation in Lhasa. Unfortunately, this was not to be. Just before reaching the city, he heard a rumor that the Chinese were aware that a British agent was approaching Lhasa from India. The pundit sent one of his servants ahead of him to see if the Lopchak mission had arrived with the remainder of his funds. The response was negative; in fact, the head of the mission had died on the way to Lhasa. Now Nain Singh's penury was to force the curtailment of his expedition.

But there was a more present danger. On reaching Lhasa, Nain Singh had the bad luck to bump into a merchant from Leh who knew his identity and true occupation. The pundit feared betrayal and made plans to leave Lhasa immediately, rather than wait in the hope that the Lopchak mission might appear. Had he been able to delay his departure, he might have been able to retrieve his funds from the mission, even in the absence of the Lopchak himself.

Instead, the pundit sent two of his men back to Leh. They carried details of all his astronomical observations and route survey, and they reached Trotter safely in January 1875. Trotter now feared for the safety of his agent, who had in fact left Lhasa abruptly with his two remaining servants only two days after arriving. The psychological strain of possible discovery (followed by the inevitable imprisonment and probable death) must have told on the pundit, particularly as he had had to start off again from Lhasa with no chance to recuperate from a four-month march across the Chang Tang.

To return to India via Peking was clearly out of the question. The remaining funds were pitifully small. The best route to take home was the shortest and quickest, not northeast through China, but south into India.

In order not to arouse suspicion, and to throw pursuers off the track should he be betrayed, Nain Singh left his bulky inessentials behind with his landlord, saying that he would collect them in a month's time after returning from a pilgrimage to a monastery north of Lhasa. The small party duly left Lhasa for the north, but as soon as darkness fell made a 180-degree turn toward India. This fall-back strategy was in accordance with his original instructions received from Walker and Trotter.

A week after leaving Lhasa, the pundit came to the Samye gompa, an ancient and famous monastery just two miles from the northern bank of the Tsangpo. He admired its high circular walls, which he estimated to be one and a half miles in circumference, and counted 1,030 *chortens* (funeral monuments) on top of it.

Nain Singh followed the course of the Tsangpo downstream for two days and then crossed it by boat. The river was sluggish, and the pundit was able to estimate its rate of flow as two-thirds of a mile per hour by throwing in a piece of wood and timing it over a fixed distance. Measuring the poles used to punt the ferry across the river gave it a depth of between eighteen and twenty feet. The river was about five hundred yards wide.

The point where the river was crossed was near the town of Chetang, and here Nain Singh left the Tsangpo. The information he was able to give about the river was valuable. He had followed it for thirty miles along a part of its course that had hitherto been unexplored. Chetang was fifty miles beyond the lowest point at which the river had been mapped to date, and from the town the pundit was able to approximate its course for a further one hundred miles by taking bearings of distant peaks, the Tsangpo being reputed to pass to one side of them.

Following the road south away from the Tsangpo, and up the valley of the Yarlung, one of its tributaries, Nain Singh crossed the main Himalayan chain by the Karkang pass, at a height of over sixteen thousand feet. He was traveling toward Tawang, accompanied by a man of some importance in that district. Tawang was a small area to the east of Bhutan and north of the Assamese plains, loosely owing an allegiance to Lhasa, and situated on a traditional trade route between India and Tibet. The merchants of Tawang were suffering at the hands of those in Lhasa and so were preventing any merchants from Tibet from proceeding onward to the Indian border, in order to retain the bulk of the trade for themselves. Because of this, the pundit, who had arrived in Tawang on 24 December, was detained there until 17 February, and not even his influential friend could prize him free before that time. Eventually, by depositing almost all of his remaining goods and by claiming that he would return for them after a pilgrimage just across the border, the pundit reached Udalguri in British territory on 1 March 1875. There he presented himself to the local assistant commander, who telegraphed Trotter to announce the safe arrival of his explorer. The assistant commander also made the travel arrangements for the pundit to proceed to Gauhati, where he once again met up with the Tsangpo, now known as the Brahmaputra, and took a steamer to Calcutta.

The expedition had achieved important results, even though the pundit had been unable to reach his far-flung goal of Peking.

Nain Singh had traveled 1,405 miles between Leh and Udalguri. His survey had started at Noh, a village whose position had also been fixed by the pundit Kishen Singh on his return from Khotan. It terminated at Udalguri, the position of which was known very accurately from measurements made by the Indian Revenue Survey Department. Between these two points stretched 1,319 miles of virtually unknown country, of which 1,200 miles was completely unexplored. Prior to Nain Singh, only the small section around Tengri Nor had been surveyed, by Kishen Singh in 1872.

The pundit had located the eastern extremity of Lake Pangong, provided additional details of the Tibetan goldfields, mapped a large number of new lakes and rivers, and confirmed the existence of a chain of snow peaks to the north of the Tsangpo. More information on the course of this river through Tibet had been discovered. The route through Tawang to British India had been charted for the first time.

Nain Singh also took a large number of sextant observations, as well as pacing his route, taking compass bearings and measuring for altitude by observing the boiling point of water. All had to be made in conditions of complete secrecy. Based on the pundit's earlier observations at Lhasa, Montgomerie had concluded that Lhasa lay at longitude 90° 59' 30". All the measurements, said Trotter, showed the pundit to be "a skillfull and accurate observer."[69]

No Europeans were successful in reaching Tengri Nor until Bonvalot and Prince Henri of Orleans in 1890. A British expedition to the west of Tengri Nor almost half a century after Nain Singh (in 1922) commented that most of the information they had on the area was still derived from his expedition and that of Kishen Singh. They also verified the accuracy of the two pundits' observations.[70]

This was Nain Singh's final foray beyond the frontiers. The stress of this journey and prolonged exposure to the elements had taken their toll on his health, and his eyesight in particular had been affected by continuous observations taken at very high altitudes. But although he retired from exploration, he continued to serve the Indian government with the training of younger explorers.

Within a year of his retirement, Walker was able to write that "he is an admirable trainer and has managed to collect several young men around him and taught them all that is necessary for work of this nature, so that they are now ready for further explorations."[71] The work of teaching new recruits the fine art of secret exploration continued at least up until 1879, when "S.C.D." (Sarat Chandra Das) was given a course in surveying and observing by Nain Singh.[72]

The pundit's name was now made public and was announced in the *Geographical Magazine* in 1876.[73] Members of the GTS, including Walker and Montgomerie, urged that Nain Singh, in addition to his pension, should receive further monetary compensation from the government, as well as recognition from the Royal Geographical Society.

Montgomerie wrote to the India Office in March of 1877 from his home in Bath, pressing for a grant of land to be made to Nain Singh.[74] Unknown to Montgomerie, this had already been done. On the recommendation of Walker, the Indian government had proposed to London on 15 December

1876 that the pundit be given the grant of a village in Rohilkand together with a *jumma* (or revenue assessment from land) of Rs. 1,000. These proposals were enthusiastically endorsed by the secretary of state for India in Council, who spoke of the "high value" of the pundit's achievements. The secretary of state also expressed "warm approval of the energy and discretion shown by Colonel Walker and Colonel Montgomerie in the gradual elaboration of a system which has produced, at a minimum of cost, results of real importance, which are seldom attained elsewhere without some considerable sacrifice of resources, if not of life."[75]

The Paris Geographical Society had given Montgomerie a gold watch for him to send on to Nain Singh. Montgomerie did so, noting in a letter to Walker that "it is not a very handsome watch but the Society is not rich and they meant to pay N.S. a high compliment."[76] The award of this watch came in the same year as the award of a gold medal from the Royal Geographical Society. It was the latter award, however, which occasioned considerable dissension in the highest councils of the "Geographical."

The question at issue was who was the most meritorious—Nain Singh for his feats of exploration, or Trotter for planning the expedition and interpreting and writing up the results? Clearly each accomplishment depended upon the other, but who should achieve recognition first?

On the one side was the former president of the RGS, Sir Henry Rawlinson, who proposed that Trotter should have the Patron's Medal for 1876 because of his "having conducted the Survey operations of the late Mission to eastern Turkistan under Sir Douglas Forsyth."[77] This view was opposed by Colonel Henry Yule, whose views as a scholar carried much greater weight than those of Rawlinson. Yule wrote to Sir Rutherford Alcock at the Society, calling Nain Singh "the Pundit of Pundits," and comparing him with such giants of exploration as Livingstone and Grant. It was his "strong opinion," said Yule, "that his [Nain Singh's] great merits cannot be fully recognised by anything short of one of the Society's gold medals." Yule continued that "*either* of his great journeys in Tibet would have brought this reward to any European explorer; to have made *two* such journeys adding so enormously to accurate knowledge . . . is what no European but the first rank of travelers like Livingstone or Grant have done."[78] Yule had been in touch with Walker, who was on leave in England at the time. Walker agreed with Yule and wrote that "I shall be very glad if you can get him the gold medal of the R.G.S., or any other suitable mark of distinction, in acknowledgement of his excellent services to geographical science."[79] The letter, which did not mention Trotter, was sent along to the RGS by Yule.

Not all the scholars of the Society supported Yule. Clements Markham wrote to Colonel Walker, his cousin, apparently unaware of his relative's endorsement of Yule's position. "We are doing everything we can to get Trotter the medal this year," he said, "but unfortunately Yule has proposed the Pundit Nain Singh, and is very hot upon it. Obviously this would be unjust to Trotter, and I trust Sir Henry Rawlinson will carry the majority of the Council with him."[80] But this was not to be. In an embarrassing reverse for the president, who had already informally promised the medal to Trotter, the Council voted in favor of Nain Singh. Markham expressed his annoyance in a further letter to Walker, commenting that "Colonel Yule made a long semi-political speech magnifying the Pundit at the meeting of the Council and ignoring the fact that the utilization of his work is entirely due to the [Survey] Department."[81] When the time came for the medal to be presented by the Society, it was the president who had to address Yule, standing in for Nain Singh in the latter's absence. But Rawlinson concealed his defeat well and praised the pundit highly. He was, he said, "a man of loyalty, courage and endurance who had accomplished his explorations with frequent risk to his life."[82]

Nain Singh himself was not personally involved in the altercation. The only wish that he had expressed was to have another gold watch from the RGS to replace the one they had awarded him in 1868, which had been stolen from him. He had only had it for six months and entrusted it to a Pathan, whom he was training, to take to his home. The Pathan stole the watch, and despite all efforts, it was never recovered.[83] It was a prized possession, and its loss was a great blow to the pundit. He wrote to Colonel Smyth, who had recruited him for the Survey of India, requesting that the RGS send him a replacement, and he would bear the cost. He wanted the same inscription on it as the original and wrote in Hindi characters the English words "De President and Council of de Raeel Jographical Society of London to Pundit Nain Singh for his great Jographical exploration. 25th May, 1868." But Smyth (or the Society) never complied with his request.[84]

The medal from the RGS and the watch from the Paris Geographical Society were sent out to Nain Singh in India. There they were officially presented to him by the viceroy, Lord Lytton, at a quiet ceremony in the drawing room of Government House, Calcutta, on the afternoon of 1 January 1878.[85] On the same day, the Pundit was gazetted a Companion of the Order of the Indian Empire.[86]

Nain Singh handed a letter to the viceroy at the ceremony, asking for financial aid to send his two sons to be educated in England, "which is as cold a place as their native country." The viceroy said he "could not hold out any promises to him."[87] There is no record of any money for education being granted. Smyth speaks of two boys, whom he describes as the pundit's cousins, who were educated at a mission school in Almorah, became Christians, and then went on to study medicine in Agra.[88]

After spending several years training a new generation of explorers, Nain Singh went back home. The summer months he spent in his native village of Milam, where his cousin Mani was still Patwarie, and in the winter he migrated to the warmer weather in the plains.

He died at the village in the plains where the government had granted him land. One writer, who checked with a descendant of the pundit, says he died in 1895, of a heart attack. This writer also says that an earlier report by Colonel Smyth stating that the pundit had died in early 1882 is false.[89] But, this report does exist (the obituary is in *The Times*), and Smyth's account adds detail to it, saying that the death occurred in Moradabad and was due to cholera contracted at the January fair at Allahabad.[90] Smyth, therefore, must have checked the account in the paper with another knowledgeable contemporary, and I am inclined to think the date of 1882 is more likely to be correct.[91] The pundit was in his early to mid-fifties when he died.[92]

The last words on Nain Singh are best left to Colonel Yule, addressing the RGS at the time of its presentation of the Society's gold medal. Nain Singh, he said, "is not a topographical automaton, or merely one of a great multitude of native employe's with an average qualification. His observations have added a larger amount of important knowledge to the map of Asia then those of any other living man."[93]

Kishen Singh

The only rival that Nain Singh had for his feats of exploration was his cousin, Kishen Singh, alias the pundit "A.K."

The third and last exploration of A.K. was his crowning achievement, as well as the longest, both in distance and time elapsed, of any of the trained explorers of the Survey of India (Map 5). It began when he left Darjeeling on 24 April 1878 and ended with his return there on 12 November 1882, over four and one-half years and 2,800 miles later. His epic journey led him north from Lhasa across Tibet into China almost as far as Outer Mongolia, from where he returned by a different route to southeastern Tibet, and then continued west along the border between Tibet and Assam, in northeastern India.[94]

The arrangements for A.K's journey were initiated by Colonel (later

MAP 5
KISHEN SINGH
1878-82

General) Walker. Montgomerie had left India for medical reasons in 1873. For some years he hoped to return to the GTS, but his health failed to improve, and he retired with the rank of colonel in 1876. He died at his home in Bath, of arteritis and bronchitis, on 31 January 1878. Montgomerie's place in India had been taken by Henry Trotter, who, after mounting important explorations by the pundits as part of the second Forsyth Expedition to Yarkand, left the Survey for a career in diplomacy. It was left to Walker, therefore, at the close of his own career, to organize and direct A.K.'s final journey. Walker returned from leave in 1877 and became surveyor-general of India in January 1878. By the time A.K. saw him again, in Calcutta in December 1882, Walker was on the verge of retirement, and he left India two months later, in February 1883.

Although Montgomerie was dead, Walker was still following his grand plan of exploration far beyond the frontiers of India. A.K. had penetrated some distance into northern Tibet on his first exploration of 1871-72. Additional information had been derived from the travels of Nain Singh, made in 1874-75 after the close of the second Forsyth Mission. The prime objective of A.K. was to make a further reconnaissance, to traverse Tibet from south to north, cross the Kunlun mountains, and so explore the area beyond. Specifically, he was instructed to take any practicable route across Tibet and to return by a parallel but different route. He was to avoid China proper as far as possible because Walker thought that if A.K. came upon one of the major trade roads leading into China, he might be tempted to follow it and return to India by sea from the China coast. Since most of China was already well mapped, this would not be as useful as going through unknown territory. Of this part of the Chinese empire, where Chinese Turkestan met the Gobi desert, very little was known beyond the accounts of Marco Polo, and others such as Benedict Goes in the early seventeenth century. The two French priests Huc and Gabet had crossed into northeast Tibet and reached Lhasa, but they were not trained surveyors or geographers, and their observations left a great deal to be desired. Nikolai Prejevalsky, the Russian explorer, and the Hungarian Count Szechenyi were soon to explore this region, but neither had done so at the time A.K.'s travels were planned. A.K. subsequently crossed the routes of both their expeditions.

The exploring party consisted of A.K. himself and two others, one of whom A.K. described as "my faithful companion Chumbel." One account describes Chumbel as being a "fellow villager" of A.K., but another has him coming from the village of Zaskar in Ladakh.[95] Both accounts agree that he was a loyal and reliable friend, unlike the third member of the group, a servant named Gangaram, who deserted A.K. at a critical point in the expedition. Chumbel was older than A.K. and had also accompanied Nain and Kalian Singh.

The equipment that the group took with them included a nine-inch sextant, a Tibetan tea-bowl to be used as a container for the mercury which would provide an artificial horizon; two compasses, one prismatic for taking bearings of distant peaks, and the other a pocket version for use in taking route bearings; and an aneroid barometer and some boiling-point thermometers, both to be used for calculating altitudes. Also included were a rosary to keep track of the paces marched and a prayer wheel, in the barrel of which the day's notes could be stored.

A.K. was to travel in the disguise of a merchant and was given ample funds for this purpose. The route that he eventually covered has been described in the official report as being like a triangle. The western side of the triangle went from Lhasa northeast to Lake Tosun Nor in Tsinghai. This was the apex of the triangle, but with a significant extension northward to Saitu (Tunhuang). The eastern side ran southeast from Chakangnamaga to Tachienlu (Kangting, now part of Szechuan) with the third side leading from Tachienlu back almost to Lhasa, actually closing at Chetang on the Tsangpo, about forty-seven miles southeast of Lhasa. The accuracy of A.K.'s observations could be judged, as the positions of the opening and closing points of his survey, Lhasa and Chetang, had both been established by the earlier explorations of Nain Singh.

A.K. was delayed for three months because Gangaram fell ill on the way, so that they took over four months to reach Lhasa. The route was through Phari and Gyantse, the same route as that followed by Bogle and Turner in the eighteenth century, and also by Thomas Manning, the first Englishman to reach Lhasa, in 1811. First passing over the Himalayas, A.K. then crossed the Tsangpo by a bridge "formed of two iron chains, one on each side: from the chains thick ropes are suspended to the depth of four yards: by these ropes planks, three feet long and one foot broad, are supported lengthwise so as only to admit of one person crossing at a time."[96] A.K. must have had a better head for heights than Nain Singh, who had come to the same bridge twelve years earlier and had preferred to take a boat across the river, saying that the bridge looked very insecure.

Arriving in Lhasa on 5 September, they spent over a year in the Tibetan capital. A.K. wanted to join a caravan heading for Mongolia, but there were few available at the time. A year in Lhasa was longer than anticipated, but A.K. put the extra time to good use, bringing back with him the best account of the city, its people, and their customs since the visit there of Nain Singh in 1866.

The Tibetans, A.K. reported, were a happy, carefree people, living peacefully in crowded two- or three-story dwellings, side by side with traders from China, Nepal, India, and Mongolia. The climate was very healthy, and no contagious disease had ever been known except for an outbreak of smallpox about forty years earlier. A.K.'s report said that the people were "uncommonly social and jovial," drank a fermented liquid "but are never, or very rarely indeed, drunk," and enjoyed social gatherings at which flutes and guitars would play. Both men and women would dance. In the summer, picnics could last all day. Despite these diversions, the city apparently flourished by its trade, although A.K. notes that while brick tea from China was a major import, little seemed to be manufactured for export except a few skins and a fragrant slow-burning match. Religion dominated the life of the Tibetan capital. The Potala, "built on a low isolated hill," formed a cluster of buildings, about four hundred yards long and two hundred yards wide, and shone over the city, topped by golden cupolas "which sparkling in the sunlight present a dazzling and gorgeous spectacle visible for miles around." Crowds every morning made a religious circumambulation of the city, the devout repeating the process in the evening. Smaller circuits might also be made of particular shrines. This, said A.K., "is imperative on common folk," although the wealthy could hire substitutes to walk for them.

The explorer's account of Lhasa also described the interior of the Potala, the religious observances (particularly the New Year festivals) and beliefs, details of the Tibetan government and the Chinese presence, marriage customs, language, dietary habits, and agriculture. In addition, A.K. produced a plan of Lhasa and its environs. During his stay he also acquired a sufficient knowledge of Mongolian to be able to converse with the leaders of the caravan he eventually joined, which left Lhasa on 17 September 1878 heading in the direction of the Kunlun mountains.

A.K.'s party now consisted of six men: himself, his companion Chumbel, his servant Gangaram, and three other servants. The caravan totaled 105 people in all, sixty of whom were Mongols and the rest Tibetans. The Mongols invariably rode while the Tibetans, for preference, walked leading their baggage animals. Instead of taking the more usual route northeast toward Sining, the caravan headed due north from Lhasa, along a less well traveled track. This was done to reduce the likelihood of being attacked by the robbers who plagued the trading routes, once the inhabited area around Lhasa was left behind. A.K., having been set upon during his previous expedition in 1872, was well aware of the danger. As an additional protection, the men were armed with matchlock rifles and swords. The march began each day at sunrise, and camp was made between

2 and 4 P.M. The caravan proceeded in close order by day, and guards were posted at night. If anyone was taken ill on the march and became unable to travel, they were left by the wayside with a supply of food and water. Such unfortunates were rarely heard of again.

The route from Lhasa led up and down steep hills and through narrow rock defiles, past villages and monasteries. About sixty miles from Lhasa they crossed the Lani La pass at 15,750 feet, passed through the Nyen Chen Tanglha Range, and emerged onto the Chang Tang, that great elevated plain of central and Western Tibet which is at an average altitude higher than the maximum elevation of any mountain in Colorado. Other Indian explorers had penetrated the Chang Tang to the south and west, but once A.K. was beyond Lake Tengri Nor (the caravan passed within two days' march of the site of his encounter with bandits in 1872), he was in uncharted territory.

Cultivation ceased abruptly on entering the Chang Tang. A few flowers and hardy grass and scrub were all that could grow in the thin air above fifteen thousand feet, given the intense cold, lack of rainfall, and the salt that permeated the soil. Populated villages gave way to the occasional black yak hair tents of the Tibetan nomads. Vast herds of the beasts could be seen, and their argols, or yak dung, provided the only fuel for cooking and making tea. Soon, even the nomad encampments disappeared as the caravan took off on a little-used track in order to avoid the bandits. A.K.'s ponies became affected by the cold, and one died. Snow fell, and the animals had difficulty foraging for grass. A pony and a mule got stuck in a bog and had to be abandoned. Slowed down, A.K.'s party was separated from the main caravan. Crossing a river, Chumbel lost a toe, possibly because of frostbite, perhaps severed by a sharp rock. He was able to continue, but progress was distressingly slow. Two more animals died for lack of food. The small and exhausted group reached the foothills of the Kunlun range on 25 October.

The Kunlun mountains mark the northern edge of the Chang Tang. After crossing the range, grass for the horses became more abundant, and nomads sold them fresh horses to replace those lost. Heading now in an easterly direction, parallel to the mountains, they eventually rejoined the caravan. The Mongolian members of the caravan now departed for their homes in the area, leaving just the Tibetans, and all congratulated themselves on having successfully crossed the Chang Tang without being robbed.

At this point disaster struck. Firing rifles, then attacking with swords and spears, two hundred mounted bandits charged into the camp. Attempts to drive them off failed, and the robbers departed with all A.K.'s baggage animals and most of his possessions, leaving him with only his survey instruments and a few small items such as glass beads, which were of little value. Attempts at pursuit secured only a number of lame or unfit ponies. With all their goods stolen, the Tibetan traders opted to return to Lhasa, but A.K. determined to press on, even though under the circumstances no one at Survey headquarters would have criticized him for heading home. He was forced to dismiss three of his servants. With just two loads of petty merchandise, A.K., Chumbel, and Gangaram were on their own. It was a year and seven months since they had left Darjeeling.

They were now in the Tsinghai province of China, on the edge of the Tsaidam. In many ways the Tsaidam and the adjacent Koko Nor region, both to the north of the Kunlun range, are extensions of the Chang Tang. However, by comparison the Tsaidam (or "salt marsh") is a vast oval depression of maximum dimensions about two hundred by five hundred miles, lying at an altitude of 8,500 feet, between the mountains of the Kunlun and the Altyn Tagh. What little vegetation grew there did so only because underground water was forced to the surface at certain points.

Leaving the site of the robbery on 13 December, A.K. and his two companions hired three bullocks to carry their remaining goods and crossed the marshy southeast corner of the depression, entering the basin of the Koko Nor, or "blue lake," from which the province of Tsinghai (or "blue sea") derived its name. A week later they came to Tosun Nor, next to Kurlyk Nor, which exhibited a feature characteristic of the area, one being a freshwater lake, the other salt. Here they met a Tibetan lama who had formerly lived in Gyantse, and, desperately short of funds, they agreed to look after his camels for the winter. But with the onset of spring, they left the service of the lama and marched in a northwesterly direction, first following the edge of the Tsaidam, and then crossing its northeastern extremity. Here the sandy soil was arid and barren, strewn with pebbles and coated with salt.

The party reached the village of Yembi, lying south of the Altyn Tagh mountains, in early April 1880. They stayed there for three months, hoping to be able to join a caravan going to Lop Nor. In the meantime, A.K. sold their remaining merchandise and purchased seven horses with some of the proceeds. Unfortunately, one of the party was not happy with the idea of pushing further. Gangaram had heard tales of the Moslems to the north of the mountains and was unwilling to venture among them. He had hinted to A.K., without success, that it would be best to turn back. More openly, he had suggested to Chumbel that the two of them leave A.K. and return home. Chumbel refused to listen, and so in July, when the others were temporarily absent, Gangaram deserted, taking with him all the horses, most of the money, and A.K.'s telescope. A.K. and Chumbel now had only Rs. 50 left. Virtually destitute, they once again hired themselves out as servants, tending horses and goats. After several months' employment their employer generously gave them a horse, provisions, and warm clothing. A.K. was determined to push on, even if he had to beg his way, and so they left Yembi in January 1881, still heading north.

Joining a caravan of merchants, they crossed a ridge of mountains joining the Altyn Tagh and the Nan Shan and reached the city of Tunhuang in the extreme northwest of the province of Kansu. It was 6 January 1881. Tunhuang (or Saitu) (the "City of Sands") is probably the Shachan or Sachiu of Marco Polo. The town is an oasis, situated on the trading routes connecting Lhasa with Mongolia and China with Turkestan. It was here that the Jesuit traveler Benedict Goes had succumbed to disease, or poison, in 1607. Both Count Szechenyi and then Prejevalsky had visited Tunhuang in 1879.

This was to be the northernmost point reached by the expedition. Along the whole route, A.K. had taken compass observations, along with boiling-point observations to ascertain the altitude, and had counted off his measured paces. He also had notes of a wide variety of geographic and other data. He described Tunhuang as a walled city, with four large gates, standing next to a river on a fertile plain. There was a Chinese garrison, and the population was largely Chinese, living in some two thousand single-story clay houses. A.K. said that the climate was similar to that of Yarkand. A wide variety of fruit and vegetables grew locally, cotton was cultivated, and a silk-weaving factory had recently been built. Girls, he noted, had their feet bound with strips of cloth.

After a few days he and Chumbel tried to leave Tunhuang by joining a group of traders going to Lop Nor. But a short distance outside the city they were overtaken by a horseman, dispatched by the governor, who ordered them to return. On arrival, they appeared before the governor, who said that he suspected them to be either spies or thieves. Either way, they were to remain in Tunhuang until they could provide surety for good behavior. Months passed and, unable to pay for the feed of the horses, A.K. sold them and tried to make a living as a fruit seller. He described the local people as "inhospitable and ungenerous." Meanwhile, the governor closely monitored their activities. A.K. became ill, contracting a fever which made it difficult to walk. All in all, it was the low point of the expedition. Luckily, after several months A.K's health improved, and an influential lama, whom he had known in the past, arrived in Tunhuang. The lama was from Thubden Gompa, a monastery about six hundred miles to the south, and he had come to visit the "caves of the thousand Buddhas" nearby, subsequently explored by Aurel Stein in 1907. The lama persuaded the governor to allow A.K. and Chumbel to accompany him on his return, and they were able to leave with him, in the capacity of servants, during August 1881. Tunhuang was the last point on the spur to the northwest of the apex of their triangular route. Together with the lama they now retraced their route southeast to the apex at Lake Tosun Nor, which they reached on 17 September.

For part of the way the lama forced A.K. to ride on horseback, for fear of not being able to speed away if robbers should attack. This naturally meant that he was unable to count his paces. Ever resourceful, he estimated the length of a horse's stride and counted the number of times the right foreleg hit the ground. The official report of the expedition concluded that the "results do credit alike to the explorer's ingenuity and to the horse's equability of pace."

From Lake Tosun Nor, their original route bore southwest to Lhasa. With insufficient funds to return to Tibet this way, A.K. and Chumbel continued in the lama's service, heading almost due south. This was fresh ground. A.K. became a bullock driver and was able to proceed on foot, although on some portions of the route the lama again obliged him to ride.

After recrossing the Tsaidam, they learned that their former servant Gangaram had settled in the area and was living with a group of Tibetan nomads. Apparently harboring no animosity for past misdeeds, A.K. sent a man to Gangaram, suggesting that he rejoin them, but the offer was refused.

The party now climbed over the Kunlun by the Namohon Pass, about 180 miles to the east of their earlier crossing. Once again A.K. was on the Chang Tang. Still traveling due south, they forded the Ma Chu, one of the main sources of the Huang Ho (Yellow River) and arrived at the small monastery of Thubden Gompa on 21 October. There they had to wait two months for the lama to pay them, and A.K. was able to take latitude and altitude observations for the first time in over a year.

The two set off on 16 December 1881, A.K. carrying with him a letter from the lama to an influential friend in Jyekundo (the modern Yushu), which was reached the following day. Jyekundo was a large trading village of two hundred houses and forty Tibetan and Chinese shops, strategically situated at the intersection of five routes from Sining, from Lhasa, and from Chamdo to the south. The letter from the lama provided them with an introduction to a trader about to leave for Tachienlu (the Tibetan Darchendo and the modern Kangting). They joined the trader's caravan as servants and left on the four-hundred-mile journey to southeastern Tibet.

The road (for Tibet) was a good one. Although rocky and mountainous, the inclines were not too steep, and grass and water were plentiful. There was even wood for fuel. Best of all, the area was free of bandits.

They passed many yak caravans carrying deer horns, woven fabrics, animal skins, musk, and other Tibetan products to be exchanged for Chinese tea. Monasteries passed on the road included such well-known places as Kantze and Dege Gonchen, known throughout Tibet for its printing press.

Eventually, the caravan crossed the Gi La, a high pass over a snowy range at fifteen thousand feet, and on 5 February 1882 entered Tachienlu, a small city lying in a valley surrounded by snow-capped hills. It was on the border between territory that was racially and linguistically Tibetan, and China proper. In the nineteenth century it was on the political boundary as well, but is now administered as part of Szechuan province. Composed of two-story stone and timber houses, the town was a center of the tea trade coming from China. The tea, shaped into five-pound bricks, was brought in on the backs of coolies, who had carried it for twenty days. In Tachienlu it was transshipped to animals and taken by yak into Tibet and as far afield as Kashmir. Two routes ran from Tachienlu to Lhasa, one northerly via Jyekundo, and a more widely used southern route through Batang. On the latter route, a yak caravan took about three and a half months for the approximately nine-hundred-mile journey.

General Walker had given A.K. a general letter of introduction to the French missionaries in Tachienlu, where the Vicar Apostolic for Tibet resided. A.K. learned that the Jesuit mission was located just outside the city wall and made his way there, intending to seek advice on the best way to return to India and to ask for a loan. He presented his letter of introduction to Bishop Biet, who advised him to proceed westward, through Batang to Darjeeling, rather than east to the China coast and then by ship to India.[97] A.K. had hoped that he would be able to broach the question of a substantial loan from the Bishop but did not do so, "as in the course of the conversation he did not raise the question of my means I did not think it advisable to trouble him."

The Jesuit father did, however, give A.K. a small gift of six rupees. He also wrote to another member of the mission, Abbé Desgodins, who was on a visit to India, asking him to tell General Walker that A.K. was safe, in good health, and on his way back to India. This was good news for Walker, who had not heard from his explorer in four years, particularly as rumors had just reached Nain Singh to the effect that A.K. and Chumbel had been arrested in Lhasa, after which Chumbel had been executed and A.K.'s legs had been amputated to prevent his carrying out any further explorations.

Captain Thomas George Montgomerie. *Courtesy Royal Geographical Society*

Nain Singh. *Courtesy Royal Geographical Society*

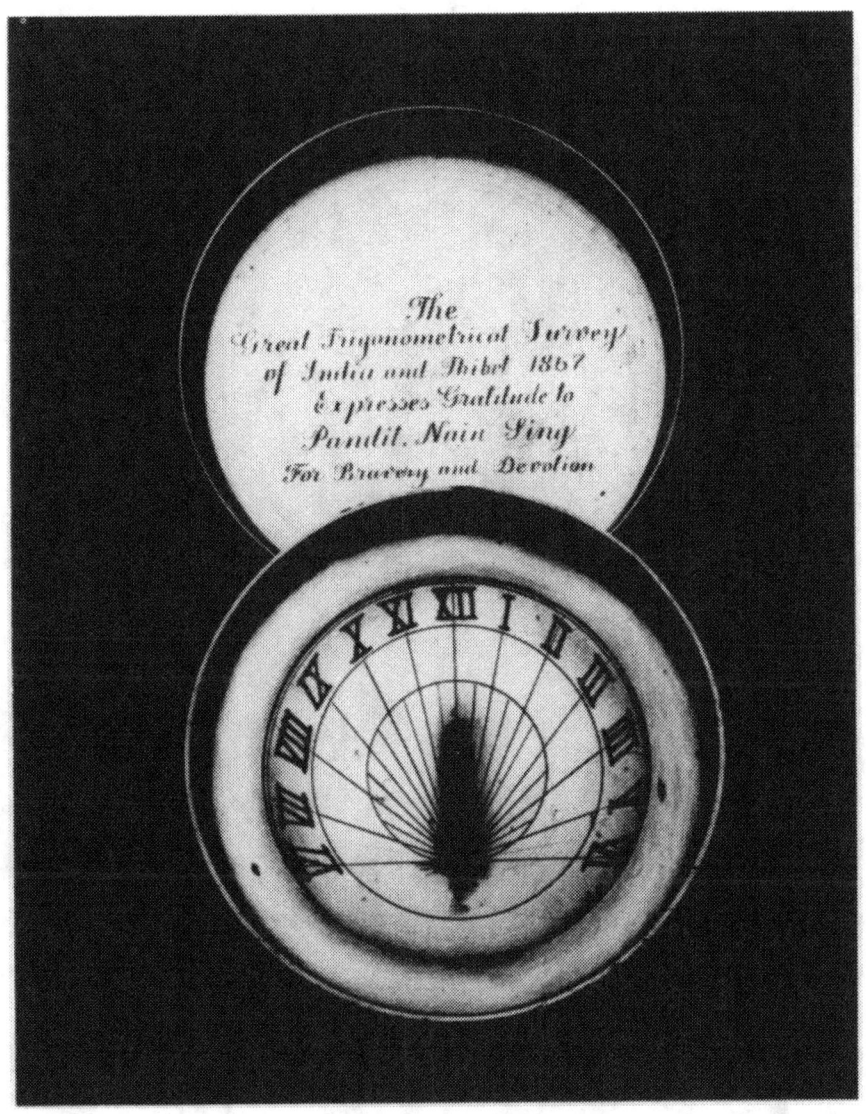

Surveying instrument purportedly presented to Nain Singh by the Great Trigonometrical Survey. *Photo by Tim O'Leary*

Sarat Chandra Das. *Courtesy Royal Geographical Society*

Drawing of a Tibetan prayer wheel, by Sarat Chandra Das. The drum of a prayer wheel, which normally contained prayers, was sometimes used by the pundits to conceal records of their explorations. *Courtesy Royal Geographical Society*

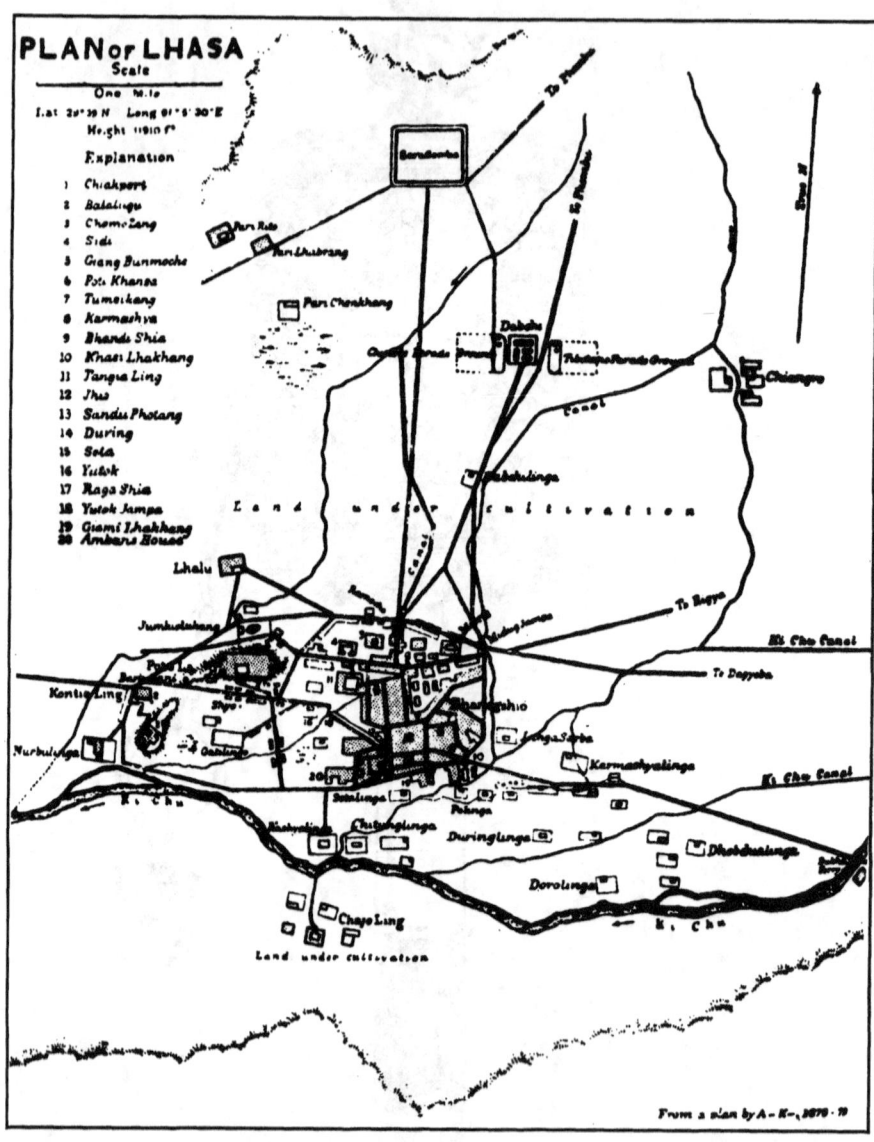

This plan of Lhasa is from the report of Kishen Singh ("A.K."), who spent over a year there in 1878-1879. Reprinted from *Journey to Lhasa and Central Tibet,* by Sarat Chandra Das.

Above, medal awarded to Ugyen Gyatso for his services to the Sikkim Expedition of 1888. Below, gold watch presented to Rinzing Namgyal, the only pundit ever to visit England, on the occasion of his visit to Queen Victoria.

Lt. Gen. James T. Walker. *Courtesy Royal Geographical Society*

The two stayed in Tachienlu for eleven days and left on 16 February 1882, initially retracing their steps to the Gi La pass and then turning westward along the road to Batang. In this part of southeastern Tibet, the rivers had carved out steep valleys for themselves, running from northwest to southeast. Up these valleys blew the warm, humid air from the Indian Ocean, producing more forest and lush vegetation than was generally the case in Tibet.

Travelers like A.K. and Chumbel, going from east to west, were forced to traverse these V-shaped canyons, crossing a river, then climbing to perhaps fifteen thousand feet before beginning the precipitous descent into the next valley. Crossing the Yalung River, one of the sources of the Yangtse, the two reached Litang, at 13,300 feet one of the highest towns in the world. Lhasa itself is situated at 12,000 feet. Batang was reached on 13 March. It was here that the expedition of Captain William Gill was halted in 1877, Gill then traveling down the "River of Golden Sand," before striking out to Bhamo in northern Burma. Count Szechenyi suffered a similar fate in Batang during his attempt to reach Lhasa in 1879-80, and followed Gill's route from Batang. A.K. noted that Batang had a monastery with about a thousand monks. The town was situated on the left bank of the Yangtse, which A.K. and his companion crossed by ferry. Shortly thereafter they had to cross both the Mekong and the Salween since these two rivers, with the Yangtse, run parallel to each other in a zone only fifty miles wide.

It was a most fearful contraption that provided the only way of crossing the Mekong. A leather rope spanned the river, about 130 paces wide at that point, running from the high to the low bank. Travelers tied a rope to themselves and then attached this rope to a bent piece of wood. The wood, in turn, was placed over the leather rope, and one then slid down to the opposite bank. A similar arrangement was in effect elsewhere.

The method for crossing the Salween, some two hundred paces wide, was only a slight improvement. Passengers sat on planks of wood, propelled by oars, while boatmen held on to a rope stretched across the river, thus preventing the plank from being swept downstream by the force of the current. After these experiences, it must have been a relief to cross the Irrawaddy and Zayul rivers by means of wooden bridges.[98]

Before reaching the Mekong, however, they turned off the "main road" to Lhasa and headed southwest in the direction of India, hoping to cross into British territory via Assam. This shortcut home to India was possibly suggested by Bishop Biet in Tachienlu, but given the unfortunate experiences of some earlier French missionaries who had tried this route, it was most likely A.K.'s own idea.

The Zayul River, which they had just crossed, flowed into Assam, where it was known as the Lohit Brahmaputra. At the village of Rima on the Zayul (which at only 4,600 feet above sea level was the lowest point reached on the journey), A.K. came into contact with traders from the Mishmi people of Assam. The Mishmis, untouched by any civilizing influences, controlled the trade in this area between Tibet and Assam by refusing passage to anyone through their territory. Some of the goods traded by the Mishmis included children, kidnapped in Assam and sold in Tibet as slaves. Nevertheless, A.K. continued south toward Assam, but only after being quarantined for twenty-two days because of his arrival from a district infected by smallpox.

On 23 May 1882, the two reached Sama, at which point only thirty miles separated them from British soil. Here they tried in vain to arrange for passage through Mishmi territory. They were told that any attempt on their part to try to reach India via Assam would simply result in their murder. The Tibetans themselves never took this route. Two French missionaries, fathers Krick and Boury, had tried to enter Tibet through Mishmi territory in 1854. Both had been killed near Sama. (A British punitive force, sent a year later, arrested and hanged the Mishmi chief responsible, after killing three of his sons.) The same route was followed by the English traveler T.T. Cooper in 1869. Although he survived to recount his experiences, he did not get as far as the French missionaries before being compelled to retrace his steps to India.

Reluctantly, A.K. and Chumbel were forced into the realization that their planned shortcut to India was too dangerous and that they would have to proceed north again, and then head west in the direction of Lhasa, leaving Tibet by the route they had entered. But no immediate progress could be made. Spring was slow in coming to the mountains, and the passes to the north were still blocked by snow. Nor did they have enough money for the long journey home. Waiting for the passes to clear, A.K. went from house to house reciting Tibetan sacred books and succeeded in earning Rs. 20.

They resumed their march on 9 July, soon crossing the Ata Gang pass over the southern Himalayan range. Then they ran into difficulties. Because of its low altitude, the area they had just left around Rima was one of the warmest in Tibet and was regarded by the Tibetans as a very unpleasant place. Consequently, criminals were transported there for life from Lhasa, many branded on the foreheads. Leaving this penal district, A.K. and Chumbel presented such a shabby and distressed appearance that they were arrested on suspicion of being escaped convicts. It was only the arrival of an influential traveler from Rima a few days later, who was able to speak for them, that permitted their release.

On 6 September they connected again with the direct road from Tachienlu to Lhasa, from which they had earlier departed in the direction of Assam, and crossed the Gia pass, which marked the boundary between the Tibetan administrative areas of U-Tsang and Kham, at the end of the month. The two then diverted off the Lhasa road to one used by pilgrims circumnavigating the mountains to the south of the city. On 8 October, they reached Chetang on the Tsangpo-Brahmaputra river, a large town of about a thousand houses, a monastery, and a fort. Chetang's position had been fixed earlier by Nain Singh. A.K. was told that there had been an iron bridge across the river, three miles from town, but that it had been destroyed by lightning.

A.K. finally closed the triangle of his great exploration on 17 October when he reached the place he had passed through on his way to Lhasa four years before. Here he ceased his route survey. After a slow march through heavy snow via Gyantse and Phari, the two arrived back in Darjeeling on 12 November 1882. According to General Walker, "they arrived in a condition bordering on destitution, their funds exhausted, their clothes in rags, and their bodies emaciated with the hardships and deprivations they had undergone."[99]

The entire journey lasted slightly over four and a half years. According to General Walker, the distance covered amounted to some 2,800 miles, excluding the mileage to the point in Tibet where the route survey began and terminated. When this figure is added to the 1,950 miles already surveyed on earlier expeditions, the total distance marched by A.K. exceeded that of any other native explorer. It was never surpassed.

Some of A.K.'s route was traversed either by Prejevalsky during 1879 to 1880, or by Gill in 1877. A.K.'s route also coincided in part with that of Evariste Huc, but Huc made no scientific measurements on his travels. However, about 1,700 miles of A.K.'s expedition was over entirely new ground, of which the only previously available maps had been those derived from the Jesuit surveys of the early eighteenth century. A.K. showed that their measurements were correct in large part.

A.K.'s stay in Lhasa produced a sketch map, which was the only plan of the city available to the Younghusband Expedition of 1903-1904. Surveyors with the Expedition praised A.K.'s work as "very accurate and reliable."[100] Perceval Landon, who accompanied the expedition as a correspondent for the *Times,* was full of praise for the work of the Indian explorers, although critical of their rather meager descriptions of the scenery in southern Tibet. "The native of India," commented Landon, "has no eye for the beauties of nature, and would as soon make a day's journey across a desert, as a park."[101] To A.K., of course, the scenery would have been nothing unusual. Growing up in the Himalayas, he and the other explorers must have become blasé at their grandeur.

A.K. took observations for latitude at twenty-two points. He also made determinations for altitude at seventy places, using the boiling-point thermometer. At Tachienlu, because A.K. was uncertain of the value of the single measurement for latitude he took there, the Survey of India used instead the figure given in du Halde's atlas, made in 1714. Nevertheless, according to the official report, A.K.'s figures produced "results highly creditable to the explorers' accuracy and skill." In the northern part of his travels, where his route had intersected that of Prejevalsky, A.K.'s observations for latitude agreed very much with those made by the Russian. The measurements for longitude were less close, but the means available to A.K., the different starting points of each expedition, and the vast distances involved must also be taken into consideration. In the southeast, A.K.'s figures agreed closely, in terms of both latitude and longitude, with those of Gill. The first European to follow A.K.'s route north from Rima in the Zayul district, the botanist-explorer Frank Kingdon-Ward, wrote of the excellence of A.K.'s report and route surveys. It was, he said, "hard to find a mistake."[102] According to Kenneth Mason, A.K.'s observations in the Batang area agreed within one mile over a distance of 120 miles with those made later, and with better instruments, by Colonel Ryder, who subsequently became surveyor-general of India. Indeed, Mason is of the opinion that, in his accuracy with a sextant, A.K. surpassed even his mentor Nain Singh.[103]

The only European who had probably taken A.K.'s route north from Lhasa to Tunhuang (and returned by the same road) was the Dutch adventurer Samuel van der Putte, who passed through Lhasa in 1729 and again in 1730. Alas, all his notes were destroyed, at his own request, leaving only a sketch map of his travels.

Shortly after A.K. left Darjeeling for Tibet in 1878, two other expeditions had set out, independently of the Survey of India. From the north, in 1879-80, the Russian Nikolai Prejevalsky, now on his third expedition to Tibet, passed through Tunhuang and crossed the Tsaidam and the Kunlun mountains. He aimed to reach Lhasa, but while traveling on the same road along which A.K. had marched in the opposite direction, he was stopped and forced to turn back, only 170 miles north of the city. Another expedition, under the Hungarian Count Bela Szechenyi, reached Tunhuang from western China in 1879. Unable to penetrate Tibet from the north, he went on to Tachienlu and then headed west, along the route taken by A.K. But like

Gill in 1877, Szechenyi was stopped at Batang. A.K. was able to go where Russians, Hungarians, and Englishmen could not.

Because of his inability to penetrate into Assam, A.K. had been forced to travel north from Rima. Major geographical advantages were to be derived from this circuitous route. Indeed, according to the official report, A.K. "solved one of the most interesting geographical problems of modern times." The problem was whether the Tsangpo river of Tibet emerged to the south as the Brahmaputra or the Irrawaddy. Most geographers, since the days of Rennell, believed that the Tsangpo and Brahmaputra were one and the same. But it was difficult to prove this, and while A.K. did not definitively solve the problem, he did provide strong evidence in favor of the majority view. On his route north from Rima, A.K. had on his left a great range of hills which was the watershed between the Tsangpo and the rivers, such as the Irrawaddy, to the east. Since A.K. observed no river cutting through this watershed, it meant that the Tsangpo, coming from the west, could not cross over to flow into the Irrawaddy in the east. A later Indian explorer, Kintup, proved the identity of the Tsangpo and the Brahmaputra of India, although his account was not given much credence at the time. In 1885-86, J.F. Needham, Assistant Political Officer at Sadiya, in the company of Captain Molesworth of the frontier police, advanced up the Lohit Brahmaputra almost as far as Rima, near where A.K. had been halted in 1882. Their travels confirmed the findings of A.K. that the Tsangpo and the Irrawaddy could not be the same. They were the first Europeans to enter Tibet by this route and survive to tell the tale, Fathers Krick and Boury having perished in the attempt. The British had been trying to follow the Lohit into Tibet since 1826, when the first expedition, under Captain Wilcox, was halted by the Mishmis. The official account of the Needham and Molesworth expedition states that their geographical information on the Lohit Brahmaputra was in complete agreement with the report of A.K.[104]

The English diplomat-explorer F.M. Bailey tried to follow the path of the Tsangpo from Tibet into Assam some forty years later, in 1912. Entering Tibet from China, he was halted at Shugden Gompa, where A.K. had been arrested in 1882. He was the first European to see the monastery. Although unable to continue his journey to the Tsangpo, Bailey was able to reach Rima, and then continue down the Lohit to Sadiya, bribing the Mishmis with opium. The following year, accompanied by Captain Moreshead, Bailey was successful in following much of the Brahmaputra up through Assam.

A.K. returned to India with all his notebooks and virtually all his instruments intact—no mean feat after being robbed once by bandits and once by his own companion, not to mention being detained under suspicion on a number of occasions. His notebooks were tiny, and he hid them on his person and concealed others in the barrel of his Buddhist prayer wheel.

He was asked on his return what debts he had incurred, so they could be settled by the Survey of India. It was quite normal for an explorer, once his goods had all been traded, to borrow in order to finance the continuation of his expedition. But despite the hardships he had suffered and the length of his absence from Survey headquarters, A.K. responded that he had no debts to repay. Looking at A.K.'s achievements as a whole, Walker was right to describe him as "accurate, truthful, brave and highly efficient."[105]

General Walker read his paper on the exploits of A.K. to a meeting of the Royal Geographical Society, held in London on 8 December 1884. In the discussion that followed the talk, the Chairman, Sir Henry Rawlinson, said that Walker's use of native agents had filled in many blanks on the map, "but his crowning success had been this marvelous journey of the Pundit A.K."[106]

As for A.K. himself, he returned to find his only son dead and his home broken up. His health was weakened by the deprivation he had suffered, and it was feared at first that he would not survive.[107]

The American diplomat and traveler William Woodville Rockhill was critical of the British treatment of their retired Indian explorers. If, Rockhill wrote, any British explorer had achieved just one-third of the accomplishments of his Indian counterpart, "medals and decorations, lucrative offices and professional promotion, freedom of cities, and every form of lionizing would have been his; as for those native explorers a small pecuniary reward and obscurity are all to which they can look forward."[108] Rockhill's strictures are exaggerated: A.K. had not opted for a career with a regular ladder of promotion, and the "freedom of a city" would not have meant a great deal. But medals and pecuniary rewards certainly did come to him.

At the Geographical Exhibition and Congress, held in Venice in 1881, the Geographical Society of Italy had placed two medals, one (first class) in gold and the other (second class) in silver, in the hands of General Walker "for award to the two native explorers whom he considers the most meritorious."[109] The gold medal was subsequently presented to A.K.[110] Nor was this A.K.'s only medal. In 1886 Ferdinand de Lesseps, the president of the Geographical Society of Paris, awarded a gold medal to A.K. "for his exploration in Eastern Tibet." The medal was received on behalf of A.K. by the British ambassador.[111] Nevertheless, it is true that, although members of the Royal Geographical Society in London were vociferous in their praise of A.K., they did not see fit to reward him with a medal, although they did so acknowledge the accomplishments of Nain Singh.

A.K. ceased his explorations in 1882, but he was kept on the books as a member of "the permanent native establishment of Trans Himalayan Explorers" until 1885, at a salary of Rs. 100 per month. In that year his salary ceased, and he retired on the income from the village of Itarhi in the Sitapur district, with the title of Rai Bahadur.[112]

The mountaineer Tom Longstaff, on an expedition to Tibet, met him twenty years later in the village of Mansiari in Kumaon, where the Bhotias of Milam (his home village) generally spent the winter. A.K., said Longstaff, "did all he could to help us with our plans."[113] At about the same time, he was placed in charge of a surveyors' cairn, built near the Milam glacier.[114] The last recorded encounter with A.K. came from the Assistant Commissioner of Kumaon, who reported that "he was very spry in retirement in his 70's, and I used to go and see him when I was on tour. He had a number of large deodar wood chests in the fine stone tea-plantation house, 50 miles over a bridle road from anywhere, that he had bought from an European. The chests were full of maps, blue books and gold medals from many of the world's geographical societies. He was most unassuming for all that, but we had great fun. He kept handy a large map of Central Asia. I used to pinpoint X or Y or Z and ask if he had ever been there. 'Oh, yes, [he would respond] I was there in 1876."[115]

FIVE
The Forsyth Missions to Yarkand and Kashgar

The Muslim insurrections in the provinces of Kansu and Shensi from 1862 onwards led to the loss of control on the part of the Chinese authorities over Chinese Turkestan.[1] Under its new ruler, Yakub Beg, fresh opportunities were presented to the Indian government. One of these was the lure of increased trade.

The possibility of increased commerce with Yarkand and Kashgar had long been viewed favorably by the government of the Punjab. The belief that there were substantial profits to be made did not die an easy death, despite the unsettled nature of the area, the immense difficulties of geography, the high tariffs charged on goods passing through Kashmir, and the small size of the population of Chinese Turkestan. Some trade had always found its way over the Karakorums between India and Kashgaria, with opium, spices, and cotton piece goods and manufactured articles being exported from India, in return for Chinese tea, silk, and carpets.

To begin with, Yakub Beg showed himself to be hostile to the Russians and reduced the quantity of their goods coming into Kashgar, thus nullifying the natural geographic advantage that Russia possessed in its trade with Chinese Turkestan. Secondly, the visits to Kashgar in 1869 of the Mirza, George Hayward, and Robert Shaw had provided more knowledge of the area, and the report of Shaw in particular was glowing in its belief in commercial promise. With the hostility between China and Yakub Beg, now seemed an opportune time to replace Chinese tea with tea from India.

In 1869, the viceroy, Lord Lawrence, left India and was replaced by Lord Mayo. Mayo saw that trade might be used by the government to help create in Chinese Turkestan a buffer zone, friendly to British interests, which would hamper any Russian expansion there. The Karakorums and the Himalayas presented almost insuperable obstacles to any projected invasion of India from Chinese Turkestan. The Indian government, however, feared that Kashgaria, if annexed by Russia, could be used for diversionary raids, pending an invasion over the easier passes of the Pamir. A friendly buffer state seemed, therefore, to have definite advantages. Perhaps Yakub Beg could even be persuaded to join in an Islamic front against Russia.

The possibility of increasing trade and establishing diplomatic ties with India was also of interest to Yakub Beg. He sent an envoy to India in 1870, who was received by both the lieutenant-governor of the Punjab and the viceroy. The envoy requested that a British officer return with him to meet Yakub Beg (now styled the "Atalik Ghazi").

T. Douglas Forsyth was a clear choice to lead the small expedition. He was commissioner of the Punjab government and had long been an ardent supporter of increased trade with Central Asia. In 1867 he had paid a visit to Leh in an attempt to get a reduction in the high tariffs imposed by the Kashmiris on goods in transit, tariffs which were hindering trade between India and Chinese Turkestan. On his return, he had set up an annual fair at Palampur (near Dharmsala) to attract merchants from Yarkand.[2] Forsyth's visit was to be strictly unofficial and for commercial purposes only. Robert Shaw, back home in England but eager to make a second visit to Yarkand, quickly volunteered his services, which were accepted. But Lord Mayo hedged the mission in with restrictions. It was told, for example, not to proceed into the interior of Chinese Turkestan unless peace prevailed throughout the area.[3]

As it happened, Forsyth never met the Atalik. By the time the mission reached Yarkand, the Atalik was off campaigning near Turfan, some six hundred miles away. Forsyth was thus obliged to retrace his steps quickly in order to recross the passes to India before they were closed by the winter snows.

Through an unfortunate mishap, even the opportunities to gather geographical information were largely lost. An application was made (probably by Forsyth) for one of Montgomerie's pundits to join the expedition.[4] After the exploits of Abdul Hamid and the Mirza, Montgomerie had no great need to dispatch more explorers to Yarkand and Kashgar, but naturally seized the chance of extending his surveys northeast from Kashgar toward the Gobi desert.[5] Accordingly, he detached Nain Singh, his most experienced explorer, from his duties and sent him to Ladakh to join the mission. Unfortunately, as soon as Nain Singh arrived in Leh, it became generally known that he was a trained surveyor and explorer, traveling incognito.[6] This aroused the suspicions of Yakub Beg's envoy Mirza Shadee, by "indicating a pursuit of knowledge other than commercial."[7] As Forsyth subsequently wrote, "the appearance openly of Pundit ——— in own [sic] camp, ostensibly to survey the whole of Yarkund, could convey but one meaning, of hostile designs, to Mirza Shadee's mind. Dr. Henderson's photographic apparatus, and his penetrating search after information, were all attributed to the same motive, and all this tended to render the Mirza keenly suspicious of our intentions."[8] To allay the suspicions of Mirza

Shadee, Nain Singh was sent back from Leh to Dehra Dun, and no Indian explorer of the GTS accompanied the mission.[9]

It had been suggested by GTS headquarters that one of their British officers might join the expedition to take astronomical observations, but since the man who volunteered was a military officer, his services were declined on the grounds that "his presence might impart a warlike character to a purely commercial and pacific enterprise."[10]

Despite these setbacks, some data were acquired. Robert Shaw, who joined the mission in Ladakh after a hurried journey from London, took several observations.[11] Dr. Henderson took the first photographs of Lake Pangong.[12] Two political agents of the Indian government also accompanied the expedition. One was Faiz Baksh, who had performed several missions for the government in the past (under the pseudonym of Ghulam Rabbani) and who made a journey from Peshawar through the Pamir to meet Forsyth in Yarkand.[13] He was not, however, a trained explorer or surveyor,[14] nor was the other political agent, Ibrahim Khan, who was sent on a circuitous route from Kashmir to Yarkand, via Gilgit and Yasin, and of which he produced a very rough report.[15]

Mayo did not contemplate a second mission, following the failure of the first. But upon his death in 1872, he was succeeded as viceroy by Lord Northbrook, a more political animal than his predecessor, who viewed with suspicion Russian moves toward Chinese Turkestan.

On their part, the Russians were alarmed at the possibility of a Moslem united front against them, headed by Yakub Beg. They were also irked by the Forsyth mission to Yarkand and believed that Britain might support the designs that Yakub Beg had on the Ili valley. The Russians, therefore, moved to extend their control over the strategic area of Ili, through which much trade between Russia and China passed, by occupying it in 1871. Faced with what looked like the preliminary move toward an attack on Kashgar, Yakub Beg agreed to receive a Russian commercial mission. A treaty was signed the following year.

The Russians now looked favorably upon the ruler in Kashgar. Although the Ili valley was Chinese territory, it had been occupied by Tungan rebels in 1864. In occupying it themselves, the Russians told Peking that they would return it as soon as China was in a position to reclaim it. Yakub Beg stood in the way of any such claim being made in the near future.[16]

Lord Northbrook was anxious to stem the flow of Russian influence in Chinese Turkestan. A good opportunity soon arrived. Relations between St. Petersburg and Yakub Beg had soured, in part because of the recognition of Yakub Beg by Russia's enemy, the sultan of Turkey, who had also bestowed on Yakub Beg the title of emir. In 1873, the emir's envoy, Syud Yakub Khan, was returning to Kashgar from negotiations in Constantinople. One result of these negotiations was the acquisition of a supply of arms for the emir from Turkey. All this was viewed with grave disfavor by the Russians, who may have been dissuaded from attacking Kashgar only because they were occupied with the assault on Khiva.

Northbrook quickly organized a new mission to Kashgar. Forsyth was again placed in charge, this time as the official envoy of a much larger enterprise, which included six European military officers and scientists, 350 men, and 550 baggage animals. The mission was charged with signing a commercial agreement with the emir. But the political task of upgrading British influence was of greater importance. The mission was also ordered to acquire scientific, strategic, and geographical data. Geographical data concerning the boundaries between Kashgaria and Afghanistan on the Pamir were particularly desired.

Accompanying Forsyth on his second mission were Lieutenant-Colonel T.E. Gordon as second-in-command; Captain Biddulph (aide-de-camp to the Viceroy); Dr. Bellew, as medical officer and historian; Captain Chapman, secretary to the mission and in charge of stores; Dr. Stoliczka, geologist; and Captain Henry Trotter (Royal Engineers) of the Great Trigonometrical Survey.[17]

The Pundits and the Forsyth Mission

Montgomerie had gone to England on leave, in poor health, in 1873, and friends there reported that his condition seemed little improved. One wrote to General Walker, saying that he had seen Montgomerie at the Royal Engineers' dinner and that he was "looking very ill, and I was sorry to see so little outward evidence of improvement in his health."[18]

After Montgomerie's departure for England, Captain Henry Trotter of the GTS was placed in charge of the trans-Himalayan explorers of the Survey of India, a position he retained until his own transfer to the Diplomatic Service in 1875. By the time of the second Forsyth mission, Walker must have realized that Montgomerie was not likely to return to India. He therefore appointed Trotter as geographer, and in charge of the pundits attached to the expedition.

Trotter was commissioned into the Bengal Engineers (later merged with other units to form the Royal Engineers) and at the age of twenty-one went out to India where he joined the Trigonometrical Survey. At the time of the second Forsyth mission, he was thirty- two years old. Trotter seems to have been a rather reserved character, with few close friends. Nevertheless, he was generally popular, always courteous, and had a good sense of humor. He once said that he had initially identified the names of many villages in Kashgaria as "Bilmen," which was what he was told by the inhabitants. "Bilmen," he admitted, turned out to mean "I don't know."[19] He was also a keen sportsman and hunter.

On hearing from Forsyth that there was to be a second mission to Kashgar, Walker urged that a Survey pundit be sent along, so as to exploit opportunities to explore new regions. Forsyth agreed and supported proposals to this effect made by Walker to the government, which accepted them.[20] It was fortuitous that instead of being at Survey headquarters in Dehra Dun, Walker was in Calcutta and met Forsyth at the time the expedition was being planned. Without this accidental circumstance, no member of the Survey of India might have joined the mission. Montgomerie believed this to be the case and wrote to Walker from England that "it was very lucky that you were in Calcutta, otherwise I am sure the Mission would have gone without a single competent surveyor or astronomer. Trotter will, I think, do what you want very well."[21] Certainly, there is no evidence that it was the government which pressed for a geographer or any pundits to be attached to the expedition.

Trotter himself was on survey duties in the Kathiawar area, some two hundred miles northwest of Bombay, when he received a telegram from Calcutta in which Walker asked him if he would like to join the Forsyth mission as geographer. Trotter leapt at the chance. Only then did he reach for an atlas in order to, as he put it, "make search as to what part of the Asiatic continent Yarkand was to be found in."[22]

Trotter left at once for Dehra Dun and spent the time before the departure of the mission practicing his skill in taking astronomical observations, preparing forms for the construction of maps on the journey, and gathering lightweight equipment. This equipment included maps on which were drawn details of the northern frontier of India to the south and of Russian observations to the north. Trotter hoped to explore the area in between and perhaps link the two surveys. Captains Chapman and Biddulph, two other members of the expedition, were also at Dehra Dun with Trotter and were given short courses in survey techniques, so that they could work independently if they were on a party detached from the main expedition.

The precise number of pundits deployed on the mission is not entirely clear. In an early letter, written to the RGS by Forsyth while on his way to Simla in April 1873, he refers to Walker as supplying him with "one of his best assistants" (i.e., Trotter) and "one of the well-known pundits."[23] The official report refers in one place to two pundits, with their assistants,[24] at another point to "two of the old Pundits with two assistants,"[25] leaping to "seven of the Survey Pundits" at yet a third place.[26] Kenneth Mason, in his review of the records, concluded that Trotter had with him three pundits, plus two assistants and "a sub-surveyor Abdul Subhan."[27]

From the records of the endeavors performed by the pundits on the expedition, it is clear that there were three members of the Singh family present: Nain (the "Chief Pundit," or simply "the Pundit"), Kishen (alias "A.K." or "Krishna"), and Kalian ("G.K.").[28] They were accompanied by one, or possibly two, subordinates. Part of the confusion over the number of pundits was likely due to the inclusion on the mission of Abdul Subhan, Faiz Baksh, and Ibrahim Khan. Faiz Baksh was present as a secretary. Ibrahim Khan was an inspector from the Punjab police. Both had been part of the first Forsyth mission, but neither was a pundit. Abdul Subhan was a native surveyor, attached to the Gwalior party of the Topographical Survey, and his services had been supplied to Trotter by the surveyor-general, Colonel Thuillier. It was intended that he should act as Trotter's assistant, but during the mission, Trotter, "thinking that he would be better employed as an explorer in these unknown regions . . . obtained permission from Sir Douglas Forsyth to start him off on independent exploration from any point on our road where a favourable opportunity should occur."[29] Such an opportunity did occur, and Abdul Subhan performed important work and, in effect, acted as a pundit. He was code-named "the Munshi"; his explorations are described below.

Trotter, like Montgomerie, was anxious to expand the survey as far as possible beyond the borders of India. The vision was breathtaking. Pundits of Moslem extraction would be utilized to the west and southwest of Kashgar.[30] To the west they were to investigate the Terek passes between the Trans-Alai and Tian Shan mountains, passes which led from the territory of the emir of Kashgar to the Russian khanate of Kokand.[31] In the southwest, much of the Pamir and the route of the Oxus were still uncharted. Here also, information was needed about the terrain and the passes through which a Russian advance might be made. The GTS hoped to provide a preliminary link between the surveys of India and those of Russia. But the real prize lay to the east of Kashgar, for from that city the dominion of the emir stretched for about seven hundred miles through places not visited by Europeans in recent history. If only they could reach Aksu, said Montgomerie, it would be a great haul.[32] Aksu, an oasis on the southern edge of the Tian Shan about 250 miles northeast of Kashgar, was an important town on the trade route between Russia and China. The last European to visit there had been Benedict Goes in 1604.

But neither Forsyth nor Trotter was prepared to stop there. Forsyth had heard that a regular caravan route ran from Karashahr (a town toward the eastern end of the Tian Shan, another 350 miles east of Aksu) to Lhasa, following a river that flowed south across the Gobi desert (i.e., the Takla Makan) to Khotan. The emir had reported that the land between Karashahr and Khotan was not a desert but a wilderness of trees, grass, and wild animals. "I am very anxious to have this explored by some competent man," wrote Forsyth on his way to start the mission; "probably we shall depute the Pundit for this purpose."[33] In fact, the rivers that carried the melted snow off the Tian Shan past Karashahr ran only intermittently, partly into the Takla Makan, partly into Lop Nor.

Most ambitious of all was the plan to send the pundits to Lop Nor and back to India via Lhasa.[34] Trotter even said that the rubber boat he had used to take soundings of Lake Pangong had been carried "in the hope of ultimately floating it on Lake Lop."[35] Given that "Lake Lop," or Lop Nor, a migratory salt lake, was the better part of a thousand miles from Yarkand, it is not surprising that this wish remained unfulfilled. Nevertheless, the pundits and the other members of the expedition reaped a substantial harvest of geographical and scientific information, which was to far exceed the mission's political and commercial achievements (Map 6).

A substantial selection of instruments was accumulated by Trotter for use on the expedition. All were as small and light as possible. They included theodolites and sextants, compasses, two telescopes (one of which was presented to the governor of Yarkand on the return journey), and two pocket chronometers. Although the watches were useful in Turkestan, they proved to be very inaccurate in the Himalayas because of the erratic changes in temperature, and Trotter preferred to rely on the pacing of the pundits, combined with sextant observations for latitude, instead of observations for longitude dependent on the chronometers. Other instruments included a plane-table (useful for drawing a map on exploratory surveys where theodolites could not be used), thermometers, barometers, and hypsometers.[36] The last named instrument was used for measuring heights and was based on the principle that the boiling point of water varies with altitude above sea level.

On the first stage of the journey, over the Karakorums from Leh to Shahidula, Trotter had hoped to extend further the triangulation of India. While some of this region had been reasonably well charted by Shaw, Hayward, Johnson, and the earlier pundits, much was lacking. But the weather made this impossible. Snow and cloud, together with the need to go where supplies were located, forced the curtailment of the triangulation. Only the pundits, generally working in pairs, were able to count their paces and take latitude observations by sextant. In so doing, the various routes of the mission over the mountains were "certainly laid down with an amount of accuracy not hitherto attained."[37] Although the pundits proved their worth early on the expedition, Trotter was disappointed. He had expected more and was afraid that, once in the dominions of the emir, political considerations would diminish or even halt opportunities for mapping the area.

The mission proceeded from Leh across the Karakorums in two groups, each group itself splitting up from time to time and sending pundits out on independent explorations, while en route to the frontier fort of Shahidula. The smaller advance party consisted of Trotter, Stoliczka, and Biddulph, accompanied by A.K. (Kishen Singh), the Munshi (Abdul Subhan), and Kalian Singh. They traveled by a circuitous route through the Changchenmo valley. The main, or headquarters, group led by Forsyth took along Nain Singh and an assistant and journeyed by the more direct and westerly route across the Karakorum pass. Nain Singh and his assistant conducted a route survey from Leh over the Saser pass to Saser. At this point they separated, Nain Singh going up the Shyok River by the winter route to Daulat Beguldi, while his assistant took the more easterly summer route to the same place. Then they proceeded to Aktagh over the Karakorum pass before starting off northwest, down the Yarkand River. After three days, they reached Kirghiz Jangal, where they turned east and headed for Shahidula. From there on, all the members of the expedition took the same route to Sanju, and on to Yarkand.

The advance party left Leh in an easterly direction for Lake Pangong on the border of Tibet. All but Kishen Singh's assistant (who took an alternative route) crossed the Chang La, before reaching the village of Tankse. Trotter floated his portable India-rubber boat on Lake Pangong, while Biddulph took soundings of the water.[38] The advance party then turned northeast to Gogra, at which point they split up. Kishen Singh went with Biddulph on the more difficult easterly route across the Aksai Chin plateau. The main group, led by Trotter and including Kishen Singh's assistant and the Munshi, took the more direct route to the west, crossing the Changchenmo and following the path by which the first Forsyth mission had returned in 1870. The two routes merged at Kizil Jilga but diverged again shortly thereafter, Biddulph and Kishen Singh following the Karakash river as it wound northeast and then northwest to Shahidula, while Trotter and the others crossed the Karatagh pass to Aktagh (about forty miles south of Shahidula) where they joined the main headquarters group, before going on

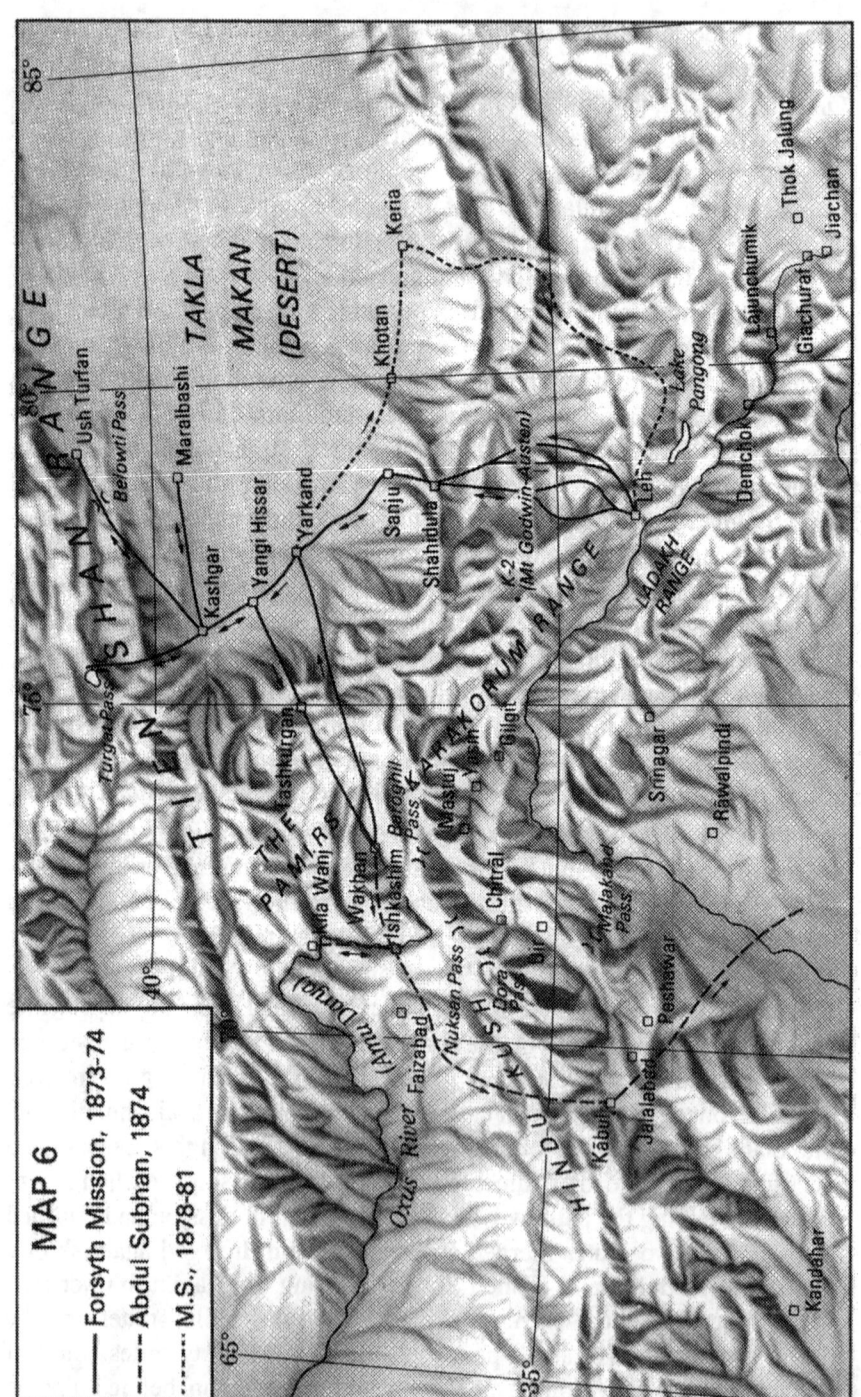

to Shahidula over the Suget pass. Trotter records that between Gogra and Suget, a period of over three weeks, he was never at an altitude of less than fifteen thousand feet, and the temperature fell to $-26°F$ at night. Stoliczka became seriously ill with spinal meningitis, and although he seemed to recover, he died in the mountains on the return journey.[39]

The mission proceeded to Suget, from where several diversionary explorations were staged before the advance to Shahidula. Bellew and Stoliczka traveled along the Karakash river in search of the jade mines. The area around Khotan had been renowned for its jade (or nephrite) for centuries. It was traditionally used for jewelry, pipe mouthpieces, small boxes, and the like. The report by Montgomerie's first explorer, Abdul Hamid, of jade in the bed of the Karakash had stimulated British interest. However, because of the expulsion of the Chinese by the emir, Bellew and Stoliczka found that most mines were no longer worked.[40]

Trotter detached the Munshi and an assistant off to the northwest. The Munshi was able to fix his position in relation to some of the Karakorum peaks already surveyed by the GTS, but only at the cost of several frostbitten fingers. Trotter himself headed up the Karakash river in order to investigate the existence of a road which was believed to run between the river and the Karatagh Lake. Trotter soon met Biddulph and Kishen Singh coming down the river. He sent the pundit off with a local guide to do some independent surveying (not very successfully, as the snow was very deep and the guide became ill) and then accompanied Biddulph to Shahidula.

From Shahidula, where the territory of the emir started, the mission proceeded across the Sanju pass to Sanju, and on to Yarkand. There they were entertained well by the governor of the city. In return, Forsyth presented him with some gifts, one of which, a large music box, was brought in playing "Come Where My Love Lies Dreaming."[41]

A great deal of information was acquired about routes across the Karakorums to Chinese Turkestan. However, the haul was not as great as Trotter anticipated, because of the weather, the terrain, and lack of time. The pundits successfully counted their paces, took compass bearings, and observed latitudes by sextant. Trotter had hoped to continue the triangulation of the GTS all the way from Leh to Shahidula, but it proved to be impossible to use his theodolite most of the time. His diary records "one almost continuous succession of disappointments."[42] It was hard work climbing to a high elevation in the thin air and galling, having done so, to find snow and cloud obscuring all the neighboring peaks. The winter days were short, and it was so cold that handling a prismatic compass became impossible. Even the Ladakhis, who were used to the climate, had to crouch behind stones to escape the icy wind on the peak of a hill.

More disappointments were to follow. From Shahidula onward, Forsyth placed increasing restrictions on Trotter's use of the pundits. No one was permitted publicly to take observations or show any of their instruments. One pundit (probably Nain Singh) was allowed to use a small pocket compass so as to get a route survey from Shahidula to Yarkand, and Trotter supplemented this with some nocturnal use of the sextant. But all these restrictions were not very encouraging and did not bode well for the geographical success of the mission. Forsyth seems to have been overly cautious and was too easily led by the emir's envoy, Syud Yakub Khan, who traveled with them to Yarkand on his way back from Constantinople. Forsyth wrote from Yarkand that "[at] the outset, I adopted as our rule the maxim that honesty is the best policy. I have told him [Syud Yakub Khan] everything about every theodolite and every pundit, and make no secret or mystery of anything, but always ask his advice before action. Sometimes he advises caution."[43] Given the experiences of previous travelers and the suspicious nature of the emir, it was not prudent to be so open about the objectives of the mission.[44] In the event, Forsyth decided that theodolites and cameras might be viewed as "instruments of the black art." Accordingly, he "enjoined on one and all the utmost caution, and decided that until we reached the royal presence, and had the opportunity of explaining the harmless nature of our scientific instruments, they should not be used."[45] Only the Munshi was permitted to travel with the mission to Kashgar, although Kishen Singh was allowed to follow a few days behind. Nain Singh and the other pundits had to remain in Yarkand.[46]

The mission set off from Yarkand on 28 November 1873. On 4 December, on a clear, cold day, they entered the fort of Yangi-shahr, the "new city" of Kashgar and the home of the emir. The walls of the old city could be discerned in the distance.

Kashgar

Shortly after the arrival of the mission, Forsyth had a formal interview alone with emir Yakub Beg. A reception for the mission as a whole soon followed. The emir put on a display of his troops and artillery, with lunch provided by the emir's commandant of artillery, Nubbi Baksh, the man who had caused so many difficulties during the Mirza's stay in Kashgar in 1869. Members of the mission were allowed to visit the old city of Kashgar and were the first Englishmen to do so. Trotter occupied his time taking observations of different kinds—astronomical readings for latitude and longitude, the determination of height by mercury and aneroid barometers, and magnetic and meteorological observations. On 20 December, Forsyth presented the Treaty of Commerce to the emir for his approval. After this, the emir gave his permission for shooting expeditions to be made outside Kashgar and said that scientific instruments could be used freely.

Forsyth quickly took advantage of this opportunity, and on the last day of the year two parties set off. Captain Trotter and Dr. Stoliczka, under the orders of Colonel Gordon, headed northwest to the Russian frontier on the Tian Shan, and Captain Biddulph struck out due east toward Maralbashi along the road to Aksu.

Gordon's objective was Lake Chadyr Kul on the Tian Shan plateau, about 110 miles northwest of Kashgar.[47] The party then hoped to return by way of the Terekty pass and the forts there. Neither Kishen Singh nor the Munshi accompanied this excursion.[48] Trotter himself made a route survey and took observations. On the orders of the emir, local leaders did not prevent him from doing so, although many of them tried to confuse him with false geographical information.

This was the first major excursion outside Kashgar to be made by the mission staff, and, according to Trotter, the emir was worried that he "might not be able to restrain the roving propensities of so many foreigners." Accordingly, Gordon had to accept the provision by the emir of baggage animals and servants. The party's movements were thus not entirely free, and although they crossed the Russian frontier by the Turgat pass, they were unable to return via the Terekty pass.

Trotter and Gordon both got a shot at specimens of *Ovis poli* (Marco Polo sheep), but neither scored a hit, and Gordon had two fingers frostbitten, caused by contact with the frozen metal of his rifle.

Although they had not seen all they had hoped to, Trotter was able to claim a survey of a road not hitherto traversed by Englishmen. It was heavily fortified to guard against a Russian attack. He also remarked that the surveys of India and Russia had now crossed each other "in friendly rivalry."[49] This information, on reaching London, led the RGS to claim prematurely that the trigonometrical surveys of India and Russia had now overlapped,[50] a notion that Trotter later took pains to dispel, pointing out that neither country had carried its triangulation into Chinese Turkestan and that both surveys relied on the much less accurate use of astronomical observations.[51] It was, however, one of the first connecting links between the two surveys.

Biddulph had set off at the same time as Trotter, accompanied only by his dog and a servant. He reached his objective, the town of Maralbashi about

120 miles east, in seven days, traveling through country wooded with stunted poplars. Everybody he met treated him well, and he made a short excursion fourteen miles beyond Maralbashi along the road to Aksu. He could have gone on to Aksu but probably believed that time did not permit. Biddulph made a route survey and took sextant observations, returning to Kashgar on 23 January.[52]

The Treaty of Commerce that Forsyth had presented was approved by the emir on 2 February 1874. Forsyth's mission in Kashgar was now completed. But because the passes to India were still blocked by winter snow, Forsyth delayed the mission's departure and organized another excursion. This exploration, led by Forsyth himself (who no doubt welcomed the chance to get out of Kashgar for a while), included Trotter, Chapman, Bellew, and Stoliczka. They left Kashgar on 14 February, leaving Biddulph and Gordon to look after things.

The emir had approved a visit to the Artysh districts encompassing the hills to the north of Kashgar. The area was well populated and appeared reasonably prosperous. On 20 February, the group met one of the main roads linking Kashgar with Aksu via Ush-Turfan. Trotter got authority from Forsyth to leave the main party and, in the company of Stoliczka, make his way in the direction of Ush-Turfan. The only restriction was that they were not to go beyond the limits of the Artysh district. Passing through a region inhabited by nomadic Kirghiz tribesmen, the activities of both men hampered by cold and snow, they succeeded in reaching the Belowti pass, fifty miles from Ush-Turfan. They returned to Kashgar on 3 March, having covered 340 miles in a little over two weeks. Trotter made a compass survey of the route, which later enabled him to make substantial corrections to the existing maps.[53]

Forsyth has said that his intention was that the mission would explore Kashgaria to the northeast and proceed via Lop Nor and through Tibet to India. "Everything," he said, "was arranged."[54] This was what Trotter had hoped for. But at the last minute the emir, perhaps because of pressure from the Russians, decided against it. In any case, it is unlikely that Forsyth intended that the entire mission force would return by this quite unknown route, particularly given the strict rules of the Indian government about entering Tibet, and so the distinction of being the first European to see Lop Nor fell to the Russian Prejevalsky, in 1877. Forsyth consoled himself with the thought that "though this is personally a great disappointment . . . our desire to visit Lake Lob has been considerably lessened by the discovery that it is only a series of marshy swamps, with here and there a stream running through it."[55] Biddulph was rather disgruntled and wrote to a friend that "we left Kashgar . . . our Aksu trip being ignored in a curious way though the Ameer had given his permission for it."[56]

On the morning of 17 March 1874, "under the usual salute," the mission left Kashgar and reached Yangi Hissar on the road to Yarkand the following day. On 21 March, Forsyth dispatched Gordon, Biddulph, and Stoliczka, together with Trotter, accompanied by the Munshi and Kishen Singh, to the Pamir. This geographical diversion, which was almost recalled by the emir, was to provide some of the most important data of the entire mission.[57]

Gordon's route was southwest from Yangi Hissar, through Tashkurgan to the Wakhan, that area which formed the northeastern extremity of Afghanistan. From there they were to continue west into Badakhshan and hoped to return to India via Kabul. On the first day of the new year, Forsyth had sent Ibrahim Khan to Kabul, requesting Emir Sher Ali to allow Gordon and his party of forty to pass through his territory. Gordon was ordered to halt in the Wakhan, where Forsyth was to join him and hoped to bring the permission of Emir Sher Ali to press forward. If the response was negative, Gordon was instructed to return to Leh through Yarkand.

The plains of Kashgaria were quickly left behind, and Gordon and Trotter soon found themselves making heavy weather through the winter snow. Their route was identical to that taken by the Mirza in the opposite direction in 1869. More settled areas where people were preparing for cultivation with the onset of spring gradually gave way to groups of Kirghiz nomads. After ten quick marches and crossing three mountain ranges, they reached Tashkurgan, situated in a stony valley. There they halted for two days. Up to this point, Kishen Singh and the Munshi had divided the work of pacing the road between them. Trotter, now that they were about to leave the dominion of the emir Yakub Beg, decided that Kishen Singh, being a Hindu, should not continue with them. Trotter obtained permission from the governor of the province for him to return to Yarkand by a different and more direct route. The Munshi, a Moslem, stayed with the group.[58]

Leaving Tashkurgan on 2 April, Gordon opted to traverse the Wakhan by the Little Pamir. This was the usual winter route, as the more northerly road over the Great Pamir via Wood's Lake (Lake Victoria) was deep in snow. Even so, the conditions were worse than they had expected, given that spring was supposed to have arrived. "Hard work," and "an uncommonly rough time of it," were the muted comments of Gordon and Biddulph. Trotter agreed, but commented "happily we are none of us any the worse for it, except that we have lost all the skin off our noses."[59] In the western part of the Wakhan, the Little and Great Pamir routes joined near the village of Kila Panjah on the Oxus. Here was the residence of the mir of Wakhan, and it was here that the exhausted group halted to replenish supplies and baggage animals. Once resupplied, they could continue, but only if authority to do so was received from Emir Sher Ali in Kabul.

Unfortunately, the dispatch from Kabul was negative. The Afghan ruler was having disagreements with Britain over the succession to his title, and he apparently felt that Russia was the rising power in the region.[60] Gordon decided to make the best of it and sent two men of Wakhan, accompanied by an Indian sepoy, up the Great Pamir route, to see if the mission could return by that route to Tashkurgan. They pronounced it practicable (to Gordon's surprise), and after paying off the entire national debt (£45) to ensure the permission of the mir of Wakhan, all the expedition members left for Tashkurgan, Yarkand, and home on 26 April.[61] All, that is, except one.

The exception was Abdul Subhan, alias "the Munshi." Before separating from Forsyth, Trotter had received permission to set the Munshi off on an independent exploration, should a good opportunity materialize. With Gordon and the rest of the group forced to return to Yarkand, now was an ideal time.

Because he was a trained surveyor, Abdul Subhan was an exception to the general rule that such individuals were not dispatched to explore beyond the frontier, the ranks of the pundits being drawn from those peoples who resided in border areas and customarily traveled across the border in pursuit of legitimate trading or religious objectives.

The Mirza and Wood had already provided a survey of the Oxus up river from Ishkashim, and so the Munshi was ordered to proceed there and continue the survey downriver as far as possible (Map 6). Shortly after leaving Ishkashim, the Oxus turned north through Shignan, to whose ruler Gordon sent a letter and a present, carried by the Munshi, hoping that this would provide his explorer with safe passage. Three days after the departure of Gordon and the others, the Munshi set off, on 29 April 1874.[62] The Munshi carried with him a prismatic compass, a boiling-point thermometer, a pocket sextant, and a watch. He was instructed to use them covertly. Unknown to the Munshi (and to Trotter), just ten days earlier the Havildar had left Faizabad in Badakhshan for Kolab, where he turned east and started to survey up the Oxus.[63] Both explorers were ignorant of the fact that they were marching toward each other, steadily narrowing the gap in this unsurveyed section downriver from Ishkashim, where the Mirza had met the Oxus in 1869. The Munshi, traveling downstream, arrived at Kila Wamur, the capital of Roshan, on 11 May. Less than two months later, the Havildar, surveying up the river, reached Kila Yaz Ghulum, the frontier village of Shignan, on 9 July. Neither explorer was able to penetrate beyond these villages, and so a gap of about twenty-five miles remained between them. No more than one long day's march remained to complete the survey of the upper course of the Oxus.

The Munshi was successful in mapping the course of the Oxus for about eighty-five miles north of Ishkashim, passing through the territories of Gharan, Shignan, and Roshan, which, Trotter wrote later in his report, "have hitherto only been known to us by name."[64]

In addition to his surveying activities, the Munshi also gleaned much political information of value. Gharan, he said, had always been under the direct rule of the mir of Badakhshan, with whom Shignan and Roshan had a tributary relationship. Furthermore, the Munshi reported that the territory of all three districts existed on both sides of the Oxus. Since the mir of Badakhshan recognized the authority of Emir Sher Ali in Kabul, this meant that Afghan territory extended across the Oxus to the land on the right bank. This information made parts of the Gorchakof-Granville Agreement of 1873 contradictory, because the agreement said both that the Oxus was to be the frontier and that Afghanistan included all land under the authority of Emir Sher Ali.

Up to this point, little had been known except for hearsay about the route of this portion of the Oxus. The achievements of the Munshi (and the Havildar) were of major geographic and political importance. Geographically, the course of the Oxus, as marked on existing maps, had to be considerably revised. These changes were of political significance, since the Oxus was to define the northern frontier of Afghanistan.

Trotter had instructed the Munshi to take a return route through Shignan, following the Shakdarah river into Wakhan and then continuing to Kashmir through Hunza.[65] This did not prove to be possible, however, and the Munshi eventually returned to India by way of Kabul.

While the Munshi was conducting his independent exploration of the Oxus, Gordon and the others were on their way back to India. The weather was mild, almost springlike. Gordon was determined to try a new route back and so headed for the Great Pamir and Lake Victoria (Wood's Lake). Biddulph, clearly a man who enjoyed his own company, took off on his third solitary expedition, down the Little Pamir road, with the intention of investigating some of the passes into Chitral before rejoining Gordon at Aktash, where the Great and Little Pamir routes converged. May 4 was set as the date for rendezvous.

Gordon, Trotter, and Stoliczka reached Lake Victoria on 1 May. Here Trotter verified the lake's position as determined by Wood and made estimations of the lake's elevation and drainage.[66] On leaving the vicinity of the lake, Trotter shot an *Ovis poli*, the only successful attempt of any member of the expedition, and possibly the first ever *Ovis poli* shot by a European.

At Aktash, they rejoined the route by which they had entered the Pamir and made a punctual rendezvous with Biddulph, who returned from a successful side trip to the Baroghil pass, the lowest of all the passes over the Hindu Kush.

Gordon had requested permission from the local chief of the Sarikol district for the group to return to Yarkand by a new and more direct route, instead of going back by way of Yangi Hissar. Permission was granted, and they arrived in Yarkand on 21 May. After a week resting and replenishing their supplies, they left on 28 May and arrived in Leh on 29 June. Unfortunately, the exertion and the climate proved too severe for Dr. Stoliczka, who expired after crossing the Karakorum pass at a distance of eleven days' march from Leh.

Forsyth and the main body of the mission had been biding their time in Yangi Hissar for spring to arrive. While laying in supplies for the return journey and waiting for word from Gordon, Forsyth and Bellew found time to visit the sand-buried city of Oordum Padshah, about fifty miles to the east. On 3 May, Forsyth learned that Gordon was not going to be able to go on to Kabul and that he was returning to Yarkand. Forsyth then headed for Yarkand himself and left there just three days ahead of Gordon's arrival. He had received approval from the emir to take a different route back from Yarkand to Leh, and so at Karghalik the mission took the road through Kugiar, via the Yangi pass to Shahidula. Nain Singh, Kalian Singh, and one assistant pundit had remained in Yarkand throughout the winter. Now that there was no necessity to curb their activities, one of them, probably Kalian Singh, resurveyed the route through Sanju to Shahidula with no attempt at concealment.[67]

The road through Kugiar had been taken by the advance baggage party (returning to Leh), of which Nain Singh was a member. He mapped the route, parts of which had never been surveyed before,[68] although a portion had been traveled by George Hayward in 1869, who had explored it from Shahidula as far as the base of the Yangi pass. Hayward reported that the road was little used in his time because of robbers from Hunza and Nagar, but that the route was practicable for baggage animals throughout, and in his opinion was "the easiest and most direct route from across the Karakorum into Eastern Turkestan."[69] As soon as the spring came, Nain Singh explored this new route, apparently then continuing on to Leh and sending back a report so favorable that Forsyth and then Trotter opted for it.[70]

The Forsyth Missions

Forsyth joined his previous route at Aktagh and then proceeded over the Karakorum pass, arriving in Leh on 17 June 1874, just twelve days before Trotter and the rest of the mission.

The commercial aims of the mission remained unfulfilled. Robert Shaw was ordered by the viceroy to go to Kashgar as the permanent British representative there, as provided for in the treaty. His first task was to exchange ratifications of the treaty. Alas, when Shaw reached Kashgar, the emir informed him that no permanent representative could be allowed until the sultan of Turkey had given his approval. The emir alleged that this had been agreed to by Forsyth, although Forsyth denied this. The Indian government pressed Shaw to return to India, having received ratification of the treaty from the emir. This he did, but the "ratification" turned out to be just a letter of greetings to the viceroy.[71]

Nevertheless, the mission did produce a huge amount of geographical and other data on Chinese Turkestan. Much of the scientific information was included in the massive official report of the mission. Geographically, many places in Kashgaria had been mapped for the first time, or had had their positions confirmed. New details had been acquired of routes from Kashgar and Yarkand through Wakhan to Badakhshan, and the course of the upper Oxus had been completely traced, with the exception of a small gap. New routes had been surveyed between Ladakh and Chinese Turkestan, and old ones had been measured more accurately. These showed the extreme unlikelihood of any Russian advance across the Karakorums. Although the Indian government continued to be concerned about Russian influence over Kashgar, particularly after the conquest of Kokand in 1876, strategic concerns shifted to the Baroghil and other passes over the Hindu Kush. Biddulph's report on his excursion to the Baroghil pass gave the clear impression that an army, even equipped with artillery, could be moved over it with ease.[72] The Mullah, who crossed the Baroghil a bare week after Biddulph, provided confirmatory evidence.[73]

But these were not the only results of the mission. One of the most important explorations was the journey of the pundit Kishen Singh, made while both Trotter and Forsyth were on their way home from Yarkand to Leh.[74]

Kishen Singh had been instructed by Forsyth to take the route to the ancient city of Khotan along the southern fringe of the Takla Makan desert, and then to continue along the road as far as possible in an easterly direction.[75] Khotan was actually an area of more than three hundred villages, the largest town of which was called Ilchi. This oasis community, lying between the Kunlun mountains and the Takla Makan desert, was on the southern route of the old "Silk Road" between China and the lands to the west. The oases were fed by the Yurungkash River which, when in full flood in early summer from the melting snows of the Kunlun, flowed across the Takla Makan to join the Tarim southeast of Aksu.

Marco Polo had seen Khotan in 1274, and Benedict Goes had followed in the seventeenth century. Once famous for its jade, Khotan had fallen upon hard times with the revolt of Yakub Beg against the Chinese. The pundit reached Khotan on 18 May, the first British agent there since the unauthorized visit of William Johnson in 1865. He had averaged about fifteen miles per day, passing through a generally well-populated region with plentiful water, pasture land, and fuel, and remained in the city until 7 June, with a two-day excursion to Karakash, which he described as a "large commercial town" fifteen miles to the northwest.

Kishen Singh's description of Khotan was a sparse one. It was, he said, "a large town, where a Governor and several hundred sepoys are posted. Numerous canals from the Karakash river intersect a large area of country around Khotan."[76] He did, however, provide a plan of the city.[77]

His measurements of the city's position were the first since those taken by Johnson. As a result, the location of Khotan on the map was shifted by more than thirty miles.[78] Trotter admitted that "[i]t may appear bold to make this extensive change in the position of a place that has been visited by a European explorer," but he had great confidence in the pundit and had, moreover, been in communication with Johnson, who readily agreed that his own observations for longitude might well have been in error.[79] The new position of Khotan was given as longitude 79° 59', latitude 37° 07'. Trotter's confidence was justified: the *Times Atlas of the World* gives the reading as 79° 57' and 37° 07'.

The pundit continued in an easterly direction, reaching the village of Keria on 18 June. From here he made a side trip of three days' journey to the Sorghak goldfields, about 160 miles (by road) from Khotan, and the most easterly point of his travels in Turkestan. Johnson had gone no further east than Keria. His report, as written up by Trotter, says little of the goldfields, except that the pundit visited them. Historically, they were well known. Kishen Singh's notes, attached to the route survey, indicate that the goldfields were worked all year round by men from Keria, who lived in temporary huts with their wives and families. The emir, Yakub Beg, had a monopoly of the gold, one-fifth of which he collected as a tax, buying the remainder at a fixed price.[80]

Leaving the goldfields, Kishen Singh retraced his steps back to Keria, where he turned south. Crossing the Kunlun from the frontier village of

Polu, he returned to Leh via Lake Pangong, confirming the existence of another route to Leh, two and a half degrees to the east of the most easterly route known to exist at that time, which was the one taken by Johnson on his visit to Khotan nine years earlier. Johnson had heard of this route while in Khotan and described it as being suitable for "wheeled conveyances," with plenty of wood, grain, and water available and not crossing any snowy ranges. Best of all, it passed to the east of Kashmir, so avoiding the onerous taxes on goods in transit.[81] Because of this, information on the road was highly desired.

Once over the Kunlun by a 17,500-foot pass, Kishen Singh was on the Chang Tang plateau. The road was usually good, and grass and fuel were, as Johnson reported, abundant. Nevertheless, for almost 250 miles he did not see a single inhabited village, just a few ruined huts, and he did not pass another traveler.

Trotter had heard that the route was little used because of fear of bandits. Even so, he surmised that much of the road was safe and extolled its virtues as a trade route between India and Tibet, one which (at least in the summer) had no really difficult passes to negotiate and which avoided crossing any of the territory of the maharaja of Kashmir. Trotter admitted, though, that this would have to await "some distant day . . . as long as Europeans are rigorously excluded from Western Tibet."[82] Eleven years later, A.D. Carey and Ney Elias took this road in the opposite direction, using the pundit's directions, which they found to be highly accurate. Arriving at Polu, they caused consternation among the Chinese authorities (who had by then reconquered the territory of the emir) and who had apparently not known of (or had forgotten) the existence of this road.[83]

The pundit was soon approaching the village of Noh, on the north bank of Lake Pangong. He was aware that he was likely to be searched, since the lake formed the boundary between Tibet and Kashmir. Accordingly, he hid his instruments and notes behind a bush on the outskirts of the village. He was searched, but of course nothing was found. He had hoped to continue to the provincial capital of Rudok, to the south of the lake, but the authorities were suspicious and tried to force him to return the way he had come. It was with great reluctance that they permitted him to go by a direct route to Leh, but avoiding Rudok. Kishen Singh retrieved his papers and equipment and arrived safely in Leh at the end of July 1874.[84]

The pundit had performed very well, and he was marked down for more ambitious explorations in the future. Trotter pronounced the route survey (which had started and concluded at known points) to be of an accuracy such as could not be expected to be generally attainable, only being possible in this case because a good portion of the route was uninhabited, and therefore the pundit could take all the observations he wanted without concealment.

The confidence placed in Kishen Singh's location of Khotan has already been noted. Trotter also used the pundit's value of the longitude of Yarkand in preference to his own observations, placing the city at 77° 15' 55" extremely close to the figures of 77° 15' 46" derived by de Filippi, using wireless telegraphy in 1914.[85] But it was not a case of total confidence. Kenneth Mason points out that "had still more reliance been placed upon the evidence collected by him [Kishen Singh], the map of the headwaters of the Yurungkash would not have remained incorrect for nearly fifty years."[86]

In May of 1878, the Royal Geographical Society awarded Trotter its prestigious Patron's Medal for his work in connection with the Forsyth Mission and for his initiative in dispatching Nain Singh across Tibet at the end of the mission.[87]

By the time Trotter received his medal, Montgomerie was dead, Forsyth (now Sir Douglas Forsyth) had returned permanently to England, and the Chinese had recaptured Kashgaria. They recovered the province of Kansu in 1873 and, by a major military effort, captured Urumchi in 1876. In May 1877, Yakub Beg expired, after taking or being given poison.

Trade between India, Yarkand, and Kashgar continued, but never even approximated Forsyth's hopes for it. The Russians had the advantage geographically, and the British were hampered by poor diplomatic relations with China.

No further surveys of Chinese Turkestan by the pundits were ever undertaken. Their attention continued to be directed toward Tibet, of which so much was still unexplored, and then to the northeast frontier of India.

Postscript

The small gap in the survey of the Oxus left uncompleted between the explorations of the Havildar and the Munshi in 1874 was finally filled in 1881 by the pundit M.S.[88] His real name was Mukhtar Shah.[89] M.S. was a well-educated Pir, or Muslim holy man, from Kashmir, and a friend of Abdul Subhan (the Munshi), who, when he found out M.S. was about to make a journey to Kolab, put him in touch with Walker at the GTS.[90] Walker learned that M.S. had traveled in the Upper Oxus region on previous occasions[91] and asked him to work for the GTS. M.S. agreed and was sent off to Dehra Dun for a few weeks' training under Nain Singh.

On 1 February 1878, M.S. left Dehra Dun for Kashmir. A famine was raging there, and it was difficult to procure supplies. He was not able to depart from Srinagar until June, when he left for Gilgit accompanied by his son and three servants, arriving in October. He left Gilgit the following month, leaving his son behind, and spent the winter in Yasin. The following September, he took the route as instructed by Walker across the Baroghil pass, passing the spot where Hayward was murdered (Map 6). At the Baroghil pass he joined his survey with that made by the Mullah in 1873. He reached the Oxus at Sarhad in the Wakhan and followed the route of the Munshi downriver, passing Kila Panjah (where Trotter was halted in 1874) to Faizabad, leaving the Oxus at Ishkashim, where it began its great bend to the north. It had been the intention of M.S. to continue down the Oxus; but in the unsettled state of the area, the governor of Shignan was refusing to allow any traffic to pass. As a result, M.S. decided to approach the "missing link" in the Oxus from the other direction. From Faizabad he continued to Kolab, crossing the Oxus at Samti, having followed the route pioneered by the Havildar, although with some additional exploration of his own.

From Kolab, however, Walker had directed M.S. to continue beyond the area explored by the Havildar, and so he took a new route up the Doaba valley for fifty miles. At the end of the valley the pass to Darwaz (and the trade route to Bokhara) was blocked by snow, and so M.S. partially retraced his steps, crossing a pass into the Dora Imam valley to the east, which ran nearly parallel to the Doaba. From here he crossed into the valley of the Oxus and marched up the north bank of the river. As far as Kila Khum, the route was unexplored. There he joined the route of the Havildar, but a few days later he was halted at Waznud, almost exactly the spot where the Havildar himself had been stopped. Again, the governor of Shignan was to blame. M.S.'s second attempt had been foiled.

The pundit retraced his steps to the Dora Imam valley and went down the valley to Kila Kisht, where he met the Oxus. He then crossed the river and struck off across Shiva, that part of Badakhshan within the loop of the Oxus, a region of which the British had been completely ignorant. Traversing high passes and green elevated valleys, the pundit eventually met the Oxus again at Kila Bar Panjah, where he was able to link up with the survey of Abdul Subhan. M.S. was now ready for his third attempt, which proved surprisingly easy. He met no obstacles as he traveled downriver as far as Waznud, where he had been stopped earlier. The last link in this portion of the upper Oxus was now completed. A complete map could be drawn from its sources to Kisht, where there was a thirty-mile gap to Samti.

M.S. now turned around and went back to Kila Wamar, where he left the

Oxus and followed the valley of the Murghab River as far as its highest inhabited point.[92] His further progress blocked by hostile Kirghiz, the pundit retraced his steps and, once on the Oxus again, turned upriver and reached Kila Bar Panjah, where he fell ill with rheumatism.[93] He spent the winter recuperating at Kila Bar Panjah. In the spring, he used his illness as an excuse to make an excursion up the Shakhdara valley "for the sake of his health." Trotter had told Abdul Subhan to survey this area, but the Munshi had not been successful. Through steep defiles, opening out to broad plateaus, M.S. was able to march for nearly fifty miles up the valley before being stopped by deep snow. Retracing his steps yet again, indefatigable despite his poor health, M.S. went back to the Oxus and continued upstream. Passing through Ishkashim and Kila Panjah, he took the Little Pamir route to Sarhad. Leaving the river, he recrossed the Baroghil pass. While camped on the far side of the pass, he heard the local people talk of a large lake to the east. M.S. promptly hired a local guide, using the excuses that he wanted to do some shooting there and also pick medicinal herbs, and set off on a two-day march to the lake. The Ghazkol lake, at nearly fifteen thousand feet, was surrounded by perpetually snow-clad peaks whose sides rose straight from the banks of the icy water. M.S. was able to fix the position of the lake and give a rough idea of its size. This information was very useful to Walker and his colleagues, who had heard of this lake from Biddulph and others but had only a very hazy idea of its location.

The pundit then returned to the Darkoth pass and closed his survey at the point he had started it some two and a half years earlier. M.S. eventually returned to Dehra Dun on 18 February 1882, through Yasin, Gilgit, and then Srinagar, where he stayed for five months for medical treatment. He had been gone four years.

In addition to finishing the last link in the mapping of the course of the upper Oxus, M.S. also provided valuable data on the geography of Badakhshan and of the small states on both sides of the Oxus. His travels confirmed or corrected route surveys of the earlier pundits. His educational background as a holy man enabled him to meet influential people in the areas through which he passed and so bring back statistics, not only of the topography but also of the religious, linguistic, and political boundaries.

M.S. volunteered for this assignment despite the risk of death, either accidental or deliberate. The area was in a disturbed state, and travelers giving the impression of conspiring with neighboring chiefs were often put to death. To be seen measuring distances or using a compass would have meant summary execution. M.S. saw two men from Darwaz arrested and their throats slowly cut because they carried suspicious papers; at that point one of his companions quickly concealed their notes and instruments under a rock. The same companion later perished while crossing the Murghab. He was on a raft, propelled across by men swimming alongside who had inflated skins strapped to their chests. The raft hit a large boulder, and M.S.'s companion fell into the water. Failing to get a grasp on the rock, worn smooth by the force of the current, he was swept downstream, his faint cries for help eventually drowned by the roar of the torrent.

Although the information M.S. brought back was very useful, it did not measure up to the surveying standards of most of his predecessors. Walker had seized on the opportunity of a volunteer who was planning to travel in an unexplored area, but there was insufficient time to train him to the usual level. His pacing was "not always strictly accurate,"[94] and he took no latitude observations.[95] It was these deficiencies that led Walker to agree with the Russians that the Aksu flowed into the Murghab. Although the survey of M.S. indicated that they were separate rivers, the Russians were trained surveyors. But Walker took the side of M.S. (and the Havildar) when a Russian map showed "an enormous bend or loop" to the east in the course of the Oxus, and then to the southwest between the point at which it was entered by the Murghab and the Vanj.[96] No such radical change in course was described in the map produced as a result of the surveys of M.S. and the Havildar, although at the point where the Murghab flows into the Oxus, the latter interrupts its northward course to flow westward, before making a ninety-degree turn and heading north again.

Colonel Tanner, who wrote the introduction to the travels of M.S., complained that native travelers only had eyes for the mundane, or the unimportant, describing in detail the number of mulberry trees in a village, but omitting to even mention the glory of a majestic snowcapped peak.[97] For the Indian traveler, familiarity perhaps bred contempt. The mountains were always there, but crops and mulberry trees were transient. Besides, it is to be doubted that the officers of the GTS asked for lyrical evocations of the landscapes or mountain ranges. In any case, M.S. was quite capable of giving a graphic account of events when he felt that circumstances warranted. Here is his description of his progress up the valley of the Murghab, as written up by Colonel Tanner:

> He had to climb along the face of a scarp with only the narrowest possible ledge for his feet and an insecure and rude hand-rail of wood to grasp; high cliffs reared themselves up overhead, and the black chasm of the Bartang, with its raging waters below, seemed ready to engulf him should he in the slightest degree lose his presence of mind.

The pathway, if such it could be called, was carried along a fault in the rock at an immense height above the river below, which, rushing along amidst huge boulders, filled the air with its noise. The precipice which overhung the black abyss was in places covered with a coating of ice, and icicles hung from every point; an oozy spring, freezing as it came into the cold air, had formed rounded bulging masses of ice, which extended over the pathway. The party cut holes in it, and roughened the surface as much as possible, and, crawling on hands and knees, traversed its slippery length and managed somehow to make their way across this dreadful place without loss. Midway the ice was so smooth and glassy, and the track so narrow, that it seemed as if the slightest breath would cause them to slip over the edge into space.[98]

For his contributions to the geography of Badakhshan, M.S. was awarded one of the two medals given to General Walker at the Venice International Geographical Congress for presentation to the native explorers of the Survey of India.

SIX
Around Everest and Kanchenjunga: Hari Ram and Rinzing Namgyal

Nepal is a landlocked, roughly rectangular country, running in a northwest to southeasterly direction to the south of the main Himalayan chain. Its northern boundary forms the border with Tibet, and with the exception of Sikkim (now an Indian protectorate) to the east, it is bounded by the Indian states of West Bengal, Bihar, and Uttar Pradesh. Approximately five hundred miles wide and one hundred miles broad, Nepal is the largest, both in size and population, of the three Himalayan states of Nepal, Sikkim, and Bhutan. Along the southern border with India is a narrow strip of territory of grass and jungle called the terai, well known both for its big game and, in the nineteenth century, for the malaria to which many British surveyors fell victim. Moving north, the terai merges into the hill country, which in turn gives way to the icy heights of the Himalayas.

In Nepal, or on its borders, are nine of the world's fourteen highest peaks, ranging from Mount Everest, the giant of them all at 29,028 feet, to Gosainthan (Shisha Pangma) at 26,291 feet, and including Annapurna, Dhaulagiri, Kanchenjunga, and Makalu. Nepal is one of the most mountainous states in the world.

From west to east the country is divided into three sections by mountain peaks and rivers. Between Nanda Devi in Kumaon and Dhaulagiri, the area is drained by the Kali and Karnali rivers, the Kali marking the western border of Nepal with India. The central section lies between Dhaulagiri and Gosainthan. Drained by the Gandak River system, the central sector includes the valley of Nepal and the capital, Kathmandu. The eastern division ends at Kanchenjunga on the Sikkim border. From here the Kosi and Arun rivers eventually flow, like the Kali, Karnali, and Gandak, into the Ganges.

Although the northern border of Nepal generally follows the crest of the Himalayas, there are places where it penetrates to the north of the main range. There are several passes of various degrees of difficulty, which carry traffic across the Himalayas between Nepal and its northern neighbor, Tibet. Used in the nineteenth century (and to a lesser extent today) by pilgrims and merchants from Tibet, Nepal, and India, these passes are more numerous along the eastern part of the border, closer to the populated areas of Tibet. Nineteenth-century travelers between Kathmandu and Lhasa would probably have taken the Kuti or Kirong passes in eastern Nepal. Fifty miles to the east of the Kuti was the Hati pass, following the course of the river Arun, although since this was a difficult pass, most wayfarers preferred the Nangpa La to the west of Everest. On the east, the Tipta La, a little to the west of Kanchenjunga, was the standard route. Other Himalayan passes of note included the Mustang pass from Kathmandu to the monastery of Tradom on the Tsangpo River, much frequented by traders and by pilgrims visiting the shrines at Muktinath. Finally, in the western part of Nepal, there existed the Takla pass between Nanda Devi and Dhaulagiri. For centuries, these passes had made Nepal one of the main links of communication between India, Tibet, and China.

The first Europeans to explore these links were the adventurous Capuchin and Jesuit missionaries of the Catholic church. Both religious orders used Nepal as a way station as they journeyed between India and Tibet or China. The first missionary to cross Nepal was probably the Jesuit John Cabral in 1628, who passed through the country on his way to India after visiting the Tibetan towns of Shigatse and Gyantse. He was followed in 1662 by his fellow Jesuits, Albert d'Orville and Johan Grueber, who traveled from China to Lhasa. Continuing to India, they entered Nepal through the Kuti pass and stayed briefly in Kathmandu. Another Jesuit, Father Santucci, stayed in Nepal for a few months in 1679. Neither of these early visitors provided any significant information about Nepal, although Grueber and d'Orville did take some observations for latitudes.

By papal decree, the mission fields of Nepal and Tibet were given into the jurisdiction of the Capuchins in 1702, and they set up a base in Lhasa that functioned intermittently between 1708 and 1760. The first fathers reached the Tibetan capital through the now customary Nepalese route in 1707-08. Others followed over the years, of whom the most famous was Orazio della Penna, who spent a decade in Lhasa. When he left Tibet in 1729, he went first to Kathmandu, working there for two years before continuing to Rome. He returned to Lhasa in 1739-40, but was forced to leave Tibet for Nepal in 1745. He died in Kathmandu. Mention should also be made of the great Jesuit traveler, Father Ippolito Desideri, who, accompanied by Father Manuel Freyre, traveled from Ladakh across Tibet to Lhasa in 1716. On reaching Lhasa, Freyre returned almost immediately to India, through Nepal. Desideri followed him five years later.

The small Capuchin mission in Lhasa eventually foundered in 1760.

After their expulsion, the Capuchins moved to Kathmandu, where one of them, Father Giuseppe da Rovato, witnessed the overthrow of the Newar kingdom by the rising power of the Gurkhas and provided some details of the topography of Nepal to the British.[1]

The Gurkhas occupied the Kathmandu valley in 1768.[2] As they continued to expand their influence, so they eventually came into conflict with British power in Bengal, recently secured by Clive's victory at the battle of Plassey in 1757. One of the major issues in dispute with the British was the question of trade, both with and through Nepal.

Trade with Nepal itself was not large. Nepal exported fruit, spices, timber, sheep, and elephants to India, while importing cloth, carpets, cutlery, and tobacco. Britain saw Nepal as a potential market for the goods of the new Industrial Revolution. More important, however, was Nepal's location as a trade route between India and Tibet, which was well on the way to becoming a dependency of China, and through Tibet to China itself. At the time, and up until 1842 with the British acquisition of the island of Hong Kong, British trade with China was conducted through Canton, under very difficult circumstances, so that the shortest trade routes to China ran over the Himalayas and across Tibet. Nepal lay astride the most important of these routes, as British India had no common border with Tibet until the conclusion of the Anglo-Nepalese War in 1816, when the British took control over Kumaon.

China was seen as a huge market for British manufactured goods, which could offset British purchases of Chinese tea. Tibetan gold and silver already flowed through Nepal and made important contributions to the Indian economy. Unfortunately, just as the East India Company became increasingly aware of the value of Nepal to trade, so this trade came to a halt.[3]

With the Kathmandu valley under siege by the Gurkhas, the Newar king appealed for help from the British. The Newars had always assisted the close commercial links between Tibet and India, links which the East India Company wished to take advantage of, but which had been disrupted by the military activities of the Gurkhas. The British therefore decided to render military assistance to the Newars, in the first of several attempts to halt Gurkha expansion.

Assistance was provided in the form of a military mission under Captain Kinloch. It was not a success. Dispatched in the rainy season of 1767, hampered by malaria, and running low on supplies, Captain Kinloch and his men were forced to withdraw to the terai before even reaching Kathmandu. A military failure, Kinloch did return with a few sketches of a portion of

Nepal's southern frontier. From the perspective of the Gurkhas, the mission confirmed the suspicions of their ruler, Prithvi Narayan Shah, about the hostility of the British.

The East India Company then decided on a less aggressive approach by accepting the services of James Logan, who was familiar with the border area and knowledgeable about past trading arrangements as well as those that still continued with the Nepali rajas opposed to the Gurkhas. In 1769 Logan was endorsed as an official emissary of the company. This approach produced no results. Logan was refused permission to enter Nepal, under Prithvi Narayan's policy of excluding Europeans in general, and the British in particular, from his territory.

This climate of hostility, fueled in part by border conflicts along the terai, looked ripe for improvement in the next decade. Warren Hastings took over the administration of Bengal in 1772 and became its first governor-general in 1774. Prithvi Narayan died in 1775. Hastings was anxious to increase India's trade with China and Tibet and twice sent George Bogle as an envoy to Tibet, in 1774 and again in 1779. Bogle brought back encouraging information, but the trade routes through Nepal were still blocked as a result of hostile relations between Nepal and both its Indian and Tibetan neighbors. Hastings sent a Mr. Foxcroft to Nepal in 1784, to see whether trade with India might be reopened, but Foxcroft apparently had no better success than Logan.[4]

Gurkha territorial conquests inevitably created conflicts not just with the British to the south, but also with Sikkim on their eastern border and the Tibetans to the north. These upset the normal trading patterns of the region. But at the same time, Tibet, Nepal, and the other Himalayan states were all fearful of the expanding British authority to the south, so that conciliatory attempts by the East India Company to reestablish good trading relationships were seen as a preliminary move toward British political and military dominance.

Continued Gurkha expansion eventually led to opportunities for the British to turn the situation to their advantage. In 1788 the Gurkhas invaded Tibet, occupying parts of the country and forcing the Tibetan government to pay an indemnity. The Tibetans appealed to the British for help which, had it been given, would have greatly improved relations with Tibet, while at the same time halting the encroachments of the Gurkhas. But Britain vacillated and stayed neutral. The Gurkhas invaded Tibet again in 1791, capturing Shigatse and sacking the monastery of the Panchen Lama at Tashilhunpo. This time, the Tibetans called on the Chinese for assistance, and a large Chinese army inflicted major defeats on the invaders from Nepal. The price the Tibetans paid was that China had now firmly established its control over Tibet. The retreating Gurkhas, hoping to get British military aid, signed a commercial agreement with the East India Company. However, Lord Cornwallis, Hastings's successor, not wishing to offend the Chinese, again opted for neutrality, although he agreed to send a military mission to mediate the conflict between Nepal and Tibet and to press for the implementation of the commercial agreement. The leader of the expedition, Captain William Kirkpatrick, was also instructed to discuss with the Gurkhas the question of trade with Tibet and to mediate boundary disputes along the terai. The Tibetan government was informed that the Kirkpatrick mission was not intended to provide military aid to the Gurkhas.

By the time Kirkpatrick reached Kathmandu, the war was over, and the Chinese had forced an ignominious treaty on Nepal. Neither side appreciated British neutrality, and the Tibetans firmly believed that the British had assisted the Gurkhas.[5] Nothing had been achieved diplomatically. Nepal and British India continued to be deeply distrustful of each other, and the Chinese and the Tibetans played on each other's fears and suspicions of British perfidy, to close Tibet to virtually all foreigners for over a century.

But all was not lost. Kirkpatrick, although not the first Englishman to enter Nepal, was the first to produce a major account of the country and its political institutions, history, trade, and topography.[6] Even more geographical data would have been acquired had not the Gurkhas rejected the idea that a military surveyor accompany Kirkpatrick.[7] As it was, Lieutenant John Gerard, in command of Kirkpatrick's escort, made a survey of the routes taken by the mission in and out of Nepal. He used a compass to take his bearings. Distance was calculated by estimating the speed of march and timing the number of hours marched per day. From these surveys, a sketch map was constructed of the routes to and from the Nepal border to Kathmandu.

Despite diplomatic setbacks, the East India Company was still anxious to open trade with Tibet and, through Tibet, with China. Bhutan had been closed by the Tibetans, and Sikkim was still an unknown quantity, so the British decided to try to breathe life into the 1792 trade agreement with Nepal. Aware of the Gurkhas' distrust of Englishmen, the company dispatched Abdul Kadir Khan, a Moslem holy man and former member of the Kirkpatrick mission. In addition to sounding out commercial possibilities, he was also to press for permission for a British Resident in Kathmandu. Kadir was received in the capital in 1795 and produced a detailed report on the commercial relations of Nepal. But permission to establish a Residency was not forthcoming.

The death of Prithvi Narayan was followed by a prolonged period of complex political rivalry in Nepal, as different factions of the ruling family vied for superiority. This factional rivalry provided an opportunity for the East India Company to press again for improved relations and commercial advantages. In 1801 a treaty was signed on behalf of the company by Captain William Knox. This treaty provided for a British Residency in Kathmandu, and Knox, who had been a member of the Kirkpatrick expedition, became the first Resident.

Knox was well received initially, but political turbulence in the city led to a change of heart on the part of the government there. His Residency harassed and hampered, Knox was forced to leave in 1803, after only a year in office; and the 1801 Treaty, now a dead letter, was formally terminated by Britain in 1804.

During Knox's brief Residency, Charles Crawford, who was in charge of the military escort, used his time to produce some important surveys of the area. He calculated the latitude and longitude of Kathmandu and produced a large-scale map of the Kathmandu valley, correcting the earlier observations of Kirkpatrick. He was also the first to survey from the hills surrounding the valley and show the great height of the Nepal Himalayas. Finally, he drew up a small-scale map of the whole country, based on information provided to him by native travelers.[8]

After the abrogation of the 1801 Treaty, Anglo-Nepalese relations continued to deteriorate. An official British document described these relations as consisting "entirely of unavailing remonstrances against aggressions on the frontier of British territory throughout its entire length."[9] The Gurkhas not only pressed against the British frontier on the south, but intruded into Sikkim on the east and extended their control west from the river Kali up to the Sutlej. With the Gurkhas now exercising their authority over the territories of Kumaon and Garhwal, they were able to close most of these areas to the British. But occasionally a brief entry could be achieved. In 1808 Robert Colebrook, the surveyor-general of Bengal, obtained permission from the governor-general to send a small party to explore the source of the Ganges. This expedition, under Lieutenant Webb and Hyder Young Hearsey, reached the source of the eastern branch of the Ganges at Badrinath and obtained a good survey of the upper Ganges before being called back by the Gurkhas and detained. The Gurkhas refused permission for a further expedition to Lake Manasarowar, but Webb was able to visit Kumaon again, taking observations of the heights of several mountains. From these observations he calculated the height of Dhaulagiri as 26,862 feet, a figure denounced as laughable by many geographers outside India, who still believed that the Andes were the world's highest range.[10]

Hyder Young Hearsey, this time traveling with William Moorcroft, slipped into Tibet in 1812. On their return, the two were arrested and detained in Kumaon. Although neither was a surveyor, some useful information was acquired. The following year, a British surveyor was allowed into the area north of Dehra Dun.

The main area of Anglo-Nepalese friction was along the terai. This came to a head after the Gurkhas crossed the border in 1811 and occupied land in British India. When the Gurkhas refused to accept an ultimatum and evacuate these and other disputed areas, war was declared in 1814. The British attacked in four columns, two of which made little progress, but eventually Sir David Ochterlony, campaigning west of the Kali River, forced the capitulation of the main Gurkha army early in 1815. The Treaty of Segauli was signed later that year, but the Nepalese then refused to ratify it. Ochterlony advanced on Kathmandu, and the treaty was finally ratified in 1816. By the provisions of the treaty, the boundaries of Nepal were fixed by the river Kali in the west and the Mechi in the east. To the west of the Kali, the British annexed Kumaon (giving British India a common border with Tibet for the first time) and returned other territories to their former rulers. Territory to the east of the Mechi and part of the terai were returned to Sikkim. Most of the terai was ceded to Britain, or to the kingdom of Oudh, although the British soon returned the bulk of theirs to Nepal. At the time that this was done, it was agreed that both sides would appoint boundary commissioners to establish "a straight line of frontier" between Britain and Nepal along the terai. The Treaty of Segauli also called for "accredited Ministers" to be exchanged, upgraded from the "confidential person" referred to in the 1801 agreement.

The most important postwar Resident for several decades was Brian Hodgson, who first went to Kathmandu as assistant to Edward Gardner in 1820. He spent almost all of the next twenty-three years in Nepal, becoming Resident in 1833. During his period of office he produced a prodigious amount of scholarship on the country, including details of its trade and trading routes with Tibet, China, and Central Asia. Little of this information, however, was geographical, although Hodgson was occasionally permitted the rare privilege of being allowed to travel beyond the confines of the Kathmandu valley.

The Nepalese continued to avoid close relations of any kind with the British, allowing no visitors into the country except for the Resident and his small entourage. Settlement of the boundary question proceeded at a snail's pace. The terai frontier with Oudh was not demarcated until the early 1830s, and that with British India some years later. The surveying of the surrounding territory, since it did not depend on the good will of the Nepalese, met with more success. The terai was mapped from 1816 onwards, and the eastern border of Nepal in 1817. The survey of Kumaon began in 1815, even before the Treaty of Segauli was signed, and was completed in 1821. One of the surveyors did attempt to enter Tibet but was stopped by Chinese officials.[11] It was during this survey that Nanda Devi was shown to be the tallest mountain of the Kumaon Himalayas, at 25,645 feet.

Meanwhile, triangulation of India was continuing unabated, and in 1840 the surveyor-general, George Everest, requested permission for his surveyors to intrude into Nepal so as to link the northern ends of the north-south meridional chains. Permission was not granted, and it was left to Everest's successor, Andrew Waugh, to link the chains along the British side of the terai between 1846 and 1855. During this survey, Waugh commented that "the lofty snow peaks situated north of Nepal are the most stupendous pinnacles of the globe. Their heights and relative elevations are therefore most interesting desiderata."[12] The surveyors did what they could by observing the distant peaks from the southern border of Nepal, but even this was possible for only a few weeks in the autumn because of the generally hazy atmosphere. Nevertheless, the position of Kanchenjunga, on the Sikkim-Nepal border, was fixed in the late 1840s, and that of Mount Everest shortly thereafter. As for a map of Nepal, the deputy surveyor-general produced one in 1855, based on the best available data, but said of it that it could not "pretend to a geographical performance of even ordinary accuracy or value."[13]

Jung Bahadur came to power as prime minister of Nepal in 1846, a position which he retained for thirty-one years. He improved relations with India, cemented by a visit to England in 1850. From a better neighbor, stopping attempts to exploit British problems in India, Nepal moved to a reliable ally at the time of the Indian Mutiny, lending troops to assist the British in regaining control over the rebels. As a reward, all the remaining portions of the terai annexed by Britain in 1815 which had not been returned in 1816 were restored to Nepal in 1860. The country remained a closed land, however. Waugh tried again to get surveyors into Nepal in 1860, to clear up questions of the identities of some peaks, but without success.[14] The movements of the Resident in Kathmandu were still restricted, with only some slight relaxation after 1865. Nepal stayed wary of British preeminence in India, so that Sir Richard Temple was led to remark, at the time of his visit to Kathmandu in 1876, "nothing, however, will dissuade the Nepalis from the belief that topographical surveys, geological examinations, and botanical collections, are either the precursors of political aggression, or else lead to complications which end in annexation."[15]

Occasionally, the curtain was lifted. The German scientist Hermann Schlagintweit received permission to proceed to Kathmandu in 1856. He spent a few weeks in the area in 1857 (the same year that his brother Adolph was murdered near Kashgar) and made some good drawings. Although he was no surveyor, he nevertheless took many observations, from which he claimed to have fixed the locations of a number of peaks in the Nepal Himalayas, locations which were eventually shown to be inaccurate by the Survey of India, but not until 1903 when the Nepalese allowed Captain Henry Wood to survey the principal peaks and discover their names.[16]

By 1870, British firsthand information on the geography of Nepal was still almost entirely limited to frontier surveys (except to the north, where no official surveys were possible) and to the routes between India and the Kathmandu valley. A few additional areas had been visited by Brian Hodgson, and the naturalist Sir Joseph Hooker had penetrated the northeast corner of Nepal from Sikkim in 1848. As one member of the Kathmandu Residency wrote in the early 1870s: "the country, except for twenty miles round the capital, is as unknown to Europeans as it was fifty years ago."[17] Nor was this situation likely to improve radically, given the prevailing attitudes of the Nepalese. Daniel Wright, Residency surgeon in Kathmandu for ten years, described Nepal as "a country where every enquiry made by a European is viewed with the most jealous suspicion, where the collection of statistics is looked on as mere folly, and where, above all, Baron Münchausen himself would have been considered a marvel of accuracy and truthfulness."[18]

Under the circumstances of the time, the only way to get at least a rough idea of the topography of Nepal was to do it secretly, by using the Indian pundits. This had started with the early exploration of the Singh cousins in 1865. But at that time Nepal was just a transit area on the way to Tibet. By 1870, the target was Nepal itself.

Hari Ram

Montgomerie's line of exploration beyond the Indian frontiers ran from Gartok in western Tibet to Lake Manasarowar, and then along the course of the Tsangpo River to Lhasa. Nain Singh and others had opened out large tracts of territory in Tibet to the north of this line. The task of Hari Ram was to investigate the territory lying inside the main line of exploration, and to provide links between this line and points already mapped in India. The connecting links of particular interest to Montgomerie were through territory in northeastern Nepal and to the southwest of Lhasa, in the triangle between Darjeeling, Shigatse, and Mount Everest.

Very little is known about Hari Ram, who also went by the code names M.H. and No. 9. Like many Pundits, he was from Kumaon,[19] a Hindu, and he entered the service of the Survey of India in 1868.[20] The first exploratory work that can be definitely attributed to Hari Ram was in 1871, but it was probably he who was responsible for an expedition to the north of Mount Everest in 1868. As Kenneth Mason notes, virtually all of Hari Ram's subsequent journeys were in that area.[21] He was able to get behind Mount Everest, that is to the northern or Tibetan side, before being apprehended by Tibetan officials about fifty miles northwest of the mountain. The officials forced him to leave Tibet, but not before he had taken observations for height and latitude. He was able to provide some details of the Himalayan watershed and on the nature of the peaks that lay out of sight behind the ranges visible from India. Hari Ram made a route survey of 1,190 miles (marching to Everest 640 miles along one route, and returning by a different one 550 miles long), which it was possible to connect to points made in the course of other surveys.[22] The success of this venture led Montgomerie to dispatch him to the same area three years later.[23]

Hari Ram left Darjeeling in the summer of 1871 and passed through Sikkim, following in part the same route as Hooker in 1848 (Map 7). But on trying to enter Tibet, he was detained by officials who refused to let him continue, on the grounds that no one knew who he was and that he was unable to provide a satisfactory reason for proceeding into Tibet. Luckily for Hari Ram, he was able to ingratiate himself with a Sikkimese official, whose wife was ill. Montgomerie always provided his agents with a supply of medicines, and Hari Ram also had with him a Hindi translation of a medical text. He matched up the symptoms with the treatment in the book and prepared the appropriate drugs. Then, as Montgomerie said, he "awaited the result in not a little trepidation." To his astonishment, the woman made a rapid recovery, and her husband provided Hari Ram with a companion to vouch for him along the border. The pair crossed the Tipta La in eastern Nepal (16,700 feet) and were allowed to continue into Tibet, although Hari Ram's baggage was searched. Following the eastern branch of the Arun, he discovered a large lake, about which Montgomerie had heard, but which was not marked on any known map. Continuing in a northeasterly direction, he reached Shigatse on 17 September, where he stayed until 29 September. He then left the city to the southwest, by a different route.[24] After passing the great Sakya monastery, he reached the Dingri Maidan, a level plain at about thirteen thousand feet above sea level, where the Gurkhas had been defeated by the Chinese in 1792. The only town was Dingri, perched on a small hill, which served as a center on the trade route from Lhasa to Kathmandu across the Kuti pass.[25]

Fearful of being trapped in Nepal by the winter snow, Hari Ram headed for the passes into Nepal. The best pass would have been through Kirong, but only officials were permitted to use it. So he took the difficult, and at times hair-raising, Kuti pass, sixty miles west of Everest, through which a branch of the Kosi ran. At one point the path ran along a perpendicular rock face and was constructed of iron pegs driven into the side of the chasm, across which were laid slabs of stone covered with earth. On a path often only nine inches wide, a false step meant hurtling to one's death in the river, which tore through the ravine 1,500 feet below.

Hari Ram arrived safely in Kathmandu in January 1872 and from there returned to Darjeeling. In the course of his explorations he therefore became one of the first people to make a complete circuit of Mount Everest, though at such a distance that Everest itself was always obscured by closer peaks.[26]

Montgomerie was able to conclude that Hari Ram's pacing and observations were all reliable, except his measurement for altitudes. His larger thermometers had all broken, and he had been forced to use a smaller and less accurate model. This expedition of "No. 9" had shed new light on thirty thousand square miles of largely unexplored territory. In particular, new positions had been located on the Himalayan watershed, and much had been discovered with respect to the role played in the mountain drainage system by the Arun and Kosi rivers. Furthermore, his route survey of 844 miles represented territory largely new to modern geography.

Montgomerie errs, though, when he speaks of Hari Ram's route through Tibet to Nepal as never having "been even seen by an European." The paths of Grueber, d'Orville, and Desideri had all preceded and overlapped, at least in part, that of Hari Ram.

The third exploration of Hari Ram was probably one of the last, if not the last, of all the pundit explorations to be personally directed by Montgomerie. Hari Ram collected his surveying instruments and instructions for his route at the GTS headquarters in Dehra Dun in the spring of 1873.[27] Montgomerie left for England early that year. Before proceeding into Nepal, Hari Ram visited his home in Kumaon. Unfortunately, there was an outbreak of cholera in the village, which led to the death of his wife. He himself was ill for two months.[28]

The pundit started his route survey at Pithoragarh, presumably his home village, on 1 July 1873, once more posing as a physician. He was accom-

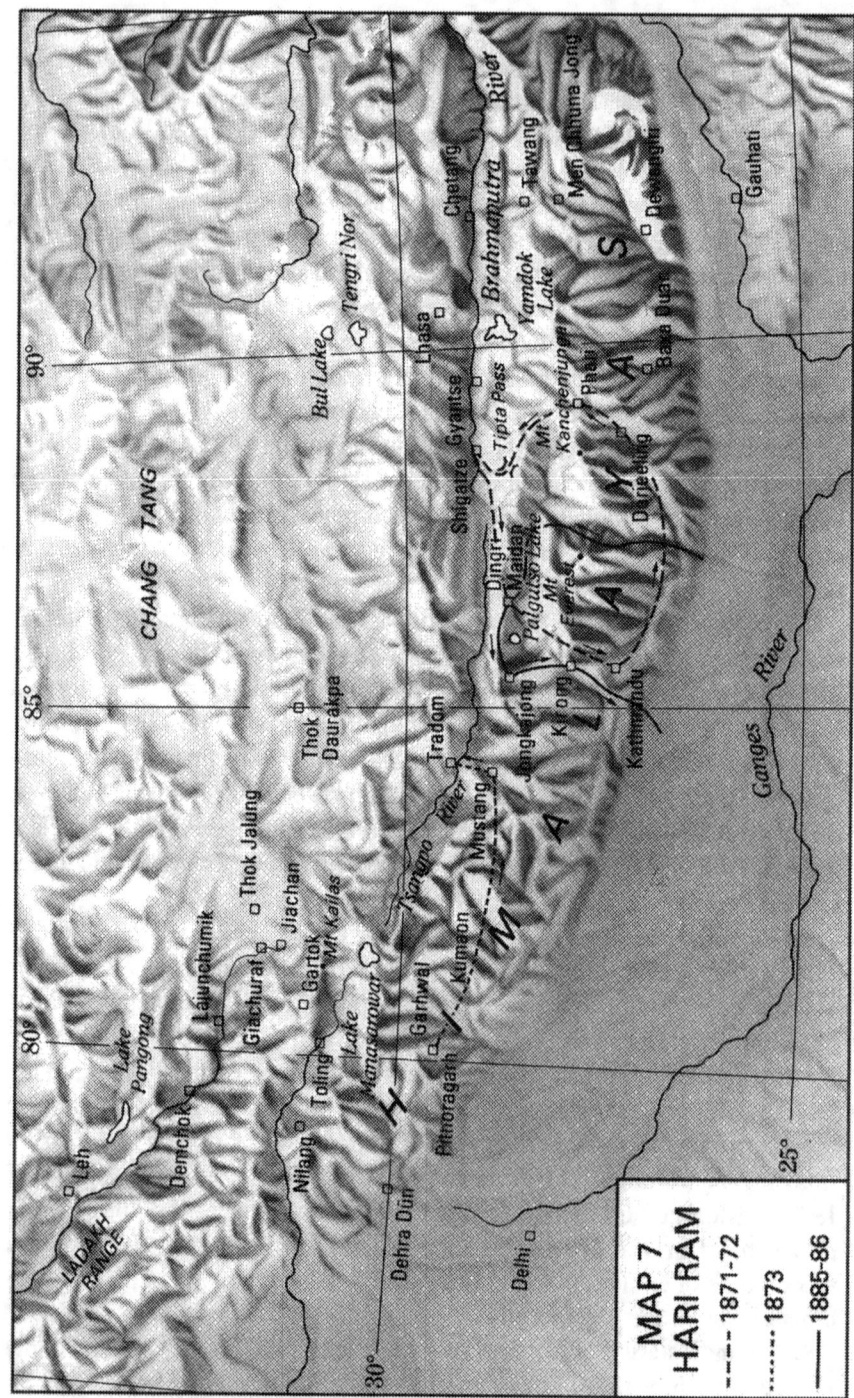

MAP 7
HARI RAM
----- 1871-72
······ 1873
——— 1885-86

panied by one or two servants. His route took him northeast to the Nepal border, marked by the river Kali. There were no customs posts or officials to impede his progress, but the river itself was a formidable obstacle. A single rope spanned the water, and the usual method called for travelers to hold on by hands and legs and carry their loads on their chests. Hari Ram admitted he "had no nerve for it" and so had a sling made, in which he was pulled across.

From now on the pundit pursued a southeasterly course, crossing rivers at right angles to their direction of flow and remaining parallel to the Himalayas. He crossed the Karnali on 6 August by means of a rope bridge two hundred feet long, and reached Jumla a few days later. In Jumla he received permission to visit the border area of Mustang, lying to the northeast on the Tibetan frontier. After making a short detour to visit the shrine at Muktinath, he arrived in Mustang on 13 September.[29] Hari Ram described the raja's palace and gave details of the commerce of Mustang, which was a center for trade between Lhasa and Nepal and, to some degree, India. The raja was under instructions from Jung Bahadur in Kathmandu to let no one (apart from the authorized traders of Mustang) across the border into Tibet. Hari Ram nevertheless succeeded in obtaining a pass, though by what means is not known. The pundit proceeded into Tibet and marched northward, crossing the Tsangpo and arriving at the monastery of Tradom on 23 September, thus linking his route survey with that of Nain Singh. Here he was detained by suspicious officials, who locked him up for the night and refused to take account of his claim that he was a physician on his way to Lhasa. Montgomerie was rather irked about this and blamed Hari Ram for not getting further east down the river onto the Dingri Maidan.[30] This is a clear indication that Montgomerie's instructions were for Hari Ram to return to the area of his earlier travels.

The following morning, the pundit was put under armed guard and escorted to the frontier, and so began his return journey to Mustang "with great reluctance and under threats of personal violence."

Hari Ram then followed the course of the Gandak River until it reached India. The results of his expedition were rather disappointing, as far as his lack of success in Tibet went. They were also overshadowed, when published in the *GTS Report for 1873-74*, by Kishen Singh's exploration of Tengri Nor (1872) and by Trotter's preliminary report of explorations made by the Forsyth Mission to Kashgar.

Nevertheless, although not exciting, Hari Ram's surveys were useful. Walker reported that the route from Pithoragarh to Jumla was new ground. From Jumla to Tradom via Muktinath was "over ground of which rude information was already forthcoming, but it required additions and rectifications," and the route through Nepal down the Gandak River was "practically new also, and . . . a useful contribution to our knowledge of the geography of the Nepaulese Dominions."[31] The "rude information," which Hari Ram was able to supplement, must have come in part from the travels of Mani Singh, after he separated from Nain Singh in Kathmandu in 1865, returning to Kumaon through Nepal, and in part from data provided by the companion of Kishen Singh, apprehended in Tibet in 1868 but allowed to proceed into Nepal and on to Muktinath.

During his explorations of 1871-72, Hari Ram had learned in Dingri that a good road ran from there to a fort at Jongka, and then into Nepal at the frontier town of Kirong, and down to Kathmandu. In his report, Montgomerie had said that this route was a "desideratum," as was the size and location of the Palgutso Lake, which lay between Dingri and Jongka fort.[32] Hari Ram had discovered, however, that this route was for the use of officials only. In 1880, the Survey of India made a further attempt to explore this area, sending a pundit into Nepal with instructions to proceed to Dingri, and then "to go to Katmandu from Dingri by some unexplored route."[33] It is not known why Hari Ram was not used at this time. Instead, the survey employed a Hindu called Sukh Darshan Singh and known by the code name G.S.S. He proved to be unreliable, and this was to be his only exploration.[34]

G.S.S. left Darjeeling on 24 May 1880, entered Nepal and marched up to the river Arun. He crossed over into Tibet by a fifteen-thousand-foot pass in mid-July. Once across the border, however, G.S.S. was refused permission to go to Dingri. Since he did not have Hari Ram's talent for persuading officials to go along with his wishes, G.S.S. remained where he was until October. He then returned to India in early 1881, traveling through Kathmandu, even though he had been expressly ordered not to visit the Nepalese capital unless he had first been to Dingri. At best, this expedition provided the Survey of India with a few more notes on routes in Nepal.[35]

Four years later, and twelve years after his last exploration, Hari Ram was reemployed and sent off in the Survey's third, and ultimately successful, attempt to gain information on the routes between Dingri, Jongka fort, and Kathmandu.

In March 1885 he was reappointed to the ranks of the permanent native establishment of Trans-Himalayan explorers, at a salary of Rs. 45 a month. His salary started as of 1 April 1885.[36] He received his orders on 12 April. They instructed him to proceed north through Nepal, following the Dudh Kosi river, and then over the border to Dingri. From Dingri he was to turn west to Jongka fort, then back across the Nepalese frontier at Kirong. At Kirong, he was to head west again, meeting one of the tributaries of the Gandak river, which he was to follow to India.[37]

Hari Ram went first of all to Kumaon from survey headquarters in Dehra Dun and hired four men (one from Kumaon and three Nepalis) to accompany him. As on previous occasions, he traveled in the disguise of a physician and carried both Indian and European medicines. Because of illness, the party did not cross the boundary of Nepal with India until 11 July. The crossing was made in the southern part of Nepal, southeast of Kathmandu. The Dudh Kosi River was soon located, and the party made good progress following it north and arrived at the fort of Khumbu, residence of the governor of the province, in mid-August.

The journey so far had been a relatively easy one, marred only by a bad fall taken by one of the men, which had broken Hari Ram's single boiling-point thermometer, even though for security (and secrecy), it had been packed inside a hollow walking stick.

The governor, however, was adamant that he would not allow them to proceed north over the Pangu pass, alleging that it had never been crossed by any "Hindustani or Gurkha." Hari Ram settled in for a lengthy stay, and once again his luck with medicine stood him in good stead. He cured the governor's daughter-in-law of goiter, and thus her husband, who was about to leave for Tibet with a caravan, became indebted to him. This proved to be the key factor in the success of Hari Ram's mission. The governor eventually consented to Hari Ram's joining his son's party, and they set off in late September.

The crossing was by a very difficult pass, the Pangu La, which the pundit could only estimate at about twenty thousand feet. Although Mount Everest was hidden from view, he was only fifteen miles from the peak, the closest that a trained observer had ever come to it.[38] The group eventually arrived at Dingri in early October. It was three weeks before the head official, or *daipon*, at Dingri returned, and then Hari Ram learned that the road to Jongka fort was still reserved for officials only, just as it had been on his last visit in 1872. The pundit, however, managed to persuade the *daipon* that he was a native of Jumla in western Nepal and that he needed to return there as soon as possible by the shortest route, which was through Jongka. The *daipon* agreed to let Hari Ram take this route, provided that the governor's son accompanied him and that local guides were hired at each village along the route, thus ensuring that the travelers should not deviate from it. The party set off on 25 October.

They passed the Palgutso lake, estimated to be nine miles long and four miles wide, and reached the fort at Jongka at the end of the month. The fort, about four hundred yards square, enclosed by a wall five feet thick and fifteen to twenty feet high, was the home of the district governor. At first, the governor would give permission for Hari Ram to enter Nepal only in the direction of Nubri, thus preventing him from following his instructions and taking the road through Kirong. Luckily, the road to Nubri was blocked by snow, and the governor succumbed to some generous gifts.

Bidding farewell to the son of the Khumbu governor, Hari Ram left Jongka on 3 November and passed through Kirong without difficulty three days later. After some side explorations in Nepal, he followed the Gandak river to Tribeni and reentered India on 13 January 1886.

This exploration was a successful and valuable one, marred only by the pundit's inability to measure altitudes. Hari Ram was not only a skilled surveyor, but also a good observer of the local scene, and his report contains many details of the commerce, government, and flora and fauna of the area through which he passed. He filled in the gap in the map of southern Tibet between Dingri, Jongka, and Kirong. He also traced the Dudh Kosi, which separates Mount Everest from Gaurisankar, to its source, for a total of 420 miles of new ground in all, and confirming observations of 100 miles that had been surveyed previously.

Apart from the Kathmandu valley, which had been well surveyed by British Residents, the only other way of mapping Nepal from inside the country itself was by the use of native agents such as Hari Ram.[39] Otherwise, reconnaissance surveys made from towers erected along the Indian side of the border had to be resorted to. Although by the late 1870s virtually the whole of Nepal had been surveyed in this way, it was admitted that the maps obtained in this manner were fragmentary and imperfect, although the triangulation to fixed peaks did enable GTS officers to correct some of the measurements of the pundits.[40]

The renewed interest on the part of the GTS in the surveying of Nepal and the region of southern Tibet around Dingri would have had, if it had been made public, adverse effects on another policy of the Indian government. At the same time that Hari Ram was exploring, another pundit, Sarat Chandra Das, was in Peking as part of a British mission headed by Colman Macaulay, an official of the Bengal government. Macaulay's task was to persuade the Chinese to issue passports for his mission to enter Tibet, under the Chefoo Convention of 1876. Not only were the areas of Hari Ram's explorations quite distant from Macaulay's projected routes into Tibet, but his discovery as a British agent, engaged in the clandestine mapping of Tibet, would have quickly undermined all Macaulay's endeavors.[41]

Rinzing Namgyal

Rinzing Namgyal was the only explorer, apart from Hari Ram, of whose work it could be said that a substantial proportion was in Nepal, although in his case it was confined to the extreme eastern part of that country, and particularly Kanchenjunga on the Sikkim-Nepal border.

The present state of Sikkim has an area of about 2,800 square miles. It is bounded on the south and southeast by the rivers Tista and Rangit, which form the frontier between Sikkim and India. In other directions, Sikkim is surrounded by high ranges, which define its horseshoe-shaped boundaries with Nepal, Tibet, and Bhutan. From these ranges, spurs penetrate in a southerly direction, dividing the country with deep valleys and high ridges. Most of Sikkim is composed of snowcapped mountains without permanent human habitation.[42]

Kanchenjunga is the dominant peak of the mountain ranges bordering Sikkim. Surveyor-General Andrew Waugh received unofficial permission to enter Sikkim during 1848-49 and made the first estimate of the height of the main peak, which at 28,176 feet "far exceeds what has hitherto been conjectured."[43] Kanchenjunga was then believed to be the highest mountain in the world. It was soon displaced from this position by Mount Everest, but for much of the nineteenth century it was not clear whether Kanchenjunga was the world's second- or third-highest peak, vying for that honor with K^2 (Mount Godwin-Austen). Kanchenjunga is now known to be number three, at 28,208 feet. On a clear day, its granite mass, topped by snow, was clearly visible from the British hill station of Darjeeling, less than one hundred miles distant.

The British connection with the area came about primarily as a result of Gurkha expansion into Sikkim in the late eighteenth century. After the defeat of Nepal in 1816, the British returned to Sikkim that territory previously annexed by the Nepalese. This move was sealed by the Treaty of Titalia (1817), by which Britain guaranteed the security of Sikkim. Britain also obtained the right to trade in Sikkim up to the Tibetan border, although this route, crossing into the Chumbi valley of Tibet from southeastern Sikkim, was not exploited until the latter half of the century.

In 1835 the small village of Dorjé-ling was ceded by the Sikkimese raja to the British as a sanatorium. The British were also now well placed to monitor internal developments in Sikkim. Situated only three hundred miles north of Calcutta, and renamed Darjeeling, the town became a popular resort offering relief from the summer heat of the plains. But because of its proximity to Tibet—the border was only thirty-five miles away—it also brought the British residents into contact with Tibetans and Tibetan culture, prompting further inquisitiveness about that closed land so close to hand.

This curiosity was not matched by a similar degree of interest on the Tibetan side. Furthermore, the Sikkimese rajas, heavily influenced by the wishes of the Tibetan government, continued to place obstacles in the way of British trade. Dr. Archibald Campbell, the superintendent of Darjeeling, reported in 1847 that the Sikkimese objected to Europeans entering their country, "even for recreation and exercise."[44] A crisis erupted in 1849 when Dr. Joseph Hooker, accompanied by Dr. Campbell, crossed over the border into Tibet. On their return, they were promptly arrested and manhandled by the Sikkimese. As a result, after some military maneuverings, Britain annexed the rest of the Sikkimese terai. In 1861 Britain imposed a treaty on Sikkim, making Britain the suzerain power in matters of foreign policy. The British were also granted the right to build a road through Sikkimese territory up to the Tibetan border.

But the raja seemed no more anxious than before to help promote trade between Tibet and India. British officials were of the belief that it was the Chinese who were blocking the development of trade and that their obstructions could best be removed if direct discussions could take place with the Tibetans. Accordingly, in 1873, John (later Sir John) Edgar, the deputy commissioner for Darjeeling, was sent on a mission to the Tibetan frontier. Although Edgar did have inconclusive talks with some Tibetan representatives, they did not allow him to enter Tibet, and fortified the passes to dissuade him from attempting to force his way in.[45]

Hopes for increased trade still continued, backed by the desire for political influence in Tibet. A road was built from Darjeeling through Sikkim to the Jelap La (pass) leading to Tibetan territory in the Chumbi valley. In 1881 the railroad from Calcutta to Siliguri was extended up to Darjeeling.

With the signing of the Chefoo Convention with China in 1876, Britain obtained the right to send a mission to Lhasa. Following the Bhutanese attack on Phari in the Chumbi valley in 1883, which resulted in a decline in the existing trade across the border, the Indian government saw the opportunity to send another mission to the Tibetan border. Colman Macaulay, the Bengal Financial Secretary, headed the delegation, which met with Tibetan officials in Sikkim. These officials blamed the Chinese for the poor relations between Tibet and British India. Macaulay urged that the British authorities in Peking press for passports for his mission to enter Tibet, as approved by the Chefoo Convention. The British Legation in Peking was not convinced of the utility of the mission and doubted if the Chinese had the ability to ensure that the Tibetans would honor the passports. Accordingly, although passports were issued, the Macaulay mission was abandoned after the British annexation of Upper Burma in 1886, in partial compensation to China for the loss of sovereignty there.[46]

In the same year, however, the Tibetans sent troops into Sikkim and built a fort within sight of Darjeeling. In part, this was a response to the Macaulay mission, which they believed heralded a British invasion of Tibet. Negotiations to persuade the Tibetan soldiers to withdraw failed, and they were forcibly expelled from Sikkim by British troops in 1888.

Talks with the Chinese over Tibet produced the Sikkim-Tibet Convention of 1890, followed by a set of Trade Regulations signed in 1893. The frontier between Sikkim and Tibet was defined, and Sikkim became a British protected state. A trade mart was to be set up at Yatung in the Chumbi valley, with a resident British official.

Sikkim was therefore satisfactorily incorporated into the frontier system of British India. The same could not be said of Tibet. Under the terms of the Convention and the Trade Regulations, matters concerning Tibet had to be dealt with not by direct British-Tibetan contact, but through China. This would probably have been acceptable if China had been in a position to have its wishes carried out in Tibet. But China was not. The Tibetans, for example, consistently flouted the Trade Regulations. Chinese loss of imperial control over Tibet, and the growing power vacuum there, coupled with British alarm over the spread of Russian influence, was eventually to lead to the invasion of Tibet by the Younghusband Expedition of 1903-1904.

The interests of the Indian government in Sikkim were, geographically, mainly concentrated in the southeastern part of the country, through which ran the best trade route along the Darjeeling-Lhasa "highway," via the Chumbi valley. The curiosity of the Survey of India, however, was elsewhere, in the unexplored areas of the west and northwest, particularly around Kanchenjunga.

Rinzing Namgyal was the Indian pundit who made the most contributions to British knowledge of the Kanchenjunga area. His family name was Kunlay Gyatso Laden La, but in the official records he was usually code named R.N. Born in the 1850s into a Sikkimese lama family, he was the brother-in-law of the explorer Ugyen Gyatso (U.G.) and the great-great-nephew of the lama who founded the monastery on the Observatory Hill in Darjeeling in the mid-eighteenth century.[47] R.N. was educated at the Bhutia Boarding School in Darjeeling, where the headmaster was Sarat Chandra Das.[48] It was probably Das who was instrumental in introducing him to the Survey of India.

After the departure of Trotter for the Diplomatic Service in 1875, the recruitment and organization of the pundits had been taken over by Lieutenant Henry Charles Baskerville Tanner and Captain Henry John Harman. They worked under the direction of Colonel Walker, who was surveyor-general of India from 1878 until his retirement in 1883.

Harman had been in India only a few months when Montgomerie recommended him for appointment to the Great Trigonometrical Survey in 1872. He was soon surveying in Kumaon and Garhwal and was then active in Assam, attached to the Daphla Expedition (1874-75) and then engaged in the exploration of the Miri Hills (1877-78).[49] Harman had been in Darjeeling since 1878 and was in charge of the Darjeeling party of the Survey of India, responsible for the mapping of Sikkim and the Sikkim-Nepal boundary. He had tried personally to reach the area round Kanchenjunga in 1881 but had been unable to do so because of poor health.[50] When Lieutenant-Colonel Tanner returned from furlough on 1 November 1882, the Darjeeling party was handed over to him. Harman himself took sick leave and died shortly thereafter.

H.C.B. Tanner was an officer in the Bengal Infantry, which he joined in 1862. He was attached to the army during the Afghan campaigns of 1877-78 and in 1879 led a detachment of troops to Gilgit, to relieve the besieged Colonel Biddulph, resident British agent there. At the time of his appointment to the Darjeeling party, he was forty-seven years old. Tanner himself played a mainly indirect role in the mapping of Sikkim, most of the actual survey work being carried out by an assistant surveyor, W. Robert.

R.N. is first identified as being on survey work in 1879, by Sarat Chandra Das, who says that R.N. was at the head of a survey party in Sikkim which met Das returning from his first visit to Tibet.[51] Although Rinzing Namgyal did not accompany Robert on his surveying expedition into Sikkim in 1881-82, he did so the following year, between October and December 1883. While on this survey, R.N. made an independent exploration of the Talung valley, the only valley in Sikkim which, according to Tanner, had never been visited by a European.[52] This survey completed the mapping of Sikkim, thus finishing the work begun by Hooker in an informal way in 1848.

During the spring and summer of 1884, R.N.'s activities shifted westward, when he accompanied Tanner on a journey to the area where the borders of British Kumaon, Tibet, and western Nepal met. From there, they hoped to gain more information on the Himalayan chain stretching along the Nepal-Tibet border.

The party crossed over into Tibet by the Lipu Lek pass but was stopped by Tibetan officials, who refused to allow them to cross the Karnali River.

On giving assurances that they would not do so, Tanner and R.N. were permitted to stay in the area for two days, sketching and observing. Tanner remarked to the suspicious Tibetan governor that the English "did not in the least desire to occupy such a bleak and comfortless land as theirs." "Bleak, do you call this?" the governor responded. "Why, you are now in the very garden of Tibet. If this you call barren, what would you say of other parts where there is literally nothing but rock and ice! Go back now to India, you have seen the most inviting part of our country, the rest is not worth a visit. We are not angry at your coming this once, but we never wish to see you again."[53]

With the expansion of British influence along the southern boundaries of the Himalayas, the Tibetans were becoming increasingly concerned about possible British occupation of Tibet. As a result, as Tanner remarked in his notes, the passes were more closely guarded, and it was no longer possible for a European to bribe officials. "The annexation of Burma," Tanner concluded, "is an event not likely to ease their minds."[54]

After a successful tour, R.N. and Tanner returned through Kumaon to Darjeeling. R.N.'s semi-independent work in Sikkim, together with his assistance in Kumaon and Tibet, had convinced Tanner that he was now ready to be deployed on a fully independent and secret expedition of his own. As a result, on 1 August 1884 R.N., who was described as being on loan from the Forest Department, was transferred to "the permanent native establishment of Trans-Himalayan Explorers" at a salary of Rs. 60 a month. When his exploration began in early October, this was increased to Rs. 100, and went back to Rs. 60 on his return.[55]

His task was to reconnoiter the last remaining unexplored area of Sikkim, to the north of Kanchenjunga, and to delineate the boundary there between Nepal and Tibet. Hooker's map showed only a blank area to the northwest of Kanchenjunga, but had on it the written information that "this country is said to present a very elevated rugged tract of lofty mountains sparingly snowed, uninhabitable by man or domestic animals."[56] The area had attracted few Europeans, as it lacked sport, was difficult to reach, and in part was barred from entry by Nepalese guards.[57]

The operation was directed by Tanner, in charge of the Darjeeling party, now more appropriately renamed the Himalayan party. R.N. and his companions encountered severe difficulties in the course of this expedition, which lasted from 2 October 1884 to 31 January 1885. At times they were trapped by snow and had to spend nights exposed to the elements, without food or fuel. Two of the party, including the leader, fell ill on the way back and died before reaching Darjeeling.

Nevertheless, despite these privations, R.N. succeeded in making the first complete circuit of Kanchenjunga and provided sketches of the mountain and of all the ridges and valleys surrounding it. His route in northeastern Nepal and northwestern Sikkim gave the first determination to the Survey of India of the boundary between those two countries and Tibet. R.N. was also able to correct some earlier observations made by William Robert and by his brother-in-law, Lama Ugyen Gyatso.[58] However, although Rinzing Namgyal had had considerable experience of surveying and was able to fix accurately the location of distant points, his knowledge of how to draw the topography of the areas he traversed was rudimentary. As a result, his map was imperfect.[59]

Within a year, R.N. was dispatched again, on another secret mission to try to discover whether the Tsangpo river of Tibet flowed into the Brahmaputra or the Irrawaddy. This mission, which was completed in 1886, and another mission on the northeast frontier of Assam in 1889 will be treated in chapter 8.

After the completion of the first of these two missions, in June 1886, the next record we have of R.N. is that he took leave for three months from 6 January 1887, after which he took up his surveying duties again in April.[60] Working again with Colonel Tanner, he surveyed western and central Nepal from tower stations of the Great Trigonometrical Survey located in the Indian plains, along the Nepalese border. In this way, R.N. and Tanner were able to extend the survey eastward to the Gandak River, covering an area of nearly twenty-six thousand square miles. High points could be fixed with reasonable accuracy, but, of course, the surveyors remained uninformed as to the course of the valleys between the mountains, relying for this information on the reports of their explorers. The work of R.N., Tanner, and others during the 1887-88 season completed the reconnaissance survey of Nepal from outside the boundaries, except for a small remaining area to the west of the Gandak.[61]

In 1899 an expedition under Douglas Freshfield made the first circuit of Kanchenjunga to be completed by Europeans. Tanner was due for retirement in 1900. R.N., who had probably been dropped from the active roster of trans-Himalayan explorers by this time, was described by Freshfield as the Kazi, or headman, of a Sikkimese village in the Tista valley. Freshfield knew of R.N.'s earlier exploits in the vicinity of Kanchenjunga and hired him, through the good offices of the district commissioner for Darjeeling, to accompany the expedition as a guide and surveyor.[62]

Freshfield seems to have had mixed views as to the character of R.N. At times he alludes to him very favorably, saying that he was "always to the front, and a capital walker,"[63] and "an energetic climber and intelligent man."[64] But on other occasions he is critical of R.N.'s work: "having during the tour had frequent opportunities of seeing the Surveyor at work, I am disposed to attribute some of the defects of his survey to his obvious predilection for sitting in a snug tent and filling in neat but somewhat subjective detail. Scrambling with his plane-table among rough ice and moraines, and out-of-door sketching were far less to his taste."[65]

Rinzing Namgyal was now middle-aged and perhaps could not scamper about as he had in his youth. As to the "defects of his survey," Freshfield generally held R.N. in high confidence. The expedition discovered and mapped large glaciers on the Nepalese flank of Kanchenjunga, never before seen by Europeans, which contradicted survey reports of the early 1880s that no glaciers existed. This error had already been pointed out by R.N. during his tour of the mountain in 1884-85. Unfortunately, he had not been properly instructed in the method of representing glaciers on a map, and Freshfield admitted that he had been confused by R.N.'s wormlike squiggles.

Another area of disagreement concerned the Jonsong pass, a very high and difficult pass just south of the border of Sikkim with Tibet. R.N. claimed to have crossed this pass in 1884, as did his brother-in-law, Ugyen Gyatso, and U.G.'s companion, Sarat Chandra Das, in 1879. But their observations and descriptions were different. Crossing the Jonsong La himself, Freshfield concluded that R.N. had indeed crossed the Jonsong, but that Ugyen Gyatso and Das must have taken another pass further to the east.

At some point R.N. made a visit to England, the only pundit ever to do so. Family tradition holds that he traveled with Sir Alfred Croft, the director of education for Bengal. While in England he met with Queen Victoria, and the occasion was commemorated by the presentation to him of a fine gold watch from Sir George Campbell, M.P., who had retired from India in 1874 as lieutenant-governor of Bengal. The watch is inscribed "To Kunlay Laden La from George Campbell on visit to Queen Victoria at St. James' Palace."[66] Both the watch and a signed photograph of the Queen are in the possession of Rinzing's descendants.

The last known reference to R.N.'s activities is in the book *The Exploration of Tibet,* by Graham Sandberg.[67] Sandberg was personally acquainted with Ugyen Gyatso and his wife and presumably knew her brother R.N. as well.[68] Sandberg recounts that when Mr. John Claude White, political officer in Sikkim, was deputed to visit Giagong on the Sikkim-Tibet border in June 1902, and to demarcate the boundary there, he was "accompanied by two experienced trained surveyors, Rinzing and Lobsang."[69] White, in his autobiography, has a chapter on the mission; but although he discusses surveying, he does not refer to any surveyor by name, and after this nothing further is heard of Rinzing Namgyal.

SEVEN
"A Hardy Son of Soft Bengal"

Babu Sarat Chandra Das was an Indian of a different order from the other pundits of the Survey of India. He was a highly educated and sophisticated man, who has been accurately described as a "traveller, and explorer . . . a linguist, a lexicographer, an ethnographer and an eminent Tibetologist."[1] Das also played an important diplomatic role during the Macaulay mission of 1885-86. When, in 1901, Kipling immortalized the pundits in *Kim,* the character of the secret agent Huree Chunder Mookerjee was most probably based on Das.[2]

Rather than coming from one of the hill peoples, accustomed to trading with Tibet, Das was born in the port town of Chittagong, Eastern Bengal, in 1849. He subsequently traveled to Calcutta and studied civil engineering at Presidency College. There he came into contact with Professor C.B. Clarke, an inspector of schools, and Alfred (later Sir Alfred) Croft, the director of public instruction. When the young Indian came down with malaria, it was Clarke who recommended him, at the age of twenty-five, for the position of headmaster at the newly established Bhutia Boarding School in Darjeeling. Das, pleased with the offer of such a responsible position and believing that the mountain air would be better for his health than the summer heat of Calcutta, accepted the post.

The school was opened in 1874 on the orders of Sir George Campbell, the lieutenant-governor of Bengal. The purpose of the school was to provide a good education to young Tibetan and Sikkimese boys resident in Sikkim or the Darjeeling area. The school also had another, less public, function. This objective was to train a cadre of personnel for use in Tibet. In a secret letter to Simla, Alfred Croft wrote that "the object of the school is to train up interpreters, geographers and explorers, who may be useful if at any future time Tibet is opened to the British."[3] John Edgar, the deputy commissioner of Darjeeling, while on his visit to the Sikkim border, spoke to Sikkimese officials in 1873 of plans to start the school, which he described as being "for the teaching of English Thibetan, and hill surveying."[4] The officials promised to send him some intelligent boys from prominent families. Lamas at the Pemionchi monastery in Sikkim also expressed an interest in learning surveying. Edgar was anxious to get at least one of the boys being educated at the monastery to Darjeeling before he became a lama.[5]

It was apparently the intention of the government to send the best graduates of the school on to Dehra Dun for more intensive training by the Survey of India in techniques of surveying and exploration. However, although a number of boys benefited from the education received at the school, only "two or three" ever went on to Dehra Dun.[6]

The Bhutia Boarding School does not seem to have been particularly successful, at least with respect to the training of the pundits. Das himself became its most famous associate. The Tibetan language teacher at the school, Lama Ugyen Gyatso, who had been hired by Edgar from the Pemionchi monastery, worked with Das on his explorations. The lama's brother-in-law, Rinzing Namgyal, was the only boy educated at the school known to have become an explorer.[7]

In April 1874, Das arrived in Darjeeling and was greeted by Edgar, who told him that the purpose of the school was to train Sikkimese boys in English so as to help promote trade with Tibet. Two years later, Edgar was to confide in Das that the school was also designed to train the boys in surveying, so that they could explore across the frontier. Das started to teach the older boys surveying, which presumably had been part of the curriculum when he was in civil engineering college in Calcutta.[8]

Das was soon active in recruiting boys from the village headmen and landowners of Sikkim, and from among Tibetan boys in Darjeeling. By August, fourteen students were enrolled, and Das had to learn Tibetan to be able to communicate with them. The following year, both Sir Richard Temple, the new lieutenant-governor of Bengal, and the viceroy, Lord Northbrook, visited the school and declared their approval of the progress being made. Temple hinted of things to come when he spoke at the school of "the great work of exploration in an unknown country which was before us."[9]

In 1876, Das went with some of the boys in his charge to Sikkim on a holiday visit. There he visited the home monastery of his colleague Lama Ugyen Gyatso. On his return to Darjeeling, Edgar loaned him some books, among which was the newly published account by Clements Markham of the travels of George Bogle and Thomas Manning to Tibet.[10] This changed Das's life. "I read the book," he related, "over and over again. It kindled in my mind a burning desire for visiting Tibet and for exploring its unknown tracts."[11] Edgar also revealed that one of the objectives in establishing the school was to train "some intelligent Bhutea lads" for trans-Himalayan exploration, and that was why Das had been hired. As a result, Das reported, "I now commenced giving lessons in surveying to the higher class boys."[12]

Das also energetically pursued his study of Tibetan and eventually applied to the Bengal government for permission to sit the language examinations in the Bhutia and Lepcha dialects of Sikkim. Although Edgar supported his application, it was rejected. Writing on behalf of the government, Colman Macaulay said that "the Examination referred to, is not open to the officers of the Subordinate Educational service."[13] Macaulay nevertheless praised Das for his diligence, and awarded him a grant of Rs. 300 to cover the costs of language study in Sikkim.

Das's second journey to Sikkim had taken place in 1877 when, accompanied by his younger brother and Ugyen Gyatso, he visited a number of monasteries, including Pemionchi.[14] Through his study of Tibetan Buddhism, Das's desire to visit Tibet and to see Lhasa grew apace. In early 1878 he confided in Ugyen Gyatso that visiting Tibet was uppermost in his mind.[15]

To cross the border into Tibet required the permission of the Bengal government. Das's first attempt to gain permission, from the new deputy commissioner at Darjeeling, Major Herbert Lewin, was dismissed out of hand, Lewin characterizing the idea as absurd and preposterous.[16] Rebuffed, but far from disheartened, Das decided to take a different initiative.

He conceived of the idea of suggesting to his assistant at the Bhutia Boarding School, Ugyen Gyatso, that he, the lama, should make a visit to Lhasa and to the great monastery of Tashilhunpo near Shigatse, the seat of the Tashi (or Panchen) Lama. Ugyen Gyatso would travel as a representative of his monastery at Pemionchi, and would carry the appropriate tribute. While in Tibet under this pretext, he would attempt to obtain for Das an invitation and a passport to enter Tibet. The lama agreed to the mission, provided that he would be given leave from the school, and funds to cover his expenses.[17]

When Alfred Croft arrived in Darjeeling in early March to inspect the school, Das told him of his plans to obtain a passport for Tibet and asked for Croft's help and support. Croft was unenthusiastic, but Das persevered and wrote Croft in mid-March, saying that he had read of the signing of the Chefoo Convention between Britain and China, authorizing a mission to Lhasa, and that if he could study Tibetan in Tibet, then he would be of use to the proposed mission as secretary. He also confided in Croft that if his request for a passport was refused, then he planned to make a secret visit to Tibet, disguised as a Nepalese merchant. Croft responded later that month. He made no promises about the British mission to Tibet, beyond commenting that if there ever was one, and if Das had indeed studied Tibetan, then he would be an obvious candidate for the post of secretary. The primary question was how to proceed to obtain permission from the government of

India for Das's visit to Tibet, and here Croft said that it would be best to await news of the fate of Ugyen Gyatso's visit to Tibet. Croft said that he would back Das, but that he was very dubious about the chances of getting a passport, given the difficulties Nain Singh had had with the Tibetans.[18]

In May 1878, the lama left for Tibet. To Croft's surprise, when he returned in September, the lama carried with him a passport issued by the Tashi Lama. The lama had requested a passport in Lhasa, but without success. In Tashilhunpo, however, he met with the prime minister to the Tashi Lama. The prime minister was interested in learning Hindu, the language of the native country of the Buddha.[19] The lama suggested Das as a teacher, and the passport was granted with the permission of the Tashi Lama, who added his name to the list of theology students at Tashilhunpo. The passport provided for assistance with ponies, baggage animals, and food and accommodations for the journey of Das and Ugyen Gyatso into and out of Tibet.[20]

With the passport in hand, permission from the Indian government to make the journey came quickly. Sir Ashley Eden reported in October that he had obtained this authority from the viceroy, Lord Lytton. It is likely that the British had in mind not only the long-term goal of establishing better relations with Tibet, but also dealing with the current problem of counteracting the hostile influence of opposition members of the Sikkimese ruling family, resident in Tibet.[21]

Das was replaced as headmaster in January 1879 and given a fictitious (although salaried) appointment as deputy inspector of schools for British Sikkim. In fact, he took leave and proceeded to Calcutta with Ugyen Gyatso. There, under the orders of Tanner and Harman, Das's rusty knowledge of surveying, dating from his student days in engineering school, was brought up to date, and adapted for secret exploration by Nain Singh.[22] Nain Singh instructed both Das and the lama in the use of the sextant, prismatic compass, and boiling-point thermometer. No mention is made of instruction in the pacing of distance and counting paces by beads, and no pacing of distances was done on their subsequent journeys.[23]

Croft wrote to Colonel Walker, now promoted to surveyor-general of India as of January 1878, listing the equipment which Das said he needed. "If you will provide him with these," Croft wrote, "he might possibly be able to do some work that your Dept. might find useful."[24] This indicates that Das was not traveling primarily as a pundit of the Survey of India. Through his own interest in Tibet and its religion, he had become motivated to travel there, and had made his own arrangements to make this possible. Approval of the visit was granted for political reasons. In any case, the request came, not from the Survey of India, but through Croft and the Bengal Education Department. Only after everything was approved was Das handed over to the Survey of India in order to maximize the value of his journey.

Sarat Chandra Das and Lama Ugyen Gyatso, together with a guide and two coolies, set out from Darjeeling in June 1879 (Map 8). They were code named S.C.D., and U.G. or the Lama. In addition to the surveying equipment, they took with them a pair of binoculars, a camera and a manual of photography, and Rs. 150 in cash.[25] The equipment provided also included two guns and two umbrellas. Das was not quite thirty years old. He apparently obtained permission from his wife to go to Tibet by telling her that it was just a few miles from Darjeeling.[26]

The party traveled due north into Sikkim, reaching Jongri on 17 June, and then turning northwest toward the Nepal border.[27] At each night's halt, Das boiled water and then measured its temperature to give their altitude. He also tried, weather permitting, to take sextant observations of the stars. U.G. was delegated to use the compass and take bearings on the march.

Two days after leaving Jongri, they crossed the frontier into Nepal without being apprehended. Several days were spent at the Gyunsar monastery, which was of the same Red Hat sect as U.G.'s home monastery at Pemionchi. The monks mistook Das for a fellow lama, and he did not disabuse them. The Gyunsar lamas were most helpful, providing new coolies and a guide named Phurchung to assist them on their journey, but the travelers left the monastery hurriedly on receipt of news that the passes were about to be closed in order to halt the spread of cattle disease into Tibet.

The journey so far had not been a particularly easy one. Mist and rain hampered the route survey in Sikkim, and Das suffered from altitude sickness over the pass into Nepal. The scenery, though, was magnificent. Lofty mountains of red rock were interspersed with small villages set in wooded valleys. As they proceeded, immense rock walls, marking the base of Kanchenjunga, could be seen to the east. By the time they reached the pass into Tibet, Das was flagging, and had to be carried up much of the snowy slope on the back of Phurchung. U.G., whose condition, Das reported, "was worse than mine on account of his corpulence," nevertheless made it up and over the pass under his own steam. On the last stage, Phurchung had to drag Das along with his hands. "In this miserable fashion," wrote Das later, "did I cross the famous Chathang-la [Jon-sang La] into Tibet, the very picture of desolation, horror and death, escaping the treacherous crevasses which abound in this dreadful region."[28] The worst was now over. Once in Tibet, they bought fresh food and three ponies. Near

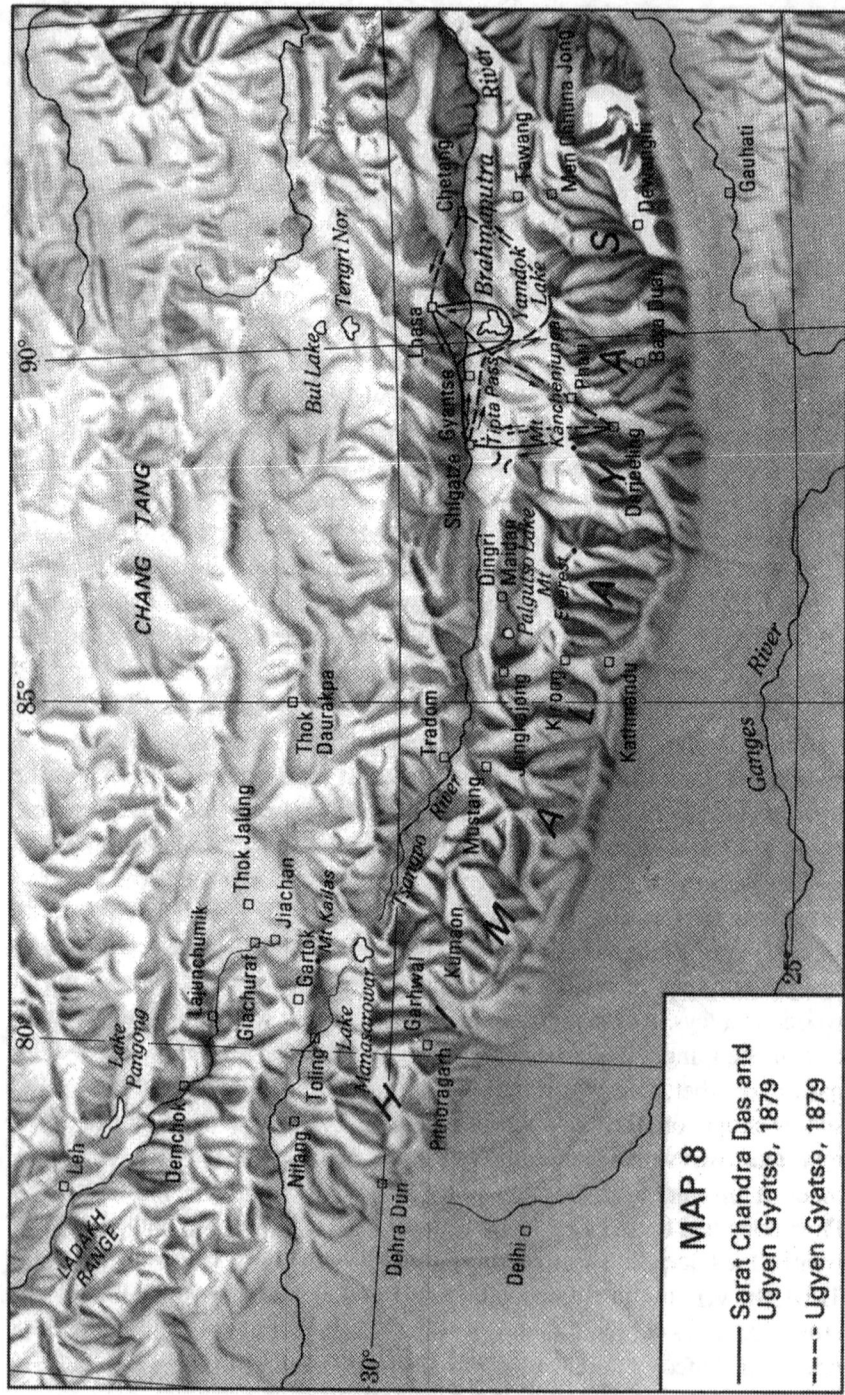

MAP 8
Sarat Chandra Das and Ugyen Gyatso, 1879
Ugyen Gyatso, 1879

Shigatse, on the morning of 7 July 1879, the great monastery of Tashilhunpo came into sight "like a dazzling hill of polished gold."[29]

Das was worried that he might be unmasked as a British agent. But in the absence of the Panchen Lama, it was the prime minister, the prime mover in securing the passport for Das, who received them both warmly, and the two remained at Tashilhunpo for two and a half months. Avid for information, the prime minister delighted in the books and toys and the magic lantern that had been carried by pony to Tashilhunpo. Eventually, he shut himself off from the outside world for two weeks, so that the visitors could spend all their time with him. Das remarked that this was an expensive undertaking, for while the prime minister was in seclusion, he was not able to receive any of the gifts of goods or money that pilgrims and other supplicants were obliged to bring with them.[30]

The day usually began with the study of Sanskrit and Hindi. Then several hours were spent on learning to operate the camera and the developing equipment. "For seven or eight days together," commented Das, "he was wholly engaged on photography to the neglect of everything else."[31] The prime minister was also entertained with the magic lantern, and received some instruction in algebra and in the use of a telescope which he had bought from a Kashmiri merchant. Here at last seemed to be a worthy successor to the Panchen Lama, who, a century earlier, had so welcomed George Bogle, ready to open Tibet to the outside world.

On the return of the Panchen Lama to Tashilhunpo in August, Das was quickly granted an audience. He described the Panchen as being "26 years of age, of a spare frame and middling stature. He has a remarkably broad forehead and large eyes, slightly oblique."[32]

No words were exchanged at the audience, but Das was soon informed that his request to stay on as a pupil at Tashilhunpo, communicated through the prime minister, had been granted. The Panchen, however, had his suspicions that the two might possibly be British agents and ordered relays of monks to camp in Das's quarters under the pretext of studying the Tibetan scriptures housed there. Das, no fool, "put to them some difficult and abstruse questions on Buddhism, . . . which soon relieved me of their presence."[33]

At this point, in late August, the plan was for U.G. to return to Darjeeling for more money and to make purchases there for the prime minister. Das would remain at Tashilhunpo, but would rendezvous with U.G. in October at Dongtse, a small village just outside Gyantse and the birthplace of the prime minister, who would be on holiday there. However, these plans had to be changed abruptly when the Panchen ordered the prime minister to make an inspection tour of districts to the north of the Tsangpo.

In the light of these developments, Das decided to leave for Darjeeling with Ugyen Gyatso. The Panchen Lama granted him the privilege of a passport which required the headman of every village on the way to provide food and shelter. He also made available ten yaks and three ponies for themselves and their baggage.

Before leaving, Das and U.G. paid a visit to the *jong,* or fort, situated between the monastery and the town. A market was set up by the fort, and Das recognized several traders from Darjeeling. Not wishing to be recognized, dressed as he was in the clothes of a lama, Das urged on his pony and passed the market "at a gallop unobserved."[34] The two continued for their first view of the Tsangpo and took a rather precarious ride on the river in a leather boat, and then returned through Shigatse to the monastery.

The following day, Das and U.G. bade farewell to the prime minister. There was an exchange of gifts, which included forty volumes of Tibetan manuscripts for Das ("a full yak load," commented Croft) and a fur-lined wool coat for the prime minister.[35] Das was urged to return the following April and to bring with him a lithographic press (on which the prime minister made a down payment), smallpox vaccine, a music box, and other goods on an itemized list. The prime minister promised to take Das with him to Lhasa the following year.

The party left Tashilhunpo in late September, traveling via Khamba Jong. The journey through Tibet was made easy by the production of the passport. Das crossed the Donkya pass into Sikkim mounted on a yak, and measured the altitude of the pass as 18,500 feet. On 10 November 1879, after an absence of five months, he returned to Darjeeling.

The route survey that was produced from the observations of Das and U.G. was useful. The road they took from the Sikkim border to Shigatse had not hitherto been surveyed. It was not very precise, however, as neither traveler had paced the route, and the distances were therefore only estimated. More important were the data on Tibetan customs, religion, and language that the two brought back. But above all, a quasi-diplomatic link had been opened with a sympathetic official in Tibet, and the way was paved for building on this contact by means of a second visit the following year.

Local disturbances in Sikkim made the idea of a return to Tibet in 1880 impossible.[36] Accordingly, Das occupied his time writing at his home in Darjeeling (aptly called *Lhasa Villa*) and improving his knowledge of Tibetan history, religion, and language. According to one report, he may have undertaken a further course in surveying techniques.[37]

By 1881, conditions in Sikkim had improved, and in July Das wrote an effusive letter to Croft, contrasting his own individual success in Tibet with the large state-supported expeditions of General Prejevalsky and Count Szechenyi, and asking the Indian government for Rs. 20,000 ("the least sum of money with which we should go") to explore, like Huc and Gabet, the territory between Lhasa and Peking.[38] The government, however, was prepared to sanction only an expedition as far as Lhasa, by way of Tashilhunpo. Das was instructed that when in Lhasa he should "cultivate the friendship of influential persons." He was told not to go beyond Lhasa just for geographical purposes, but that he could do so if necessary to pursue his studies. Under those circumstances, he could take the observations for a route survey, but should make no map.[39] Clearly, the British were more interested in Das as a scholar and diplomat than they were enthusiastic about his abilities as a surveyor.

On 7 November 1881, Das and U.G., again accompanied by their guide Phurchung, left Darjeeling for Tibet.[40] They carried with them Rs. 5,000 in gold, coral, pearls, and other salable commodities to cover their expenses on route. This was a considerable improvement over the financial arrangements made for the first journey, the cost of which Das had borne in part out of his own pocket. Das's salary was now doubled to Rs. 300 per month, with Rs. 100 per month to be paid as a pension to his widow, if he should die before returning. U.G. was to receive a salary of Rs. 100, and his widow Rs. 25.[41]

Once beyond the environs of Darjeeling, Das exchanged his Indian attire for the clothes of a Tibetan lama. The route taken to Tibet was similar to that used in 1879, passing through Sikkim into Nepal, and then to the west of Kanchenjunga. When in Nepal, they came to Phurchung's home village, where the guide celebrated by getting drunk. Indeed, he was frequently inebriated during the journey. Nevertheless, this did not prevent him from carrying Das, and at times Ugyen Gyatso, on his back over particularly wearying terrain. Das arrived safely at Tashilhunpo on 9 December, "with the measured steps and grave demeanor" befitting a lama.[42]

Das's friend, the prime minister, was temporarily absent in his hometown of Dongtse, but had left instructions that the visitors should be cared for. Das busied himself with renewing old acquaintances and learning more of the religious practices at Tashilhunpo. He also resumed his studies of Tibetan and Sanskrit books. While waiting for the return of the prime minister, Das found out that his heavy luggage, which had been dispatched separately from Darjeeling in the care of Rinzing Namgyal, had been held up on the frontier by orders of a Tibetan official at Khamba Jong. This luggage contained, among other things, the smallpox vaccine and the lithographic press requested by the prime minister. Das sent Phurchung to Khamba Jong to secure the release of his luggage, but he returned in January without having succeeded in doing so.

Meanwhile, Das had received a request from the prime minister to come to him at Dongtse, which was about thirty-five miles southeast of Tashilhunpo on the road to Gyantse. On arrival, Das and U.G. were immediately welcomed by the prime minister and soon picked up their discussions from where they had left off in 1879. The prime minister showed Das a book he was writing, which included a section on photography, complete with diagrams borrowed from the photography manual Das had brought with him on his first journey. The prime minister also got Das to read English to him and said that he hoped he could get another leave from the Panchen Lama, so as to improve his ability with the language. Both Das and U.G. expressed an interest in visiting Gyantse, about ten miles away. This was quickly arranged, and U.G. left ahead of the others.

Das followed U.G. to Gyantse after a few days and learned that U.G. had been inquiring locally about the state of the road to Lhasa, and the best time to visit the capital. U.G. had also struck up a friendship with a Tibetan army officer, got him drunk, and discovered details of the Tibetan and Chinese military garrison in Gyantse.

After returning to Dongtse, Das and U.G. left with the prime minister in the direction of Tashilhunpo. The prime minister asked to be shown the operation of the prismatic compass. U.G. obliged, but expressed regret that he had no tape measure for measuring distances. The prime minister said he would like to have some surveying instruments, plus a medicine chest and a book on astronomy. U.G. quickly reported that he would willingly bring them from Calcutta but that he did not wish to leave Das alone, with his desire to visit Lhasa unfulfilled. "That is easily provided for," said the prime minister, and he indicated that Das could probably go to Lhasa with the Panchen, who would be traveling there for the ordination of the new Dalai Lama.[43]

The lithographic press had, in the meantime, arrived at Tashilhunpo, and the prime minister enthusiastically joined Das in assembling it. The remaining luggage, however, was still stuck at the frontier. The prime minister was anxious to see what the luggage contained and so insisted on sending U.G. himself, who was provided with a suitable passport. On January 28 U.G. left Tashilhunpo, accompanied by Phurchung. Das continued his studies, trying to teach the prime minister the rudiments of telegraphy, as well as practicing English and arithmetic, all the while looking forward avidly to his promised visit to Lhasa.

It began on 26 April 1882. Das left Tashilhunpo for Dongtse, there to make the final arrangements with the prime minister. These were accomplished without delay. The auguries, however, were not good, as travelers reported that smallpox was raging in Lhasa. Das decided to press on. Passing quickly through Gyantse, he turned east and, following the route taken by Nain Singh in late 1865, crossed the Karo La pass and soon arrived at Nagartse on the west bank of the Yamdok Lake. This was called "scorpion lake" by the Tibetans, because of its irregular shape, with a large curved piece of land stretching into the water. This was initially assumed to be an island but was later seen to be connected to the shore by two promontories. Das named the lake "Yamdok-Croft" after his benefactor. But here he fell ill with a high fever. Luckily, he was traveling in the company of a lady who was the wife of a high-ranking official in Lhasa, and whose cousin was the abbess of the nearby monastery of Samding. Although she left him alone by the lake, for fear that he had contracted smallpox, she did write Das a letter of introduction to the abbess at Samding. Here he was warmly received and cared for. It was none too soon. Near death, he remained there for ten days, eventually recovering after medication which included "a sacred pill [*rinsel*] containing a particle of Kashyapa Buddha's relics."[44] Das also arranged for the purchase on his behalf of five hundred freshly caught fish, which were promptly returned to the lake in a life-saving gesture, earning him great merit according to the Buddhist religion. As he left Samding for Lhasa, Das shuddered as he saw that portion of the lake into which the bodies of the dead were thrown.

Heading north and then northeast by the deep turquoise blue water of the lake, Das soon reached the Tsangpo and saw the iron chain bridge across it, also observed by Nain Singh in 1866. The river was full of melting snow, overflowing the boundaries of the bridge, so Das crossed by boat. On 30 May, Das at last reached Lhasa, the city of his dreams. Jostling with merchants and travelers going to the city, he entered unquestioned, his fatigued appearance and dark goggles making people believe he was a sick man. Das found accommodation at a building where lamas from Tashilhunpo lodged, donned his lama robes, and soon set about exploring the city, mapping its streets and temples, buying Tibetan books, and participating in a religious ritual at the Jokhang, the main temple, or "cathedral," of Lhasa. A brief and formal audience with the Dalai Lama was easily arranged. Das described him as a "child of eight with a bright and fair complexion and rosy cheeks."[45]

In the nineteenth century, Dalai Lamas rarely reached the age of majority—dying, often in suspicious circumstances, frequently before the age of eighteen. However, Thupten Gyatso, the thirteenth Dalai Lama, and the one with whom Das had an audience, lived until 1933.

Because his servants became alarmed by the spread of smallpox in Lhasa, Das was forced to cut his stay short and return to Tashilhunpo. He stopped on the way at Dongtse to pay a courtesy call on his friend the prime minister, but found him suffering from smallpox. He was eventually to recover. In the meantime, Das pressed on toward Shigatse and was reunited both with Phurchung and Ugyen Gyatso, who gave him letters from India. At this point, rumors began circulating that Das was a British agent, and so he decided it was time to leave. Sending U.G. ahead to India with the botanical and other scientific data which the Lama had collected, Das left Tashilhunpo with Phurchung on 18 October. Before leaving Tibet, he was determined to visit the famous monastery of Samye, the first monastery built in Tibet, about A.D. 775, which lay on the north bank of the Tsangpo, about thirty miles southeast of Lhasa. The itinerary this time was along the southern shores of Yamdok Lake, before turning northeast to Samye. Das reached Samye on 29 October 1882, only eighteen days after A.K. had passed by it on his way back to India at the end of a journey that had lasted over four years.

Das spent several days exploring the monastery and making excursions into the surrounding countryside. On one of these excursions, he followed the Tsangpo as far downriver as Chetang, fulfilling in part a promise made to Croft years earlier.[46] At Chetang, a Kashmiri voiced his suspicions as to his true identity, and so he left rapidly and returned to Tashilhunpo by a different route. Through the intervention of the prime minister, he quickly obtained a passport from the Shape at Shigatse (the Panchen Lama having died in the meantime) giving him permission to proceed to India, and then to return again to Tibet. Das was now determined to leave for Darjeeling but decided to make yet another diversion on the way home and visit the Sakya monastery, founded in 1073, and the seat of the Red Hat sect of Tibetan Buddhism.

Accompanied by Phurchung, he bade farewell to Tashilhunpo on 30 November and turned southwest to Sakya. The party spent the night at a house near the monastery. Das was able to pay a brief visit to the monastery, but then pressed on south and east to Khamba Jong, reaching the Sikkim border on 10 December and Darjeeling on 27 December, after an absence of nearly fourteen months.

Das was a contrast to most of the other pundits. He was not an Indian from one of the hill peoples, peoples accustomed to traveling in Tibet but usually ill equipped from the educational and social standpoint to return with useful political information. Das was a Bengali from Chittagong, an educated man, a schoolmaster who taught himself colloquial Tibetan, and who was able, because of his knowledge of the religious customs of Tibet, to participate in the lives of the Tibetan ruling elite. Because of their lowly backgrounds, neither Nain Singh nor Kishen Singh had been able to provide this kind of insight into the life of the capital. By comparison with other travelers of the time, often lavishly equipped and backed by their governments, Das's success in reaching Lhasa was particularly significant. True, he was an Asiatic and therefore had an advantage not possessed by Europeans who tried to break into Tibet. But this should not detract from the hazards he surmounted on his journeys or the information he returned.

While Das was in Tibet in 1879, the Russian Nikolai Prejevalsky tried to enter the country but was turned back by the Tibetans. Das reported that the arrival of Prejevalsky's party on the northern outskirts of Tibet had caused consternation and that the great monasteries had sent three thousand monks to halt his progress.[47] Prejevalsky died on his next attempt to reach Lhasa a few years later. Earlier that year, a Hungarian expedition under Count Bela Szechenyi had raised the alarm in Lhasa as it skirted the edges of Tibet from north to east. Szechenyi tried to enter Tibet from western China in late 1879 but, like Prejevalsky, was forced to abandon the attempt.[48] The first Englishman to see the city, and the last for nearly a hundred years, was Thomas Manning, in 1811. The only other Europeans to gain entry to Lhasa that century were Huc and Gabet in 1846. In the late 1880s, the American diplomat and explorer William Woodville Rockhill, who had met Das in Peking in 1885, made two attempts to reach Lhasa but was foiled by lack of money and the hostility of the Tibetans. As the century drew to a close, others followed with similar lack of success.[49]

Das returned, like George Bogle and Samuel Turner, with a high opinion of the Tibetan people. "Humanity, and an unartificial gentleness of disposition," he wrote, "are the constant inheritance of a Tibetan. Without being officious, they are obliging; the higher ranks are unassuming, the inferior, respectful in their behavior; nor are they at all deficient in attention to the female sex; in this respect their conduct is equally remote from rudeness and adulation."[50]

In addition to the geographical and other data that Das returned with, he also acquired over "two hundred volumes, manuscripts or block-prints," many in Sanskrit and not seen in India for centuries.[51] From these materials, Das was able to produce a great deal of scholarly material, including a voluminous Tibetan-English dictionary, "a work embracing a mass of new and important collections on the language," which was published in Calcutta in 1902.[52]

Unfortunately, the later discovery of the real nature of Das's mission by the Tibetan authorities only increased their desire to exclude travelers from visiting Tibet and brought down severe penalties on those who had assisted him.[53] Indeed, the Japanese monk Ekai Kawaguchi, who had studied under Das in 1898-99 in Darjeeling before proceeding to Lhasa, was questioned by Tibetan officials about Das. Kawaguchi observed that the realization that Das was not a pilgrim, but an employee of the Indian government, had made the exclusion policy "so strict that it now seems as though Tibet has been converted into a nation of detectives and constables."[54]

L. Austine Waddell, who was a member of the Younghusband Expedition to Tibet of 1903-04, was told by the Tibetan governor of Lhasa about the fate of those who had befriended Das. The prime minister at Tashilhunpo was subjected to daily public beatings in the market place in Lhasa and then murdered and his body thrown into a river. Worst of all, he was denied reincarnation forever. The governor of Gyantse and his wife, who had helped Das at the instigation of the prime minister, were imprisoned for life, their servants mutilated and left to die.[55]

When the British finally prised open the doors to Tibet with the Younghusband Expedition, they were indebted for many of the details on their maps, and for the description of Lhasa, to the work of Sarat Chandra Das and other pundits.[56]

Ironically, it was there that the tragic finale was played out when British forces discovered in a Lhasa prison the chief of Dongtse and his son, both incarcerated for helping Das. The *North China Herald* reported that "the old man was brought into durbar, weak and tottering, his chains having been removed from his limbs that morning for the first time in twenty years. He came in beaming with happiness and blinking at the unaccountable light like a blind man whose sight had been miraculously restored."[57]

Although his days as an explorer came to an end after his return from Lhasa, Das continued to be of assistance to the government of India. Officially, he was still employed by the Education Department of the Bengal Government, but as secret government communications showed, he was "almost exclusively employed on political duties in the direction of Tibet."[58]

In October 1884, he accompanied Colman Macaulay to the Tibetan border of Sikkim. There they met a Tibetan official who told them that it was only the Chinese who were preventing a great improvement in relations between Britain and Tibet. Encouraged by this, particularly in the light of the friendly correspondence between the new regent in Tashilhunpo and the Bengal government (reminiscent of the period after the visit of Samuel Turner in 1783), Macaulay waxed optimistic about the prospects for the development of trade with Tibet. This optimism did not convince everyone; but the secretary of state, Lord Randolph Churchill, agreed that Macaulay should go to Peking in pursuit of passports for Tibet, as sanctioned by the Chinese under the separate article of the Chefoo Convention. Das was deputed to accompany Macaulay. They arrived in Peking in October 1885.[59] His depth of learning plus his tact and diplomacy made Das very much sought after by the lamas in Peking, so that he took up residence in the Yellow Temple there. While in the temple, he gained much useful intelligence information. In order to pass this on to his superiors he had to travel, wearing his yellow monk's robes, in a "closed cart" to a friend's house, change into Indian clothes, and then proceed in another closed vehicle to the British Legation.[60]

Macaulay believed that the Chinese were trying to impose isolation on Tibet. The Chinese, given the weak state of their government, certainly did not want to encourage foreigners to travel in Tibet, but Das perceived correctly that the isolation of Tibet was imposed primarily by the Tibetans themselves, fearing for their religion. The Chinese realized that even if they did grant passports for a British mission, the Tibetans would ignore them and resist the mission by force. Although, under pressure, passports were granted and Das's views ignored, a major clash with Tibet was only avoided, at least for the time being, because the mission was abandoned in 1886 as part of a larger settlement with the Chinese over Burma.

Das returned to Darjeeling and settled down to a life of scholarship, together with work for the Bengal government as a Tibetan translator. In 1892, he founded and became secretary of the Buddhist Text Society of India. But there is also evidence from Das himself that he was still engaged in intelligence activities concerning Tibet. These activities, like his own earlier explorations, were sanctioned directly by the Indian government and were not done under the auspices of the Survey of India. In the early 1890s, for example, Das sent a lama to explore the Chang Tang, north and west of Tashilhunpo. Das also speaks of having a "small office establishment" which he used "to keep communication with Tibet."[61] This was possibly the Darjeeling branch of the Bengal Secretariat Press of Calcutta. The main office had published the confidential report of Das's explorations, and since Rinzing Namgyal was known to have been employed at the Darjeeling branch in the 1890s, it is reasonable to assume that Das was there too.[62] The government rewarded him for his services with the title of Rai Bahadur and created him a Companion of the Order of the Indian Empire.

In 1887, the Royal Geographical Society awarded Das the Back Premium "for his researches in Tibet." The Premium consisted of the annual interest on a legacy of £600 bequeathed by Admiral Sir George Back. However, although this award to Das was a mark of the society's recognition of his achievements, it was not a gold medal, his desire for which was later transmitted to the society in no uncertain terms.[63] In 1886, Das was presented with the Marquess of Dufferin and Ava's Silver Medal, and the following year he received the Siamese King Chulalonkorn's Tushiti Mala Decorations.[64] In 1905, at a meeting in Calcutta of the Asiatic Society of Bengal, he was presented with a diploma from the Imperial Russian Archaeological Society, electing him a foreign corresponding member.[65]

Many years later, probably in 1914 or 1915, Das moved his principal residence from "Lhasa Villa" in Darjeeling to Manicktala Street in Calcutta.[66] There, in 1915, he renewed his friendship with Ekai Kawaguchi, who persuaded him to return with him to Japan. In 1916 Das did so, despite having only recently recovered from a serious illness. He died a few months later, probably in Japan, on 5 January 1917.[67]

Lama Ugyen Gyatso

Until 1882, Ugyen Gyatso had traveled primarily in the company of Das, acting as his secretary, surveyor, and, when necessary, translator. By 1883, the year of his only independent exploration, U.G. was aged thirty-two. He had been born into an old and distinguished Sikkimese-Tibetan family whose forebears had founded the Tashi monastery near Sakhyong some ten or twelve generations earlier, followed by the Samduk Lhakhang at Phari. In the seventeenth century, one of his ancestors had been granted the *jaghirs* of Lingdam and Yangang, which still remained in the possession of the family. More recently, his great uncle had founded the monastery at Yangang, where Ugyen Gyatso was born in 1851. He entered the Pemionchi monastery at the age of ten and remained there for twelve years, studying for the priesthood.

In 1872 he was deputed by the monastery to make a visit to Tibet, in order to obtain a copy of the Tengyur, one of the great collections of the Buddhist scriptures. After a year he returned with the complete set of 225 volumes, and in the following year he paid his first visit to Darjeeling, traveling in the entourage of the raja of Sikkim. While in Darjeeling, he met the lieutenant-governor of Bengal, Sir George Campbell. Later that year he accompanied John Ware Edgar, the deputy commissioner, on a tour of Sikkim up to the Tibetan border. When Edgar applied to the Sikkim raja for a teacher of Tibetan at the Bhutia Boarding School in Darjeeling, U.G. was selected, and he began work there in April 1874 when the school opened with Das as headmaster.[68]

The last exploration of U.G. took place in 1883, when he again entered Tibet from Sikkim (Map 8).[69] In addition to his monthly salary of Rs. 100, he was to receive one rupee for each mile of exploration and Rs. 4 per day when halting.[70] On this journey he was accompanied by his wife and his brother-in-law.[71] He received some additional training from Colonel Tanner of the Survey of India in the use of the prismatic compass and in the use of the hypsometer (an instrument used to determine altitude by measuring the boiling point of liquids).[72] His route, however, was planned, not by the survey, but by Alfred Croft, the director of public instruction for Bengal, who had worked closely with Das on his travels. Colman Macaulay provided him with instructions for collecting further samples for the Calcutta Botanical Society.[73]

The party left Darjeeling on 9 June 1883, after letting it be known that they intended to travel to U.G.'s home village of Yangang. They did indeed reach Yangang but, after spending nine days there, continued north to the Sikkim-Tibet border. After bribing officials, they entered Tibet by the Donkya Pass on 19 June. U.G. suffered from altitude sickness on the pass, but from here on, as instructed, he began to take observations and collect botanical specimens. From this pass in northeast Sikkim, they headed north and then northwest to Khamba Jong. Here U.G. met with the Jongpen (administrator) whose permission he needed in order to proceed further into Tibet. The presence of U.G.'s wife, plus a few presents, helped convince the Jongpen that U.G. was a genuine pilgrim. Changing their yaks for faster-moving ponies, they left for Gyantse to the northeast.

The route lay across a gravel-covered plain, interspersed by an occasional village. Soon Gyantse came into view, surrounded by gardens and fruit orchards. Avoiding the town for fear of recognition, U.G. stayed for just a few days with friends in an adjacent monastery. After surveying around the town, the group left for Shigatse, fifty miles to the northwest. The dreary gravel plains were lightened by spectacular mountain chains to either side, and cultivation became more common the closer they came to Shigatse. U.G. stayed in Shigatse for seven nights, and visited Tashilhunpo, but his report, as written up by Colonel Holdich, makes no reference to seeing acquaintances from previous visits there with Das.

Leaving Shigatse, U.G. continued his zigzag progress toward Lhasa, this time moving east, parallel to the Tsangpo. Along the way he renewed friendships in villages familiar to him from previous travels. "It is surprising," notes Holdich, "how many of these friends were of the gentle and more hospitable sex."[74] Eight days after departing from Shigatse, U.G. reached the Yamdok Lake, 13,800 feet above sea level. He eventually traveled around the whole of this odd, scorpion-shaped lake, and his mapping of it was one of the major achievements of the expedition. His complete circuit of the lake was the first to be provided to the Indian Survey, although Das had traversed much of it in 1882.[75] From the western side of the lake a mountainous peninsula jutted northeast. One arm of the peninsula then turned in on itself, bending back and rejoining the shore to the south, and so enclosing another lake, the Dumo Lake, within it. The Dumo Lake, about twenty-four miles in circumference, was said by U.G. to be a very eerie place. Underground noises and rockfalls into the water constantly disturbed the silence, and the landslips had raised the surface of the lake, which had no outlet, to a level five hundred feet above that of the Yamdok Lake. U.G. reported that the superstitious Tibetans believed that the Dumo Lake would one day overflow and flood all of Tibet.

U.G. did not finish his circuit of the Yamdok Lake at this time, but instead turned south to the Pho Mo Chang Tang Lake, which at a height of over sixteen thousand feet was one of the highest in Tibet. U.G. and his party left the lake by a depression in the hills to the southeast and continued in that general direction toward Bhutan. Once away from the highest elevations, the ground was lush with grass, flowers, and shrubs. This was the valley of the Lhobra River, the upper course of which was now mapped by U.G. for the first time. The southernmost point of the journey was reached at Lhakhang Jong, two days north of the Bhutan frontier, and it was here that U.G. ran into trouble.

He had visited two monasteries in the vicinity and, on returning to his lodgings, found two officials searching his luggage. His wife had done her best to hide his incriminating notes and instruments, but enough was discovered to lead the officials to denounce him as a British spy. He, his wife, and his brother-in-law were promptly arrested and imprisoned.

The Jongpens then surprisingly decided to treat them all very leniently, possibly because continued detention might cause more problems than it was worth. U.G. made a few bribes, and the Jongpens let them go, after burning U.G.'s notebook and extracting from him a promise not to go to Lhasa. He was allowed to keep all his instruments and botanical specimens. U.G. left Lhakhang Jong as rapidly as possible—and headed for Lhasa.[76]

His route was an ascent to the northeast, out of the fertile valley to a barren, stony plateau, whose only inhabitants were wild goats and antelope. But a few miles farther brought him to the head of the Yarlung River and then a descent into the Yarlung valley, flourishing with monasteries, villages, and abundant cultivation. On his way he came close to the route traversed by Hari Ram in 1871-72, and in the Yarlung valley itself he closed with a survey made earlier by Nain Singh. The party joined the Tsangpo at Chetang, but then detoured away from Lhasa in an easterly direction. The Tsangpo was crossed by boat, and on the northern bank, U.G. explored some areas already visited by Kishen Singh on his major exploration to the north of Tibet a few years earlier.

Now turning westward, but remaining on the north bank, U.G. visited the celebrated monastery of Samye (seen by Das in 1882) and thence made his way by a rather circuitous route to Lhasa itself.

U.G. entered Lhasa secretly, under cover of darkness, avoiding the official gates to the city, and threw bones to the packs of dogs that might otherwise have torn him to pieces. At 2 A.M. he rested under a tree, only to discover in the morning that it was a meeting place for thieves and bandits and that he was lucky not to have been murdered. Finally, he found shelter with a friend at the Drepung monastery to the west of the city.

U.G. took two days to make a survey of Lhasa, "under cover of an umbrella . . . sufficient to disguise his proceedings."[77] He also acquired a good deal of information about the life of the city.

On one of his walks through Lhasa, U.G. was unlucky enough to be recognized by a beggar who knew he came from Darjeeling. The beggar shouted that U.G. must be a spy and demanded money to keep quiet. U.G. paid up, but the experience made him apprehensive. He stayed indoors and made preparations to leave. At dawn on 20 October, he visited the Jokhang and prayed for a safe journey home. He then left Lhasa to the east, riding on a pony and still taking bearings from under cover of his umbrella.

After thirty miles, he crossed the Tsangpo and was soon on the northern bank of the Yamdok Lake. He took the longer, clockwise route around the lake and so completed his mapping of its circumference. The weather was fierce as he left the lake at its southwestern corner and headed for home. One of the donkeys fell and broke a leg, leading to an overnight halt on the open plain without food or shelter. After a miserable night he pressed on, and it was only a matter of days before he came to the lower altitudes and warm weather of the Chumbi valley, an indentation of Tibet between Sikkim and Bhutan. Passing Phari by night to avoid detection, U.G. crossed into Sikkim and was soon resting in his own monastery of Pemionchi. Finally, he returned safely to Darjeeling on 15 December 1883, after an absence of just over six months.

U.G.'s original written account of his expedition contained much material on the social and religious customs prevalent in Tibet. This material was omitted when Colonel Holdich wrote up the official report, and remains unpublished.

Holdich described the Lama's account as "one of the best records of Tibetan travel that has yet been achieved by any agent of the Survey of India."[78] U.G. had provided much valuable geographical information, crossing parts of Tibet by routes until that time completely unknown. In so doing, he had crossed the paths of several earlier Indian explorers, thus linking up their surveys and providing a check on their observations. His survey of the Yamdok Lake was most useful, particularly his complete circuit of the Dumo Lake, enclosed within the two peninsulas jutting into the main lake. He also mapped the most direct route from Lhasa to Darjeeling.

U.G.'s earlier explorations had been rather overshadowed by the work of his companion, Sarat Chandra Das, even though he himself was reported to be the better linguist.[79] It was Ugyen Gyatso who obtained most of the geographical information from the two journeys he made with Das. One member of the survey of India, who knew both, said of the two that "the Lama [Ugyen] was the harassed and hard-working surveyor; the Babu the light-hearted observer."[80] This exploration of 1883, which was to be his last, showed that U.G. was fully capable of first-class independent work.

Lama Ugyen Gyatso continued to be of assistance even after his own active exploring career ended. He helped take down the account of the explorer Kintup (who was illiterate) in 1884[81] and in putting together a description of the course of the lower part of the Tsangpo written by the Mongolian, Lama Serap Gyatso.[82] He subsequently helped Das in the preparation of Das's great Tibetan-English dictionary. At the same time he remained available to the government for service as a translator and interpreter. In October-November 1884 he accompanied Colman Macaulay to Sikkim and the Tibetan frontier on a mission similar to Edgar's, of which he had also been a part a decade earlier. The Macaulay mission visited Yangang, and Macaulay recorded that "Ugyen Gyatso, who is himself a Lama, is the great man here,—he owns the living, in fact, of the monastery,—and he introduced the head Lama, who is really his own nominee."[83] He acted as chief interpreter on the Sikkim Expedition of 1888 and was of help in the interrogation of prisoners, and in supplying details of the road from the Jelep pass on the Sikkim border up through the Chumbi valley.[84] He was awarded the silver campaign medal for his services. His records also apparently established the basis for a revised map of eastern Tibet.[85]

Official recognition of his services came in 1893, when he was awarded a silver medal by the Indian government. In the accompanying letter, the viceroy spoke of "the distinguished services rendered by you in obtaining geographical and statistical information in the little known regions on the North East Frontier of India during explorations carried on at great personal risk and hardship."[86] On 30 October 1893, the acting lieutenant-governor of Bengal, Anthony MacDonnell, invested the lama with the title of Rai Bahadur. He was also presented with a reward of Rs. 1,000 by Colonel Thuillier, the surveyor-general.[87]

In June 1895 he was appointed assistant manager of government estates, Darjeeling, and in April 1896 to the post of assistant manager Kalimpong Government Khas-mehals. A few years later he became the manager of the government estates.

Rai Lama Ugyen Gyatso Bahadur eventually retired to Yangang, where he died about 1915. He was survived by two widows, both of whom were granted pensions by the Indian government. In spite of his having two wives, he had no children, other than an adopted daughter. Choki, his first wife, died in 1921.[88]

EIGHT
The Tsangpo-Brahmaputra Controversy: Lala, Nem Singh, and Kintup

A glance at the map of Asia shows the river of Tibet, the Tsangpo, flowing through the country from west to east before turning south into India. The map also reveals the remarkable spectacle of three more great rivers—the Yangtse, Mekong, and Salween—flowing parallel to each other north to south, each separated from its neighbor by only fifty miles. To the west of the Salween is the Irrawaddy, reaching down to Rangoon from the mountains of the Burma-China frontier. Further west still, four more rivers, the Lohit, Dibong, Dihang, and Subansiri, run south from the Assam-China border to the plains of India, where they unite to form the Brahmaputra. The great "desideratum" for eighteenth-century European geographers was the connection between the Tsangpo and the other rivers of Asia. How did the Tsangpo reach the sea? The principal questions were whether it joined the Irrawaddy or the Brahmaputra and, if it flowed into the Brahmaputra, by what route did it do so, and which of the several possibilities was the connecting channel between the two?

The first reasonably accurate map of Tibet was produced by the French geographer d'Anville. This map, based on data provided by the Jesuits in China in the early eighteenth century, showed the Tsangpo linked to the Irrawaddy. This view was at variance with evidence provided by Catholic missionaries in Lhasa, which connected the Tsangpo with the Brahmaputra. The correctness of this belief of early missionaries to Tibet was reaffirmed by James Rennell, the first surveyor-general of India. In 1765, Rennell explored up the Brahmaputra into Assam. From information provided by the people living in the areas through which he passed, coupled with other data as to the course of the Irrawaddy, Rennell concluded that there was now the "strongest presumptive proof" that the Tsangpo and the Brahmaputra were one and the same river, although he noted that a positive verification of this could be obtained only by actually following the course of the river, "a circumstance unlikely ever to happen to any Europeans, or their dependents."[1] Rennell was subsequently proved to be right in identifying the Tsangpo with the Brahmaputra, and although the course of the river is now well known, there are still small sections of the Tsangpo never directly observed by Europeans.

Although some continental European geographers, most notably Heinrich Klaproth and Elisée Réclus, followed d'Anville and continued to identify the Tsangpo with the Irrawaddy, Rennell's view linking the Tsangpo to the Brahmaputra was the one that became generally accepted. Nevertheless, since no one had followed the route of the Tsangpo into Assam, some doubts persisted. And even among the majority, who agreed with Rennell, there was disagreement as to whether the Dihang or the Subansiri was the channel carrying the Tsangpo into the Brahmaputra.

It proved to be well nigh impossible to remove all remaining doubt concerning the validity of Rennell's thesis. The Assam region of northeast India lay to the south of the eastern chain of the Himalayas. Although the altitude of the Himalayan chain along the northeast frontier was lower than elsewhere, the region was in many ways considerably more difficult to explore. At the lower levels, closest to the plains, a profusion of tropical growth including bamboo thickets and twenty-foot-high grass greeted the surveyor or explorer. Only an elephant or a buffalo could make any headway. In the higher elevations, tall trees crowded together, their trunks festooned with creepers. In this frontier area lived tribal peoples, some of whom had little contact with either the Tibetans across the border or the peoples of the Indian plains to the south, and who were suspicious of even their immediate neighbors, let alone outsiders.

The British viewed Assam as a buffer area between India and Tibet, and although some attempts were made in the eighteenth century to establish commercial relations, the policy was generally one of nonintervention. This policy was broken as a result of the Burmese invasions of Assam in 1817 and 1819. Because these attacks threatened the security of Bengal, British forces intervened in 1824 and eventually expelled the Burmese, forcing them in 1826 to sign the Treaty of Yandabo by which Burma agreed to relinquish all claims to Assam and to abstain from any further interference in the area.[2] Even so, British incursions into the tribal areas of the Assam Himalayas continued to be infrequent, to say the least. When an official from Sadiya ventured up the Dihang in 1884, he found that he was the first Englishman in the region for thirty years.[3]

In the course of pursuing armed action against the Burmese, Lieutenant Wilcox, a military surveyor, was directed to discover the source of the Brahmaputra. In 1826 he proceeded up the Dihang until stopped by the Abors, who inhabited the land on both sides of the river. In the same year, he also explored up the Lohit branch of the Brahmaputra into Mishmi country, and in 1827 he reached a western branch of the Irrawaddy. As a result of these expeditions, Wilcox concluded that the Tsangpo did indeed flow, via the Dihang, into the Brahmaputra.[4]

A similar view was expressed a decade later by Captain Robert Pemberton who in 1837 had been sent on a mission to Bhutan, Assam's western neighbor, in order to halt incursions being made by the Bhutanese into Assam. While in Bhutan he obtained information from Tibetans familiar with both the Tsangpo and the Brahmaputra, all of whom believed that the two rivers were one and the same.

By the early 1870s, the Survey of India was ready to try to resolve the issue by adopting the methods that had proved successful elsewhere in exploring beyond the Indian frontier. Efforts were made to locate "natives of Assam," who could be trained to make a clandestine reconnaissance of "the portion of the Brahmaputra River which as yet has not been explored."[5] But Walker was forced to report that district officers in Assam had great difficulty in finding suitable persons. "No-one," he said, "has been found who could be trusted to make his way any distance beyond the border."[6] When British officials did succeed in recruiting Assamese natives for training, it was only to find that they were unwilling to leave when the time came for exploration. The natives alleged that the hill country was divided into warring clans, who only entered each other's territory by special arrangement, even for the purposes of trade. Permission was never given to strangers.[7]

Because of this inability to find local people, recourse was made to Nain Singh, the most experienced of all the pundits, even though he was not familiar with the area. In 1873, Trotter had dispatched him to Lhasa, where his primary task was to join the triennial tribute mission from Lhasa to Peking. But he was instructed that if this should not prove to be possible, then he was to follow the course of the Tsangpo downriver into India. Nain Singh reached Lhasa but was forced to make an abrupt departure from the capital, without joining the tribute mission. He headed for his secondary objective and succeeded in getting as far as the town of Chetang in late 1874 before lack of funds compelled him to leave the river and return by a more direct route to India. Chetang, about fifty miles southeast of Lhasa, was the lowest point of the river surveyed up to that time by any explorer. Nain Singh reported that the Tsangpo was visible for a further thirty miles below Chetang and that the local inhabitants believed that the river flowed into Assam.[8]

Nain Singh returned to India just as the explorer Lala was ready to start his first independent exploration. The official account of this expedition describes Lala as a "hill man of Sirmur," an area of the foothills of the Himalayas, northwest of Dehra Dun.[9] He had worked for the Survey of India in Kumaon and had been under consideration for the Forsyth Expedition in 1873. According to Montgomerie, Lala was a hill *duffadar* (a petty officer of native police) who "went to Abysinnia with Carter, and as far as I know has no objection to going anywhere."[10]

Lala set out from Darjeeling on 29 March, shortly after Nain Singh had reentered British territory at Udalguri on 1 March 1875, arriving in Calcutta ten days later. Whether they actually met is unknown, but the results of Nain Singh's expedition must have been transmitted to Darjeeling, for Lala's report mentions at one point that he intended "to follow the route of Pandit Nain Singh."[11]

The official reports of Lala's travels generally restrict themselves to identifying where he went, without saying where he was ordered to go.[12] It can only be surmised, therefore, that he was directed to proceed north through Sikkim and to survey the hitherto uncharted road from the Sikkim-Tibet border to Shigatse (Map 9). At Shigatse he would be close to the right bank of the Tsangpo, from where he must have been told to follow the course of the river downstream as far as possible. He was specifically forbidden to visit Lhasa.[13]

Lala was accompanied by a man who spoke Tibetan, as well as three coolies. Hidden in his luggage were a sextant, two compasses, a watch, and four thermometers. The first part of his route lay almost due north from Darjeeling through Sikkim to the Tibetan frontier, much of which was identical to the route taken by Hooker in 1848-49.

The journey was to be beset with serious difficulties, the first of which occurred at Lachen, a village in Sikkim which, although some twenty-five miles south of the border, served as the Tibetan frontier post. Because this route to Tibet was reserved for official travelers, Lala was detained, together with a party of Tibetan merchants returning from Calcutta with indigo, cutlery, and cloth, who had decided to avoid the regular commercial route through Phari because of the higher taxes levied there. After a detention of six days, Lala was allowed to press on toward Tibet.

The party crossed the Kangra La at over 16,500 feet and descended onto the Tibetan plain. Soon within sight of the fort of Khamba Jong, they were accosted by five armed horsemen and once again found themselves under arrest. The governor questioned Lala about his business in Tibet and his eventual destination. What Lala's disguise was is not known. After fifteen days confined in a village outside the fort and threatened with violence, Lala was sent under armed guard to Shigatse. From the point of view of his

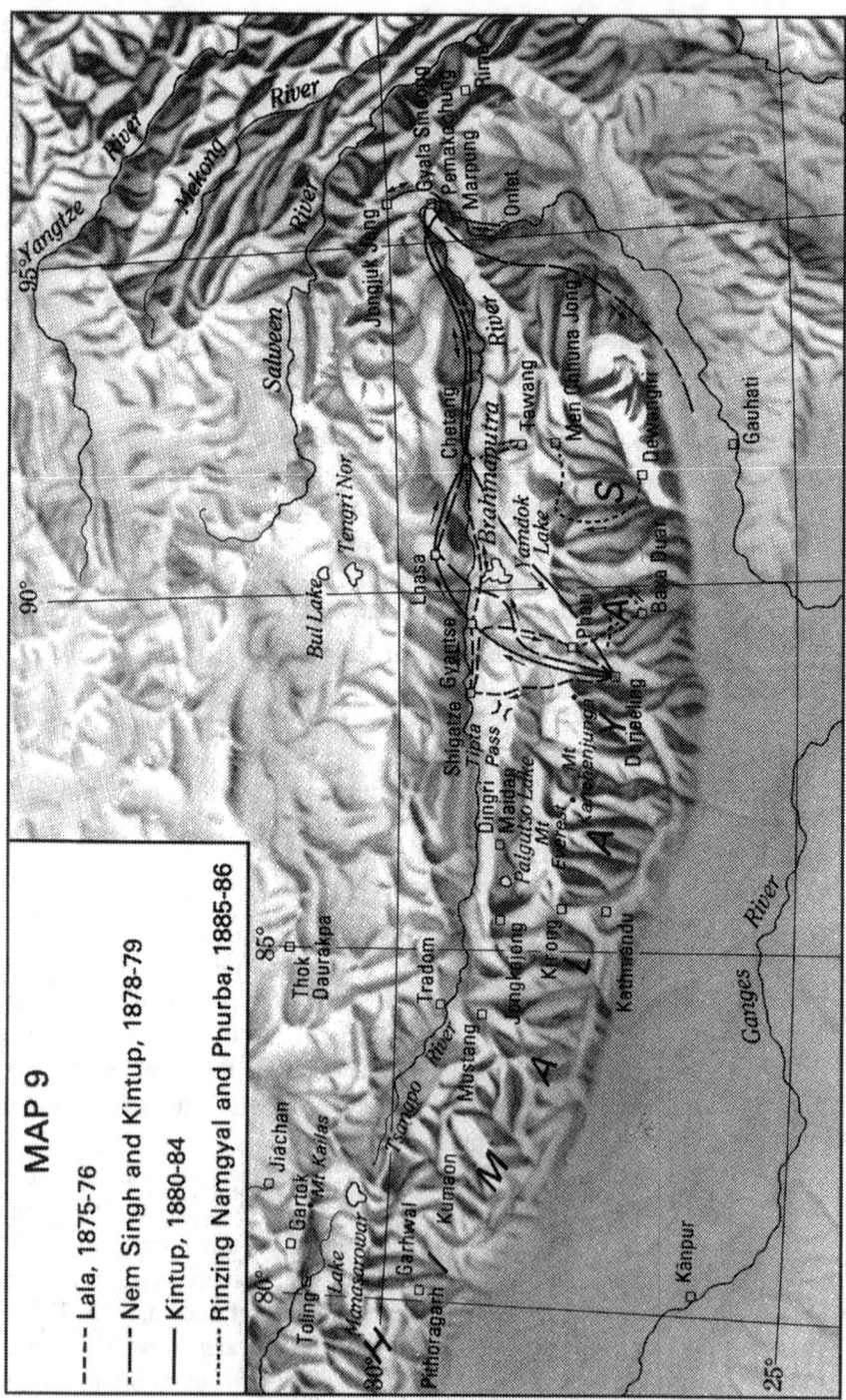

MAP 9

---- Lala, 1875-76
—·— Nem Singh and Kintup, 1878-79
——— Kintup, 1880-84
······ Rinzing Namgyal and Phurba, 1885-86

survey, this was a stroke of luck, since it was where he was headed anyway. Arriving in Shigatse in the middle of May, the party was detained for more than five months. Lala occupied his time by collecting information about the town and the great monastery of Tashilhunpo nearby. At last a party of merchants arrived, whom Lala persuaded to vouch for him (probably by bribery). As a result, Lala and his companions were allowed to depart.

They left in early November and proceeded along the right bank of the Tsangpo for about fifty miles to a point where the road separated from the river in a southeasterly direction. Lala followed this road, which led him to the northern bank of Lake Yamdok. Here he could see yaks, sheep, and goats grazing on the slopes of the mountain rising from the water of the lake. Local inhabitants provided the first information that the mountain was not an island as had been believed, but that the animals could walk to it across a land connection. The Survey of India doubted the accuracy of this report, but it was subsequently confirmed by the journeys of Sarat Chandra Das (1882) and Ugyen Gyatso (1883).

Leaving the shore of Lake Yamdok, the road turned northeast and rejoined the Tsangpo where the great chain bridge carried traffic across the river to Lhasa. Lala and his companions, however, took a branch in the road to the east, along the bank of the Tsangpo down a hitherto unmapped section of the river and soon reached the monastery at Samye, the point at which Nain Singh's route had joined the Tsangpo a few months before. From here they followed in the footsteps of Nain Singh to Chetang, the farthest point downstream yet surveyed by the pundits. Lala was told by the people of Chetang that the Tsangpo flowed "east by north . . . for 15 marches" and then "turned south, and, passing through a wild mountainous region, entered a country governed by the English."[14]

Unfortunately, the survey was not destined to be carried further by Lala. He was warned that it was extremely dangerous for a small group to proceed into a lawless area infested by thieves. Lala stayed in Chetang for six days and, when his funds began to run low, decided to return to India by following the route of Nain Singh. Leaving in mid-December 1875, Lala proceeded south, actually by a route slightly different from that of Nain Singh; but on arrival at Tawang, he was arrested by Tibetan officials and incarcerated in a public flour mill. The authorities refused to allow him to continue south. After a month, he was dispatched under armed guard toward Lhasa. Fortunately, some inaccuracy in the documents carried by the guard led to the party's release along the road back to Chetang. Realizing that it would now be the height of folly to try again to go south to India, Lala retraced his steps to Chetang and then back to Shigatse. It was rough going, particularly traversing the desolate terrain to Chetang while freezing gales blew with such force for several hours each day that travel became unthinkable.

It was the end of March 1876 before all was in order for the party's departure from Shigatse. Traveling with a band of merchants, they followed the route taken by Samuel Turner in 1783 and retraced in part the steps of Nain Singh on his first expedition of 1865. Marching first southeast to Gyantse, they then headed south for Phari in the Chumbi valley. It was not a smooth journey. At Phari, Lala came under suspicion and was again arrested and detained for a month before one of the village headmen spoke up for him and obtained his release from Chinese officials. Lala was then able finally to make his way to Kalimpong, where the commissioner for Darjeeling was in camp. It was July 1876, and he had been gone for a year and four months.

When the observations taken on the expedition were analyzed, a number of discrepancies appeared on comparison with the measurements made by Hooker. Since Lala was considered to be generally very reliable, it seemed that some systematic error must have crept in, probably during that portion of his route between Khamba Jong and Shigatse, when he was under guard and not able to take bearings or count paces with his usual care.

It was not safe for Lala to retrace this route. But the Survey of India decided that a bias might be detected if he were just to resurvey his route as far as the Tibetan border, where his observations could be compared with Hooker's.

Lala left Darjeeling on 29 September 1877.[15] He was again stopped by Tibetan officials, just as in 1875. Initially they refused to allow him to proceed, but on receipt of a bribe permitted him to pass. Otherwise, the journey was uneventful, and he returned to Darjeeling at the end of December. From these new observations the survey was able to correct the bias that had occurred in his expedition of 1875-76.[16]

Lala had traversed some new ground, of which that along the course of the Tsangpo between Shigatse and Chetang was of particular interest. He had not, however, succeeded in carrying the survey of the river any further downstream beyond the point reached by Nain Singh in 1874.

Lieutenant Henry Harman decided that the time was now ripe to push forward with a two-pronged assault to determine finally the course of the Tsangpo. His plan was to have explorers sent in from the north to carry the survey down the Tsangpo, while he himself would attempt to explore upriver from India.

Harman had been placed in charge of survey operations in the Assam valley in October 1874. Shortly thereafter he was seconded to Major Godwin-Austen, who was in command of the survey party attached to the military expedition proceeding into the territory of the Daflas. The Daflas lived to the west of the Dihang, next to the Abors. Harman found the Daflas to be friendly, but they lived in fear of their more powerful and warlike neighbors. Much of the area was such thick jungle that progress of the survey was slowed to only one hundred yards per day, and Harman reported that even his dog had to be carried in places.[17]

Harman rejoined the civilian survey in March 1875. An attempt to survey into Abor territory was rebuffed by Abor chiefs, after negotiation. In 1876, a small area of Abor territory was surveyed, the survey party being accompanied by a military escort. A full survey of the Brahmaputra was now completed to within a few miles of Sadiya, near where the Dihang, Dibong, and Lohit converged.

Harman had even brought Lala with him to Assam in January 1877. Lala was sent up to Sadiya, but for reasons unknown it proved impossible for him to be dispatched further.[18]

The heat and the dense jungle took their toll of Harman, and Walker summoned him to the hill town of Mussoorie, adjacent to Dehra Dun, where he could write up his results in the cool air of the hills. Here he recuperated and, while doing so, laid his plans for continuing the survey of the Tsangpo-Brahmaputra. These plans were submitted first to the government of India and to the chief commissioner of Assam, after which Harman went in person to Simla, the summer capital of the British Raj, to explain his proposals in detail to the Foreign Department of the Indian government.[19]

Later that year (1877), Harman was back in Assam. His principal task was to determine which of the rivers flowing into the Brahmaputra connected it with the Tsangpo. The Dihang was the prime candidate, although some, including Godwin-Austen, favored the Subansiri.[20] Because direct observation was very difficult as a result of political difficulties in penetrating areas inhabited by such primitive peoples as the Abors, an indirect approach was adopted. The assumption was that if the Dihang were the connecting channel to the Tsangpo, then it would have to carry a much larger volume of water than the other rivers, as it would drain a much larger area of land.

Early the following year, Harman undertook the task of ascertaining the flow of the tributaries of the Brahmaputra. His measurements confirmed that the flow of the Dihang was greater than that of any other river flowing into the Brahmaputra and that the Dihang was therefore the most likely link to the great river of Tibet.[21] The discharge of the Dihang was estimated at 55,500 cubic feet per second, far more than that of the Lohit (33,800), more than double the discharge of the Dibong (27,200), and more than three times the volume of the Subansiri.[22]

These figures provided strong evidence that if indeed the Tsangpo joined the Brahmaputra, then most likely it was the Dihang which connected them and not the Subansiri. But Walker, now surveyor-general of India, was cautious and pointed out that on the prior question of whether the Tsangpo flowed into the Brahmaputra or the Irrawaddy, "the evidence is not yet conclusive."[23] Captain Woodthorpe, who had served with Harman on some of his Assam surveys, and who himself believed that the Tsangpo and Dihang and Brahmaputra were a single river, nevertheless commented "mere theories on geographical questions, however, apparently well based on observation, have so often proved false, that it will only be by a much more extended exploration than we were able to make that the much-vexed question of the course of the Sanpo will be finally set at rest."[24] It was just such an "extended exploration" that Harman had planned and began to set in operation when he returned to Darjeeling in April 1878.

In Darjeeling, Harman decided to learn Tibetan and hired as his teacher a lama from the Pemionchi monastery, where Lama Ugyen Gyatso had trained for the priesthood. The lama's name was Nem Singh, and he was described by Harman as being about thirty years old, a Sikkim Bhotia, quite well educated and with a smattering of English. He worked for the Public Works Department as an overseer of gangs of coolie laborers and also assisted from time to time as an interpreter at the Court of Darjeeling.[25] F.M. Bailey says that his real name was Nyima Tsering, "an ordinary Tibetan name which means 'Sunday Long Life.'"[26]

Harman began teaching Nem Singh the rudiments of surveying. He proved to be a good pupil, and Harman soon asked if he would be interested in joining the survey as an explorer. Nem Singh quickly accepted. In accordance with now standard procedure, he was code named G.M.N., the consonants of his name in reverse order.[27] He was not able to get in as much practical experience of surveying as had been hoped, because the summer of 1878 was particularly wet. No sun or stars were seen for twenty-seven consecutive days. But Harman was anxious not to lose a dry season and so sent Nem Singh off on 6 August. This lack of training was to mar the results of the exploration.

Nem Singh's paramount objective was to carry the survey of the Tsangpo downriver from Chetang as far as possible. Chetang was the great stumbling block. No one seemed to be able to progress beyond it. Nain Singh had fixed its position in 1874, and Lala had also reached it, a year later. But these were not major accomplishments, bearing in mind that Catholic missionaries such as Desideri had visited Chetang early in the preceding century.

Nem Singh's secondary tasks were to make a circuit of Lake Yamdok and to provide a detailed description of the iron chain bridge over the Tsangpo at Chaksam.[28]

Nem Singh was accompanied by an assistant, Kintup, who was later to be sent out again by Harman on what turned out to be a very unfortunate assignment. The two left Darjeeling for the Chumbi valley and passed through Phari without incident. Nem Singh then met Lake Yamdok on its west bank and left the lake on reaching the northern shore, failing, for no clear reason, to attempt a circuit of the lake. He did, however, provide a good description of the great chain bridge, which he crossed on his way to Lhasa. It was, he said, "the most wonderful he had ever seen," made of four iron chains about three hundred paces long, the iron being an inch thick.[29] From the two chains on each side a rope footway was suspended. The chains were wrapped around huge bollards of wood which in turn were sunk into the masonry of a pier on each side of the river. Only one person could cross at a time, and during the rainy season boats were used, as one pier was cut off from the bank by floodwaters.

Harman reported that Nem Singh spent "a considerable time" in Lhasa, making presents (presumably out of Survey funds) to the lamas. Eventually, he left the city and made his way to Chetang. In October he started out downriver.[30] At last the survey was to be carried forward.

About thirty miles from Chetang, the road ceased to follow the Tsangpo and instead went north, eventually bending back to rejoin the river. The point where the road diverged from the river was the farthest place that Nain Singh had observed visually from Chetang. He had reported that the river then turned in a southeasterly direction, an observation that had led some in the survey to hypothesize that it flowed into the Subansiri. Nem Singh showed, however, that this southeasterly flow continued for only a very short distance before the river turned due east and then made a sharp bend northeast. This was a major discovery. Pressing on, he soon reached the point where the course of the Tsangpo changed yet again, from northeast to southeast, cutting through the highest points of the eastern Himalayas, between Namcha Barwa (25,445 feet) and Gyala Peri (23,460 feet).

Nem Singh continued for another twenty miles downriver before stopping at the village of Gyala Sindong, which he estimated to be 287 miles from Chetang. Here he was halted by mountains and rugged terrain. The local people said the Tsangpo eventually "entered a land ruled by the British."[31] This could have made either the Dihang or the Subansiri the connecting channel. In practice, the latter was an unlikely candidate, for given what was now known about the route of the Tsangpo, it would have to bend back on itself to make the link with the Subansiri. On the other hand, commented Harman about the Tsangpo, "very agreeable results are found by turning it into the Dihang."[32] The volume of the Subansiri (although small if it was assumed to be the effluent of the Tsangpo) was now accounted for, since it would drain that area described by the bend of the Tsangpo around Namcha Barwa. Furthermore, if Nem Singh had located the position of Gyala Sindong accurately, then only about a hundred miles of the Tsangpo remained unsurveyed between this point and the highest point fixed upriver along the Dihang.[33]

Even though Nem Singh was the first explorer to get beyond Chetang, Harman was not pleased either with him or his results. Nem Singh was unable to provide much information about his return route; he failed at times to make proper entries of his observations in his field book; his dates were wrong; his measurements of the altitude of the sun were "very doubtful"; and no sense at all could be made of his astronomical work.[34]

While traveling along the great bend of the Tsangpo, the pundit had been in great fear of robbers and had moved with such haste to leave the vicinity that his bearings proved to be quite inaccurate. Nem Singh had in fact put the peak of the bend at longitude 94° east. This was too far west, but it was not for over thirty years, until the Abor Expedition of 1911-12, that it was corrected to 95°.[35]

Although Harman thought that in general his route could be relied upon, Nem Singh was sacked from the Survey shortly after his return in January 1879. The explorer was very upset. He had done his best, he said. Harman relented, perhaps remembering that it was he who had sent Nem Singh off before his training was complete. The explorer was rehired and sent to Nain Singh for proper instruction in surveying.[36]

Writing in 1880, Harman said that Nem Singh had "prosecuted his studies with vigor and has gone away on a most important journey, guided by a Lama who has traversed the whole route Nem Singh has to follow."[37] Kenneth Mason dates his second journey as 1879-80 and reports that no account was ever published.[38] The lama to whom Harman referred was probably Ugyen Gyatso. Little is known of Nem Singh's third and final expedition, in 1880, except that it included a traverse from Shigatse to Khamba Jong.[39]

Nem Singh's major exploration remained his survey down the course of the Tsangpo. For all its faults, this route, which carried the survey of the river for nearly three hundred miles into virtually unknown territory and showed the great bend to the northeast, was a major contribution to solving the question of the course of the Tsangpo-Brahmaputra river.

It was at this point, just when the identity of the Tsangpo with the Brahmaputra seemed a foregone conclusion, that a counterclaim was put forward, reviving the old argument that the Tsangpo flowed, not into the Brahmaputra at all, but into the Irrawaddy. This view was tenaciously held by Robert Gordon, an engineer with the Public Works Department, employed in Burma on the lower reaches of the Irrawaddy. Gordon's thesis was first advanced in a massive volume issued by the government of British Burma.[40] Later, in a presentation to the Royal Geographical Society, Gordon claimed that the exponents of the Tsangpo-Brahmaputra theory simply ignored unfavorable evidence. He based his own arguments on the size of the discharge of the Irrawaddy and on views put forward by ancient Chinese geographers. He also disputed the accuracy of Harman's measurements of the discharges of the four major rivers flowing into the Brahmaputra. Gordon was familiar with many of the reports of the pundit surveys and sometimes quoted these selectively to support his thesis. His treatment of the exploration of Nem Singh is a good example. Gordon believed that the Tsangpo flowed further north and east than was generally believed, before turning south to join the Irrawaddy. He therefore approvingly quoted Nem Singh's report on his discovery of the bend in the Tsangpo to the northeast, but made no mention of Nem Singh's other observation that the river subsequently turned to the southeast at longitude 94° east.[41]

Gordon also referred in his paper to the observations of "the Surveyor Alaga," who had shown the immense size of the upper Irrawaddy. From such data Gordon deduced that the Tsangpo must flow into it. There was no other explanation, he said, for the volume of water carried by the Irrawaddy. If the Irrawaddy was not the effluent of the Tsangpo, stated Gordon, then "we have here an exceedingly large river, certified to by independent testimony from various sources . . . with almost no gathering ground for its waters."[42]

Alaga was a Burmese native explorer who had been sent to explore the upper reaches of the Irrawaddy in 1879.[43] Early that year, Walker had instructed a British surveyor in Rangoon, Captain J.E. Sandeman, to train a Burmese for this purpose. Sandeman quickly located Alaga, an intelligent Burmese, whom he trained during the spring and summer. In October 1879, Alaga set off with his nephew M___o. He was also accompanied by an older man, known only as A⎯⎯e M⎯⎯e, who had been trading in timber up and around Bhamo for years. The party were to proceed from Rangoon to Bhamo, commence their survey there, and take it as far up the Irrawaddy as possible. This they did, and returned safely to Rangoon in April 1880, having got as far north as latitude 26°. Although this was not sufficient distance to discover the source of the Irrawaddy, their observations, inconclusive though they were, in Sandeman's opinion tended to support the views of Rennell and Walker connecting the Tsangpo to the Brahmaputra, rather than the theory of Gordon.[44]

Meanwhile, the basic triangulation of Assam had been completed by the summer of 1878. Harman was then transferred to the Darjeeling district. The year 1878 was the year in which General Walker was named surveyor-general of India. In the same year, the three separate departments, the Great Trigonometrical Survey, the Topographical Survey, and the Revenue Survey, were amalgamated into a single entity known as the Survey of India.

This reorganization led to increased demands on Harman's time, and his health began to suffer from the strain of overwork. Nevertheless, the following year he embarked on a survey of northern Sikkim. He left Darjeeling in October 1879, with a view to triangulating some hitherto unsurveyed Himalayan peaks during the brief period of clear weather between the end of the monsoon rains and the start of the winter snows. A month later, he reached the foot of the Donkya pass on the Sikkim-Tibet border.[45] The following day he reached the top of the pass, but because it was farther and higher than he had expected, he did not arrive until late afternoon. The pass revealed a magnificent view of distant snowy peaks, none of which had been fixed trigonometrically. At this point Harman made the decision which was ultimately to cost him his life. Rather than return to camp, he opted to bivouac on the pass overnight. He and his two Tibetan companions had only one blanket among them. The pass was more than fourteen thousand feet high, and it was a cloudless and very cold night. The three lit a fire and slept close to it, but, unfortunately, the fire went out during the night, and Harman's feet were severely frostbitten. General Walker recounted the circumstances: "He awoke at daybreak quite unconscious of the injury he had received, and he lay watching with great delight the peaks of the distant range in Tibet coming gradually into view; when they became sufficiently lighted up for him to commence his observations, he sprang on his feet to set to work; the same instant he found his feet fail him, and fell flat on his face to the ground. The Tibetans understood at once what happened, and they set to work rubbing his feet vigorously and endeavoring to restore the circulation; but all their efforts were unsuccessful."[46] Despite his injuries and great pain, Harman continued his work in Sikkim for a further two months, getting about on ponies, with the help of crutches, or on the backs of coolies.[47] He eventually lost four and a half toes.[48]

Once back in Darjeeling and rested, Harman declared that he was fit as ever and rededicated himself to solving the problem of the route of the Tsangpo. He decided once again to make use of Kintup, who had traveled with Nem Singh as his assistant in 1878-79. Nem Singh himself was off on another expedition, and in any case the results of his journey down the Tsangpo had not been as good as had been expected. Kintup, however, had shown himself to be a reliable companion and helper. He was also, of course, familiar with the route of the Tsangpo as far as Gyala Sindong. Kintup would no doubt have been employed as an explorer in his own right, but he was illiterate and could not take down any field observations. Harman therefore teamed him up with a Chinese lama, for whom he was to act as a servant and assistant.[49]

Kintup (or KP as he was known in the official archives) was a native of upper Sikkim and had acted as a guide for travelers there. He had a shop in Darjeeling where he practiced his trade as a tailor.[50] L. Austine Waddell of the Indian Medical Department, who employed Kintup in later years, said that his "sturdy courage and roving propensities . . . attracted the notice of Captain Harman, R.E."[51] Waddell described Kintup as dependable, thickset, active, of medium height, and with a look of dogged determination. He had weather-beaten features, a few bristles on his upper lip, and a deep-chested voice, with the alertness of a mountaineer and the strength of a lion.[52] He was thirty-one years old.[53]

Kintup and the Chinese lama were instructed to proceed to Gyala Sindong and then to press on, tracing the route of the Tsangpo into Assam. But in case that proved impossible, Harman devised an ingenious contingency plan. The two were to prepare a large number of specially marked logs, and after sending a message to Harman, those logs were to be thrown into the Tsangpo. Harman, alerted to this, would station men at the point where the Dihang entered Assam. Finding one of the logs would prove beyond all doubt that the Dihang did indeed join the Tsangpo to the Brahmaputra.[54]

The pair left Darjeeling in the summer of 1880 and made their way north, crossing the Donkya pass (where Harman had been frostbitten less than a year before) and entering Tibet on 7 August (Map 9). The Chinese lama traveled under the pretense that he was going to visit his sister and that Kintup was accompanying him.[55] Once across the border, they joined a group of merchants for the seven-day journey to Gyantse. In Gyantse, Kintup assumed the disguise of a pilgrim going to Lhasa. The two stayed for nearly a week in the capital while the lama was entertained by old friends at the Sera monastery, one of the three great monasteries (together with Drepung and Ganden) on the outskirts of Lhasa. By the end of August they reached Chetang, after an uneventful journey. At Chetang they were delayed for three weeks, as the lama was ill, and here for the first time the official narrative reported that Kintup "was very badly treated" by his companion.[56]

Once the lama was recovered, they continued downriver, begging for food in the manner of pilgrims. A major delay occurred in the small village of Thun Tsung, where they stayed initially for two days. The Chinese lama began an affair with his host's wife, which continued for four months until her husband found out. Kintup had to pay Rs. 25 in compensation to the man before they could leave. They reached Gyala Sindong in March 1881. This was the farthest point down the Tsangpo yet explored, reached by Nem Singh in 1878.

From Gyala Sindong they continued downriver for a further fifteen miles to the village of Pemakochung, where there was a small monastery. Pemakochung was to become famous, for Kintup's narrative reported that just two miles away the Tsangpo "falls over a cliff . . . from a height of about 150 feet."[57] For over a quarter of a century this was to conjure up in the minds of explorers the vision of a massive waterfall, rivaling the great Victoria Falls on the Zambezi.

After viewing the falls, Kintup and the lama retraced their steps upriver and then turned inland to Jongjuk Jong, northeast of the most northerly point on the Tsangpo. The Jongpon allowed them into the fort and housed them in the servants' quarters. There Kintup hid his pistol and three compasses. The lama spent some time with the Jongpon, and the two seem to have become friends, for the lama told the official the nature of his exploring activities. Soon one of the Jongpon's servants came to Kintup, and Kintup was forced to disclose the hiding place of one compass and his pistol. Shortly afterwards, on 24 May 1881, the lama told Kintup that he was leaving on business but would return in two or three days. That was the last that was ever heard of him. Kintup was kept in detention for two months, stitching clothes, before he learned that the lama had actually sold him to the Jongpon as a slave. Forced to work as a servant, Kintup bided his time and waited for an opportunity to escape. It was not until the evening of 7 March 1882 that he managed to slip away.

He fled first to a village on the Tsangpo just downriver from Pemakochung, from where he traveled on for twenty miles before turning east into mountainous country. He then retraced his steps to the Tsangpo and pressed on downriver to Marpung. He was now thirty-five miles down the river from Gyala Sindong, and it was here that his pursuers caught up with him.

There was a monastery in Marpung of thirty monks. Exhausted and at his wits' end, Kintup went to the head lama and begged his assistance. He said that he was on a pilgrimage and asked the lama not to hand him over to the Jongpon's men. The lama agreed to pay Rs. 50 to the Jongpon for Kintup.

Although Kintup had successfully evaded the clutches of the Jongpon, he had only exchanged one form of slavery for another. Now he had to work for the lama as a servant. After four and a half months, he asked the lama for a month's leave so that he could make a pilgrimage. The lama, impressed by his piety, agreed.

By now it was August 1882. Kintup had been absent from India for two years and had twice been sold into slavery. He could easily have been forgiven if he had seized this opportunity to return home as quickly as possible.

But Kintup had not forgotten that his instructions were to survey the Tsangpo. Since it was not feasible for him to travel alone and without funds down the river to Assam, he decided to carry out Harman's contingency plan and throw marked logs into the river. But first of all the logs had to be collected, and then Harman must be alerted, so that men could be stationed on the Brahmaputra to watch for their arrival.

Crossing over to the left bank of the Tsangpo, Kintup went to the monastery at Giling, where he stayed for five days under the pretense of being in search of salt. Instead, he spent his time making five hundred logs (no mean feat in five days), each one foot long, shaped in a particular way.[58]

Kintup had been supplied with five hundred tin tubes, each containing an identification paper. He also had a gouge for drilling holes in the logs, into which the tubes were to be inserted. Kintup had lost the gouge, but retained the tubes. He therefore bound a tube with strips of bamboo to the outside of each log.[59] The logs were then hidden in a cave, "where no human foot had yet trodden." It would seem very unlikely that anyone could cut five hundred logs, shape them, attach the tubes with bamboo, and carry them into hiding in a cave, all in five days. Even working twelve hours per day, this would have allowed only seven minutes per log. The solution to the problem lies in Kintup's report. It was probably garbled in transcription. Although the narrative states that he stayed at Giling "five days making the 500 logs," it also notes that he returned to Marpung "after an absence of one month and four days."[60] Since Giling is only ten miles from Marpung, the likelihood is that Kintup actually spent about a month preparing his logs.

He returned to the monastery at Marpung and worked for the lama for another two months. He then asked for and was granted two months' leave, ostensibly to make another pilgrimage, this time to Tsari, upriver. But his real destination was Lhasa. Kintup gives no dates, but it can be estimated that he probably reached the capital in December 1882. In Lhasa, he learned of a Sikkimese kazi (judge) there, whose wife was about to return to Darjeeling. At this point it would have been easiest for Kintup to join the group going to Darjeeling. After his ordeal, no one at the survey would have blamed him for the failure of the mission. But Kintup decided to persevere. The kazi agreed to take down a letter dictated by Kintup and have his wife give it to Nem Singh in Darjeeling. Kintup's note read as follows: "Sir, The Lama who was sent with me sold me to a Jongpon as a slave and himself fled away with the Government things that were in his charge. On account of which the journey proved a bad one; however, I, Kinthup, have prepared the 500 logs according to the order of the late Captain Harman, and am prepared to throw 50 logs per day into the Tsang-po from Bipung in Pemako, from the 5th to the 15th of the tenth Tibetan month of the year called *Chhuluk*, of the Tibetan calculation."[61]

Nem Singh was asked to pass on this message to Harman. The letter reached Nem Singh, but it was never delivered to Harman. By a stroke of ill luck, Harman had left India in December 1882, just before the letter arrived. This was to be his last journey, and he departed believing that Kintup and the lama must have been arrested and allowed neither to proceed nor to return to him.[62]

Harman had initially convinced himself that he was fully recovered from the frostbite and exposure he received on the Donkya pass. He even set out on an expedition to Kanchenjunga in 1881. But his health gave out, and he had to be carried back to Darjeeling. There he remained for a year. Realizing at last that he was a dying man, he resigned from the survey and left for Europe. Cared for in his final months by his sisters, he died in Florence, Italy, on 14 April 1883, of tubercular pneumonia.[63]

Nem Singh either failed to pass the letter on to anyone else in the survey, or if he did, no attention was paid to it. According to F.M. Bailey, by the time Nem Singh received Kintup's letter, the date for throwing the logs into the Tsangpo had already passed, and so he threw the letter away.[64] This is unlikely, even given the slow speed of communication in Tibet, unless the kazi's wife delayed her departure. *Chhuluk* is the "water-sheep" year of the Tibetan calendar, or 1883, and with the new year beginning in February, Kintup's date would have been about mid-November on the Indian calendar.[65]

Unaware that Harman had left India and that no one was going to be watching for the arrival of his logs, Kintup returned by a new route to the lama at the Marpung monastery. Since he could not return unnoticed to his cache of logs, he had first to return himself voluntarily into slavery. He worked for the lama for another nine months, at the end of which time the lama, who had been impressed by Kintup's devotion to his "pilgrimages," set him free.

Kintup stayed on, working at the monastery for another month to earn some money. He then left, headed for the cave where he had hidden his special logs, retrieved them, and threw them into the river at a rate of fifty per day. He remained in the area for a month, earning additional funds to support him on his journey home.

Kintup's intention at this point seems to have been to try to follow the Tsangpo into India. He pressed on downriver, but the road deteriorated, becoming only a track, impassable even by horses. He was soon entering the territory of the hostile Abors, whom he described as "almost naked, wearing nothing but a wrapper over the lower part of the body. They always carry a sword and bow, and even at night they keep their weapons near them."[66] Even so, Kintup was successful in getting as far as Onlet, about ninety-five miles (as the crow flies) from Gyala Sindong, and only a little over forty miles from the boundary of British India.

Here he was forced to turn back, because the Abors did not allow people from the area from which he had come to pass through their territory.[67] He went back to Pemakochung, stayed two months to earn more money, and then returned to his home village, via Lhasa. Once home, he discovered that his mother had died during his wanderings. It took him two and a half months to complete her funeral arrangements, before he left and found Nem Singh and A.W. Paul (the Deputy Commissioner of Darjeeling) at the monastery of Namchi in Sikkim. He traveled with them for a month and on 17 November 1884, after an absence of more than four years, arrrived back in Darjeeling. His return passed without notice, and he languished in obscurity.

Less than a year after Kintup returned, another explorer was dispatched with the same objective—to trace the route of the Tsangpo. Colonel Tanner had assumed charge of the triangulation of the Himalayas after the death of Harman. Tanner had worked closely with Rinzing Namgyal (R.N.) in the past, and he now transferred him from his surveying duties to the list of active explorers, at a salary of Rs. 60 per month.[68] His instructions were to travel east from Darjeeling across Bhutan to Gyala Sindong, explored by Nem Singh in 1878-79. Since no one had bothered to cross-examine Kintup, this was, as far as anybody knew, the lowest point on the river reached by a pundit. At Gyala Sindong, R.N. was to cross the Tsangpo to its left bank and then to follow it down into India, without recrossing the river.[69]

R.N. received his instructions from Tanner in August 1885. On 1 November he left Darjeeling in a party composed of three companions, five permanent servants, and a number of coolies.[70] Now on active duty, he received Rs. 100 a month.[71] For part of his exploration, he was also accompanied by another explorer, a Bhotia from Sikkim called Phurba, whose code name was P.A.[72]

The objectives of the exploration were not accomplished. R.N. made two attempts to cross from Bhutan into Tibet, but was stopped on both occasions. P.A. traveled for part of the time with R.N. and also made two independent survey operations. The two returned to Darjeeling on 3 June 1886.[73]

R.N.'s first attempt to enter Tibet was foiled because of an ongoing dispute between Bhutan and Tibet. At his second attempt, he found the frontier on a state of alert. The Tibetans were preparing for the advance into Tibet of the Macaulay Mission, which had assembled in force at Darjeeling early in 1886. They had also heard rumors of Russians to the north. As a result of these fears of invasion, the borders were closed to all traders and pilgrims.[74]

Nevertheless, significant results were achieved from this expedition, even though the primary objective was not met (Map 9). Bhutan was a small Himalayan state lying between Sikkim, Tibet, Bengal, and Assam. Contacts with Bhutan had greatly expanded following the British occupation of Assam in 1826. Disputes over the frontier had also increased, resulting in a number of British missions to Bhutan. Up to the time of Rinzing Namgyal's expedition, British knowledge of the geography of Bhutan was still largely based on what had been learned by the Pemberton Mission of 1837-38. Additions had been made to this by Godwin-Austen (who accompanied the Eden Mission of 1863-64 and participated in survey work during the ensuing Anglo-Bhutanese War of 1864-65), by Pundit Nain Singh in 1875, and by Harman's distant observations of peaks in Bhutan made from the plains of Bengal and Assam. Now the route surveys of R.N. and P.A., apart from covering much new ground, tied together the separate observations of Pemberton, Godwin-Austen, and Nain Singh, as well as linking up with the survey of U.G. just to the north of the Bhutan-Tibet border.[75] In addition, R.N. returned with much useful data on the politics and administration of Bhutan. Atkinson, who wrote up the narratives of both R.N. and P.A., was able to produce a new sketch map of Bhutan.[76]

At the time that R.N. returned to Darjeeling, Tanner was there acting as survey officer to the Macaulay Mission, waiting for orders to proceed into Tibet. At this point, Tanner probably learned of Kintup's return. Perhaps he had even known of it for some time but had had no opportunity or incentive to take down his narrative. Now, having processed R.N.'s report, and with the Macaulay Mission going nowhere, Tanner had time on his hands. Furthermore, since R.N. had not been able to reach the Tsangpo, Tanner now had a good reason to question the one pundit who had succeeded in pushing downriver past Gyala Sindong. Tanner sent for Kintup. It was nearly two years since the explorer had returned.[77]

It must be remembered that Kintup was illiterate. He returned without any written observations, field notes, route bearings, or notations of temperature and altitude. His companion, whose status as a lama would have carried some weight, was not to be found. Kintup had been gone a long time, and Harman, the one man who would have trusted him, was dead and buried in Europe. Harman's superior, General Walker, had retired as surveyor-general in 1883.[78] And so, perhaps, it was not surprising that two years passed before his story was finally taken down.

Kintup first dictated an account of his travels to Lama Ugyen Gyatso, which was translated into English by Norpu, an employee of the Survey of India.[79] This narrative was then compiled into a brief report published in 1888 in the general report of the Survey of India for 1886-87, which was accompanied by a map sketching "the course of the Sangpo from information supplied by K.P." The full narrative of Kintup's expedition was only published the following year, five years after his return.

Kintup was rewarded with a grant of Rs. 3,000.[80] Nevertheless, because he was illiterate and not a trained explorer, his observations were given less weight than those of other pundits. He went on one further expedition, in a minor capacity, and then resumed earning his living as a tailor, or as a guide and assistant to British sportsmen and travelers.

Colonel Tanner, who wrote up Kintup's narrative for publication, reported that both Ugyen Gyatso and Rinzing Namgyal had said that Kintup's dates and distances "may be relied on as fairly true." Tanner himself commented, "I have no doubt that his account is a *bona-fide* story of his travels."[81] This statement was slightly, but significantly, changed the following year to read that Kintup's information "can *only* be regarded as a *bona-fide* story of his travels."[82] In other words, Kintup was believed to be telling the truth to the best of his ability, but because of his lack of education and training, little reliance could be placed on his observations. Consequently, there was a reluctance to consider that he had significantly advanced the resolution of the Tsangpo-Brahmaputra problem

In fact, although uneducated, Kintup was highly intelligent. Perhaps because he did not have the ability to write anything down and so remind himself at leisure, his powers of memory were highly developed. This was clear from the amount of data in his narrative on events, dates, names of villages, and other geographical details, all taken down years after his journey. Decades later, this narrative proved to be amazingly accurate.

Ironically, the one statement in his narrative that attracted the most attention was precisely that which was subsequently shown to be false. Kintup had stated that about two miles from Pemakochung the Tsangpo "falls over a cliff . . . from a height of 150 feet. There is a big lake at the foot of the falls where rainbows are always observable."[83] A great waterfall on the Brahmaputra, perhaps rivaling the largest known, was what many geographers were anticipating, and they seized on Kintup's observation with excitement.

Their anticipation stemmed in part from a commentary on the 1878-79 exploration of Nem Singh. This journey virtually assured the continuity of the Tsangpo with the Brahmaputra, but given the known altitudes of the Tsangpo at Lhasa, Chetang, and Gyala Sindong, this meant that the river had to drop seven or eight thousand feet before entering the plains of Assam. "This interval," trumpeted writers in the *Proceedings* of the Royal Geographical Society, "must include some grand development of fluvial topography,"[84] with the unexplored portion of the river concealing "a scene of wonderful sublimity—one of the last, and perhaps the grandest, of nature's secrets."[85] However, in the official report of Nem Singh's expedition, appearing in 1880, Harman sounded a distinctly cautious note, saying that "if the Tsangpo be the Dihang branch of the Brahmaputra, then it has a fall of about 7,000 feet in about 160 miles, or 40 feet per mile, which is not a very great fall for Himalayan rivers."[86] But Kintup's report specifically stated that a waterfall of 150 feet existed, and the Survey of India said that Kintup was reliable. It was not until much later that a waterfall of this size was shown to be illusory and that Kintup had been a victim of an error made when his oral narrative was taken down. He had never claimed to have seen a waterfall of 150 feet. But this did not come to light until 1913, and so the belief in some massive cataract continued for decades.[87]

The next attempt "to solve one of the great geographical mysteries of the age, the problem of the Tsangpo falls," was planned in 1905, in the aftermath of the occupation of Lhasa by the Younghusband Expedition. Captain C.H.D. Ryder of the Survey of India had suggested that he lead an expedition down the Tsangpo, to be escorted by one hundred Gurkhas. J.F. Needham, a British official in Assam, was to travel up the Dihang from Sadiya to meet Ryder in Tibet.[88] But the expedition was vetoed by the

Indian government, which did not want to run the risk of military involvement with the people on the Assam frontier.[89] As a result, it was not until well into the twentieth century that Kintup was finally vindicated.

Meanwhile, additional information continued to be acquired supporting the identity of the Tsangpo with the Brahmaputra. Even while Kintup was being held in slavery, Sarat Chandra Das had traveled downriver from Chetang for about twenty-five miles in 1882, and the following year Ugyen Gyatso had succeeded in getting another twenty miles or so beyond that. But the most rewarding journey of all was made by the explorer Kishen Singh (A.K.), who arrived back in India after a four-year journey.[90]

On his return route to Darjeeling, A.K. had passed through southeastern Tibet, close to the border with Assam.[91] His intention had been to proceed directly through Tibet to Assam, but he was prevented from doing so by the Mishmi people on the Assam border. Turning to the northwest, he crossed the Tsangpo at Chetang and continued to Darjeeling. From the route which A.K. took it was clear that he would have had to have crossed the Tsangpo twice if it ran into the Irrawaddy. In fact, he crossed it only once. When this information was joined with Harman's measurements of the effluents of the Brahmaputra, the identity of the Tsangpo with the Dihang/Brahmaputra seemed settled "once for all."[92]

But Robert Gordon did not give up. It was his original report that had rekindled the idea that the Tsangpo might flow into the Irrawaddy. Now he counterattacked with a closely argued paper read in front of the members of the Royal Geographical Society on 9 March 1885.[93] This was just three months after Walker's paper to the society had detailed how the travels of A.K. proved that the Tsangpo could not possibly join the Irrawaddy.

Gordon again produced as evidence the views of the ancient Chinese geographers. He also made a numerical analysis of the discharge of the rivers in the area, using his own measurements of the Irrawaddy, selectively quoting the observations made by others of the tributaries of the Brahmaputra, and criticizing the work done by Harman. Harman's observations, alleged Gordon, were not truly representative because they were made during the dry season.[94] Finally, Gordon quoted at length from the Survey of India's analysis of the route of A.K. to show that, in his view, the survey had misinterpreted the results of the expedition, which in fact (alleged Gordon) served to corroborate his theory linking the Tsangpo to the Irrawaddy.

This was too much for Walker, who was sitting in the audience, and who had been provided in advance with a copy of Gordon's paper. Walker demolished Gordon's arguments one by one. Ancient Chinese geographers, he said, knew virtually nothing of the Brahmaputra. As for Gordon's interpretation of A.K.'s expedition, A.K., he said, would "certainly wonder greatly when he hears this." Hennessey, of the Survey of India, had written the official report of A.K.'s travels. "Is it possible to believe for a moment," demanded Walker, "that the Pandit's work is better understood by Mr. Gordon, who has never seen or corresponded with him, than it is by Mr. Hennessey, who has known him intimately for many years, and has supervised the mapping of all his explorations?"[95]

Walker concluded by referring to the route by which Gordon proposed the Tsangpo flowed eastward toward Burma and commented sarcastically that to do this it would "have either to take a flying leap over the Brahmaputra or to burrow under that river."[96]

After this onslaught, no other member of the society was prepared to comment. Gordon apparently made no rejoinder, and the president diplomatically concluded the meeting by saying that the matter would be settled finally only by actual exploration down the Tsangpo. But from this time on, little was heard to challenge the view that the Tsangpo and the Brahmaputra were one and the same.

The final blow to any hopes that Gordon might have retained for his theory came only a few months later. In his paper, Gordon had been critical of the observations made by the Pundit A.K. A.K. had shown that the Tsangpo could not flow round to the north of the Lohit Brahmaputra to join the Irrawaddy. Gordon agreed that this was true and alleged that the Lohit was not in fact the Brahmaputra, but that it flowed into the Tsangpo on its way to the Irrawaddy.

This theory was immediately challenged by J.F. Needham, an assistant political officer at Sadiya in Upper Assam, who set off in December 1885 in the company of Captain E.H. Molesworth and a detachment of native police by a route that closely followed the Lohit Brahmaputra. The expedition traveled through Mishmi country to the outskirts of Rima on the Tibetan side of the border. On their return in January 1886 they were able to confirm the observations of A.K. and prove that the river flowing through Rima (the Zayul) was the Lohit Brahmaputra. This left no space on the map for any imaginary line connecting the Tsangpo to the Irrawaddy.[97] The identity of the Tsangpo with the Dihang was no longer open to question.[98]

Kintup, the man who had effectively been the first to prove that this was the case, remained in relative obscurity. Colonel Tanner, who had compiled his report, had faith in Kintup's account of his travels, as did others in the survey. Tanner believed in the existence of the waterfall because of Kintup's description of the rainbow there. Outside the survey, however, his account was given little credence.[99]

In 1889, Kintup accompanied Rinzing Namgyal on another expedition. The two were dispatched by Tanner to Sadiya, where they reported to Needham. Their objective was to travel with Needham up the Dihang. They were to survey the unknown area up to the lowest point reached by Kintup and beyond that to verify his earlier data.[100] But the expedition never took place, as it was vetoed on political grounds by the chief commissioner for Assam.[101] Rinzing Namgyal did collect some information from Mishmi and Abor traders in Sadiya, on the basis of which a revised map of the lower Tsangpo was drawn up.[102] Needham, who took the opportunity to question Kintup in the company of a group of Abors, concluded that Kintup had not traveled any distance south of Gyala Sindong.[103]

Kintup subsequently accompanied Major Waddell of the Indian Medical Corps on a number of expeditions. At one point, Waddell dispatched Kintup into Tibet across the Gora pass in eastern Sikkim. Waddell wanted to use the pass, which he had heard was unguarded, for his own secret incursions into Tibet. Kintup crossed the pass and penetrated seven days' march beyond the frontier before being arrested and imprisoned by Tibetan authorities. He eventually managed to escape and return to Sikkim.[104] When Waddell was ordered to join the Younghusband Expedition in 1903, he arrived at Siliguri railway station, near Darjeeling, to find his "trusty old servant" waiting for him. Kintup accompanied Waddell to Lhasa.[105]

Several questions about the Tsangpo, however, remained unresolved. What was the route it took to the Dihang? Did it travel through rocky gorges and deep defiles, through a series of rapids? And did the mighty falls which Kintup had apparently discovered really exist?

Attempts to proceed down the Tsangpo were abandoned, to be replaced by efforts at exploration from other directions. An attempt made in 1899 failed when Major Davies (who was mapping the province of Yunnan in southwestern China) was ordered, together with Captain Ryder of the Survey of India, to approach the Tsangpo from the east, but was turned back by the Tibetans.[106]

Another attempt to penetrate the area, this time from the south, was made in 1901. Under the direction of J.F. Needham, two Gurkhas, trained by the Survey of India, traveled up the Dihang as far as Kebang, about forty-five miles northwest of Sadiya, before being turned back by the Abors.[107] After this, apart from the abortive attempt in connection with the Younghusband Expedition, nothing was done until 1911 and the Abor Expedition.

In 1910, the Chinese began to extend their control over the districts of Pome and Zayul, and down the Lohit Brahmaputra. This extension of Chinese influence threatened the security of the northeast frontier of British India and forced the Indian government to reconsider its policy of noninterference with the tribal peoples of the Assam Himalayan region. Against this background, the catalyst was provided by the killing in 1911 of Noel Williamson, who had taken over the position of assistant political officer at Sadiya from J.F. Needham. Williamson had set out up the Dihang to check on Chinese infiltration into Abor territory when he and his party were murdered by the Abors. As a result, in the same year a punitive expedition was sent against the Abors, together with friendly missions to the neighboring tribes. Apart from simple retribution, the task of the Abor Expedition was to survey the Indian frontier with Tibet, assess the degree of Chinese influence in the area, and, finally, to map the route of the Dihang, as it connected the Tsangpo to the Brahmaputra. In order to assist the expedition, Kintup's narrative was republished in 1911.

The main force of the Expedition penetrated into Abor territory up the Dihang only as far as Kebang. Other detachments explored the tributaries of the Dihang. One party proceeded a considerable distance north up the river, marching to the village of Singging, about forty miles north of the southernmost point reached by Kintup. Opinions differed as to whether Kintup had actually traveled in the area. The unit was accompanied by Mr. Bentinck, the expedition's political officer. He could find little correspondence between what he saw and the observations of Kintup. "When his [Kintup's] journey into Aborland is described," he commented with sarcasm to an audience at the Royal Geographical Society, "as 'one of the romances of the Survey of India,' I am prepared to let it go at that."[108] Sir Thomas Holdich, who was present at the meeting, spoke up in support of Kintup, reminding the audience that Kintup had dictated from memory, years after his explorations occurred. Another member of the Abor Expedition wrote in to the society alleging that "the names of the villages along its course [the Dihang] agree remarkably well with the names given by Kinthup."[109]

At the same RGS meeting, the question of the identity of the Tsangpo with the Dihang was again raised, this time by Captain Bethell, who had been part of the Younghusband Expedition and was familiar with the size of the Tsangpo near Lhasa. It was, he said, "a very big river indeed." Eight years later, he participated in the expedition against the Abors and saw the Dihang at the point where it entered the plains of Assam. Instead of being an even mightier river, it seemed to have less volume than it did seven hundred miles upstream in Tibet. Although Bethell had no answer to the problem of where the Tsangpo went if it did not join the Dihang, he did succeed in demonstrating that all doubts about the link between the Tsangpo and the Brahmaputra could not be finally laid to rest until the connection had actually been surveyed.[110]

Just such an attempt had been made in 1911 by Frederick Bailey. Bailey was an army officer who had formed what was to be a lifelong interest in Tibet while he was attached to the Younghusband Expedition. When this was concluded, he joined Rawlings's expedition to western Tibet and then transferred to the Political Department of the Indian government. He was appointed British trade agent at Gyantse in 1905. After more than three years in Tibet—first in Gyantse and then in the Chumbi valley—Bailey took leave in England. While working in Tibet, Bailey had read all he could find about the country, learned the language, and resolved "to solve the question of the falls on the great river."[111] Bailey was aware of the unsuccessful attempt made by Davies and Ryder to approach the Tsangpo through China. Large expeditions, he thought, were doomed to failure because of the animosity they invoked from both the Chinese and the Tibetans. But perhaps a single individual, able to speak colloquial Tibetan, familiar with the customs of the country, and traveling with just one servant, might be able to slip through. By January 1911, Bailey was ready to put his ideas to the test and use the remaining part of his leave to explore the Tsangpo on his way back to India.

Carrying surveying instruments loaned by the Royal Geographical Society, Bailey took the Trans-Siberia railway to Peking, continued by train to Hankou and thence by boat up the Yangtse. Pressing on by sedan chair and on foot, Bailey reached Tachienlu in western China in May and Batang, on the Tibetan frontier, in June. Shortly afterwards he crossed the frontier into southeastern Tibet. Bailey was soon traveling through territory traversed by A.K., and even though thirty years had elapsed, he was able to verify the accuracy of A.K.'s descriptions of the names and locations of villages on his route. After crossing the Mekong by rope bridge, Bailey soon came to the Zayul River (Lohit Brahmaputra), which he followed upstream. By late June he reached Shugden Gompa (monastery). There he discovered that a river not far to the north, the Ngagong Chu, ran into the Tsangpo. Once on the Tsangpo, he could search for and identify Kintup's waterfall. "I was now," Bailey stated, "on the very verge of the country into which it had been my object to enter."[112]

Unfortunately, the areas through which Bailey proposed to journey were very disturbed, with pitched battles occurring as local tribesmen resisted the imposition of Chinese control. The head of the monastery (who was also the local jongpon) believed that Bailey would either be killed by the tribespeople or executed by the Chinese as a spy. In either case, it would be he who got the blame for allowing Bailey into the area. Bailey thought the story about disturbances was made up for his benefit, but later discovered that it was true. Dispirited, after having traveled halfway around the world only to be turned back when almost within sight of his goal, Bailey retraced his steps downriver and then followed the Lohit through Mishmi country to Sadiya along the route taken by Needham in 1885-86. He arrived in Sadiya in August 1911. His journey, often through unexplored territory, had been undertaken without any official backing, and Bailey was reprimanded for overstaying his leave. Geographically, however, the government found his explorations of value in supplying much needed information about the India-China-Tibet border area.[113] Bailey's contributions were soon recognized by the award of two medals—the Gill Memorial Medal of the RGS and the Macgregor Medal from the Royal United Service Institute of India.

It was while Bailey was in China that Williamson was murdered and the expedition launched to punish the Abors. One of the instructions to the expeditionary force was that it should "explore and survey as much of the country as possible, visiting, if practicable, the Pemakoi falls and incidentally settling the question of the identity of the Tsangpo and Brahmaputra rivers."[114] For Bailey, the Abor Expedition came at a fortuitous time and provided him with a second, and this time successful, opportunity to solve the riddle of the Tsangpo falls.

But first Bailey left Sadiya for Calcutta. There he was called upon to explain his overstay of leave, following which he was posted to Aligarh, 125 miles southwest of Delhi. After only ten days there he was summoned to Simla and told to produce a report of his journey as quickly as possible. While in Simla, Bailey used his influence with the foreign secretary, Sir Henry McMahon, to obtain a posting to the Abor Expedition. By 9 October 1911, he was back in Sadiya.[115]

When he reported to the camp of General Hamilton Bower, the commander of the Abor Expedition, Bailey found that he was regarded as just "that damn fellow from Simla."[116] In order to keep him busy, Bailey was sent off into the territory of the Chulikattas, to see if they intended to rise in support of the Abors. He found to the contrary that they were pleased at the prospect of the Abors, their enemies, being eliminated. With this business concluded, he was told to go back to Simla. From Simla Bailey returned to Aligarh.

It appeared that his plan had been thwarted yet again. But the survey parties sent out during the cold weather of 1911-12 did not finish their operations that season, and as a result, Bailey was ordered back to Sadiya in the autumn of 1912. There he was appointed intelligence officer of the Mishmi Exploration Survey, which was instructed to make a deeper foray into Chulikatta territory and so complete the mapping of the basin of the Dihang River. About one hundred miles due north of Sadiya, the force entered the village of Mipi, where Bailey was surprised to find a small community of Tibetans. It was February 1913. Bailey met one Tibetan who was a frequent traveler up and down the Tsangpo, and who was able to confirm many of Kintup's observations made in Abor country. He had even heard a story about logs being thrown into the river by Kintup. The man believed, wrote Bailey, that "these logs were afterwards found at Buddh-Gaza, together with others which had been thrown into the upper waters of the Ganges and Lohit, thus proving that these rivers united in the most holy of Buddhist places." Bailey commented, "we may, perhaps, allow rumors in Tibet to add a little romance to the foundations laid by Kintup's journey."[117]

Bailey was delighted to be able to practice his Tibetan and befriended the headman of the village, who offered to provide guides into Tibet. Here, he realized, "was my chance of getting through to Tibet from the Assamese side."[118]

Bailey wrote a report, combining details of Kintup's explorations with what the headman could tell him of the route to the Tsangpo. This report, appended to the report of the expedition written by the commander, Captain G.A. Nevill, would provide the justification for a subsequent request to follow up these routes.

Realizing that he could not accomplish a journey to the Tsangpo alone, Bailey asked a member of the survey team, Captain Henry Morshead, to join him. Morshead jumped at the chance. The two decided to remain at Mipi after the mission withdrew in April, and then proceed into Tibet. Nevill telegraphed this request to Simla. Simla responded by approving the expedition, but refusing permission to enter Tibet. Another telegram arrived forty-eight hours later, ordering Bailey to await further orders. Nevill was sympathetic to the mission, and the three of them decided to assume that Sir Henry McMahon had sent the first telegram, that he really wanted them to enter Tibet, but was forced to say the opposite in order to cover himself in case they were attacked. There was a lot of wishful thinking involved in this interpretation, as they had no idea even of who had written the order.

The second telegram was easier to deal with. Nevill volunteered to say that they had left before it arrived. Hastily assembling their supplies, Bailey and Morshead left Mipi on 16 May 1913 "with ten coolies and three local guides, in pouring rain."[119] At last the solution to the problem of the Tsangpo falls was in sight.

The two worked well together, and each praised the other in their subsequent reports to the government. Bailey did the work of negotiating with the tribal people and collecting specimens of the flora and fauna, while

Morshead kept up a survey of the route. Morshead was tireless, and apparently indifferent to physical discomfort. Bailey at times worried that Morshead's lack of concern for his own health could jeopardize their mission. Morshead, said Bailey, "would stand there covered with leeches and with blood oozing out of his boots as oblivious as a small child whose face is smeared with jam."[120]

The pair pushed on north, traveling to the east of the Tsangpo, before meeting up the river at Rinchenpung. Shortly thereafter they were detained by the chief minister of the Poba people, who forced them to accompany him to the "capital," the village of Showa, northeast of the Tsangpo. The minister was suspicious that they were working for the Chinese, who had only recently withdrawn from the area. The pair were released after a few days (after Bailey managed to gloss over the discovery of Chinese characters inscribed on Morshead's stick of Indian ink) but were not permitted to continue up the Tsangpo.

Morshead befriended the minister and showed him his survey instruments. The minister voiced no objection to Morshead's surveying and then recollected that "once many years previously a Chinaman had come from the west and had attempted to march through the country counting his paces and writing the numbers down in a book, but that in accordance with the custom of the time he had been bundled out of the country by the way he came, with the intimation that such things were not done in Pome."[121] This was a clear reference to the Chinese lama with whom Kintup had traveled. Jongjuk, where the incident had occurred, was only a few miles away. If the minister's story was correct, then the Chinese lama's abrupt abandonment of Kintup was not due to his betrayal of confidence to the jongpon at Jongjuk, but to the discovery of the true nature of his travels. The lama possibly fled for his life, rather than selling Kintup into slavery for profit.

From Showa they passed through Jongjuk and traveled westward round the great northern bend of the river, meeting up with it again at Pe. They were now in a position to follow the Tsangpo downriver to the falls.

Bailey and Morshead soon arrived at Gyala Sindong, Kintup's description of which, said Bailey, "is accurate." The two continued from Gyala to Pemakochung, spending the night in the same cave as Kintup and the lama. It was at Pemakochung that Kintup had made his famous and tantalizing observation that "the Tsangpo is two chains distant from the monastery and about 2 miles off it falls over a cliff called Sinji-Chogyal [Shingche Chogye] from a height of about 150 feet. There is a big lake at the foot of the falls where rainbows are always observable."[122]

At Sindong, on the opposite bank of the river from Gyala, Kintup had said that there was "a waterfall which drops from a height of about 100 feet into a stream."[123] Bailey saw the waterfall at Sindong, which was on an insignificant stream. The real falls had to be at Pemakochung. So it was with great anticipation that Bailey hoisted himself onto a rock one hundred feet above the water. It was July, and the river was full with the snow melt from the Himalayas. The view was frightening. Below him the foaming white water thrust violently through a narrow gorge fifty yards in width, dropping some thirty feet over a series of rapids. Spray, colored with rainbows, filled the air halfway up to Bailey's vantage point. But the cliff called Sinji Chogyal, over which the Tsangpo was supposed to drop 150 feet, was nowhere to be seen.[124]

Both Bailey and Morshead concluded at the time that Kintup had been confused.[125] Falls called Sinji Chogyal were discovered, but only on a small stream that entered the river opposite Gyala. It was here that Kintup had referred to a waterfall dropping into a stream, and it was here, Bailey and Morshead were told, that people believed that the god Shingche Chogye lived, behind the waterfall.[126] Bailey learned that two or three hundred pilgrims came to the spot every May on pilgrimage. The pilgrims burnt butter lamps and tried to see the god behind the waterfall. The falls were about thirty feet high, according to Bailey, with a chain hung with bells across them. Morshead observed three successive cascades of fifty feet each.[127] The god was either painted or carved into the rock behind the falls, but the volume of water made this impossible to discern.

Bailey was able to push down the river for a further twelve miles beyond Pemakochung before being stopped by a shortage of supplies and an impenetrable rhododendron forest.[128] He estimated that now only about forty-five miles of the river remained unexplored and gave up hope that Kintup's falls lay in this area. Everyone living in the region agreed that the rapids continued for some distance, but that there was no waterfall at any point. Kintup, it seemed, had unwittingly led everybody astray.

Bailey and Morshead retraced their steps up river and proceeded to Chetang. From here back to India they followed part way in the footsteps of Nain Singh, through the Yarlung valley to Tawang and into India via Bhutan. Looking thoroughly disreputable, they reached a junction on the Eastern Bengal State Railway on 15 November 1913, after a journey of 1,680 miles, much of which, with the exception of some parts visited by early eighteenth-century Catholic missionaries, had never before been seen by Europeans.[129]

Bailey's report provided the government of India with a great deal of political information about the administration of the areas through which he and Morshead had passed. Of particular interest was Bailey's assessment of the degree of Tibetan influence to the south of the main line of the Assam Himalayas. This assessment, together with information on Tawang, was important to Sir Henry McMahon in his construction in 1914 of the "McMahon Line," delimiting the boundary between India and China along the northeast frontier.[130]

In addition, the expedition had surveyed a large area of previously unexplored territory. Some 380 miles of the Tsangpo had been properly mapped for the first time. Interesting examples of new flora and fauna had also been acquired.[131]

But above all, the identity of the Tsangpo with the Brahmaputra, linked by the Dihang, had finally been proved. This was true even though a small part of the river had still not been actually observed. Bailey estimated that the unmapped section of the river was about forty-five miles in length.[132] Actually, it was less than that. Bailey was calculating the distance that he and Morshead had been unable to survey. Another survey team had pushed up the Dihang at the same time that Bailey and Morshead were traveling down the river. The gap between the two surveys was only about ten miles.[133]

But what of Kintup? How could he have been so wrong about the falls, and given this egregious error, could his other data be trusted? Had he really traveled down the Tsangpo as far as Onlet, or just stood on a hill and had the names of villages read out to him? Apart from the question of the falls, Bailey was impressed by the agreement he found between his own observations and those of Kintup. Although Kintup consistently underestimated his distance, Bailey called his descriptions "quite accurate."[134] One section which was very inaccurate was that immediately to the south of Jongjuk. But given that Kintup was fleeing from captivity and in fear of his life, this was hardly unexpected.[135] With respect to that part of the river traversed by Kintup but which Bailey had not seen, he was prepared to give Kintup the benefit of the doubt. Given that Kintup was illiterate and that his account was not taken down until years after his travels, Bailey said, "it is not surprising that he has made some mistakes and that on several occasions he has omitted complete marches. The surprising thing is that he was able to remember so much about his journey which has given us the only knowledge we have had of that country for thirty years."[136]

Confirmation of just how right Bailey was to have faith in Kintup was provided by George Dunbar, who was a member of the post-Abor Expedition survey party that proceeded up the Dihang during the cold weather season of 1912-13. Dunbar carried a copy of Kintup's narrative with him.[137]

The Tsangpo and the Brahmaputra 245

He was able to match up many details of what he saw, in the way of bridges, villages, and monasteries, with the narrative. Dunbar discovered that two villages Kintup had not mentioned, and for which his veracity had been doubted by Bentinck, had not even been built in 1884. Sometimes the names were incorrect, because of Kintup's unfamiliarity with the Abor dialect. It was this confusion over place names that had led Needham to doubt Kintup's story when he met him in 1889.

In total, the survey was able to identify all but about 20 of the 150 villages east of Chetang whose names had been provided by Kintup. Some of those twenty, the survey concluded, had just been caves or camps, or represented villages abandoned in the intervening thirty years.[138] At Marpung, Dunbar even donated fifty rupees to the head of the monastery, whose predecessor had sheltered the explorer from his pursuers.[139] The sum was the same paid by the monastery for Kintup in 1882. Kintup, concluded Dunbar, was "more often than not the complete Baedeker, endowed with the greatest determination and courage."[140]

If final proof of Kintup's veracity was needed, it came at Dalbuing (called Tarpin by Kintup) close to Olon (Onlet), the southernmost point reached by the pundit, where a survey party discovered that the villagers were still talking about a traveler from Tibet who had arrived thirty years before and had not been allowed to pass through.[141]

But the question of Kintup and the falls still remained. Now that it had been proved that he did indeed make the journey as claimed in his narrative, and that his account was, under the circumstances, remarkably accurate, how could he have reported observing a nonexistent 150-foot waterfall? Bailey was determined to find out.

He and Morshead reached Calcutta on 17 November 1913.[142] Shortly thereafter a telegram arrived from McMahon, ordering them to Simla, where they arrived on 26 November.[143] There Bailey resolved to find Kintup, if he was still alive, and question him about what he had seen. From Bailey's perspective this was important not just to set the record straight, but also to defend himself against those who still clung to a belief in the existence of the falls. Sir Thomas Holdich, perhaps out of loyalty to Kintup, had given an interview to the press the day after Bailey and Morshead returned to Calcutta, in which he questioned Bailey's statement that the falls did not exist. Unless they had actually visited the site of Kintup's falls, said Holdich, "the evidence as to their non-existence is imperfect."[144] Sir Thomas Holdich had served for thirty-two years with the Survey of India. He was the great authority on the northwest frontier and the recipient of a gold medal from the Royal Geographical Society.[145] He was also the author of a book on the exploration of Tibet.[146] His views were bound to carry weight. Bailey read the newspaper article and commented to Morshead "it looks as if we've just been wasting the last six months."[147]

Enquiries were made through the Survey of India, but they had no knowledge of Kintup. Bailey then wrote to a Sikkimese friend of his, a well-connected landlord, who soon located Kintup, alive and well, but living in poor circumstances in Darjeeling, where he worked as a tailor. Funds were authorized by Sir Sidney Burrard, the surveyor-general, for Kintup to come to Simla in May 1914.[148]

Bailey interviewed Kintup on the evening of his arrival in Simla. It must have been a marvelous moment for him to meet this legendary figure in whose footsteps he had followed. Soon all became clear. Kintup was able to recount vividly, even after thirty years, the 150-foot stream falling over the cliff at Gyala, concealing the god Shingche Chogye, and the thirty-foot rapids below Pemakochung. He had never, he said, reported that he had seen a 150-foot waterfall on the main river. Indeed, he compared what he had seen with the height of the house in which he and Bailey were sitting that evening.[149] Obviously, what had happened was that either Lama Ugyen Gyatso, who had taken down his narrative, or Norpu, who had translated it into English, had combined the separate observations of the falls at Gyala and the rapids below Pemakochung into one giant cataract. They must not have read his narrative back to him, and Kintup, unable to read it himself, never knew that he had created a mirage that had led on geographers and explorers for three decades.

Kintup was vindicated, and Bailey decided that something must be done for him so that he could end his years in a degree of comfort. Burrard agreed.[150] Bailey and Burrard argued with the government for a small pension for Kintup. The government was adamantly opposed to the idea, claiming that Kintup might live to be ninety. Eventually the government agreed to a lump sum payment of Rs. 1,000. This turned out to be all for the best. After being honored by the viceroy and presented with a parchment certificate of honor by Burrard, Kintup returned to Darjeeling, where he died a few months later.[151]

Armed with the new information provided by Kintup, Bailey returned to London on leave and read a full account of his expedition to the RGS on 22 June 1914.[152] Morshead was in the audience, and the two had prepared for a confrontation with Sir Thomas Holdich, who was also present. It never happened. Holdich praised the two for their explorations and confined himself to expressing his disappointment that the falls did not exist. For his work, the society awarded Bailey the Patron's Gold Medal in 1916.[153]

Morshead received the Macgregor Medal. Bailey continued to distinguish himself on the frontier as political officer in Sikkim (1921-28), Resident in Kashmir (1932-33), and envoy to the court of Nepal (1935-38). He died in 1967 at the age of 85. Morshead was not so fortunate. He was murdered in the jungle near Maymyo in Burma, "during an early Sunday morning ride," on 17 May 1931.[154]

NINE
Questions of Secrecy

There was a natural desire on the part of the personnel of the Survey of India to obtain as much credit as possible from the exploits of their trans-Himalayan explorers. The whole idea of using Indian explorers to map the territories beyond the frontiers came from within the survey, as did their recruitment and training, most of the decisions on the objectives of their missions, and the analysis of their results. Men such as Montgomerie, Trotter, and Walker naturally wanted to publicize their own achievements and those of the pundits, particularly through the meetings and publications of the Royal Geographical Society. The RGS was the world's foremost institution for the dissemination of new geographical information, and its gatherings were attended by the leading figures in every area of exploration. To be invited to present a paper to the society, and then to have the paper published in its *Journal*, was highly prized, and the award of one of the society's gold medals would add luster to any career.

Officials of the British and Indian governments, on the other hand, took a different view. At the very least, they thought, premature revelation of, for example, the methods used by the pundits to gain clandestine entry into Tibet could endanger lives on future expeditions. Many of the reports submitted by the pundits contained geographical information that could be of military value to the Russians. Maps might reveal the details of strategic passes, information that would be vital to an enemy bent on the invasion of India.[1] Other reports included political revelations and comments about foreign governments that, if read by the individuals concerned, could prove embarrassing to the British government, and certainly not conducive to the maintenance of good diplomatic relations. From the government's point of view, therefore, these reports of the Survey of India were best published in limited quantities for circulation within the official community, to be released to the general public only after careful scrutiny and the excision of all sensitive or offensive material. The attitudes of the government and the Survey of India were so opposed that it was inevitable that conflict would occur.

In the early years of the pundits, information on their activities was published freely. There is no record either of the government requiring that material for publication should first be submitted for official approval or of any retribution taken when material that might best have been kept secret appeared in publicly available journals. In 1863, Montgomerie's letter proposing to train Indians to explore beyond the frontiers and to equip them with surveying instruments was read by Walker to a meeting of the Asiatic Society of Bengal and published in their proceedings for that year. The letter even revealed that Chinese Turkestan should be the explorers' first objective, followed by western Tibet and then Lhasa.[2]

Montgomerie's first explorer, the Munshi Abdul Hamid, was in fact sent to Yarkand in Chinese Turkestan in 1863. He perished on his return journey, and it can only be assumed as a possibility that there might have been a connection between the publication of Montgomerie's letter and the mysterious demise of the Munshi.

Political material on Yarkand and of the Chinese administration in Turkestan were passed over to the Punjab government before the rest of the Munshi's papers were forwarded to Montgomerie. From these, Montgomerie compiled a report which was read to the RGS on 14 May 1866.[3] This report revealed the basic principles behind the deceptions employed by the native explorers in order to gain entry and survey territory forbidden to Europeans. These principles were that the explorers should be of an occupation and religion identical to those of legitimate travelers (the Munshi was a Muslim, traveling to a Muslim region, and accompanied a caravan disguised as a merchant) and that surveying instruments were to be concealed among their possessions. In the case of the Munshi, Montgomerie's presentation also included the details that the head of his spiked staff, an item usually carried by travelers, was larger than usual, and flat so as to accommodate a compass. The account also included a map of the Munshi's route.

Montgomerie, already the recipient of a gold medal from the RGS, was eager to bask in the glory of the accolades received at this meeting, where Sir Roderick Murchison, the society's president, together with Sir Andrew Waugh and Sir Henry Rawlinson, were fulsome in their praise. There was certainly no harm in revealing the identity of the explorer, for the Munshi was dead. But disclosing the details of concealed surveying instruments and disguises was another matter.

Montgomerie made further revelations with respect to Nain Singh's first expedition, made between 1865 and 1866. Entering Tibet from Nepal, Nain Singh explored along the road from Gartok to Lhasa. Montgomerie's account of this major achievement appeared in the survey report for 1866-67, published in 1867.[4] He also read the report verbatim to a meeting of the RGS on 23 March 1868, and it was published without change in the society's journal later that year.[5]

In this account, Montgomerie discusses the lies and disguises that enabled Nain Singh to enter Tibet and reside at Lhasa. There is a list of the surveying equipment carried on the expedition, about which Montgomerie revealed that the prayer wheel carried, not the usual scrolls of Buddhist prayers, but strips of paper on which bearings and paces were written. In addition, Montgomerie noted that because border officials never examined prayer wheels, the survey had constructed some which were fitted with compasses, for use on future expeditions. Montgomerie also explained how the traditional rosary of 108 beads contained only 100 in the "Survey version," every tenth bead being larger than the rest, so that Nain Singh could easily keep track of his paces. About the only secret information not revealed to anyone who cared to read the *Journal* was the pundit's name and his home village, which was only referred to as being "one of the upper valleys of the Himalayas . . . [whose] countrymen [have] always been granted by the Chinese authorities the privilege of travelling and trading in Nari-Khorsum, the upper basin of the Sutlej."[6]

Montgomerie's paper on the next expedition of Nain Singh, which was made to the goldfields of Western Tibet in 1867, was read to the RGS on 12 April 1869. Again, information about the disguise used was given, but beyond a mention of hidden instruments, no further details of the equipment were provided.[7] A similar paper, recounting Kalian Singh's travels in Tibet in 1868, followed a year later.[8] The RGS itself edited the report and printed only a summary in its *Proceedings*. What was omitted was only that which was not germane to the main expedition, and the report was later published in full in the *Journal of the Asiatic Society of Bengal*.[9]

The account of the Mirza's travels in the region between India and Russia and on to Kashgar, made between 1867 and 1869, was delivered to the society on 24 April 1871.[10] For the first time it appears that, for political reasons, material in Montgomerie's report was not recounted to the RGS. A description of the mir of Badakhshan given in the official survey report ("small eyes and a scanty beard . . . given to drinking . . . allows his petty officials to do very much as they like: he is consequently unpopular") does not appear in the society's *Journal*.[11] But there is no indication as to who made the cuts, some of which, in any case, seem designed to reduce the size of a lengthy narrative. Nevertheless, even though some political material was eliminated from the public version, very full details of the Mirza's itinerary were given, plus a good deal of background information on the explorer himself. Furthermore, Walker, who was present at the meeting, spoke up on the covert uses to which the rosary and the prayer wheel were put by the pundits, and this information was subsequently printed in the *Proceedings*.[12]

No pattern of vetting material developed at this time. Montgomerie read his account of the mission of the Havildar across the northwest frontier to the RGS in May 1872, and it was identical to the official report.[13] The same was true of Hari Ram's travels around Mount Everest, made in 1871.[14] This account of Hari Ram's explorations was published in the *Journal* of the RGS in 1875, together with details of his subsequent travels in 1873 and Kishen Singh's journey to Lake Tengri Nor in 1871-72.[15] The only difference between the official report (included in the Survey Report for 1873-74) and the version published by the RGS was that the RGS account omitted the reference to an outbreak of cholera in Kumaon, which killed Hari Ram's wife. Both accounts were described as "Extracts from an Explorer's Narrative," but no fuller version was published in any form.

Possibly Montgomerie, if he stopped to consider the question, thought that the Chinese authorities did not read the *Journal* of the RGS and that even if they did, then lack of concern or sheer bureaucratic inefficiency would prevent the information from being acted upon. Montgomerie did admit at one point that the activities of his explorers had been "somewhat impeded by the publicity given to the results of former expeditions,"[16] but this was likely due to the jealousy of one of Nain Singh's acquaintances in India, who might have informed Tibetan officials of his activities.[17]

Established procedures existed for the handling of secret material. After the 1858 mutiny, the powers of the government of India were transferred to the British Crown, and a new India Office was created, headed by a secretary of state with a position in the Cabinet. The Political and Secret Department of the India Office, which took over the functions of the former Secret Committee of the East India Company, was especially concerned with frontier matters and countries bordering on India. It was the custom of this department to review secret material on these areas received from India and then to pass on nonpolitical scientific data to both the India Office's Geographical Department and to the Royal Geographical Society. Not surprisingly, some explorers sought to circumvent this cumbersome bureaucracy. This had occurred in the case of T.T. Cooper, a traveler who was not connected to the Survey of India but who had hoped to reach Lhasa from China and then continue to India. Although he was unsuccessful in attaining these goals, his Chinese passport being ignored by the Tibetans, he wrote an interesting account of his journey.[18] In 1870, the secretary of state wrote to India, complaining that only one copy of Cooper's diary of his travels had arrived in London and that it had been sent by Cooper himself not to the India Office, but to the RGS. The government in London had received only an abbreviated account of Cooper's travels and clearly did not wish to learn the details at second hand from the Royal Geographical Society.[19]

The release of information on the activities of the pundits was not initially criticized by the authorities. For one thing, in the accounts of the Munshi's visit to Yarkand and Nain Singh's journey to Lhasa, there was little political information, beyond the fact that illegal entries had been made into territory claimed by China, which could embarrass the Indian or British government. Nor were the geographical data perceived as being of any great value to a foreign power. But in the case of Afghanistan and the northwest frontier, the usefulness of geographical data to the Russians was a major consideration. Russia had occupied Tashkent in 1865. Two years later the Central Asian Khanate of Bokhara submitted, and the Russians constituted the new province of Russian Turkestan. It was only a matter of time before Khiva fell. With the czarist empire advancing to the Afghan border and posing an increasing threat to the security of India, the Indian government had no wish to disturb diplomatic relations with the Afghan rulers or to provide Russian generals with details of the terrain between Russian and Indian territory.

It was out of this context that friction grew between the government of India and the Great Trigonometrical Survey, revolving particularly around the superintendent of the GTS, Colonel James Walker. In 1867, Walker had been castigated by the viceroy for dispatching the Mirza to Afghanistan and Turkestan without the prior approval of the lieutenant-governor of the Punjab.[20] In this instance, ruffled feathers were smoothed. But a major row broke out in 1876. This concerned a publication entitled *Secret and Confidential Report on the Trans-Himalayan Explorations by Employé's of the Great Trigonometrical Survey of India, during 1873-74-75*. This report contained the narratives of three important expeditions—those of the Havildar to the upper Oxus and Badakhshan, of the Mullah across the Wakhan to the Baroghil pass, and of Nain Singh from Leh to Lhasa. All three explorers had returned to India in late 1874 or early 1875, and Captain Henry Trotter, who had just completed his work on the results of the Forsyth mission, was persuaded by Walker to stay on to analyze the data and write up the narratives of the three pundits. The report was printed by the government in Calcutta in 1876.

In February 1876, the viceroy, Lord Northbrook, discovered that some copies of the report were in circulation within days after publication, and before a copy had been seen by him. The viceroy, who was at that time unaware of the contents of the report, immediately issued an order reconfirming that all reports of surveys beyond the frontier were to be considered confidential and that they were not to be distributed to anyone without the written permission of the Foreign Department of the government of India.[21] This decision was communicated by the government to Colonel Walker a few days later.[22]

When Trotter's report was formally submitted to the Foreign Department, it quickly became apparent that its publication was open to serious objections. As the department later related to London: "[F]irst, there were remarks of a political character, which, if generally known, could not fail to be productive of much mischief. Such, for example, are the observations at Page 9 of the Havildar's journey, where the late Naib Muhhamad Alum Khan, then the most trusted and powerful of the Afghan Nobles, is described as 'detested throughout the whole of his Government for his cruelty, oppression, and gross debaucheries.'"[23]

Other similarly embarrassing passages were contained in the report. But the report was also open to the more general objection that it was a collection of narratives by "secret Agents" which included the methods employed by them to escape detection, and that as such, the report as it stood was "entirely unsuitable for publication." To render it publishable the Foreign Department decided that "the report should be revised and confined to recording geographical results without any narrative of the journey accomplished, or any other matter of a personal character."[24]

Walker was strongly opposed to this decision. He was willing to remove objectionable passages, but he claimed that the pundits' narratives were "the backbone of the Report," and that if the rules of the Foreign Department were strictly adhered to, then four-fifths of the report would have to be omitted.[25]

The Foreign Department agreed with Walker that the excision of embarrassing comments about foreign dignitaries would remove one of their objections to publication. But no agreement could be reached with the superintendent of the GTS over the narratives of his explorers. From Colonel Walker's perspective, simply to list the geographical results of the expeditions would eliminate all details of the methods by which these results were obtained, and this was the unique contribution of the Survey of India. In the absence of any willingness on the part of Walker to implement the guidelines laid down, the Foreign Department had no choice but to leave the report with its original, unexpurgated text, but at the same time to label it "secret and confidential" so as not to permit its public circulation in any form.[26]

Walker's bluff had been called. He had refused to produce a watered-down version of the report, and so could not now publish any information whatsoever about the results of an extremely important series of explorations conducted over the preceding three years.[27]

The Foreign Department justified its decision by pointing out that the explorations were not only of geographical but also of political value and that the interests of the empire would be harmed if these explorations had to be halted. Publication of this report could lead to exposure of the explorers, or at least to added difficulties being placed in their way. One government official, in a minute to the Foreign Department, said that it was simply not possible to render the report suitable for publication by the mere elimination of embarrassing paragraphs, "for the objection taken by Govt. was not so much to any particular passages as to the publication to the world of the personal adventures and experiences of our spies, for spies they are, though the Survey Dept. euphemistically terms them 'explorers.'"[28]

The Foreign Department concurred. If only, they bemoaned, "we could send our Agents into Central Asia as Captain Prshevalski is sent into Mongolia, openly and with a military escort at his back, the case would be different: but it is not so." Unable to follow the example of the Russians, Britain had to use deception and cunning, in the light of which, the Foreign Department concluded, it was not possible freely to publish "the adventures of our Agents, whose very names, before long, become by-words in the mouths of persons interested in watching their movements."[29]

There the question seemed to rest. As the Indian government summed up:

> We are convinced that, whether in the interests of the British Empire in India or in the interests of the intrepid explorers whose lives are endangered for our sake, it is essential that a veil should be drawn over the proceedings by means of which our intelligence in respect to Trans-Himalayan countries is acquired. And we have no doubt that the distinguished officers, under whose orders the explorations have been conducted, will find some harmless way of placing their stores of information at the command of the literary and scientific world, without bringing into jeopardy those objects which the researches in question are mainly designed to serve.[30]

In the light of this authoritative statement, the sudden publication in the public press of material apparently drawn from Trotter's secret and confidential report caused great consternation. News items in the *Pall Mall Budget* of 7 April 1876, and the *Daily News* both contained information on the Baroghil pass on the northwest frontier, which the *Pall Mall Budget* described as the "key to one of the chief gates of India." The *Pall Mall Budget* also specifically referred to the travels of the Mullah in 1874, indicating to the authorities that the writer had apparently had access to Trotter's report. Between them, the two papers discussed the advantages and disadvantages of the Baroghil pass as an invasion route. With the Russians in mind, the Indian Government commented that "it seems scarcely necessary to remark that the premature publication of such information and comments, before we are ready for action, may prove of the utmost political embarrassment to us."[31]

Even worse, an article appeared in London in the *Times* indicating that the Russian geographer Colonel Venioukoff was very familiar with British explorations of the Upper Oxus. Indeed, said the Colonel, "the English having investigated this country for many years past, the greater part of what we have gleaned of its political arrangements is derived from the information collected by their agents."[32] The colonel mentioned by name the Mirza, the Havildar, and the Munshi, among others.

From this evidence the government concluded that someone was leaking secret information from Trotter's report to the press and to the Russians, either directly or indirectly. Equally likely, it seemed that the most probable source of the leak was either Colonel Walker, superintendent of the GTS, or possibly Captain Trotter, the author of the report.

Walker had always believed in the swapping of geographical data with the Russians. If they could provide good maps of their frontier areas adjacent to British interests, then he was happy to have them, and to provide his data in return. Over a decade earlier, he had noted that the Russian government differentiated between geographical and other information, with the geographical material going to the Imperial Russian Geographical Society for publication by them. Walker wrote: "it is from the [Russian] Geographical Society therefore that whatever information is from time to time acquired of the countries between the Russian and British frontiers may be most readily obtained."[33] So that he could share in this information, Walker traveled to St. Petersburg in 1864. There he was elected a member of the Geographical Society, and with the help of Lord Napier, the British ambassador, and a gift of maps from the India Office, Walker acquired maps and data not only from the Geographical Society but also from the War Office in the Russian capital. There he was given free access to the Topographical Department, after explaining that he "did not seek topographical information on the interior of Russia."[34]

After his visit to St. Petersburg, Walker developed a network of informal contacts with the Russians. Material on the pundits, including details on the clandestine use of the prayer wheel, was sent to the secretary of the Imperial Russian Geographical Society, Baron Frederick Osten Sacken, in St. Petersburg in 1869. The prayer wheel itself followed a year later.[35] Walker was also in correspondence in Moscow with the Russian Central Asian explorer Alexis Fedchenko, before his death in 1873.[36] Walker's revised map of Turkestan, published in 1874, was compiled in part with the help of maps and information from Russian sources, including route maps and sketches supplied by Baron Osten Sacken and Fedchenko to illustrate their own explorations.[37] Walker also kept in close contact with the German cartographer August Petermann, the editor of the important geographical journal *Petermann's Mitteilungen,* and sent him a map of Turkestan, plus the report of the 1867-68 travels of Nain and Kalian Singh to the goldfields of western Tibet.[38] In the case of British geographers, Walker kept in touch with his old colleague Montgomerie, who had been living in semi-retirement in England since early 1873. There was also constant correspondence between Walker and his cousin Clements Markham, geographer at the India Office, editor (since 1872) of the *Geographical Magazine,* and the author of a book on the history of the Survey of India.[39]

Walker was therefore used to sharing geographical information with professional colleagues, regardless of nationality. The fact that the Russians, unlike the British, had no need to acquire this information by secret means was not a distinction that Walker considered to be a vital one. Otherwise, he would not have sent a Russian geographer one of the prayer wheels used to conceal the compass and survey notes of the pundits. Nor, perhaps, did Walker appreciate that the Russians did not need to fear that their recently mapped territories might be subject to attack from India.

An inquiry was launched by the government of India to determine how copies of Trotter's report had fallen into public hands. The initial inquiry was directed to Captain Thuillier, who was standing in for Walker as superintendent of the GTS, while Walker was on leave. On 21 June 1876, A.O. Hume, on behalf of the government of India, asked Thuillier to whom might copies of the secret report have been circulated. Thuillier responded a few days later, reporting that fourteen copies had been sent out. The recipients, he said, included a number of officers within the GTS (including a copy to Montgomerie in England), plus one copy to Clements Markham at the India Office in London and one to the chief commissioner of Assam.[40] Further correspondence established both that Colonel Walker was the man responsible for this dissemination of the report, and that it had been done *after* the receipt by him of the government letter of 28 February expressly forbidding him to do so. As Hume remarked in a minute attached to the correspondence, "no copies ought to have been distributed after the receipt of our orders."[41]

The government was also aware that a copy of the report had been received by the *Pioneer Mail and Indian Weekly News* newspaper in Allahabad, which was proceeding to publish it verbatim. For all these unauthorized disclosures, Colonel Walker was held to be ultimately responsible.[42]

Walker was certainly guilty of disseminating Trotter's report to unauthorized persons, despite strict instructions to the contrary. If the government's belief that Clements Markham had sent a copy of the report to the *Pioneer* was correct, then Walker was also to blame for its publication there, for he had sent the report to Markham in the first instance.

But Walker could certainly not be held responsible for all the information about the pundits appearing in the public press. True, the *Pall Mall Budget* did refer specifically to the travels of the Havildar into Chitral in 1870, and to the journey of the Mullah to Chitral and the Baroghil pass in 1874. But much of the work of the Havildar was already in the public domain, since the account of his exploration was published in the *Journal* of the RGS in 1872. Furthermore, although the full account of the Mullah's work was contained in Trotter's report, a summary of his explorations had been included in the general report of the Great Trigonometrical Survey of India for 1874-75, which was published in 1876. All the details contained in the *Pall Mall Budget* were available from this summary.

Walker could not therefore be directly blamed for the appearance of material in the press. At worst, he might have been responsible for releasing the general report of the GTS for 1874-75, but since this was not a secret document, a copy would have been sent to the RGS.

A further publication cited by the government was the report of Colonel Venioukoff in the London *Times*. Venioukoff knew not only the code names of the explorers and details of their routes, but also the real names of the Havildar (Hyder Shah) and the Munshi (Abdul Subhan), which the code names were designed to conceal. But as Trotter pointed out, in a handwritten note in the government files, Venioukoff could not possibly have got the real name of the Havildar from the report, because it did not appear there. Trotter believed that the name had been taken from names of authorities used by Colonel Walker to compile his map of Turkestan, and listed on the map, which had been published two years earlier.[43]

As for the real name of the Munshi, and the details of his explorations along the Oxus, both were contained in the official account of the Forsyth expedition published in India in 1875, which was, according to Trotter, on sale in Calcutta.[44] Sir Henry Rawlinson had also referred to the travels of Trotter's "moonshi, Abdul Subhan," in his address to the RGS, which was duly published in the *Proceedings* in 1875.[45] Information on the pundits passed through official hands like water through a sieve. Walker was just one of these officials. But he had made the mistake of flagrantly violating a clear instruction of the viceroy.

The viceroy took a very dim view of this, referred to Walker as a "disobedient officer," and called for his severe censure. At least one member of the Foreign Department demanded that he be dismissed from his position.[46] Only Walker's professional excellence and long record of distinguished service saved his career from being abruptly terminated. He was warned that he would not be so lucky if the offense were to be repeated a second time. In its letter of 18 October 1876, addressed to Captain Thuillier, the government delivered a very sharp rebuke to the superintendent of the GTS, saying: "I am directed to convey to you, for communication to Colonel Walker, an expression of the grave displeasure of the Government of India at the serious breach of duty committed by him, and to state that His Excellency in Council only refrains from directing his removal from the charge of the Trigonometrical Survey Department in consideration of his long and distinguished service in the past. Any repetition of such conduct will be visited with the most serious consequences."[47]

Now that the Indian government had ascertained the extent of the damage and the individual responsible for it, it was time for the India Office in London to be brought abreast of developments.[48]

The viceroy's letter explaining the problems that had caused the delay in transmitting copies of Trotter's secret report to London was sent from Simla on 5 October 1876. It was received at the India Office on 30 October. There the Political and Secret Department, in a minute to the secretary of state, described the affair as "a grave scandal," but suggested that the resolution of the problem was best left to the government of India, which should be able to devise a form of publication other than "submission to the strong will of a subordinate officer." Publication of strictly geographical information, at some point, was not in itself objectionable, but this should not be done prematurely and should not contain details of the methods by which the information was acquired. Looking at matters from a global perspective, rather than the more parochial view of the Survey of India, the minute summed up by stating that "the curiosity of the public should certainly be regarded as a secondary consideration to the political interests of the Empire, if not to the safety of the Agents employed on a difficult and hazardous service."[49] An appendix to the minute spoke of Walker's actions as "most improper" and alleged that he had pursued an indiscreet course of "self-glorification," which might well compromise the interests of the state.[50] In response, the secretary of state for India, Lord Salisbury, expressed his complete agreement with the viceroy's handling of the matter, and of the viceroy's right to determine the manner of publication of the Survey reports. Lord Salisbury also agreed that "any repetition of a proceeding as insubordinate and detrimental to the interests of the public service shall entail upon the officer responsible for it severe marks of the displeasure of Government."[51]

To preserve what was left of the confidentiality of Trotter's report, Clements Markham, at the Geographical Department, was ordered by the Political and Secret Department to transfer the report to them.[52]

Trotter had planned to read a paper to the RGS on 14 May 1877, outlining the geographical achievements of the Forsyth Mission to Kashgar.[53] He was required, however, to meet with a member of the Secret Committee of the India Office, to go through the paper and ensure that its contents were suitable for publication.[54] However, when Trotter addressed the RGS on 14 May, he did not present a paper on the Forsyth Mission, but instead one on Nain Singh's journey from Leh to Lhasa. Bearing in mind that Trotter's paper on the Forsyth Mission, when it was delivered to the society the following year, was drawn from an account Trotter had already written up in 1874-75, it is possible that he was required to make such substantial changes to it that it could not be readied for delivery in time, and that Trotter therefore substituted a paper on Nain Singh. An alternative explanation was provided by Sir Rutherford Alcock, who said at the May 1877 meeting that Trotter's paper "was of more limited scope than intended, owing to [his] being called to accompany Sir Arnold Kemball to the seat of war in Asia Minor."[55]

On the other hand, the paper on Nain Singh was itself only an abbreviated version of the full account given in the secret and confidential report of 1873-74-75.[56] Details of the deceptions used by Nain Singh were omitted, although his name was given, since he had by now retired from active service. Trotter's paper on the Forsyth Mission, when it was finally delivered on 13 May 1878, was titled "On the Geographical Results of the Mission to Kashgar under Sir T. Douglas Forsyth in 1873-74." The paper referred generally to the surveying activities of the pundits and gave some account of the independent activities of the Munshi along the Oxus and Kishen Singh's journey to Khotan. The Havildar was referred to, although he was not part of the mission, but no details were given. For details of the routes followed by the pundits, Trotter referred the audience to his fuller narratives, while admitting that "not many copies were printed, and but very few have been made available to the general public."[57]

Unlike the journey of Nain Singh to Lhasa, a fairly full (although not complete) account of which was published by the RGS, no full account of the travels of either the Havildar or the Mullah was ever made public.[58] This indicated the sensitivity with which the government regarded Afghanistan and the northwest frontier in the light of Russian expansion toward the borders of British India. Even when the narratives of the pundits were collected and published by the Survey of India in 1915, the volume was titled "Explorations in Tibet and Neighbouring Regions" and excluded all the travels of the Mirza, the Mullah, the Munshi, and the Havildar.[59]

Even years later, the report was still being treated as secret. In the summer of 1881, Trelawney Saunders of the India Office Statistics and Commerce Department requested a copy of the report on behalf of Colonel Yule. Yule wanted to inspect the report for material it might contain on Chitral. Saunders supported Yule's request, saying that the geographical information could be of great interest. The report had passed through his hands, he said, but he had not been able to obtain a copy since "its circulation was . . . interdicted by Lord Salisbury" in 1876.[60] Saunders' request was granted, but under stringent security. "Details of a geographical nature alone" were to be extracted from the report and were not to be released outside the Statistics Department. The secretary of that department was to be held responsible for the difficult, if not impossible, task of ensuring compliance with these instructions, and he was to return the report to the Political and Secret Department "without unnecessary delay."[61]

Despite their condemnation of Walker's actions, the authorities in London were quite prepared to give Walker due credit for the work of the pundits. In a letter to the viceroy sent in March 1877, the India Office spoke of its "warm approval of the energy and discretion shown by Colonel Walker and Captain Montgomerie in the gradual elaboration of a system which has produced, at a minimum of cost, results of real importance, which are seldom attained elsewhere without some considerable sacrifice of resources, if not of life."[62]

The furor over the premature release of Trotter's report the previous year had died down by the spring of 1877. Perhaps the government realized that not all the blame for the leaks of information could be laid at the feet of Colonel Walker. If this was so, then the letter sought to make amends and grant due recognition to a man who had helped conceive and implement a system of exploration, the results of which were of such great utility to the governments in London and Calcutta.

Questions of Secrecy

Certainly some saw the dispatch from London in this light. Markham's deputy at the India Office, C.E.D. Black, sent Walker a copy of the dispatch, together with a letter saying that he hoped it would "atone somewhat for the nasty rudeness you experienced from the same Government."[63] There were indications that Walker was actively combating the censure he had received from the viceroy. Montgomerie, in a letter to Walker, said that he was "curious to hear what the end of your inquiries as to the Trotter Exploration Report is and how the Pioneer got hold of it all etc."[64] On 13 April 1877, Henry Yule wrote to Walker saying "I hope you will have succeeded in getting the Government to remove the censure they cast on you about the 'confidential' documents."[65] But a letter from Clements Markham, written the same day, urged Walker to let the whole affair just blow over. True, said Markham, "the Viceroy has behaved most shamefully in writing that insolent letter to you," but the secretary of state, Lord Salisbury, was "a thorough Philistine," and would support the viceroy, "his dyspeptic nominee." Markham urged Walker to let the matter be, particularly as Henry Thuillier was retiring as surveyor-general "and it is of consequence that you succeed him."[66]

Markham reiterated his hope in another letter the following month: "I trust that nothing will prevent your succeeding to Thuillier: indeed I do not see how anything can, for there is no one else. But the injustice and discourtesy with which Lord Lytton has treated you is certainly very discouraging. It would be laughable if it were not so serious."[67]

Walker did succeed Thuillier as surveyor-general of India, on 1 January 1878. But the new surveyor-general, chafing at the restrictions imposed upon him relating to the publication of the pundits' explorations, attempted to get around these rules where possible.

The second case of alleged unauthorized disclosure occurred less than a year after Walker's appointment as surveyor-general. This concerned a report of the explorations of the Mullah up the Indus River to Gilgit and Yasin in 1876.

In the course of a friendly and informal letter to Walker inviting him to stay at his house, should he come to Simla, A.O. Hume came to the point: "There is only one nasty question—the For. Office are down upon you again for publishing that exploration of the Moollah without permission. We cannot here trace that you did ask for or obtain permission—so we have been obliged to ask you for an explanation." Hume told Walker "in strict confidence" that the last time this happened, the Foreign Department recommended that he be dismissed, and that "the pigs have now routed out this new offence." Hume wanted to believe that the Foreign Department was mistaken and asked Walker: "is it really so? I am in hopes you will be able to show you are all right." Failing this, Hume pleaded with Walker: "If you are at fault, pray don't argue the question, but say it was, as it must have been an oversight, and that you will take care it does not occur again."[68]

The official letter from Hume followed a few days later, asking Walker whether he had obtained the permission of the government before publishing the narrative of the Mullah and if not, why not.[69]

The publication in question was a brief account of the Mullah's explorations, with a sketch map, which Walker had inserted in the general report of the Trigonometrical Survey for 1876-77. The account did not reveal the true name of the Mullah.[70]

Walker replied that the government itself had already printed the full report, which had also revealed the name of the Mullah.[71] Walker contended that since he had then asked the Foreign Department to recall the report and remove the Mullah's name from it, it therefore seemed all right to go ahead and print an abridged version of the narrative.[72]

No, it was not all right, the government responded. The surveyor-general, just because of an error by the Foreign Department, was not relieved "from the obligation of obeying the strict and unmistakable orders of the Government of India," to which, in the future, he must adhere "with the most undeviating strictness."[73]

Walker's second offense had escaped another severe censure, or worse, in part because he could point to a lapse on the part of the government. Another reason was that, fortuitously for Walker, a letter had recently arrived from the secretary of state in London, applauding his work with the pundits. It would have been inappropriate to send this on to the surveyor-general at the same time as a letter of censure, and so the latter was written in a firm, but less harsh tone.[74]

It was Walker's high-handed methods and predisposition to flout the rules that angered many in the Foreign Department, rather than the publication itself. When Walker asked for permission the following year to publish details of new explorations by the Mullah, the government rapidly agreed, requesting only that the names of the Mullah's servants, and those who had assisted them, be omitted.[75]

Walker appears to have kept control of himself for the remainder of his tenure as surveyor-general, at least as far as the available evidence of his handling the pundits' reports goes. The last exploration of the Mullah, made when he again traveled up the valley of the Indus in 1878, was published with a map as an appendix to the report on the operations of the Trigonometrical Survey for 1878-79.[76] As such, it could be removed prior to the public circulation of the report. A three-page summary was included in the *Proceedings* of the RGS.[77]

In 1879, he forwarded Lieutenant Harman's report on the explorations of Nem Singh (NMG) to the government, asking for permission to publish it in the annual survey report.[78] At least one member of the government opposed publication, pointing out that it would contravene the 1876 rules. Furthermore, the memo argued, "it cannot be politic to allow a single individual beyond those in whom the Government of India reposes implicit confidence, to have access to information which, as a matter of fact, concerns the Government of India alone, and in which that Government has so deep an interest."[79]

Others, however, disagreed, saying that there was no objection to publication, providing that the name of the explorer was disguised in a more effective manner than by merely leaving out the vowels.[80] Their views carried the day. Nem Singh's narrative, when it appeared as an appendix to the Survey Report, in fact did little more to conceal his identity other than referring to him only as G____M____N.[81] Summaries of this account subsequently appeared in various geographical journals.[82] This arrangement of having a full account published as an appendix to the annual survey report, with an abbreviated version made available to the general public, was followed for several subsequent explorers.

With General Walker taking leave in February 1883, pending retirement the following year, the rules over publication and dissemination of the pundits' narratives were, to a degree, relaxed. While still in office, Walker had suggested that Colonel Henry Yule write to the secretary of state for India requesting that the details of recent explorations by Kishen Singh (A.K.) be made available for publication in full. A.K. had returned in 1882 from an epic four-year journey which had carried him across Tibet and far to the north.

In his letter, Yule argued that the rules about publication had originally been laid down by Lord Northbrook in 1876 and had been reaffirmed by Lord Lytton. In both cases, Yule continued, "the reports in question treated of the countries beyond our NW frontier in the direction of Badakhshan and W. Turkestan, where great susceptibility might be supposed to exist." By implication, no such "great susceptibility" was seen by Yule to exist in the case of Tibet or China. Furthermore, said Yule in words that could have been penned by Walker himself, it was an arduous task for survey officers to labor to prepare the reports if they did not feel that by so doing they were preparing a permanent record of achievements "highly appreciated all over Europe," and that if this promise was not held out to them, then "it will be difficult to get the work done efficiently."[83]

The government of India, to whom Yule's request was forwarded, noted that during Walker's tenure as surveyor-general, "he several times tried to evade and upset the well known and stringent orders of Government regarding the publication of narratives and reports of trans-frontier explorations." [84] The Foreign Department, however, decided to treat the case on its merits and to wait until the report of A.K. had actually been received.

Yule's request was under consideration at the same time as the secretary of state was demanding to know why confidential information about the Afghan boundary had been released from India for publication in the newspapers.[85]

The Foreign Department was in a quandary. There appeared to be no way to plug all the leaks of confidential information, in the face of opposition from the Survey of India and other interested parties such as the Royal Geographical Society. Henry Durand, foreign secretary to the government of India, in a discussion on the wisdom of publishing trans-frontier maps, noted that "The tendencies of the Survey Department are always toward publication, the production of good maps reflecting credit upon them personally, and it is difficult to keep up a steady pressure against imprudent divulging of information when the Surveyor General is all for showing his most valuable treasures to the world in general."[86]

The Foreign Department therefore looked for an accommodation, particularly now that Walker had retired, which would guarantee them control over the most sensitive details of explorations beyond the frontier, but at the same time go some way toward satisfying the desires of the survey and the RGS for publication.

A.K.'s report was received in August 1884. At this time, the Foreign Department reviewed both the specific report of A.K. and the general rules governing the publication of details of the pundits' explorations. In the case of A.K., it was decided to relax the rules to allow publication. Objectionable passages must first be removed—for example, one referring to the murder of two Europeans in Batang in 1881. The Foreign Department also made it clear that one factor in their decision was that General Walker was no longer in office and therefore not in a position to abuse any concessions made by the government.[87]

With respect to the general principles governing publication, the Foreign Department reiterated that the 1876 rules were still necessary, both because the reports of the pundits "frequently contain remarks of a political character which it would be mischievous to publish," and because "they often explain the contrivances resorted to by explorers for the purpose of eluding detection." Ideally, therefore, the reports should have confined themselves to geographical matters only. But the Foreign Department realized that if this rule were strictly applied, the reports would have been unintelligible and uninteresting. Furthermore, "it is also regarded as a hardship by the employes of Government who have collected them, in many cases in the face of very serious obstacles and at imminent peril of their lives."

A compromise was therefore proposed. Narratives of the pundits' journeys could be published, including some personal details, providing three criteria were met: political details had to be omitted, together with details of the devices and disguises used to avoid detection and the real names of the explorers. The Foreign Department would scrutinize each report to ensure that these three criteria were rigidly adhered to.[88] The India Office felt that these proposals were "fair . . . as long as great care is exercised to exclude all political allusions . . ."[89]

Lord Kimberley, the secretary of state for India, had taken the opportunity on the occasion of the retirement of Walker as surveyor-general to express his praise both for the man and the institution he had directed. Kimberley, in his dispatch to India, had referred to progress in acquiring "geographical knowledge of countries beyond the British frontier [obtained] through the praiseworthy efforts of European and Native explorers." Referring specifically to A.K.'s journey through Tibet, Kimberley remarked: "I trust that it will be found consistent with the considerations which have to be regarded in such a matter that a full narrative of this remarkable journey should be published at an early date."[90] Accordingly, the original account, written up by J.B.N. Hennessey, was published after the excision of some twenty-eight passages.[91] An abbreviated version was delivered to a meeting of the RGS on 8 December 1884 and published in their *Proceedings*.[92] The views of the India Office were therefore highly consistent with the proposals for the relaxation of the rules made by the Foreign Department in India. The proposals were agreed to by the end of 1884.[93]

Nevertheless, despite this new policy, which permitted the publication of the pundits' narratives, confusion persisted as a result of different judgments as to whether a particular document should be considered "confidential," and if so, whether it might be released to the Royal Geographical Society.[94] The new secretary of state, Viscount Cross, suggested that material should not be kept secret unless there were "very special grounds," in which case it might be best to print only a very few copies, say twelve to fifteen.[95]

The narrative of Kintup's long voyage down the Tsangpo (1880-84) was only summarized in the survey's *General Report* for 1886-87. The full version appeared in a book, published by the survey in 1889, the number of copies of which was restricted to 150.[96] Publications of the visits of Sarat Chandra Das and Ugyen Gyatso to Tibet were further restricted. Some references to their first expedition of 1879 were made in a secret report attached to the *General Report* for 1881-82. The full narrative was published in an edition limited to twenty-five copies. Even of the summary only twenty-six copies were printed.[97] In the case of their second visit (1881-83), the account was issued in two reports, each limited to one hundred copies.[98] None of these three reports of the two travels of Das and Ugyen Gyatso was reprinted in the 1915 *Records of the Survey of India*.[99]

Cross appointed a special committee to consider the question of the handling of confidential documents. Colonel Yule was a member of the committee, which was chaired by Sir Donald Stewart, former commander-in-chief of military forces in India. The committee made a number of recommendations, one of which, designed to help track down the source of leaked information and prevent its spread, said that "the responsible officer of the Record Department . . . should make it his business to visit occasionally bookstalls and shops, and libraries advertised for sale, in order to keep a watch on the unauthorised publicity or disposal of any such confidential documents." This recommendation, which would have committed a civil servant to a lifetime of snooping around antiquarian bookstores, was later toned down to read only that "the Political Department be instructed to keep themselves in communication, as far as possible, with booksellers by whom confidential documents are occasionally bought or offered for sale."[100]

Even with the more formalized procedures to stop the release of confidential information, leaks still occurred. In 1888, the Foreign Department in India objected to the India Office in London concerning the office's presentation of a gazetteer of maps on Afghanistan to the Royal Geographical Society.[101] The following year, the secretary of state complained to India in the case of a report of pundits' explorations in Sikkim, Bhutan, and Tibet first that two maps contained in the report were based on confidential information[102] and second, that the report was sent to the RGS (after which a review appeared in *The Times*) more than two weeks before a copy reached the India Office.[103] Discussions over what the RGS could receive (statistical and geographical data) and could not receive (political information) and as to who was to be responsible for separating the one from the other, continued for some time. These discussions, however, did not, by and large, concern themselves with the accounts of the pundits, whose explorations were now coming to a close.

TEN
Conclusion

Thirty years elapsed between the first experimental dispatch of a pundit and the pundits' last known exploration, spanning the time between 1863, when Montgomerie sent Abdul Hamid off to Yarkand, and 1892-93, when Hari Ram and his son traveled in Nepal and Tibet.[1] The Survey of India's primary focus of attention for geographical exploration varied during these three decades. Although the first pundit, Abdul Hamid, was directed into Chinese Turkestan, this region was generally of secondary interest to the survey. The Mullah was sent there in 1873 on a return route to India after his explorations in Chitral, but other than that, the only pundit surveys in the area were part of the second Forsyth Mission to Kashgar of 1873-74. The Forsyth Mission produced substantial scientific data on Chinese Turkestan, and large Russian state-supported expeditions followed, thus eliminating the need for further use of the pundits.[2]

The northwest frontier of India and Afghanistan received several pundit expeditions in the 1860s and 1870s. This was particularly true of northern Afghanistan and of Badakhshan, the Pamir, and the Oxus boundary with Russia. Exploration of this region by the pundits came to an end only in 1881 with the surveying by Mukhtar Shah (M.S.) of the last unmapped section of the Oxus.

Tibet, of all the territories to which the pundits were sent, remained consistently of the highest priority to the Survey of India, although the survey's focus of interest in Tibet changed over the years. The pundits of the 1860s and 1870s concentrated their activities on Lhasa, and that large part of Tibet to the west of the capital. Nain Singh was dispatched to Lhasa in 1865, and he and other members of his family explored western and central Tibet later that decade and into the 1870s. By the mid-1870s, however, the primary focus of attention was switching to the region to the east of Lhasa, particularly on the route of the Tsangpo as it left Tibetan territory for British India. It was Nain Singh himself who initiated this exploration when he arrived at the town of Chetang, fifty miles southeast of Lhasa, in 1874. During the next decade, Lala, Nem Singh, Kintup, and Rinzing Namgyal were all directed to this area to solve the controversy over the route of the Tsangpo/Brahmaputra.

Other areas were also traversed by the pundits, who journeyed through Nepal, Sikkim, Bhutan, Burma, and into Chinese territory to the north of Tibet. Tibet itself, however, remained the primary goal.

In the 1890s, as the employment of the pundits drew to an end, there was a brief transition period between their use for independent explorations and the total abandonment of them in favor of purely British expeditions. One such journey which exemplified this transition period was that of Atma Ram, a surveying assistant who accompanied Captain Hamilton Bower into Tibet in 1891-92.[3]

Bower's objective, which was sanctioned by the viceroy, was to provide a better idea of the nature of the Tibetan plateau to the north of the line mapped by Nain Singh in 1874-75. In addition to Atma Ram, half of whose salary was provided by the Intelligence Branch of the Army Quartermaster-General's Department,[4] Bower was accompanied by a British physician on loan from the Indian Medical Service and by a number of servants.[5]

The expedition succeeded in attaining its basic goal, covering several hundred miles of the vast, lake-studded Tibetan plateau, parallel to Nain Singh's route and never before penetrated by a European. The expedition reached Lake Tengri Nor, where they were prevented by the Tibetan authorities (who took precious little notice of Bower's Chinese passport) from getting any closer to Lhasa. They then continued to Tachienlu, from where Bower traveled to Shanghai, returning to India by sea after an absence of a little over a year.

Atma Ram was commended by both Bower and the Survey of India for the painstaking care and accuracy with which he carried out his survey, pacing for over two thousand miles, much of which was above fourteen thousand feet in altitude, and often under conditions of great cold and hardship. Bower produced a brief confidential report on Tibet which, among other things, compared the ease with which Lhasa could be occupied by an invading force from India, by comparison with the difficulties the Russians would face if they made an attempt to reach Lhasa across the Chang Tang. The material in this report was excluded from the book of his journey that Bower wrote for public consumption.[6]

By now the era of the pundits was coming to an end. Military advances into Afghanistan during the second Afghan War (1878-80) had greatly furthered the mapping of that country, and demarcation of its northern boundary began in 1884. No pundits were dispatched to Afghanistan after 1881.

Far to the east, Bhutan remained largely unknown territory. Problems with Bhutanese raids into Assam had led to a British mission under Sir

Ashley Eden being sent there in 1864, the poor reception of which resulted in armed conflict between Britain and Bhutan in 1865. A treaty was signed the following year, by which Bhutan ceded territory to British India, but the small Himalayan kingdom then closed its doors to outsiders. The clandestine visits of the pundits Rinzing Namgyal and P.A. (1885-86) provided reasonably good geographical information on the western part of the country, when combined with observations made by the Eden mission (and the earlier mission of Robert Pemberton of 1837-38), but the eastern sector was less well known. John Claude White, when appointed political officer in 1906, became the first British visitor to the country since Eden, and could still write that at that time Bhutan was a place "hitherto almost unexplored."[7]

In the case of Sikkim, poor relations with Britain had resulted in a military mission, again under Sir Ashley Eden, which occupied Sikkim by force in 1860-61. A treaty was signed at Tumlong in the latter year, which brought Sikkim under the control of the government of India, allowed British travelers into Sikkim, and gave Britain the right to construct a road through Sikkim to the Tibetan border.

Nepal, the third and largest of the small states in the foothills of the Himalayas, remained off limits to official surveys until the twentieth century. Virtually all cartographical information about the country came from the incursions of pundits such as Hari Ram, or from observations made from along the Indian side of the border.

From 1870 onward, Chinese Turkestan had been visited by several major Russian scientific expeditions, some of which had also penetrated northern Tibet. In Tibet itself, the authorities were able to keep all Europeans out of Lhasa, but the boundaries of the country were penetrated by travelers on many occasions, including important British expeditions by Wellby and Malcolm, Deasy, and Rawling.

In 1896, Captain Wellby and Lieutenant Malcolm crossed through Tibet to China, from west to east, taking an even more northerly route than Bower.[8] They took with them a sub-surveyor from the Survey of India, who used a plane-table while Wellby and Malcolm observed for latitude and height. Captain Deasy explored west and northwest Tibet between 1896 and 1899.[9] He also took along a sub-surveyor from the Survey of India on at least two of his expeditions. Captain Rawling and Lieutenant Hargreaves surveyed a great deal of western Tibet in 1903.[10] Again, the Survey of India loaned a sub-surveyor to the expedition, who assisted in the mapping operations.

During the three decades of their operations, the pundits were able to go to places where virtually no European could venture. In so doing, they traversed more than twenty-five thousand miles of territory, much of which was completely new ground to European exploration. The list is lengthy of westerners who tried to follow in the footsteps of the pundits, but failed.

One who actually preceded the first pundit was the Lazarist priest Auguste Desgodins, who set out from western China to enter Tibet in 1861, but was turned back in 1862. Another attempt the following year was no more successful.[11]

A similar attempt to penetrate Tibet from the east was made by a British merchant, T.T. Cooper, in 1868. He hoped to pass through Tibet to Assam, but was stopped from doing so by the Tibetans.[12] Cooper also tried to make the journey in the reverse direction the following year.[13]

The pace stepped up in the 1870s when the Russian explorer Nikolai Prejevalsky, on the edge of the northern plateau of Tibet, and just twenty-seven days' ride from Lhasa, was forced to retrace his steps because of a shortage of supplies.[14] Supported by his government and the Imperial Russian Geographical Society, Prejevalsky tried again four years later, in 1877, but could only reach Lop Nor before turning back due to a lack of guides, and because his baggage animals were dying. Another try later the same year was halted by the authorities in St. Petersburg for political reasons.[15] Not giving up, and goaded by news that the Hungarian Count Bela Szechenyi was heading toward Lhasa from Sining, Prejevalsky sped toward Lhasa in 1879, but was stopped, less than one week north of the city, by Tibetan soldiers.[16] Prejevalsky's Chinese passport, approved for travel to Tibet, was simply ignored by Tibetan officials, who denied that it had any validity.[17]

Prejevalsky did not give up. He knew of the journeys of the pundits in Tibet and wanted a Russian success to offset British achievements.[18] But his 1884 expedition to eastern Tibet was halted some four hundred miles northeast of Lhasa by a combination of difficult terrain and hostile Khampa tribesmen.[19]

Spurred on by the exploits of Arthur Carey and Douglas Dalgleish in northern Tibet, British successes in an area the Russian considered to be his territory, Prejevalsky decided to pry open the gates of Lhasa by military force.[20] Alas, Prejevalsky died in 1888, before even reaching Chinese Turkestan, on the shores of Lake Issyk Kul, and for fear of exacerbating relations with Britain, his successors were restricted by the Russian government to scientific research in the northern parts of Tibet.[21]

While Prejevalsky was in the middle of his repeated attempts, two other men, one British and one Hungarian, both of whom held Chinese passports valid for Tibet, were heading toward Lhasa. Captain W.J. Gill hoped to penetrate Tibet from western China, but discovered in Batang that the Tibetans were aware of his activities and were determined to resist him. Gill gave up, and instead continued his journey to Burma through Yunnan.[22] Two years later, in 1879, Bela Szechenyi had a similar experience on arriving at Batang, and followed Gill's route to Burma.[23]

A decade later, William Woodville Rockhill, an American diplomat at the U.S. Legation in Peking who had a scholarly interest in China and Tibet, decided to try to reach Lhasa from the north, reasoning that Huc and Gabet had been successful in reaching Lhasa in 1846 because their route had led through northern Tibet, which was less well populated than the area to the south. Perhaps because he had read about the pundits, Rockhill disguised himself as a Chinese pilgrim. Although he reached the edge of northern Tibet, he had to abandon his goal because of a shortage of supplies and of the funds to buy more.[24]

Two years later, in 1891, Rockhill tried again, this time attempting to enter Tibet from the northeast and cross the country in a southwesterly direction, avoiding Lhasa, and departing through Nepal or Sikkim. By omitting Lhasa from his itinerary, Rockhill believed he could avoid being apprehended. However, like Hamilton Bower before him, he was stopped some thirty or forty miles from Lake Tengri Nor and forced to turn east, into China, following the route taken by Bower earlier the same year.[25]

Between Rockhill's two attempts, the Frenchmen Gabriel Bonvalot and Prince Henri of Orleans also reached Lake Tengri Nor, but were no more successful than Bower or Rockhill in getting any closer to Lhasa.[26]

In 1892, a missionary named Annie Taylor entered Tibet from the north, but was taken prisoner when a few days from Lhasa and forced to proceed to western China.[27]

The great Swedish explorer Sven Hedin set out on his first major expedition to Central Asia and Tibet in 1893. After nearly perishing through lack of water while crossing the Takla Makan desert, Hedin returned to Kashgar, and set out for Tibet in 1895. He succeeded in exploring the Lop Nor area and parts of northern Tibet during the following year, before returning to Europe via Sining and Peking.[28] His second expedition left Lop Nor for Lhasa in 1901, but was stopped by the Tibetans less than 130 miles from the city and forced to turn west towards Ladakh.[29] Although Hedin subsequently explored much of southern and western Tibet, he never reached Lhasa.

Others, less well equipped than Hedin, Prejevalsky, or Szechenyi, also attempted to reach Lhasa in the last decade of the nineteenth century. None was successful. In 1897, the truculent and egocentric British traveler A. Henry Savage-Landor crossed into Tibet from Kumaon and traveled past Lake Manasarowar some way down the Tsangpo river before being arrested. Savage-Landor was detained by the Tibetans and (if one believes his story) tortured by them before being returned to India.[30]

Dr. Susie Rijnhart was a Canadian missionary, working near the Kumbum monastery to the northeast of Tibet. In October 1896, she and her Dutch husband had been visited briefly by Captain Wellby and Lieutenant Malcolm as they crossed Tibet from west to east. Only one month later, they were hosts to Sven Hedin, on his way to northern Tibet. In 1890, the Rijnharts themselves left for Lhasa, some eight hundred miles to the southwest, to spread the gospel. The attempt ended in tragedy. Not only were they stopped two hundred miles from the capital, but their baby son died on route, and Susie Rijnhart's husband perished on the return journey, while fording a river.[31]

No European was to reach Lhasa in the latter half of the nineteenth century. Those who came closest to this goal were the Littledales, an English couple who passed beyond Lake Tengri Nor in 1895 and came within about fifty miles of the city before being turned back.[32]

With the dawn of the twentieth century, British officers, well armed and well provisioned, were able to ride around much of Tibet virtually at will, and there was no longer a need for the clandestine surveying techniques of the Indian explorers. With the Younghusband Expedition of 1903-04, Lhasa itself was occupied by British forces, and the Tibetans were forced to permit a British Trade Agent in Gyantse.

The pundits, because they were Asiatic and were disguised as bona fide travelers, were able to go where Europeans could not. They left an immense achievement behind them, including geographical and other details on a vast region of largely unknown territory, concentrated in Tibet but including much of Afghanistan, the Central Asian Khanates, the Pamir, Chinese Turkestan, Nepal, Sikkim, Bhutan, and Assam. This was an area of over one million square miles, more than ten times the size of Great Britain. Unlike Britain, however, this was the domain of the world's greatest mountain peaks, of vast deserts and of cold and desolate high altitude plateaus, often infested with brigands and administered by hostile authorities. Information on the topography of this region, the customs of its inhabitants, and the nature of its government and military resources was garnered under conditions of extreme deprivation and great danger. Some pundits paid with their lives; others lost their health. Their actions may have helped, in a small way, to raise British consciousness of Indians in general.

Surely, wrote one civil servant, "men of the same race as Col. Montgomerie's Native trans-Himalayan explorers can . . . be entrusted with responsible offices in the survey of the plains of India."[33] The last word is perhaps best left to Perceval Landon, who accompanied the Younghusband Expedition to Lhasa as a correspondent of *The Times*: "When the story of Asian exploration is finally and worthily written, the work of these lonely spies . . . must receive a place of honor second to none."[34]

Notes

Abbreviations

D.Dn.	Dehra Dun
GJ	*Geographical Journal*
GRGTS	*General Report on the Operations of the Great Trigonometrical Survey of India*
GRSI	*General Report on the Operations of the Survey of India*
JASB	*Journal of the Asiatic Society of Bengal*
JRASB	*Journal of the Royal Asiatic Society of Bengal*
JRGS	*Journal of the Royal Geographical Society*
L/P & S/	*Letters Political and Secret*
PASB	*Proceedings of the Asiatic Society of Bengal*
PRGS	*Proceedings of the Royal Geographical Society*

1. The Great Trigonometrical Survey of India

1. Rockhill, *Journey of William of Rubruck*, 151-52.
2. Wessels, however, believes he did visit Lhasa. See Wessels, *Early Jesuit Travellers*, 188-89.
3. Maclagan, *Jesuits and the Great Mogul*, 339-40.
4. Wessels, *Early Jesuit Travellers*, 39.
5. Maclagan, *Jesuits and the Great Mogul*, 344. For a full account of Andrade and the Tsaparang mission, see Wessels, *Early Jesuit Travellers*, ch. 2 and 3.
6. Wessels, *Early Jesuit Travellers*, 101.
7. See de Filippi, *Account of Tibet*, 365, ft. 4.
8. Maclagan, *Jesuits and the Great Mogul*, 355-57; Wessels, *Early Jesuit Travellers*, ch. 5.
9. Kircher, *China Monumentis*. Kircher published only an abstract of the letters Grueber had addressed to him. All were subsequently published by Melchisedech Thevenot in his *Relations de Divers Voyages Curieux*, Paris, 1663-1672. See Markham, *Mission of George Bogle*, lvii, ft. 3. The letters were also published in Italian in a volume edited by Jacopo Carlieri entitled *Notizie Varie dell' Imperio della China*, Florence, 1687. See Markham, *Mission of George Bogle*, ft. 1. An abstract of these letters, taken from both Kircher and Thevenot, was translated into English and printed in vol. 4 of Astley, *Voyages and Travels*, 651-55. Markham (*Mission of George Bogle*, 295-02) reprints the material in Astley. See also Wessels, *Early Jesuit Travellers*, ch. 6.
10. Wessels, *Early Jesuit Travellers*, 208.
11. Ibid., 206.
12. Markham, *Mission of George Bogle*, 304.
13. Ibid., 303 and 307.
14. Maclagan, *Jesuits and the Great Mogul*, 362.
15. de Filippi, *Account of Tibet*, 28-30. Freyre wrote a report of his experiences, which was only rediscovered two centuries later. (Ibid., 44-45.) A translation from the Latin is available (Ibid., 349-61).
16. Ibid., 372, ft. 75.
17. See Petech, *China and Tibet*, ch. 2-5.
18. Markham, *Mission of George Bogle*, lxii-lxv.
19. *Description géographique, historique, chronologique, politique et physique de l'empire de la Chine et de la Tartarie chinoise* . . . 4 vols. Paris, 1735.

20. J.B. du Halde, *The General History of China*. 4 vols. London, 1736.
21. J.B.B. d'Anville, *Nouvel atlas de la Chine, de la Tartarie chinoise et du Thibet*. The Hague, 1737.
22. Astley, *Voyages and Travels*, 449-68.
23. Ibid., between 456 and 457.
24. Ibid., 653; Markham, *Mission of George Bogle*, 299-300.
25. Astley, *Voyages and Travels*, 649-64. The letters of della Penna were later published by Heinrich Klaproth in the *Journal Asiatique*, of which he was the editor. Markham (*Mission of George Bogle*, lx, ft. 1) gives the location as second series, vol. 14, p. 177. Markham made a translation from *Journal Asiatique* and included it in the appendix to his book (pp. 309-40).
26. Antonio Giorgi, *Alphabetum Tibetanum Missionum Apostolicarum Commodo Editum*. Rome, 1762. Part two of the book was first published, in Rome, in 1759.
27. Markham, *Mission of George Bogle*, p. lx, footnote.
28. de Filippi, *Account of Tibet*, 36.
29. Ibid., xvi and 33.
30. Carlo Puini, ed. "Il Tibet (Geografia, Storia, Religione, Costumi) secondo la Relazione del Viaggio del P. Ippolito Desideri (1715-1721)." *Memorie della Societá Geografica Italiana* 10. Rome, 1904.
31. See note 7. A summary was published by Wessels in 1924 (*Early Jesuit Travellers*, ch. 7).
32. For a complete bibliography of Desideri, see de Filippi, *Account of Tibet*, xv-xviii. An English-language summary of one of Desideri's letters was published in Astley's *Voyages and Travels* (vol. 4, 655-58), and the same letter is reprinted by Markham (*Mission of George Bogle*, appendix, pp. 302-8).
33. For early contacts between Britain and Tibet, see Lamb, *British India and Tibet*. Also Cammann, *Trade through the Himalayas*.
34. Lamb, *British India and Tibet*, xii.
35. Markham, *Mission of George Bogle*, ch. 13.
36. Cammann, *Trade through the Himalayas*, 31, ft. 22.
37. Richardson, *Tibet and Its History*, 65.
38. See Samuel Turner, *Embassy to the Teshoo Lama*.
39. See note 9.
40. See Lamb, *British India and Tibet*, ch. 2 and 3.
41. See Moorcroft, "Journey to Lake Manasarovara." Also Pearse, "Moorcroft and Hearsey's visit."
42. See Lloyd, *Journey from Caunpoor*.
43. William Webb, "Passage of the Himalaya Mountains," *Quarterly Review* 22 (1820): 417.
44. Ibid., 421-22.
45. Lamb, *British India and Tibet*, 57-58.
46. Ibid., 58-61.
47. H. Strachey, "Journey to Cho Lagan."
48. R. Strachey, "Journey to the Lakes Rakas-Tal and Manasarowar."
49. R. Strachey, "Trip to the Niti Pass." See also H. Strachey, "Physical Geography of Western Tibet."
50. See A. and R. Schlagintweit, "Journey from Milum to Johar."
51. Smith, "Trip to Thibet."
52. *Travels in Central Asia by Meer Izzut-Oolah in the Years 1812-13*. Calcutta, 1872.
53. For an interesting discussion of Gardiner's travels and their authenticity, see Keay, *When Men and Mountains Meet*, ch. 6 and 7.
54. J.T. Walker. *Account of the Operations of the Great Trigonometrical Survey of India*, vol. 1 (Dehra Dun, 1870): xv.
55. Phillimore, *Historical Records* vol. 2, 238.
56. Ibid., vol. 3, 194.
57. Ibid., vol. 4, 370.
58. Ibid., vol. 3, 404.
59. The family name, however, was pronounced "*Everest*."
60. Quoted in Phillimore, *Historical Records*, vol. 5, 513.
61. Ibid., 221.

62. Ibid., 223.
63. Ibid., 485.
64. Purdon, "Valley of Kashmir," 16.
65. *The Great Trigonometrical Survey,* a pamphlet, n.p. 186-, 30.
66. Phillimore, *Historical Records,* vol. 5, 238.
67. *PRGS* 4 (1860): 30.
68. Ibid., 32.
69. *JRGS* 35 (1863): civ.
70. Phillimore, *Historical Records,* vol. 5, 474.
71. Ibid., 480.
72. Phillimore, "Kashmir and Jammu," 101.
73. Phillimore, *Historical Records,* vol. 5, 507.

74. Johnson's travels and those of other explorers were later to be denounced by the People's Republic of China as illegal intelligence operations carried out by agents of "British imperialism." See *Report of the Officials of the Government of India and the People's Republic of China on the Boundary Question* (New Delhi, 1962): CR116-CR118. See also *Beijing Review* 26 (June 27, 1983): 26.

75. Phillimore, *Historical Records,* vol. 1, 286-87.
76. Ibid., vol. 2, 282.
77. Ibid., 354-55.
78. H.H. Wilson, ed. *Travels in the Himalayan Provinces of Hindustan and the Punjab by Mr. William Moorcroft and Mr. George Trebeck,* vol. 1 (London, 1841): xviii.

79. Izzet Ullah was a merchant and was also employed by the Intelligence Department of the East India Company. See Datta, *Ladakh and Western Himalayan Politics,* 94-95.

80. William Moorcroft, "Journey to Lake Manasarovara," 382.
81. British Library, Add. Mss. 33,837 f60. Letter to G.T. Metcalfe dated 8 November 1820.
82. Phillimore, *Historical Records,* vol. 4, 290.
83. Wade, *Narrative of the Services,* 11-12.
84. Burnes, *Travel into Bokhara,* vol. 1, ix.
85. Phillimore, *Historical Records,* vol. 5, 446-47.

86. This report is to be found in the Proceedings of the Government of India, Foreign Department, Political, 1861, P/204/55, pp. 91-101. India Office Library and Records.

87. Ibid., 102.
88. Curzon, "The Pamirs," 251.
89. *PRGS* 10 (1865-6): 184.
90. *PASB* 2 (1862): 212.
91. Ibid., 213.

92. Memoranda on the Progress of the Trigonometrical Survey in Kashmir; Selections from the Records of the Punjab Government, vol. 5, no. 7 (1860): 17, Indian Office Library and Records. See also Dehra Dun 53A.

93. Montgomerie, "Geographical Position of Yarkund," 157.
94. D.Dn. 53, no. 120 ff.
95. *PASB* 2 (1862): 209-13.
96. Letter of Waugh to the Government of India, 17 September 1860, D.Dn. vol. 2, no. 57.
97. Royal Geographical Society. Journal ms. 1866; Thuillier, 2d folio of page 3.
98. Yule, *Late Colonel T.G. Montgomerie.*
99. Walker to Waugh, 11 May 1858, D.Dn. 710, no. 202.
100. *JRGS* 62 (1862): 307.
101. *PASB* 2 (1863): 175-79.
102. *JRGS* 36 (1866): 163.
103. Ibid., 164. (For a discussion of route surveys and how to conduct them, see the chapter titled "Exploratory Survey" in Arthur R.F. Hinks, *Maps and Survey.* Cambridge, 1933.)
104. Ibid., 167.
105. Mason, "Kishen Singh," 431.
106. See Blakiston, *Five Months on the Yang-Tsze,* v. See also Sarel, "Notes on the Yang-tsze-Kiang."

107. *Treaties, Conventions, Etc., between China and Foreign States*, vol. 1, 2d ed. (Shanghai, 1917). Reprint. New York, 1973. p. 407.

108. Blakiston, *Five Months on the Yang-Tsze*, 357. However, another member of the party said that they planned to get passports in Chengdu, the capital of Szechuan, from "the Viceroy for Tibet." See Barton, "Notes on the Yang-tsze-Kiang, etc.," 26.

109. Letter of 25 July 1861 to the secretary of state for War, London. Foreign Department Proceedings, Part B, June 1861, nos. 90-92.

110. Letter of 25 May 1861. Ibid.

111. Letter of 5 June 1861. Ibid.

112. Foreign Department Proceedings, part B, October 1861, no. 186.

113. Letter of Lieut-Col. Ramsay to C.U. Aitchison of 24 August 1861. Foreign Department Proceedings, Part A, September 1861, no. 51. See also Blakiston, *Five Months on the Yang-Tsze*, 304.

114. Foreign Department Proceedings, Political A, no. 176. Letter of C.U. Aitchison to Smyth of 9 August 1861. Also part B, Aitchison to Smyth, 6 September 1861.

115. Ibid., Smyth to Aitchison, no. 173, 17 July 1861.

116. Ibid., Durand to Smyth, no. 193, 24 October 1861.

117. Smyth to Walker, 28 October 1862, D.Dn. vol. 8, no. 95.

118. Foreign Proceedings, Political A, Smyth to Durand, no. 42, 9 May 1863.

119. Ibid., Durand to Smyth, no. 43, 20 May 1863.

120. Ibid., nos. 53-54, 29 March 1864.

121. Ibid.

122. In 1861 the Lazarist priests Charles Renou and Auguste Desgodins had obtained passports valid for Tibet. Renou's passport was signed by the president of the Chinese Foreign Ministry in Peking, and that of Desgodins was signed by the acting governor-general of Szechuan. But despite these documents, in June 1862 they were both halted on the Tibetan border by officials sent from Lhasa and were forced to return to China. See Petech, "European Travellers to Tibet," 219-21.

2. First Attempts: Abdul Hamid and Nain Singh

1. See *PASB* 2 (1863): 175-78. Also T.G. Montgomerie, "Geographical Position of Yarkund," 157-72.

2. See *PRGS* 19 (1875): 343-44.

3. See *PRGS* 13 (1868-69): 198.

4. *JRGS* 36 (1866): 158.

5. Ibid., 158-59.

6. Ms. of Montgomerie (1866) in the archives of the RGS, London.

7. See Thuillier and Smyth, *Manual of Surveying for India*, 441-47.

8. David Fraser, *The Marches of Hindustan, the Record of a Journey in Thibet, Trans-Himalayan India, Chinese Turkestan, Russian Turkestan and Persia* (Edinburgh and London, 1907): 263-64.

9. Montgomerie erroneously calculates the number of days as 25. *JRGS* 36 (1866): 166.

10. Foreign Department Proceedings, March 1868, letter to Walker of 13 March 1868.

11. *JRGS* 36 (1868): 165.

12. Abdul Hamid is not recorded in the two-volume work published by the Survey of India, *Exploration in Tibet and Neighbouring Regions* (Dehra Dun, 1915) (*Records of the Survey of India*, vol. 8). This is a major source for the study of the Pundits. Chronologically, the first individual referred to in this source is a Mongolian lama by the name of Serap Gyatsho. He was not, however, a true explorer or an employee of the Survey of India. He lived in the area of the lower Tsangpo River between 1856 and 1868 and some thirty years later provided information of marginal utility concerning this region to an explorer of the Survey of India. See Burrard and Hayden, *Geography and Geology*, part 2, 325-27.

13. *JRGS* 36 (1866): 163.

14. Phillimore, *Historical Records*, vol. 5, 516.

15. Phillimore is confused over the dates, having him leave India on February 20, and marry in England on February 11. Ibid., 513 and 516.

16. *PRGS* 10, no. 4 (1865-66): 162-65.

Notes to Pages 38-45

17. Yule, *Late Colonel T.G. Montgomerie.*
18. Edmund Smyth in *PRGS* n.s. 4 (1882): 316.
19. See Sherring, *Western Tibet and the British Borderland,* ch. 4 and 17.
20. See Webber, *Forests of Upper India,* 92.
21. See ch. 1. Also, Letters no. 87 and 88, Proceedings of the Government of India, Foreign Department, Political, 1861, P/204/55; Letter no. 32, Political Despatches to India, 1862, L/P & S/6/456; and Despatch no. 19, Selections from Despatches to India, 1864, p. 164.
22. Black, *Memoir on the Indian Surveys,* 49. Also *PRGS* n.s. 1 (1879): 448.
23. Webber, *Forests of Upper India,* 92-93. Rawat, *Indian Explorers,* 5. The latter author is a descendant of the two original recruits.
24. "Report on the Trans-Himalayan Explorations during 1865-67." *GRGTS 1866-7* (1867).
25. Phillimore, *Historical Records,* vol. 5, 488. Mason also agrees that they were cousins, although Montgomerie was under the impression that Mani was the younger brother of Nain Singh. See Mason, *Abode of Snow,* 84-85.
26. H. Strachey, "Map of the British Himalayan Frontier," 536.
27. H. Schlagintweit, A. Schlagintweit, and R. Schlagintweit, *Results of a Scientific Mission,* vol. 1, 38.
28. D.Dn. vol. 8, 1860-1870, no. 102.
29. Schlagintweit, Schlagintweit, and Schlagintweit, *Results of a Scientific Mission,* 39. See also Moorcroft, "Journey to Lake Manasarovara," 490-93; Phillimore, *Historical Records,* vol. 2, 430-31; and *GJ* 27 (1906): 502-3.
30. D.Dn. 8, (1860-1870), no. 102.
31. Phillimore, *Historical Records,* vol. 5, 448.
32. Smyth, *PRGS* n.s. 4 (1882): 316.
33. Buckland, *Dictionary of Indian Biography,* 390. RGS reports refer to the Singhs as Brahmins, or members of the priestly caste, as does Phillimore, *Historical Records,* vol. 5, 448.
34. Phillimore, *Historical Records,* vol. 5, 448; see also Markham, *Memoir on the Indian Surveys,* 149.
35. Letter of T.G. Montgomerie dated 3 March 1876, Foreign Department Proceedings, General, January 1878, nos. 89-97.
36. Letter of Walker dated 9 December 1862, D.Dn. vol. 31, 1860-1870, no. 16.
37. See Montgomerie, "Narrative Report of a Route-Survey"; also *JRGS* 38 (1868): 129-53. This account is also reprinted in S.G. Burrard, *Records of the Survey of India,* vol. 8, part 1, 1-24.
38. Foreign Department Proceedings, December 1863, Political A, no. 43.
39. Letter of Montgomerie to Walker, 7 February 1865, D.Dn. vol. 51.
40. Ibid.
41. I have drawn my information from Karan, *Changing Face of Tibet*; Snellgrove and Richardson, *Cultural History of Tibet*; and Vaurie, *Tibet and Its Birds.*
42. *GRGTS, 1866-7* (1867): 1.
43. Mason, *Abode of Snow,* 85. Edmund Smyth (*PRGS* [1882]: 316) says that they crossed into Tibet over the Johar pass before being recognized as explorers. He dates this as January 1865 and says they returned twice. The sequence of events is unclear. Webber, *Forests of Upper India,* 163, says that he saw the Singhs in Milam in late summer 1864 waiting for the chronometer to be repaired, but Mason (who had access to the confidential records) writes that the attempt to cross the border was made at the end of 1864, although the chronometer was still broken. Montgomerie, in his letter to Walker (7 February 1865, D.Dn. 51), does not mention the border attempt and gives the impression that the two returned to Dehra Dun in December in order to get the chronometer repaired.
44. Montgomerie to Walker, 7 February 1865.
45. Montgomerie, *JRGS* (1868): 130-31.
46. The Singhs were designated "Trans-Himalayan Party No. 2." The no. 1 party was an Englishman, A. Cameron, who was to proceed via Lahoul into Central Asia. He obtained a large quantity of medicines and instruments, but became ill before reaching the border and left for Calcutta. Montgomerie disapproved of Cameron, saying that he was not likely to succeed on his expedition "even under the most favorable circumstances." Montgomerie to Walker, 9 February 1865, D.Dn. 51, no. 124-25.

47. *JRGS* (1868): 157.
48. No account of his travels has been published. However, his route is marked on the map which accompanies Montgomerie's article in *JRGS* 38 (1868).
49. The first Europeans after Desideri were the members of the Gartok expedition of 1904-1905. See Rawling, *Great Plateau*. I have drawn upon this book to supplement Nain Singh's description of the route.
50. de Filippi, *Account of Tibet*, 128.
51. Only extracts from the Pundit's diary have been published. See note 37.
52. *PRGS* 12 (1867-68): 173.
53. Pelliot, *Huc and Gabet*, 228.
54. For example, see Markham, *Memoir on the Indian Surveys*, 154. Markham also prematurely elevates Montgomerie to the rank of colonel.
55. Phillimore, *Historical Records*, vol. 5, 516.
56. The position of Lhasa, as calculated from the Pundit's observations, was north latitude 29° 39' and east longitude 90° 59'. The accepted position today is latitude 29° 41', north longitude 91° 10' east. The Pundit estimated that the city was at an altitude of 11,400 feet.
57. Sandberg, *Exploration of Tibet*, 147.
58. The letter (dated 29 January 1868) is in the archives of the RGS. It was also printed, with minor changes, in *PRGS* 12 (1867-68): 172-73.
59. Ibid., 167.
60. *JRGS* 38 (1868): clxxxii and cxxx.
61. Letter from Foreign Department of 23 August 1867, Foreign Department Proceedings, March 1868.

3. Across the Northwest Frontier

1. For further reading see Gillard, *Struggle for Asia*; Spear, *Oxford History of Modern India*; Spate, *India and Pakistan*; Lamb, *Asian Frontiers*; Sykes, *History of Persia*; Fraser-Tytler, *Afghanistan*; and Yapp, *Strategies of British India*.
2. See Great Britain Foreign Office, *British and Foreign State Papers, 1872-3* 63 (London, 1879): 724-27, 743-44.
3. The ferry was probably still operating in 1853, according to one Indian agent employed by the British. See "Travels of Khwajah Ahmud Shah Nukshbundee Syud," 344-58.
4. RGS archives. Montgomerie to Sir Roderick Murchison, letter of 29 January 1868.
5. Nain and Mani Singh, on reporting back to Montgomerie at Dehra Dun in May 1868, were sent out again almost immediately to explore the reports Montgomerie had heard of goldfields in Western Tibet. They were joined by Nain Singh's brother Kalian. Shortly after returning from this expedition, Kalian Singh left in 1868 on a solitary mission to Rudok in Western Tibet, and then attempted to reach Lhasa. These Tibetan explorations of the Singh family are recounted in Chapter 4. Hari Ram (also known as M.H., or No. 9) started his long career as a Survey explorer in 1868, and although no report of his first expedition was ever published, it was probably he who headed into Tibet from Darjeeling and reconnoitered the area north of Mount Everest. (See Mason, "Kishen Singh and the Indian Explorers," footnote to 433.)
6. Major T.G. Montgomerie, *Report on the Trans-Himalayan Explorations in Connection with the Great Trigonometrical Survey of India during 1869*, Cambridge University Library, Mayo Papers, Add 7490, p. liii. This report is the primary source for the travels of the Mirza between 1868 and 1869. An almost identical version was published in *JRGS* 41 (1871): 132-93.
7. Letter from Walker to the Home Department, government of India, of 26 July 1867, Foreign Department Proceedings, March 1868. There were close connections between British and Russian geographers. Walker corresponded at length with the Imperial Russian Geographical Society, and visited St. Petersburg when he was on leave from India in the early 1870s.
8. Mayo papers. Cambridge University Library. Add 7490.
9. Letter of Montgomerie to Sir Roderick Murchison, 28 July 1870, RGS Archives.
10. Mayo Papers, Add 7490.

11. Excluding the possibility that Alexander Gardiner might have been there in the 1820s or 1830s. See the discussion about Gardiner in ch. 7 of Keay, *When Men and Mountains Meet*.

12. Pundit Munphool's report is most readily available in *JRGS* 42 (1872): 440-48. That of Faiz Buksh follows (pp. 448-73). The RGS had originally turned down Munphool's report, saying that it was mainly political and "thus unfitted for publication by our Society." RGS archives, letter of Rawlinson dated 8 January 1869.

13. Montgomerie, *Report* (1869), liii.

14. *PRGS* 15 (1871): 203. This is the first reference to this failed attempt.

15. Ibid., 203-4.

16. Phillimore, *Historical Records*, vol. 5, 215.

17. Lieut. J.T. Walker, "Some Account of the Survey of the Northern Trans-Indus Frontier, from Peshawar to Dera Ismael Khan, in 1849-53," in *Selections from the Public Correspondence of the Punjab Administration* 2, no. 7 (Lahore, 1854).

18. Phillimore, *Historical Records*, vol. 5, 448.

19. Letter of 25 September 1856, D.Dn. vol. 709, no. 255.

20. Letter of 16 October 1856, D.Dn. vol. 710, no. 160.

21. Letter from Waugh to Walker of 8 December 1856, D.Dn. vol. 691, no. 212.

22. Letter from Walker to Waugh of 20 October 1857, D.Dn. vol. 710.

23. Letter from Walker to Waugh of 24 May 1858, D.Dn. vol. 710, no. 203.

24. Foreign Department Proceedings, March 1868.

25. Ibid.

26. Lawrence Collection, Mss. Eur. F90/53.

27. Foreign Department Proceedings, March 1868.

28. Memo of T.G. Montgomerie, *Secret Home Correspondence*, L/P&S/3/92, vol. 81, 1874.

29. L/P&S/5/260, vol. 2, 1867, Pol. 121.

30. Lawrence Collection. Mss. Eur. F90/52 and F90/54.

31. Montgomerie, *Report* (1869), lxvi.

32. Arthur Connolly, quoted in J.W. Kaye, *History of the War in Afghanistan*, vol. 1 (London: 1874): 212. Connolly was actually referring to Herat.

33. Lieutenant Rattray, quoted in Kaye, vol. 2, 13-14.

34. Yate, *Northern Afghanistan*, 317-18.

35. Montgomerie, *Report* (1869), lxviii.

36. Gordon, *Roof of the World*, 110-11.

37. Montgomerie, *Report* (1869), lxix and lxxvi.

38. T.G. Montgomerie, *Report on the Trans-Himalayan Explorations in connection with the GTS of India, during 1868* (Dehra Dun, 1869): vii.

39. *JRGS* 39 (1869): clxxix.

40. Alexander Gardiner may have visited Yarkand in the 1820s, but he was an American. In 1859, a Lieutenant Valikhanoff went to Kashgar "in the guise of a trader." See Kuropatkin, *Kashgaria*, 5. According to Kuropatkin, a Russian embassy arrived in the city in the same year as the Mirza but "was not received in a thoroughly friendly manner" (ibid., 6). A year after the Mirza's visit, a Greek traveler crossed the Pamirs and visited Kashgar. See Potagos, *Dix Années*. Also, *PRGS* (1880): 386-87; and *JRGS* 42 (1872): 473.

41. Montgomerie, *Report* (1869), lxi.

42. Owen Lattimore, in his introduction to Norins, *Gateway to Asia*, 11.

43. Shaw died at the age of thirty-eight in Mandalay, shortly after his appointment as Political Resident to the court of the Burmese king. See *PRGS* 1 (1879): 523.

44. Shaw, *Visits to High Tartary*, 300-301.

45. Shaw, "Visit to Yarkand and Kashgar," 135.

46. Gordon, *Roof of the World*, 125.

47. *PRGS* 15 (1871): 201-2.

48. See the introductory essay by Yule to the new edition of Wood, *Oxus*, liii.

49. Ibid., lv, ft. 1.

50. Ibid., lv-lvi.

51. Trotter, "Geographical Results," 226.

52. Letter of Montgomerie to Sir Roderick Murchison, dated 28 July 1870, RGS Archives.
53. Montgomerie, *Report* (1869), lx.
54. Ibid., lix.
55. See Yule, *Late Colonel T.G. Montgomerie*, liii.
56. *GRGTS (1868)*: 7.
57. Montgomerie to Murchison, RGS archives.
58. *PRGS* 15 (1871): 198-204.
59. Letter of Lord Mayo to the Foreign Secretary, 20 May 1871, Mayo Papers.
60. Mason, *GJ* 62 (1923): 434. Montgomerie only found out about the Mirza's murder while on leave in England. He wrote to General Walker that "I shall be very sorry if the old fellow has been murdered, and you must see if you can get something done for his family." Letters of General Walker, RGS archives.
61. These details are drawn from Montgomerie, "Havildar's Journey," 180-99. This article is identical to the official report and is the primary source for the travels of the Havildar. See also Mason, *GJ* 62 (1923): 435; extract from a letter of Montgomerie to Walker, April 1875, made by Phillimore (RGS archives).
62. Phillimore, *Historical Records*, vol. 5, p. 215.
63. MacNair, "Visit to Kafiristan," 1-18. MacNair was an English employee of the Survey of India, who made his expedition while on leave, and probably without the authorization of the Indian government, but with the assistance and encouragement of the Survey of India. (See the obituary of Thomas Holdich, written by Kenneth Mason, *GJ* 45, no. 3 [1930]: 211.) MacNair was accompanied by the "Syud" and the "Meah," two native explorers, the former being described by the RGS as "one of Major Holdich's best men" (*PRGS* n.s. 5 [1883]: 553. See also *PRGS* n.s. 6 [1884]: 369-70, 750). MacNair himself traveled in the disguise of a native doctor or *hakim* (not to be confused with "the Hakim," a native explorer active on the Northwest Frontier at the same time as MacNair. See *PRGS* n.s. 6 [1884]: 370, 750.). Both native explorers were given grants of money by the Survey after the conclusion of their successful journey with MacNair (*GRSI, 1884-85* [Calcutta, 1886] p. 10). MacNair himself was presented with the Murchison Award by the Royal Geographical Society in 1884. He died in Mussoorie of typhoid five years later (*PRGS* n.s. 11 [1889]: 612).
64. Robertson, *Chitral*.
65. Ibid., 1.
66. Ibid., 3.
67. *PRGS* 16 (1872): 261.
68. *JRGS* 42 (1872): 187.
69. Ibid., 189.
70. *GRGTS 1870-1*, 24.
71. *GRGTS 1872-3*, ix.
72. *JRGS* 42 (1872): cxcvi.
73. *PRGS* 16 (1872): 260.
74. Montgomerie to Walker, 22 April 1875. Extract made by Phillimore, RGS archives. Captain Trotter, Montgomerie's successor, notes that with reference to the Havildar's mission from Kabul to Bokhara, "no account of this journey has been published, as the greater portion of the route traversed has previously been described by others" (*Report on Trans-Himalayan Exploration during 1873-74-75* [Calcutta, 1876]: 4, ft. 1). Although the precise route of the Havildar is not known, it is unlikely that Montgomerie would have sent him through an area already mapped. Walker described the details of the route survey as being "somewhat meagre, [but] not without interest" (*GRGTS 1872-3*, x).
75. *GJ* 62 (1923): 435.
76. Captain Henry Trotter, "The Havildar's Journey from Badakhshan to Kolab, Darwaz, and Kubadian," in *Report on the Trans-Himalayan Exploration by Employees of the GTS of India during 1873-74-75* (Calcutta, 1876): 4. See also Trotter's note in *GJ* 48, no. 3 (1916): 229.
77. J.T. Walker, *GRGTS, 1874-5*, no. 13—Geographical, p. 20 footnote. I assume that Kubadian is the modern "im Nasir Khisrav." They are both on the left bank of the Kafirnigan River, a tributary of the Oxus, about forty miles north of the junction.
78. *PRGS* (1879): 600-601.
79. See Mason, *GJ* 62 (1923): 434.

80. These details, together with the account of the Mullah's exploration, are drawn from Captain Henry Trotter, *Trans-Himalayan Explorations,* 24-37. See also *Narrative of Surveys,* 11.
81. See ch. 5.
82. Trotter, *Trans-Himalayan Explorations,* 38.
83. See ch. 4.
84. *Narrative of Surveys,* 1.
85. *Narrative of Surveys,* 24-5.
86. *Narrative of Surveys,* 28.
87. *GRGTS 1876-77,* 21-22. See also the *Abstract of the Reports of the Surveys and of other Geographical Operations in India, for 1876-77* (London, 1878): 57-60. The publication of the first report led to a charge leveled against Walker that he had breached security. (See ch. 9.)
88. Burrard and Hayden, *Geography and Geology,* 172.
89. At least, the last exploration of which an account is available.
90. Lieutenant-Colonel H.C.B. Tanner, deputy superintendent of the Survey of India, supplied the footnotes to the account of the Mullah's explorations. See *The "Mullah's" Narrative of his journey up the Swat Valley to Kalam and Ushu, and across to the Indus Valley via the Kandia Valley, etc.,* in 1878, published in *Report on Trans-Himalayan Explorations to accompany the GRSI, 1878-79* (Calcutta, 1880): xix-xxxv.
91. *Narrative of Surveys,* xix.
92. *Narrative of Surveys,* xx.
93. *GRSI 1878-79,* 57.
94. Letter from Lieutenant-General J.T. Walker to the Secretary to the government of India, dated 2 May 1882, L/E/7/17, p. 1.
95. D.Dn. 594 Accounts, 1880-1890. He may also have assisted the Survey in the demarcation of the Afghan frontier during 1883-84. See *GRSI 1883-84* (Dehra Dun, 1885): 8.
96. Mention should also be made of the "Bozdar," a pundit who explored parts of the northwest frontier, but about whose work little is known. He was given a grant of land by the Survey of India and awarded the title of Khan Bahadur, in 1883 or 1884. (See *GRSI 1883-84* [Dehra Dun, 1885]: 7; also Black, *Memoir on the Indian Surveys,* 149; also *PRGS* n.s. 6 [1884]: 370).

4. To Tibet and Beyond: The Singh Family

1. The Aksai Chin plateau in the northwest is currently under Chinese administration, but was considered part of Ladakh on nineteenth-century maps.
2. These are twentieth-century figures, taken from the map in Karan, *Changing Face of Tibet,* 54.
3. Spate, *India and Pakistan.* Spate was speaking of Ladakh, but the climates are similar.
4. Stein, *Tibetan Civilization,* 25.
5. The site of Tsaparang was first investigated by G. Macworth Young, in 1912. See *Journal of the Punjab Historical Society* 7 (1919): 177-98.
6. For more details, see Datta, *Ladakh and Western Himalayan Politics.* Also Ahmad, "Tibet and Ladakh: A History," 23-58.
7. Moorcroft, "Journey to Lake Manasarovara."
8. For example, the brothers Alexander, James, and Patrick Gerard, Captain William Webb, and G.W. Traill.
9. Lakes Manasarowar and Rakas Tal were visited by Henry Strachey in 1846, followed by his brother Richard in 1848, and by Smith and Harrison in 1863. The Schlagintweit brothers also briefly entered the area in 1855. See ch. 1, notes 47-51.
10. See Sherring, *Western Tibet and the British Borderland,* 272.
11. Phillimore, *Historical Records,* vol. 5, 237.
12. Ibid.
13. Longstaff, *This My Voyage,* 112.
14. Details of this expedition are to be found in Montgomerie, "Trans-Himalayan Explorations during 1867," 146-96.
15. *JRGS* 39 (1869): 147-48.
16. Mason says that he saw a document stating that the two were brothers (*GJ* 62 [1923] 432 ft.),

although a family descendant, Indra Singh Rawat, is of the opinion that they were second cousins. (*Indian Explorers*, 147).

17. *The Times*, 17 February 1869. By this time, *The Times* was aware of the letter presented to the meeting of the RGS on 23 March 1868, to which Montgomerie's papers on the results of Nain Singh's visit to Lhasa of 1865 were delivered. The letter, from M.C. Morrison, consul in Peking, criticized Montgomerie for not applying for passports so that the expeditions to Tibet could be undertaken openly, saying that "the assumption of false character (especially on the part of surveyors) must tend to excite suspicions in the minds of the Chinese" (*PRGS* 12 [1867-68]: 171-72 ft.). Morrison was clearly unaware of Montgomerie's application for passports, and its lack of success, if indeed such an application was made. However, it is not likely that any request for passports to allow the British, or their agents, to survey Tibet would have been granted, and even if it had been, the passports would have carried little or no weight with the Tibetans.

18. *JRGS* 39 (1869): 148.
19. *The Times*, 17 February 1869.
20. Rawling, *Great Plateau*, 283.
21. Hedin, *Trans-Himalaya*, vol. 3, p. 332. Rawling, *Great Plateau*, 286-89.
22. For details of trade between Western Tibet and India, see "Report on the Trans-Himalayan Operations (Trigonometrical) conducted by Mr. E.C. Ryall in Hundes," printed in the *GRSI, 1877-78* (Calcutta, 1879): p. viii, footnotes. Although little gold was exported directly to India, it had in the past found its way there via Nepal. See Cammann, *Trade through the Himalayas*, 56.
23. George Rawlinson, ed. *The History of Herodotus*, vol. 2 (New York, 1885): 408.
24. See Schiern, "Tradition of the Gold Digging Ants," 225-32.
25. Francke, *History of Western Tibet*, 14.
26. Maclaren, "Tibetan Goldfields," 825-26.
27. Ibid.
28. Fisher, Rose, and Huttenback, *Himalayan Battleground*, 171-74.
29. Letter of Montgomerie to Sir Roderick Murchison of 24 January 1869, RGS Archives.
30. According to Maclaren, "Tibetan Goldfields," 826.
31. Burrard and Hayden, *Geography and Geology*, 266. According to one writer, Thok Jalung had ceased to be worked by 1906. See Holdich, *Tibet the Mysterious*, 242.
32. Montgomerie's report refers to Demchok "in Ladakh." However, contemporary maps of British India, drawn up on the basis of the pundits' observations, show Demchok as part of Tibet (see, for example, the map of Turkestan, compiled in 1872 by J.T. Walker, superintendent of the GTS). Demchok is currently administered by China as part of Tibet, but is claimed by India.
33. The position of Gartok was determined to be longitude 80° 23' 33", latitude 31° 44' 4", very close to the current *Times Atlas* figures of 80° 21" and 31° 46'.
34. Sherring, *Western Tibet and the British Borderland*, 302.
35. Lamb, *Britain and Chinese Central Asia*, 273-74.
36. Ibid., 355-57.
37. See note 29.
38. T.G. Montgomerie, "Trans-Himalayan and Trans-Frontier Explorations," *GRGTS, 1871-1872* (Dehra Dun, 1873): 18-19.
39. T.G. Montgomerie, *Report on the Trans-Himalayan Explorations in Connection with the Great Trigonometrical Survey of India during 1868* (Dehra Dun, 1869): viii. Most of the report is reprinted in the *PRGS* 14 (1869-70): 207-14. The *Proceedings* include a summary of the discussion that followed the presentation of Montgomerie's report. The report is also reprinted in a slightly abbreviated form in the *Records of the Survey of India* 8, part 1, 109-14, and is reprinted in its entirety in *JASB* 39, no. 2 (1870): 47-60.
40. Father Andrade of the Tsaparang Mission had established a branch at Rudok in 1627. Started by two missionaries, it survived only a brief while. Rudok remained unvisited by Europeans until the twentieth century. Even the Littledales, who observed the town in 1895, did not actually enter it. See Littledale, "Journey across Tibet," 477.
41. Letter to Sir Roderick Murchison of 28 January 1870, RGS Archives. The sportsman might possibly have been Captain H.U. Smith, who visited Western Tibet in 1865 after plying Tibetan border guards and a "high priest" with brandy. See Smith, "Trip to Thibet," 121.

42. See Littledale, "Journey across Tibet," 477. Also Sherring, *Western Tibet and the British Borderland*, 298-99.
43. Montgomerie, *Report* (1869), iii.
44. Karan, *Changing Face of Tibet*, 6-7.
45. Montgomerie, *Report* (1869), v.
46. Mason mistakenly believes this route was taken by Kalian Singh. See *GJ* 62 (1923): 433.
47. They probably didn't. Hedin notes that later maps did not differ from those based on Nain Singh's observations. See Hedin, *Southern Tibet*, vol. 3, 136.
48. See ch. 2.
49. Montgomerie, *Report* (1869), vii.
50. Kishen Singh was the explorer whom Clements Markham called "D" in his *Mission of George Bogle*, cxvi, and also in *Memoir on the Indian Surveys*, 157. Walker identified "D" as Kishen Singh in *PRGS* n.s. 7 (1885): 83.
51. Kishen was the brother of Mani Singh, according to Kenneth Mason, who says that their father was Devi (or Deb) Singh (*GJ* 62 [1923]: 429-30). Indra Singh Rawat, however, refers to Kishen as being "first cousin" to Mani (*Indian Explorers*, xvi). Kishen's first exploration was in 1869, from his home village of Milam to Rakas Tal and along the Karnali River to Kathai Ghat. This journey covered about four hundred miles, but no account of it was ever published. (See *PRGS* [1885]: 83.)
52. Mason says he was born in the early 1840s, but Rawat claims that he was only twenty-one in 1871 (*Indian Explorers*, 63). Mason is generally the more accurate.
53. I have used the account drawn from the *Records of the Survey of India*, vol. 8, part 1, pp. 133-40. This is also reported, with minor changes, in the *GRGTS, 1873-74*, iii-x; and in *JRGS* 45 (1875): 315-30. Mason (*GJ* 62: 436) errs in referring to the party as being composed of Kishen Singh and the "semi-Tibetan," and the *Records* are mistaken in referring to Kishen as being one of the assistants (p. 133).
54. *Records*, 133.
55. See ch. 3. Hari Ram was also active during 1869-72 (see ch. 6).
56. Geographical Despatch to India, no. 18, 31 July 1873, *Selections from Despatches*, 1873, p. 82.
57. *Records*, 140.
58. The activities of the pundits on the Forsyth missions are detailed in ch. 5.
59. This exploration of Nain Singh is recounted in Henry Trotter, "Account of the Pundit's Journey," in *Secret and Confidential Report*, 1-3, and 46-91. My citations refer to this account. It has also been reprinted, in a virtually identical form, in *Records*, vol. 8, part 1, 160-95. Trotter read an abbreviated version to the Royal Geographical Society on 14 May 1877, which was published in *JRGS* 47 (1877): 86-136.
60. Letter dated 7 May 1873, Royal Society.
61. Trotter, *Report*, 3.
62. Ibid., 46.
63. J.T. Walker, *GRGTS, 1874-75* (Dehra Dun, 1876): 20.
64. Trotter, *Report*, 47.
65. Godwin-Austen was halted at the border by the Tibetans, "but I held out for one march towards the place [Rudok], and gained my point, but not before showing some anger at their absurd wishes." See *JRGS* 37 (1867): 357.
66. On this segment of the journey, Nain Singh passed the Tashi Bup Tso (Lake). Sven Hedin subsequently castigated the pundit for the vagueness of the details of the lake's dimensions, but as Kishen Singh pointed out in response, the pundit did in fact estimate its length and breadth. See *GJ* 35 (1910): 594. Hedin was a frequent critic of Nain Singh and the other pundits, although he also praised them on many occasions—for example when speaking of Nain Singh's "long and brilliant work in Tibet" (*Southern Tibet* 3, 148). For years Hedin and the Survey of India sniped at each other over the accomplishments of the Indian explorers. See, for example, the debate in *GJ* 33 (1909): 406-7, 418-19, 424-25, 431, 436-40.
67. Trotter, *Report*, 58.
68. At least, on some Western maps. See the *Times Atlas of The World* (London, 1958), vol. 1, map 23.

69. Trotter, *Report*, 85.
70. Morshead, "Topographical Results," 113 and 115.
71. Letter to Colonel Yule, dated 14 July 1876, correspondence files of the RGS.
72. H.J. Harman, *Geographical Explorations: Thibet*, (published as a secret report with the *Annual Report of the Survey of India, 1881-82*), n.p., n.d., p. 1. See also Black, *Memoir on the Indian Surveys*, 158.
73. Vol. 3, p. 136.
74. See Selections from Despatches, Geographical Despatch to India No. 23, dated 17 May 1877, V/6/305, p. 164; and letter of Montgomerie to Walker of 19 April 1877 in the RGS archives.
75. Geographical Despatch to India No. 15, dated 8 March 1877, V/6/305, p. 159. See also letter of Walker to Yule, 14 July 1876, RGS correspondence files.
76. Letter to Walker of 19 April 1877, RGS archives.
77. Proposal dated 23 March 1876, RGS correspondence files.
78. Letter of 18 July 1876, RGS correspondence files.
79. Letter of 14 July 1876, RGS correspondence files.
80. Letter of 13 April 1877, RGS correspondence files.
81. Letter of 4 May 1877, RGS correspondence files.
82. *PRGS* 47 (1877): cxxv.
83. See letter of Walker to Yule, 14 July 1876, RGS correspondence files.
84. *PRGS* n.s. 4 (1882): 317.
85. Foreign Department Proceedings and General, January 1878, nos. 89-97.
86. Although he had favored Nain Singh over Trotter for the 1877 RGS medal, on this occasion Walker urged that an award (he mentions the Companion of the Order of the Star of India) not be made to the Pundit, as Montgomerie deserved it more. An attempt was made to halt the award, but it was too late. See note 81.
87. See note 88.
88. *PRGS* n.s. 4 (1882): 317.
89. Allen, *Mountain in Tibet*, 137. See also Rawat, *Indian Explorers*, 61.
90. The obituary is in *The Times* for 15 March 1882. Smyth's obituary of Nain Singh is in *PRGS* n.s. 4 (1882): 315-17.
91. Another contemporary account, by General Walker, also gives the date of death as between 1 October 1881 and 30 September 1882. See *PRGS* n.s. 5 (1883): 369.
92. One of the pundits' prayer wheels, probably that of Nain Singh, was subsequently loaned by the government of India for exhibition in London at the Festival of Britain in 1951. *Festival of Britain: 1951. Catalogue of Exhibits: South Bank Exhibition* (London, 1951): 89.
93. *JRGS* 47 (1877): cxxvi.
94. The first full account of A.K.'s travels was published as *Account of Exploration in Great Tibet and Mongolia by A-K, 1879-82: In connection with the Trigonometrical Branch, Survey of India* (Dehra Dun: 1884), p. 88. By the time A.K. reached Dehra Dun, General Walker was on the verge of retirement, and so A.K.'s report was written up by J.B.N. Hennessey. From this report, certain "objectionable passages," such as that dealing with the murder of two Europeans at Batang, were removed at the request of the government of India (Foreign Department Proceedings, External A, September 1884, nos. 233-35, National Archives of India). General Walker's copy of the original document (in the RGS archives) shows where the offending passages were. The amended version was published under Hennessey's name as *Report on the Explorations in Great Tibet and Mongolia, made by A.K. in 1879-82: In connection with the Trigonometrical Branch, Survey of India* (Dehra Dun, 1884): 121. The latter version was republished in the *Records of the Survey of India*, vol. 8, part 2 (Dehra Dun, 1915): 215-323. It is identical to the earlier version except that full names are given (e.g., Kishen Singh instead of "A.K."). An account summarizing the travels of A.K., together with some additional data, was written by General Walker and presented to the RGS at its meeting on 8 December 1884. This account, together with the ensuing discussion, was subsequently published by the Society. See Walker, "Four Years' Journeyings," 65-92. I have used both Walker's and Hennessey's accounts.
95. Black, *Memoir on the Indian Surveys*, 152-53. Rawat, *Indian Explorers*, xviii. The statement in the latter source might be interpreted to mean "a village in the Zanskar region of Ladakh."
96. *Records*, 239.

97. According to one account "[F]or days he hung around the door at the bishop's house, afraid to disclose his identity, lest the Tibetans should learn his true character" (Rockhill, *Land of the Lamas*, 288).
98. A.K. gives Chinese names for these rivers.
99. *PRGS* 7, no. 2 (February 1885): 77-78.
100. *GJ* 25, no. 2 (1905): 179.
101. Landon, *Lhasa*, 22.
102. See *Himalayan Journal* 6 (1934): 152. However, north of Shugden Gompa, Kingdon-Ward admits, A.K.'s materials were of little utility. See "The Himalaya East of the Tsangpo," *GJ* 84 (1934): 379.
103. Mason, "Kishen Singh," 439.
104. *Mr. J.F. Needham's Journey along the Lohit Brahmaputra, between Sadiya in Upper Assam and Rima in Southeastern Tibet*, Supplementary Papers of the Royal Geographical Society, vol. 2 (1887-89): 498.
105. Mason, *Abode of Snow*, 88.
106. *PRGS* n.s. 7 (1885): 92.
107. Mason, *GJ* (1923): 439.
108. Rockhill, *Land of the Lamas*, 288. Rockhill is generally critical of A.K.'s observations. He quotes Walker's article in *PRGS* n.s. 7 (1885), which has A.K. giving the number of houses in Kantse as 2,500 (p. 73). Rockhill says that he observed Kantse to have "not more than 300" (p. 239). But the error is Walker's, not A.K.'s, for the original report of A.K. (p. 263) gives the number as "about 200."
109. *GRSI, 1880-81* (Calcutta, 1882): Appendix, p. 3.
110. *GRSI, 1882-83* (Calcutta, 1884): 6.
111. *PRGS* n.s. 8 (1886): 471.
112. See D.Dn. vol. 593, Accounts, 1880-1890, for April 1884 and July 1885.
113. Longstaff, *This My Voyage*, 71.
114. "Observations of Glacier Movements in the Himalayas," in *GJ* 31 (1908): 316.
115. See *GJ* 134 (1968): 327.

5. The Pundits and the Forsyth Missions

1. For more details, see ch. 3.
2. See his "Memorandum on Routes from the Punjab to Eastern Turkestan," published in *Selections from the Records of the Government of the Punjab and its Dependencies*, n.s. 11, 1868.
3. See Trotter, "Amir Yakoub Khan," 101.
4. *Selections from the Records of the Government of India: Home Department*, no. 83 (Calcutta, 1871): 5, v/23/17.
5. Memorandum of 27 April 1870 from Forsyth to the Foreign Department of the Government of India, in *Secret Letters and Enclosures from India*, L/P & S/5/264, 1870.
6. Letter from Forsyth to Sir Roderick Murchison, *PRGS* 15 (1871): 23.
7. See note 4.
8. Forsyth in L/P & S/18 c14.
9. Alder's *British India's Northern Frontier* provides very useful background details on the two Forsyth missions.
10. See note 4.
11. Shaw assigned a longitude of 76° to Yarkand, by comparison with the Mirza's 77° 30'. A recalculation of Shaw's observations at Greenwich led to the adoption of a mean longitude of 77°. See *JRGS* 41 (1871): clxxi-clxxii. Shaw also made a useful contribution to the geography of the Karakorum and the Kunlun, when he was detached from the mission returning from Yarkand.
12. See E. Forsyth, ed., *Autobiography and Reminiscences* 62.
13. His report is titled *Journey from Peshawar to Kashgar and Yarkand in Eastern Turkestan, or Little Bokhara, through Afghanistan, Balkh, Badakhshan, Wakhan, Pamir, and Sarkol*, and is published in *JRGS* 42 (1872): 448-73. It can also be found in *Selections from the Records of the Government of the Punjab*, Confidential Series no. A-6 (Lahore, 1873): IOR Neg. 3717.

14. According to Curzon, Faiz Baksh confused two itineraries. See Curzon, "Source of the Oxus," 252-53.
15. "Route of Ibrahim Khan from Kashmir through Yassin to Yarkand in 1870," *PRGS* 15 (1871): 387-92.
16. Most of the Ili valley was returned to China by the 1881 Treaty of St. Petersburg, in return for which Russia received commercial privileges in Kashgaria.
17. *Report of a Mission to Yarkund in 1873, under command of Sir. T.D. Forsyth, K.C.S.I., C.B., Bengal Civil Service, with Historical and Geographical Information regarding the Possessions of the Ameer of Yarkund*, (Calcutta, 1875). Henceforth referred to as *Report*.
18. Letter from Heaviside to Walker dated 11 June 1874, Extracts from letters to Walker made by Colonel Phillimore, Royal Society.
19. Trotter, "Amir Yakoub Khan," 95.
20. *GRGTS, 1872-73* (Dehra Dun, 1873): 30.
21. Letter from Montgomerie to Walker of 7 May 1873.
22. *JRGS* 48 (1878): 173.
23. *PRGS* 17 (1873): 286.
24. *Report*, 233.
25. *Report*, 235. The *GRGTS, 1872-73* also refers to "four of the Pundits" (p. 30).
26. *Report*, 2.
27. *GJ* 62 (1923): 436.
28. Trotter, *Confidential Report* 46. There is a fleeting reference in the *Report* to a "No. 4," whom a later source identifies as Kishen Singh (*Records of the Survey of India*, vol. 8, part 1, p. 160).
29. Captain H. Trotter, "Narrative of Munshi Abdul Subhan's Journey from Panjeh [Wakhan] to Shighnan and Roshan with a short account of his return to India via Kabul," in *Political and Secret Letters and Enclosures received from India*, vol. 4, filed with no. 22 (India, 21 June 1875): 393-422.
30. Letter of Forsyth to the RGS, 14 May 1877, *PRGS* 21 (1876-77): 347.
31. *GRGTS, 1873-74* (Dehra Dun, 1874): 33.
32. Letter of Montgomerie to Walker, 7 May 1873, Extracts made by Colonel Phillimore, Royal Society.
33. Letter to RGS, 2 April 1873, *PRGS* 17 (1873): 286.
34. See *GRGTS, 1872-3*, 29; and *Report*, 235. See also *PRGS* 21 (1876-77): 348.
35. *Report*, 239.
36. *Report*, 234-35.
37. *JRGS* 48 (1878): 189.
38. *JRGS* 47 (1877): clxxxii.
39. *JRGS* 48 (1878): 189-90. *Report*, 237. Also V. Ball, *Scientific Results*, 23 and 29.
40. *Report*, 237-40; Ball, *Scientific Results*, 23.
41. Gordon, *Roof of the World*, 36-37.
42. *Report*, 237.
43. Letter to Sir Robert Montgomerie dated 23 November 1873, *PRGS* 17 (1874): 224.
44. Forsyth was later rather defensive about his lack of ability to do more in the way of exploration. See "On the Buried Cities in the Shifting Sands of the Great Desert of Gobi," *JRGS* 47 (1877): 15-17.
45. *Report*, 5.
46. Forsyth defends his cautious approach in his *Autobiography* (pp. 245-51). Certainly the mission was able to make extended excursions from Yarkand and Kashgar, which would have been put at risk by the covert use of the pundits.
47. Details of the visit to Lake Chadyr Kul are in the *Report*, 214-16 and 249-53.
48. While Trotter was away, Kishen Singh mapped some villages to the southeast of Kashgar and investigated their irrigation systems. *Report*, 253.
49. Ibid.
50. Ibid., 415.
51. Trotter, "Geographical Results," 187.
52. See *Report*, 217-21; also *PRGS* 18 (1874): 425-28.
53. See *Report*, 17-19 and 253-61; *JRGS* 48 (1878): 195-98.
54. *PRGS* 22 (1878): 290. See also Forsyth's *Autobiography*, 192.

55. *PRGS* 18 (1874): 440. See also *JRGS* 47 (1877): 16.
56. Ibid., 434.
57. Forsyth, *Autobiography*, 250.
58. *Report*, 262.
59. *PRGS* 18 (1874): 433.
60. Gordon, *Varied Life*, 119-21.
61. Ibid., 122-23. See also *PRGS* 18 (1874): 429, 434, and 439.
62. Trotter, *Narrative of Munshi Abdul Subhan's Journey*, 394.
63. The Havildar's route was selected by Montgomerie before he retired to England. The Havildar left on his travels from Peshawar in September 1873, by which time Trotter was heavily involved with the Forsyth mission.
64. Trotter, *JRGS* 48 (1878): 210.
65. Trotter, *Narrative of Munshi Abdul Subhan's Journey*, 393. The Munshi was subsequently employed again. During 1876-77 he participated in surveying a dangerous area of Udaipur. (See Black, *Memoir on the Indian Surveys*, 69.) He was then engaged in mapping parts of Afghanistan where it was not feasible to employ Europeans. The last report on the Munshi came from Trotter, who told a meeting of the RGS more than twenty years after his travels in the Pamir that the Munshi was "now in the service of the Amir of Afghanistan." (See the discussion following Curzon's paper "Source of the Oxus," 262.)
66. *Report*, 283-84. For Trotter's error in height, see Pamir Boundary Commission, *GJ* (1899): 52.
67. *Report*, 241.
68. Ibid.
69. Hayward, "Journey from Leh," 55. See also *Report*, 22.
70. *PRGS* 21 (1876-77): 348. *Report*, 22 and 312.
71. See Alder, *British India's Northern Frontier*, 50-53.
72. Ibid., 111-12.
73. Trotter, *Confidential Report* 35-36. Also, see ch. 3.
74. See H. Trotter, "Account of P. Kishen Singh's Explorations in Western Tibet made in connection with the Mission to Yarkand and Kashgar, 1873-74," *Records of the Survey of India*, vol. 8, part 1 (Dehra Dun, 1915): 149-58; also in *Report*, 247-49, 289-90, 314-17, 348-49, 442-44; also in Trotter, *JRGS* 48 (1878): 184-87, 232-33.
75. Walker, *GRGTS, 1873-74* (Dehra Dun, 1874): 34. Walker is incorrect, however, in saying that the Pundit went via Sanju to Khotan. He took the direct route through Guma. Forsyth also sent other Indians to the Khotan area, who returned with additional information. See *Autobiography*, 238-40.
76. *Report*, 442.
77. *Report*, opposite p. 247.
78. Trotter later used this to defend the pundits against charges made by Sven Hedin that their measurements were "worthless." Hedin made the allegation at a meeting of the RGS on 8 February 1909. See *GJ* 33 (1909): 419.
79. *Report*, 289.
80. *Report*, 443.
81. Rawlinson, "On the Recent Journey of Mr. W.H. Johnson from Leh; in Ladakh, to Ilchi in Chinese Turkistan," *PRGS* 11 (1867): 9.
82. *Report*, 249.
83. A.D. Carey, "Journey round Chinese Turkistan," 731-52.
84. One part of his report on the area around Rudok is still a bone of contention between the Chinese and Indian governments, with the Chinese citing his report in favor of their case over the boundary in the area, and the Indians denying that any such case can be made. See *Report of the Officials of the Governments of India and the People's Republic of China on the Boundary Question*, Ministry of External Affairs, Government of India, 1961, pp. 260, 341 and CR-113.
85. See *Report*, 287. The *Times* atlas gives the longitude of Yarkand as 77° 16'.
86. *GJ* 62 (1923): 437.
87. *PRGS* 22 (1878): 296-99. Nain Singh's expedition has been described in ch. 4.
88. The account of the exploration of M.S. is drawn from *Secret and Confidential Reports of Trans-Himalayan Explorations in Badakshan* (1883). The introductory comments (pp. 1-23) are by Colonel H.C.B. Tanner (referred to henceforth as *Introduction*). The Journal and the Itinerary are paginated

Notes to Pages 164-178

(1)-(82) and prepared under the supervision of J.B.N. Hennessey. I am grateful to Dr. Gary Alder for allowing me to photocopy this report.

89. See Kenneth Mason, *GJ* 62 (1923): 439. Mason also notes that the report of M.S. was never issued to the public.

90. The *Report* refers to Abdul Subhan as "A__S__, an employe of the Survey Department in Geographical Exploration" (p. 1). One reason for the journey may have been that M.S. wished to visit the graves of his ancestors, although this might have been just an excuse put forward during his travels. See p. (6).

91. *PRGS* 6 (1884): 508.

92. At this point M.S. became confused and failed to identify the Aksu on the upper course of the Murghab. Faced with the observations of a Russian expedition, Walker later admitted the error. See *PRGS* 6 (1884): 136-37 and 508. Also *PRGS* 8 (1896): 253.

93. According to Black. See his *Memoir on the Indian Surveys*, 143.

94. Tanner, *Introduction*, 7.

95. Hennessey, *Itinerary*, (57).

96. *PRGS* 6 (1884): 368-69.

97. Tanner, *Introduction*, 22-3.

98. Tanner, *Introduction*, 15.

6. Around Everest and Kanchenjunga: Hari Ram and Rinzing Namgyal

1. "An Account of the Kingdom of Nepal," *Asiatic Researches* 2 (1792): 169-92. For additional information on Catholic missionary activity, see H. Hosten, "Letters and Other Papers of Fr. Ippolito Desideri, S.J., a Missionary in Tibet (1713-21)," *JRASB, Letters* 4, no. 4 (1938): 567-767; Maclagan, *Jesuits and the Great Mogul*; Markham, *Mission of George Bogle*; and Wessels, *Early Jesuit Travellers*.

2. The Gurkhas then expelled the Capuchin mission from Nepal.

3. The following works are useful for the eighteenth- and nineteenth-century history of Nepal, and its relations with the British: Chaudhuri, *Anglo Nepalese Relations*; Husain, *British India's Relations*; Lamb, "Tibet in Anglo-Chinese Relations"; Landon, *Nepal*; Mojumdar, *Anglo-Nepalese Relations* Rose, *Nepal: Strategy for Survival*; Sanwal, *Nepal and the East India Company*.

4. For details of the Kinloch, Logan, and Foxcroft missions, see Chaudhuri, *Anglo Nepalese Relations*, 13-39 and 59-60.

5. Lamb, *JRASB*, 174.

6. Kirkpatrick, *Kingdom of Nepaul*.

7. Chaudhuri, *Anglo Nepalese Relations*, 71.

8. Phillimore, *Historical Records*, vol. 2, 70.

9. Aitchison, *Collection of Treaties*, 37.

10. Mason, *Abode of Snow*, 64-65. Its official height is now given as 26,795 feet.

11. Phillimore, *Historical Records*, vol. 3, 45.

12. Phillimore, *Historical Records*, vol. 4, 81.

13. Ibid., 318.

14. Ibid., 82.

15. Temple, *Journals Kept*, vol. 2, 255.

16. Phillimore, *Historical Records*, vol. 4, 95 and 528; Mason, *Abode of Snow*, 122.

17. Quoted in Campbell, "Sketch of Political Relations," 26.

18. Wright, *History of Nepal*, 2. A few mountaineers climbed around Kanchenjunga between 1885 and 1918, most notably Douglas Freshfield in 1899. A detachment from the Survey of India was granted entry to Nepal in the mid-1920s, but only under Indian officers, and with no British supervision. This produced a good reconnaissance survey, but as late as the mid-1950s one expert observer could still say of the Nepal Himalayas that "it is not yet possible to give a fully trustworthy account of the geography or structure of the ranges" (Mason, *Abode of Snow*, 28).

19. Rawat, *Indian Explorers*, xviii.

20. Mason, *GJ* (1923): 433 ft.

21. Ibid.

22. T.G. Montgomerie, *Report on the Trans-Himalayan Explorations in connection with the Great Trigonometrical Survey of India, during 1868* (Dehra Dun, 1869): vi. See also *The Times*, London, for 24 February 1870.

23. See *Memorandum on the Trans-Himalayan Explorations for 1871* by Major T.G. Montgomerie in *GRGTS, 1871-1872* (Dehra Dun, 1872). Reprinted (with the addition of the explorer's name) in *Records of the Survey of India*, vol. 8, part 1, pp. 116-31. A slightly amended version is in *JRGS* 45 (1875): 330-49, under the title of "Journey to Shigatze, in Tibet, and Return by Dingri-Maidan into Nepaul, in 1871, by the Native Explorer No. 9." My citations are drawn from the first reference.

24. Montgomerie states that he did so, "resuming his route survey on the 30th September from a point he had previously visited" (*Memorandum*, 2b), thus providing additional confirmatory evidence that the 1868 explorer in this region was indeed Hari Ram.

25. For more information on Dingri, see Aziz, *Tibetan Frontier Families*, ch. 1 and 2.

26. The first close-up circuit was made a century later by an American team. See *The New York Times*, 12 June 1982.

27. No record is available of these instructions.

28. See *Report of Hari Ram's Journey from Pithoragarh in Kumaon via Jumla to Tra-dom and back along the Kali Gandak to British Territory in 1873*, in *Records of the Survey of India*, vol. 8, part 1, 141-47. The information about the outbreak of cholera and the name of the explorer are given in this report. Neither piece of information is supplied in the otherwise identical article in the *JRGS* 45 (1875): 350-63, although this article does say that the report was communicated to the RGS by Montgomerie. The *JRGS* article is also reprinted in the *GRGTS, 1873-74*, x-xvi.

29. For a more recent account of Mustang, see Peissel, *Mustang*. Peissel confuses the dates of Hari Ram's expedition and misquotes Sven Hedin (p. 279).

30. Letter of Montgomerie to J.T. Walker, April 1875, Summary made by Phillimore, Royal Society.

31. *GRGTS, 1873-74*, 33.

32. *GRGTS, 1871-72*, 4b. According to Clements Markham, Nain Singh had attempted to take this route from Kirong to Jongka, an "important Chinese post," in 1865 but was refused permission to do so. See Markham, *Narratives*, p. cx.

33. See "Account (drawn up by Captain H.J. Harman, R.E., Assistant Superintendent, Survey of India) of explorations during 1880-81, by explorer G__S__S," in *Secret and Confidential Reports of Trans-Himalayan Explorations in Badakhshan and beyond the frontier of Sikkim, prepared for publication with the annual report for 1881-82 of the Survey of India* (n.p.; n.d.): 7. See also *PRGS* (1883): 370.

34. His name is provided by Kenneth Mason in *GJ* 62 (1923): 438. Mason adds that "his work was valueless."

35. Some years after the expedition of G.S.S., the Survey was still bemoaning the lack of observations of the peaks "in the remote and little known region towards the head of the Arun river." See "Extract from the Narrative Report of Colonel H.C.B. Tanner, S.C., Deputy Superintendent, in charge Himalaya party, - season 1884-85," in the *GRSI, 1884-85* (Calcutta, 1886): xliv.

36. D.Dn. vol. 593, Accounts, 1880-90.

37. "Report on routes by Explorer Hari Ram from (1) Dagmara thana via the Dudh Kosi river and Pangula pass to Ting-ri in Tibet; (2) Ting-ri to Kirong via Jongkha fort; (3) Kirong via the Trisuli river to Arughat on the Buria Gandak; (4) Arughat to Nubri on the Buria Gandak; and (5) Arughat via the Buria Gandak to Deo Ghat, and thence down the Narayani to Tribeni: compiled by Mr. C. Wood, in 1885-86," *Records of the Survey of India*, vol. 8., part 2, 383-99.

38. This remained true for over twenty years. See Burrard and Hayden, *Geography and Geology* 152.

39. Hari Ram made a fifth journey, this time with his son Ganga Datt (code named T.G.) in 1892-93. (See Kenneth Mason, *GJ* 62 [1923]: 438 ft.) For his source, Mason cites the Special Report of the Survey of India for 1895. This Report is not present in the India Office Library or the British Library. There is a reference in the India Office Library, in the Indian Foreign External Proceedings (June 1895, Nos. 24-28, P/4815), which is an index entry under "matters of routine" referring to "explorations in Nepal and Tibet made by explorer M.H. and his son in 1892-93." The full account of the explorations is in the Proceedings of the Government of India, Foreign Department, External B, 21 November 1894 and

17 May 1895. These documents remain in India. These explorations of Hari Ram and his son in 1892-93 are the last known independent exploits of the trans-Himalayan explorers.

40. See "Notes by Colonel H.C.B. Tanner, on Reconnaissances and Explorations in Nepal, Sikkim, Bhutan and Assam," in *GRSI, 1887-88* (Calcutta, 1889): xlvii.

41. The passports were eventually granted, but Macaulay never entered Tibet. For an analysis of the events, see Lamb, *Britain and Chinese Central Asia*, ch. 6.

42. For additional information, see Risley, *Gazeteer of Sikkim*.

43. Phillimore, *Historical Records*, vol. 5, 83.

44. Ibid.

45. Edgar, *Visit to Sikhim*.

46. Macaulay, *Mission to Sikkim*. The analysis of the Edgar and Macaulay missions by Lamb is invaluable. See his *Britain and Chinese Central Asia*, especially ch. 5-7.

47. I am indebted for much of this early background, and other material, to Nicholas Rhodes, whose wife, Deki, is a great-great-niece of Rinzing Namgyal.

48. See the remarks by A.W. Paul in *GJ* 19 (1902): 473.

49. Harman's obituary, written by Walker, is in *The Royal Engineers Journal* 13, no. 150 (May 1883): 112-15.

50. *GRSI, 1881-82* (Calcutta, 1883): 41. See also ch. 8.

51. See Das, "Narrative of a Journey," 79. Das used R.N. to organize the conveying of his baggage to Tibet on his second journey there. Das, *Journey to Lhasa and Central Tibet*, 140.

52. "Extract from the Narrative Report of Colonel H.C.B. Tanner, S.C., Deputy Superintendent, in charge Darjeeling and Nepal Boundary Survey; - season 1883-84," in *GRSI, 1883-84* (Dehra Dun, 1885): xxix.

53. "Extract from the Narrative Report of Colonel H.C.B. Tanner, S.C., Deputy Superintendent, in charge Himalaya party, - season 1884-85," in *GRSI, 1884-85*: xlvi.

54. Ibid., xlv.

55. D.Dn. 593, Accounts, 1880-90.

56. Hooker, *Himalayan Journals*, vol. 1.

57. Freshfield, "Round Kanchinjinga," 162-63.

58. "Original Narrative Account of Rinzin Nimgyl of his exploration of the country to the North and North-West of Kinchinjunga made in the autumn of 1884, with notes by Colonel H.C.B. Tanner, and Mr. W. Robert, Survey of India," in *Records of the Survey of India*, vol. 8, part 2, 360-62. Also printed (without the identification of R.N., and with some different spellings of place names) in *GRSI, 1884-85*: xlviii-lii.

59. See the comments by Tanner, in *GRSI, 1887-88* (Calcutta, 1889): xlviii. His work was incorporated into the maps of the time.

60. D.Dn. 594, Accounts, 1880-90.

61. See "Notes by Colonel H.C.B. Tanner, on Reconnaissances and Explorations in Nepal, Sikkim, Bhutan and Assam," in *GRSI, 1887-88* (Calcutta, 1889): xlvii-xlviii.

62. Freshfield, *Round Kanchenjunga*, 191. See also his article "Round Kanchinjinga."

63. Freshfield, *Round Kanchenjunga*, 156.

64. Ibid., 210.

65. Ibid., 27-28.

66. Information and photograph provided by courtesy of Nicholas Rhodes.

67. Reprint. Delhi, 1973.

68. Ibid., 187.

69. Ibid., 265.

7. "A Hardy Son of Soft Bengal"

The title, describing Sarat Chandra Das, is from the poem "A Lay of Lachen" by Colman Macaulay, in Das, *Indian Pandits*, iii.

1. Mahadevprasad Saha, in the foreword to Das, *Autobiography*, iii. Much of my information on Das's early life is drawn from this source.

2. Huree Chunder Mookerjee may have been a composite character. Perceval Landon, for example, believed that Kipling based his fictional figure on Kishen Singh. See his *Lhasa*, 23-24. But with his educational background and love of books, "Hurree Babu" is closer to Das.

3. A.W. Croft to A.C. Lyall, Foreign Office, Simla, dated 12 April 1879, Foreign Department Proceedings, Secret. January 1882, nos. 722-25.

4. Edgar, *Visit to Sikkim*, 23.

5. Ibid., 23 and 68.

6. According to Graham Sandberg. See his book, *Exploration of Tibet*, 163.

7. The Bhutia Boarding School eventually merged with the Government Middle English School in 1891 to form the Government High School. See Dozey, *Concise History*, 109.

8. Das, *Autobiography*, 17. See also his *Indian Pandits*, xviii.

9. Das, *Indian Pandits*, 16.

10. Markham, *Mission of George Bogle*.

11. Das, *Autobiography*, 17.

12. Ibid.

13. Ibid., 18.

14. An account of this excursion is in his *Autobiography*, 8-11.

15. Ibid., 18.

16. Ibid., 19.

17. Ibid.

18. Croft's letter is reprinted in Das's *Autobiography*, 20-21.

19. This is based on a conversation which L.A. Waddell, a member of the Younghusband Expedition, had with the Tibetan governor of Lhasa. See his *Lhasa and Its Mysteries*, 7-9.

20. See Das, *Autobiography*, 23 and 29. Also the remarks by Croft, printed in the *Journal of the Buddhist Text and Anthropological Society* 7, part 1 (1900): i.

21. See Lamb, *Britain and Chinese Central Asia*, 152-3.

22. Captain H.J. Harman, *Geographical Explorations: Thibet*, published as a Secret and Confidential Report with the *Annual Report of the Survey of India, 1881-81* (n.p.; n.d.): 1. See also *GJ* 4 (1894): 61.

23. Harman, *Geographical Explorations*, 1.

24. Letter of Croft to Walker, 15 February 1879, RGS archives.

25. Ibid., and Das, *Autobiography*, 28. A complete list of the equipment requested by Das is appended to Croft's letter to Walker. It is doubtful that everything asked for was supplied. The two umbrellas are referred to by Das in *Journal of the Buddhist Text and Anthropological Society* 7, part 1 (1900): 12. Das carried a revolver, while U.G. was given a pistol (presumably only a single-shot weapon) (Ibid., 23).

26. Das, *Autobiography*, iii (foreword by Mahadevprasad Saha).

27. The account of Das's travels, written on his return, was never issued to the public. It was published in a restricted edition of twenty-five copies, for official use only, at the Bengal Secretariat Press in Calcutta, 1881, and titled *Narrative of a Journey to Tashilunpo in 1879*. I have used the account published by Das in the *Journal of the Buddhist Text and Anthropological Society* (of which he was editor) between 1899 and 1904 (vol. 7, part 1 [1899]: 1-30; vol. 7, part 2 [1901]: 1-56; and vol. 7, part 3 [1904]: 57-80). Citations are to this source. A version of his journey is also published in his *Autobiography*. Excerpts of the narrative were reprinted by Freshfield in *Round Kanchenjunga*, 309-24. A summary of the expedition, for restricted circulation, was written by Captain H.J. Harman and titled "Account of the Journey of Babu D__C__S__ and Lama O__G__U__ from Darjeeling to Shigatze in Thibet and back to Darjeeling during 1879," and published as part of a *Secret and Confidential Report of Trans-Himalayan Explorations in Badakhshan and Beyond the Frontiers of Sikkim* (1883).

28. *Journal of the Buddhist Text and Anthropological Society* 7, no. 1: 13-15. It was only in this later reprint that Das identified the Chathang La with the Jonsong La. The Survey of India believed they were two different passes (*Report 1883-84*, 7). Freshfield agreed, saying that the Chathang La was the one most likely used by Das, and that it lay to the west of the Jonsong (*Round Kanchenjunga*, 24-25). The later report of Das's travels refers only to the Chathang La. (See Das, *Autobiography*, 43.) Although Freshfield disagreed with Das on this point, he nevertheless considered his later narratives to be of great

value, and it was he, as a member of the Council of the Royal Geographical Society, who initiated the move by the RGS to publish the account of the travels by Das ("that bold Bengalee") made in 1881-83. See *GJ* 25, no. 5 (1905): 494.

29. *Journal of the Buddhist Text and Anthropological Society* 7, no. 1: 30.

30. Ibid., 7, no. 2: 11.

31. Ibid., 12.

32. Ibid., 21.

33. Ibid., 23.

34. Ibid., 52.

35. Croft to Lyall, 20 July 1881, Foreign Department Proceedings, Secret, January 1882, nos. 722-25.

36. See the comment by Croft in Das, *Autobiography*, 28. However, in 1880 another explorer of the Survey of India, Nem Singh (known as G.M.N. or N.M.G. in the government files), did succeed in making a journey from Shigatse to Khamba jong. Nem Singh, like Ugyen Gyatso, was a Sikkimese monk from the Pemionchi monastery. Further details of his explorations are not known, although he traveled by a route to the east of that followed by Das and U.G., and his observations were incorporated in the maps of the time. See the memorandum by Captain Harman in *Report of Trans-Himalayan Explorations in Badakhshan and Beyond the Frontiers of Sikkim* (1883): 7.

37. See the anonymous review of Das's book (as cited in note 40) in *The Athenaeum* 3918 (29 November 1902): 725.

38. Das, *Autobiography*, 29-31.

39. Ibid., 31-32.

40. The full account of this second expedition is embodied in two government reports. See *Narrative of a Journey to Lhasa in 1881-82* (Calcutta, 1885); and *Narrative of a Journey round Lake Yamdo (Palti) and in Lhoka, Yarlung and Sakya in 1882* (Calcutta, 1887). These were published in a very limited edition of one hundred copies each, for confidential circulation, although, according to one observer, "copies were actually to be purchased in the open market at St. Petersburg soon after it was printed" (Colquhoun, "Heart of the Forbidden Country," 43). An abridged version for the general public with much of Das's idiosyncratic language altered was eventually produced some twenty years after Das's travels under the editorship of W.W. Rockhill, titled *Journey to Lhasa and Central Tibet* (London, 1902), revised and reprinted 1904. Rockhill replaced Das's language with his own flat prose, leading one reviewer of the book to label it a "dreary monograph . . . one of the dullest achievements of human industry" (*Edinburgh Review* 201, no. 412 [1905]: 344). Freshfield reprinted part of the *Narrative of a Journey to Lhasa*, retaining the original language, in his *Round Kangchenjunga* (pp. 324-50). Excerpts were also published by Graham Sandberg in the magazine *Nineteenth Century* 26 (1889): 681-94 and in the *Contemporary Review* 58 (July-December 1890): 64-82. Das himself wrote a short article of his return journey, titled "An Account of Travels on the Shores of Lake Yamdo-Croft," which was published in *JASB* 67 (1898): 256-73.

41. Das, *Autobiography*, 27 and 32. Also, see Foreign Department Proceedings, Secret, May 1883.

42. Das, *Narrative of a Journey to Lhasa*, 46.

43. Ibid., 79.

44. Ibid., 111.

45. Ibid., 153.

46. See letter of Croft to Walker of 15 February 1879. "He [Das] tells me that his desire is after spending six months . . . in Tibet proper, to endeavor to reach India by following the course of the Sanpoo River." RGS archives.

47. *Journal of the Buddhist Text and Anthropological Society* 7, no. 2 (1901): 25.

48. Petech, "China and European Travellers," 233-36.

49. For an entertaining account of these attempts, see Hopkirk, *Trespassers*.

50. Das, "Lake Yamdo-Croft," 261.

51. Das, *Journey to Lhasa*, x.

52. From the preface to Das, *Tibetan-English Dictionary*.

53. Petech, "China and European Travellers," 252.

54. Kawaguchi, *Three Years in Tibet*, 405.

55. Waddell, *Lhasa and Its Mysteries*, 7-9. According to another member of the Younghusband

Expedition, the prime minister was executed and his servants tortured (Landon, *Lhasa*, 235-39). See also Bell, *Tibet Past and Present*, 59.

56. See the comments by Younghusband, "Geographical Results," 481. In comparing accounts of Lhasa given by Nain Singh, Kishen Singh, and Das against those supplied by participants on the Younghusband Expedition, Sandberg commented that "the native explorers in question seem on the whole to have been a little more exact than the English visitors" (Sandberg, *Tibet and the Tibetans*, iii).

57. "The Tibet Mission. Release of Prisoners," in the *North China Herald* 73 (Shanghai, 14 October 1904): 870.

58. Letter from J.W. Edgar to H.M. Durand, Secretary to the Government of India, 23 January 1886, Foreign Department Proceedings, Secret, February 1886, 229-31.

59. Lamb, *Britain and Tibet*, 155-66.

60. Michie, *Englishman in China* vol. 2, 308-9.

61. Letter of Das to the RGS, dated 29 November 1893, RGS archives.

62. Information provided by Nicholas Rhodes.

63. Knowing that the RGS was planning to publish his narratives, Das suggested to the Society that the award of one of its Gold Medals might be appropriate. See the letter to the Society written by R.C. Datt, 13 October 1893, RGS archives. Datt writes, "I am empowered by Mr. Sarat Chandra Das to mention that he attaches the highest value to a Gold Medal from the Society, and that (as he puts it) it has been his ambition to obtain it."

64. Das, *Autobiography*, v.

65. *Journal and Proceedings of the Asiatic Society of Bengal* 1, no. 8 (1905): 49.

66. In his *Grammar of the Tibetan Language*, Das implies that he was resident at Lhasa Villa in April 1914.

67. Das, *Autobiography*, iii-iv.

68. I am grateful to Nicholas Rhodes for providing most of this information on the early life of Ugyen Gyatso, primarily from his copy of U.G.'s service book.

69. See "The Narrative Account of Lama Ugyen Gyatso's third Season's Explorations in Tibet in 1883," compiled by Lt.-Col. Holdich, R.E., published in *Records of the Survey of India* 8, part 2 (Dehra Dun, 1915): 339-57. My citations are to this source which, apart from giving the full name of the lama and having an introductory summary, is identical to the original publication, prepared by Colonel H.R. Thuillier and published in *Report of the Explorations . . . in Sikkim, Bhutan and Tibet* (Dehra Dun, 1889): 18-37.

70. Letter of Colonel H.C.B. Tanner, 14 October 1884. Courtesy of Nicholas Rhodes.

71. U.G.'s wife Choki had two brothers, one of whom was Rinzing Namgyal. Although U.G.'s companion on this expedition could have been Rinzing Namgyal, it was most likely Choki's eldest brother, Khyung Dung Ringzing Laden La. The evidence for this lies in the *Narrative Account* of the expedition, which on p. 345 refers to U.G. as "travelling over the same route as the explorer Rinzin Nimgyl," and then on the following page speaks of U.G. being "with his brother-in-law and his wife." It is reasonable to assume that had the brother-in-law been Rinzing Namgyal, he would have been so identified.

72. U.G. had had a partial training in surveying techniques, but apparently not enough to become really proficient. Because of this, data from some earlier journeys had been lost. See the notes by Colonel Tanner in *GRSI, 1883-84* (Dehra Dun, 1885): xlvii.

73. *Narrative Account*, 339.

74. Ibid., 343.

75. Tanner was therefore incorrect in stating in 1885 that only the northwestern shore of the lake had been explored. See the notes by Tanner in *GRSI, 1883-84*, xliv.

76. *Narrative Account*, 345-46.

77. Ibid., 351.

78. Ibid., 357.

79. *GJ* 4 (1894): 62.

80. Holdich, *Exploration of Tibet*, 250.

81. Morshead, *North East Frontier*, 12. Kintup's explorations are recounted in ch. 8.

82. This account was published in H.R. Thuillier, *Report on the Explorations of Lama Serap Gyatsho, 1856-68 . . . in Sikkim, Bhutan, and Tibet* (Dehra Dun, 1889): 5-7. Reprinted in *Records of the Survey of India*, Vol. 8, part 2, 325-27.

83. Macaulay, *Mission to Sikkim*, 3-4.
84. *GJ* 4 (1894): 62.
85. Ibid.
86. As reported in a letter from Das to the RGS, dated 29 November 1893, RGS archives.
87. Ibid. His father, Sir Henry Thuillier, had been surveyor-general from 1861 to 1878. See also *GJ* 4 (1894): 61-62.
88. Much of the information on U.G.'s later years was provided to me by Nicholas Rhodes.

8. The Tsangpo-Brahmaputra Controversy: Lala, Nem Singh, and Kintup

1. Rennell, *Map of Hindoostan*, 91. See also his article "Account of the Ganges," 87-114.
2. Article 2. See House of Commons Sessional Papers, vol. 25 (London, 1826-67): 2-5.
3. Needham, "Excursion in the Abor Hills," 327.
4. Wilcox, "Survey of Assam."
5. *GRGTS, 1872-3* (Dehra Dun, 1873): 30. In 1867, Montgomerie had said that "every endeavour will be made to supply this missing link" in the exploration of the course of the Tsangpo. See *JRGS* 38 (1868): 219.
6. Walker, "Lu River of Tibet," 354.
7. *Royal Engineers Journal* 13, no. 150 (May 1, 1883): 113.
8. For more details of this expedition, see ch. 4.
9. See "Report on Explorations of Lala in South-Eastern Tibet, 1875-76, compiled under the supervision of J.B.N. Hennessey, Esqr., M.A., F.R.S.," in *Records of the Survey of India*, vol. 8, part 1, 197-98. The *Narrative* of his route-survey is in the same volume, pp. 199-206. These are reprinted from the *GRSI, 1878-9* (Calcutta, 1880): Appendix pp. vii-xv.
10. Letter of Montgomerie to Walker, 7 May 1873, Extracts from the correspondence of J.T. Walker, copied by R.H. Phillimore, archives of the Royal Geographical Society. Montgomerie is possibly referring to the British expedition to Ethiopia led by Sir Robert Napier in 1868.
11. *Narrative*, 203.
12. This is perhaps due to the delay in publishing the account of his expedition. Although Lala's expedition took place during 1875-76, the official account of it was not published until 1880. See note 9.
13. *Narrative*, 203.
14. Ibid.
15. "Narrative of the Second Expedition of Explorer Lala, in 1877," in *Records of the Survey of India*, vol. 8, part 1, 207-8.
16. See *Report on Explorations of Lala in South-Eastern Tibet, 1875-76*, 198.
17. *GRGTS, 1874-5* (Calcutta, 1876): 6-7.
18. Gordon, *Report on the Irrawaddy River*, 152-54.
19. *GRGTS, 1876-7* (Calcutta, 1878): 4-5. Harman had taken medical leave on 10 June 1877. See ibid., 12a.
20. See Godwin-Austen, "Lower Course of the Brahmaputra" 144.
21. *GRSI, 1877-78* (Calcutta, 1879): 16-17.
22. Details of the measurements were written up by Harman in his article "Discharges of the Large Rivers," 4-15. See also Burrard and Hayden, *Geography and Geology* footnote to 158.
23. *GRSI, 1877-78* (Calcutta, 1879): 17.
24. Ibid., 122.
25. "Report on the Exploration of Nem Singh in Eastern Tibet, 1878-79, drawn up by Lieut. H.J. Harman, R.E., Survey of India," in *Records of the Survey of India* vol. 8, part 1, 209. This report is a reprint of the original official account published in the *GRSI, 1878-9* (Calcutta, 1880): Appendix pp. I-IV, except that in this latter publication, Nem Singh is identified only by the initials G__M__N__. My citations are to the reprint.
26. Bailey, *China-Tibet-Assam*, 10. Bailey says he was called "Namsring" in the Survey reports, but I have not found any references to this name.
27. In some documents he was called not G.M.N., but N.M.G. This has led at least one writer, Sven Hedin, to believe that there were two different people. (See *Southern Tibet* 2, p. 281, ft. 2.) Hedin cites *PRGS* (1879): 593-95. This article was probably drawn from a paper delivered by Walker to the

Asiatic Society of Bengal, in which Walker refers to the explorer as N.M.G. and incorrectly dates his travels as 1877, rather than 1878. Hedin therefore believed that there were two explorations by two explorers in different years. The accounts, however, are clearly of a single exploration, and the map attached to Walker's article dates the journey as 1878. See "Exploration of the Great Sanpo River of Tibet during 1877 [sic], in connection with the operations of the Survey of India.—By Major-Genl. J.T. Walker, C.B., R.E., F.R.S.," in *PASB* (1879): 203-5.

28. *Report*, 209.
29. *Report*, 213.
30. *Report*, 210.
31. *Report*, 212.
32. Ibid.
33. Walker, "Great Sanpo River," 204.
34. *Report*, 210.
35. See *GJ* 41 (1913): 292. Nem Singh gave the latitude of Gyala Sindong as about 29° 40', which is quite accurate.
36. *Report*, 209-10.
37. *Report*, 210.
38. Mason, "Kishen Singh," footnote to 438.
39. See *PRGS* 5 (1883): 370; also *GRSI, 1881-82* (Calcutta, 1883): Appendix p. 42. Since Ugyen Gyatso had followed the Shigatse-Khamba Jong route in 1879, it is possible that these two journeys of Nem Singh were in fact a single exploration, made by him in 1880. Lama Ugyen Gyatso had returned to Darjeeling in November 1879.
40. Gordon, *Report on the Irrawaddy River*. According to Gordon, the first part of the report was written mainly in 1877, and an abstract of this was sent to Walker in early 1878 at the request of C.U. Aitchison, Chief Commissioner of British Burma (*Report*, part 1, 151).
41. Gordon, "Irawadi River," 313.
42. Ibid., 304.
43. Details of his explorations are in *GRSI, 1879-80* (Calcutta, 1881): 42-43 and Appendix pp. 29-42. See also Sandeman, "River Irawadi," 257-73; and *PRGS* n.s. 3 (1881): 400.
44. Sandeman also dispatched another explorer, "a Musselman," up the Irrawaddy in 1880-81, but he failed to make any new progress. *PRGS* (1882): 268.
45. *GRSI, 1879-80*, 30.
46. "Captain Henry John Harman, Royal Engineers," *Royal Engineers Journal* 13, no. 150 (May 1, 1883): 114.
47. *GRSI, 1879-80*, 31.
48. *PRGS* n.s. 6 (1884): 446.
49. Bailey describes the Lama as "Mongolian." See "Story of Kintup," 427.
50. Dunbar, *Frontiers*, 188.
51. Waddell, *Among the Himalayas*, 66.
52. Ibid.; see also the anonymous writer of the article "Surveying Tibet: the Story of a Secret Service" in the *North China Herald* 72 (Shanghai: 15 January 1904): 81.
53. *GJ* 44 (1914): 236.
54. *GRSI, 1886-87* (Calcutta, 1888): 8, 69, and lxxxix.
55. An abbreviated version of the explorations of Kintup and the Chinese lama was published in the *GRSI, 1886-87* (Calcutta, 1888): lxxxix-xcii. The full account was later issued in *Report on the Explorations of Lama Serap Gyatsho, 1856-68; Explorer K—P, 1880-84; Lama U.G., 1883; Explorer R.N., 1885-86; Explorer P.A., 1885-86; in Sikkim, Bhutan and Tibet*, Prepared in the Office of the Trigonometrical Branch, Survey of India, Lieut.-Colonel G. Strahan, and published under the direction of Colonel H.R. Thuillier (Dehra Dun, 1889): 3 and 7-17. Reprinted in *Records of the Survey of India*, vol. 8, part 2, under the title "Kinthup's Narrative of a Journey from Darjeeling to Gyala Sindong (Gyala and Sengdam), Tsari and the Lower Tsang-po, 1880-84. Compiled by Col. H.C.B. Tanner," 329-38. My citations are to this last source.
56. *Narrative*, 329.
57. Ibid., 332.
58. Ibid., 334.

59. Bailey, "Story of Kintup," 429.
60. *Narrative*, 334.
61. Ibid., 336. The reference to the "late" Captain Harman must have been inserted when Kintup's narrative was taken down, as Harman was still alive when the letter was written.
62. *Royal Engineers Journal* 13, no. 150 (May 1, 1883): 113.
63. Ibid., 112 and 115. Also *PRGS* n.s. 5 (1883): 488.
64. Bailey, "Story of Kintup," 430.
65. Ibid., 430; and Waddell, *Buddhism of Tibet* 452-54.
66. *Narrative*, 337.
67. G.F.T. Oakes, "Note in Vindication of Kinthup," in *Records of the Survey of India*, vol. 7, 1913-14, (Calcutta: 1916): 175.
68. D.Dn. vol. 593, Accounts, 1880-1890.
69. *GRSI, 1885-86* (Calcutta, 1886): 55.
70. G.W.E. Atkinson, "Narrative Account of Rinzin Nimgyl's Explorations in Sikkim, Bhutan and Tibet, in 1885-86," in H.R. Thuillier, *Report on the Explorations . . . in Sikkim, Bhutan, and Tibet* (Dehra Dun, 1889): 4, 37-55. This source also includes "Narrative Account of Phurba's Explorations in Tibet and Bhutan in 1885-86," pp. 4, 55-57. Both accounts are reprinted in *Records of the Survey of India*, Vol. 8, part 2, 363-379 and 379-381. My citations are to this latter source.
71. D.Dn. vol. 593, Accounts, 1880-1890.
72. See note 70.
73. *Records*, 375.
74. *GRSI, 1885-86* (Calcutta, 1886): 55.
75. Ibid., lxxxvi. See also Black, *Memoir on the Indian Surveys*, 162-63.
76. Sketch Map to Illustrate Colonel Tanner's Memorandum on Explorations in Bhutan and Tibet by R.N. and P.A. during 1885-86, Dehra Dun, December 1887, North Eastern Trans-Frontier, Sheet No. 7.
77. *GRSI, 1885-86* (Calcutta, 1886): 53.
78. Walker retired 12 February 1883 and received the honorary rank of general one year later.
79. *Records of the Survey of India*, vol. 8, part 2, 329; *GRSI, 1886-87* (Calcutta, 1888): lxxxix.
80. *GJ* 4 (1894): 62.
81. *GRSI, 1886-87* (Calcutta, 1888): lxxxix.
82. *Narrative*, 329. Emphasis my own.
83. Ibid., 332.
84. *PRGS* n.s. 1 (1879): 274.
85. Ibid., 354.
86. *Records of the Survey of India*, vol. 8, part 1, 212. See also Burrard and Hayden, *Geography and Geology* 159. Burrard and Hayden agreed with Harman. Even the RGS at one point agreed that the drop in altitude of the Tsangpo was not "an excessive slope compared with other Himalayan rivers" (*PRGS* n.s. 1 [1879]: 594).
87. Other evidence for the existence of an "immense waterfall" had been provided, before Kintup's return, by Father Desgodins, a French missionary on the boundary of eastern Tibet. See *PRGS* n.s. 3 (1881): 315.
88. Lamb, *McMahon Line*, 59-60; and Younghusband, *India and Tibet*, 328-29.
89. According to F.M. Bailey, the ambush of a small supply column, thought to be the work of Tibetans, but quite probably the result of a mistake by the expedition's own mounted infantry, caused Younghusband to reconsider the wisdom of the Tsangpo exploration. The expedition under Captain Rawling, which Bailey joined, was allowed to proceed, as it passed through thinly inhabited country. Bailey, *No Passport to Tibet*, 23-25.
90. Kishen Singh was just in time to recount his travels to Harman before Harman left for Europe. See *Royal Engineers Journal* 13, no. 150 (May 1, 1883): 113.
91. For a full account of this expedition of Kishen Singh, see ch. 4.
92. Sir Henry Rawlinson's comment at the RGS meeting when Walker presented this paper on the explorations of A.K. See *PRGS* n.s. 7 (1885): 87.
93. Gordon, "Irawadi River," 292-331.
94. Ibid., 322.

95. Ibid., 327-28.
96. Ibid., 327.
97. Needham was incorrect, however, in assuming that the Lohit was the Brahmaputra, instead of a tributary of that river. "Mr. J.F. Needham's Journey along the Lohit Brahmaputra between Sadiya in Upper Assam and Rima in South-Eastern Tibet," *Royal Geographical Society Supplementary Papers* 2 (1887-89): 486-555. The identity of the river flowing through Rima with the Lohit Brahmaputra had already been demonstrated by the travels of the French missionary Abbé Krick more than thirty years before, but his book had passed unnoticed in England (Krick, *Voyage au Thibet*). See Walker, "Lu River of Tibet," 355. Abbé Krick, together with his companion, Father Boury, was murdered by Mishmis in 1854.
98. If further confirmation was needed, it was provided in 1896 by the discovery in the Dihang of a woodblock used for printing and inscribed in Tibetan, which Sarat Chandra Das concluded had floated down river from a monastery in Tibet. See Das, "Identity of the Great Tsang-po," 126-29.
99. The RGS stated in 1891 that "the lower part of the Sanpo river . . . was left in great uncertainty by the explorations of the Indian surveyor, Kinthup, who *claimed* to have followed the course of the river to where it bursts through the Himalayan chain" (*PRGS*, n.s. 13 [1891]: 685 [emphasis added]). Even Needham, who knew him well, was skeptical. "I have very recently seen K.P., and . . . I am convinced that he did *not* descend the river Dibong [sic], *for any distance*, south of Gia la Sindong" (*PRGS* n.s. 11 [1889]: 440).
100. *GRSI, 1888-89* (Calcutta, 1890): xlv-xlvii. Reprinted in *Records of the Survey of India*, vol. 8, part 2, 401-3. The "Revised Sketch Map of the Course of the Sangpo" was published in December 1889.
101. Probably because the chief commissioner had been rapped over the knuckles by the Foreign Department (government of India) for allowing Needham's earlier expedition up the Lohit to proceed without official sanction. See the letter of 14 September 1886 from the Foreign Department to the chief commissioner. L/P & S/7 vol. 48, no. 1377. See also Reid, *Frontier Areas*, 186.
102. See *GRSI, 1889*, 71.
103. Letter of 6 May 1889 to the RGS, published in *PRGS* n.s. 11 (1889): 440-41.
104. Waddell, *Among the Himalayas*, 226-29. See also Mason, *Abode of Snow*, 123.
105. Waddell, *Lhasa and its Mysteries*, 435.
106. Ryder, "Exploration in Western China," 109-26.
107. *GJ* 17 (1901): 525-26 and 656-57; also 41 (1913): 98. See also Holdich, "North-Eastern Frontier," 384.
108. Bentinck, "Abor Expedition," 106.
109. Field, "Exploration of the Upper Dihong," 293.
110. *GJ* 41 (1913): 111.
111. Bailey, *China-Tibet-Assam*, 16.
112. Ibid., 108. Bailey also wrote a short paper for presentation to the RGS. See "Journey through a Portion of South-Eastern Tibet and the Mishmi Hills," *GJ* 39 (1912): 334-46. This exploration is also described by Bailey's biographer Arthur Swinson in his book *Beyond the Frontiers*, ch. 4 and 5.
113. Sandes, *Military Engineer in India*, vol. 1, 251.
114. Reid, *Frontier Areas*, 226.
115. Swinson, *Beyond the Frontiers*, 77-80.
116. Bailey, *No Passport to Tibet*, 28. This book is Bailey's account of his 1913 expedition to the Tsangpo.
117. Letter from Bailey to the RGS, 18 April 1913. See *GJ* 42 (1913): 87-88.
118. Bailey, *No Passport to Tibet*, 38.
119. Morshead, "South-East Tibet," 23.
120. Bailey, *No Passport to Tibet*, 55. Morshead died in 1931. An obituary recorded that while on one of the Mount Everest expeditions of the early 1920s, he lost three fingers to frostbite, owing to a "light-hearted neglect of precautions" (*GJ* 78 [1931]: 320).
121. Morshead, *Report*, 3.
122. Kinthup's *Narrative*, 332.
123. Ibid.
124. Bailey, *Report*, 6.
125. Bailey, *Report*, 11; and Morshead, *Report*, 41.
126. Bailey, *Report*, 41. See also Waddell, "Falls of the Tsang-po," 258-59.

127. Bailey, *Report*, 7. Morshead, *Royal Engineers' Journal* 33 (1921): 29.
128. Bailey's experience ended Sir Thomas Holdich's flight of fancy. Holdich had written that "this is the natural highway from India to Tibet and western China, and we should have a Tibetan branch of the Assam railway, and a spacious hotel for sightseers and sportsmen at the falls" (*Tibet the Mysterious*, 219). The idea of a railroad linking India to China was not a new one, but Bailey's report on the difficulty of the terrain put an end to speculation that it would be built in the near future. See Yate, "Bailey's Latest Exploration," 192.
129. Morshead, *Report*, 36.
130. Lamb, *McMahon Line*, vol. 2, 320 and 536-37.
131. Bailey, "Exploration on the Tsangpo," 341-64.
132. Bailey, "Exploration of the Tsang-po," 184, and "Falls of the Tsang-po," 91.
133. Dunbar, *Frontiers*, 256. In the epilogue to his book, Bailey also gives the figure of ten miles (*No Passport to Tibet*, 28). This gap was further narrowed to five miles in 1924 by Frank Kingdon-Ward and Lord Cawdor. See Kingdon-Ward, *Riddle of the Tsangpo Gorges*, 244.
134. Bailey, *Report*, 40.
135. G.F.T. Oakes, "Note in Vindication of Kinthup," in *Records of the Survey of India*, vol. 7, 1913-14, (Calcutta: 1916): 174.
136. Bailey, *Report*, 42.
137. Dunbar, *Frontiers*, 187.
138. Oakes, "Note in Vindication of Kinthup," 174-75.
139. Dunbar, *Frontiers*, 264.
140. Ibid., 256.
141. Ibid., 257; and Oakes, "Note in Vindication of Kinthup," 175.
142. Yate, "Bailey's Latest Exploration," 196.
143. Lamb, *McMahon Line*, vol. 2, 536.
144. Bailey, *No Passport to Tibet*, 276.
145. Sandes, *Military Engineer in India*, 236-39.
146. Holdich, *Tibet the Mysterious*.
147. Bailey, *No Passport to Tibet*, 276.
148. Ibid., 279. Also Morshead ("South-East Tibet," 38), who gives the dates. Bailey has said it was 1913 ("Story of Kintup," 431).
149. Bailey, "Story of Kintup," 431: *No Passport to Tibet*, 280.
150. Letter from Burrard to Bailey, 10 October 1914, Bailey Mss. Eur. F 157/274.
151. Bailey, *No Passport to Tibet*, 280. Also *GJ* 44 (1914): 236; Morshead, "South East Tibet," 38. Morshead gives his date of death as 3 November 1919.
152. Bailey, "Exploration on the Tsangpo," 341-64.
153. Bailey was already the recipient of the RGS Gill Memorial Award in 1912, given for his exploration of Mishmi territory in 1911.
154. *GJ* 78 (1931): 320. See also I. Morshead, *Life and Murder*.

9. Questions of Secrecy

1. At least as early as 1810, the government placed some maps of India with the Army Quartermaster General's Department, to prevent them from circulating freely. See J.T. Walker, *General Account of the Operations of the Great Trigonometrical Survey*, vol. 1 (Calcutta, 1870): xxviii.
2. *PASB* 2 (1863): 175-79.
3. Montgomerie, "Geographical Position of Yarkund," 157-72. See also *PRGS* 10 (1865-66): 162-65.
4. *GRGTS, 1866-7* (Calcutta, 1867): i-xxix.
5. *JRGS* 38 (1868): 129-219.
6. Ibid., 129.
7. *JRGS* 39 (1869): 146-62.
8. *PRGS* 14 (1869-70): 207-14.
9. *JRGS* 39, no. 2 (1870): 47-60.

10. *JRGS* 41 (1871): 132-85.
11. T.G. Montgomerie, *Report on the Trans-Himalayan Explorations in Connection with the Great Trigonometrical Survey of India, during 1869* (n.p., n.d.): lxviii.
12. *PRGS* 15 (1871): 204.
13. *JRGS* 42 (1872): 180-99.
14. *JRGS* 45 (1875): 330-49.
15. Ibid., 350-363; 315-330.
16. Montgomerie, *Report* (1868), vii.
17. See *JRGS* 39 (1869): 150.
18. Cooper, *Travels of a Pioneer*.
19. See L/P & S/6, vol. 457, pp. 1553-54, 1759-60.
20. See ch. 3.
21. Minutes of 23 February and 13 March 1876, Foreign Department Proceedings, July 1877, Secret nos. 1-20. (The report itself is dated at the end by the printers "16-2-75" or 16 February 1875. Since Nain Singh did not return to Calcutta until March 1875, the date of printing is clearly a misprint for 1876. The viceroy's minute was written only seven days after publication.)
22. Ibid., Minute of 28 February.
23. Ibid., Secret no. 16. Also Letter no. 46 (Secret) of the Government of India Foreign Department to the Secretary of State for India, 5 October 1876, L/P & S/7/10, vol. 10, 1876.
24. Ibid., Letter no. 46.
25. Ibid., Walker to A.O. Hume, 27 March 1876, in Secret no. 16.
26. Ibid., Letter no. 46.
27. Ibid., Letter of Hume to Officiating Superintendent, GTS, dated 21 June 1876, in Secret no. 16.
28. Ibid., Minute of "F.H." dated 13 April 1876, in Secret no. 16. See also ibid., Letter No. 46.
29. Ibid., Letter No. 46.
30. Ibid.
31. Ibid.
32. Article datelined Berlin, 15 April 1876, included as an attachment to ibid., Letter no. 46.
33. D.Dn. vol. 113, no. 12 ff. (See also "Notes on the Maps of Central Asia and Turkestan which have been compiled and published in the Office of the Great Trigonometrical Survey of India under the superintendence of Colonel J.T. Walker, R.E." in the *GRGTS, 1872-3* [Calcutta, 1874]: i-iv.)
34. Ibid.
35. Letters of Osten Sacken to Walker of 3 November 1869 and 11 January 1870, Extracts from Survey of India volumes, Dehra Dun 240/1, Colonel Walker's Europe letters, copied by R.H. Phillimore, 2 March 1964. Courtesy of the Royal Society.
36. Letter to Walker from Olga Fedchenko, November 1873; Walker's letters, ibid.
37. *GRGTS, 1872-73* (Calcutta, 1874): v-vi.
38. Letter to Walker from Petermann dated 27 March 1869; Walker's letters, ibid.
39. Markham, *Memoir on the Indian Surveys*.
40. Secret no. 16, Foreign Department Proceedings.
41. Ibid.
42. Ibid. See also Letter no. 46. Lord Lytton subsequently abolished the "close relationship" which he claimed had existed between Lord Northbrook and *The Pioneer*. (Letter of Lytton to Lord Salisbury, 27 March 1878, Lytton Papers, Mss. Eur. E 218/3/3.)
43. See L/P & S/7/10.
44. Ibid. The complete report of the Munshi was never made public. (It is located in L/P & S/7/4, 393-422.)
45. *PRGS* 20, no. 1 (1875): 16.
46. In Letter no. 46 of 5 October 1876, Foreign Department Proceedings.
47. Ibid.
48. Ibid.
49. Minute paper, Political Department, 30 October 1876, L/P & S/7/322.
50. Ibid.
51. Letter no. 16 (Secret) of 16 February 1877, L/P & S/7/343.
52. Political Department Reference Paper of 1 November 1876, L/P & S/7/10.

53. At least, this is the impression left by Sir Douglas Forsyth in his letter read to the Society. See *PRGS* 21 (1876-77): 347.

54. Letter of A.W. Moore to Trotter dated 14 April 1877, Political and Secret Semi-Official Correspondence, Second Series (Political Department), L/P & S/8/11.

55. *Geographical Magazine* 4, no. 7 (July 1877): 191.

56. *JRGS* 57 (1877): 86-136.

57. *JRGS* 48 (1878): 174. Trotter is referring to his *Account of the Survey Operations in Connection with the Mission to Yarkand and Kashghar in 1873-74* (Calcutta, 1875).

58. This was also true of the pundit M—S—, who surveyed the last gap in the upper Oxus in 1881. Only twenty-five copies of his secret and confidential report were published (see ch. 5, note 88), and he received only the briefest mention in the *PRGS* (*PRGS* n.s. 5 [1883]: 384).

59. *Records of the Survey of India*, vol. 8 (Dehra Dun, 1915).

60. Letter of 29 June 1881, L/P & S/7/10.

61. Minute Paper, Secret Department, August 1886, and minute of 10 August 1886, L/P & S/7/10.

62. Letter to the governor-general from the India Office, dated 8 March 1877, Walker letters, vol. 1, RGS archives.

63. Letter of 9 March 1877, Walker letters, vol. 1, RGS archives.

64. Letter of T.G. Montgomerie, dated 19 April 1877, Walker letters, vol. 1, RGS archives.

65. Letter of 13 April 1877, Walker letters, vol. 1, RGS archives.

66. Letter of 13 April 1877, Walker letters, vol. 1, RGS archives. H.E.L. Thuillier was the father of H.R. Thuillier, Walker's deputy in the Great Trigonometrical Survey.

67. Letter of 4 May 1877, Walker letters, vol. 1, RGS archives.

68. Letter of Hume to Walker, 5 July 1878, Walker letters, vol. 2, RGS archives.

69. Letter of Hume to Walker, 11 July 1878, Foreign Department Proceedings, October 1878, Secret no. 3.

70. *GRGTS, 1876-77* (Calcutta, 1878): 21-22. A virtually identical version was reproduced in the *Abstract of the Reports of the Surveys and of other Geographical Operations in India, for 1876-77* (pp. 57-60), which was published in London in the same year. This was also reprinted, with the map, in Calcutta in *JASB* 47 (1878): 78-80. Although the correspondence with Walker does not refer to it, the Foreign Department may also have been exercised over the publication of the map of the Mullah's explorations, which appeared, among other places, in the *Geographical Magazine* for May 1878. The department was certainly aware of this publication. See Memo no. 25 of 5 August 1878 from the Foreign Department to the secretary of state for India. L/P & S/7 vol. 19, 1878, no. 71.

71. *Narrative of Surveys*.

72. Letter of Walker to Hume, 15 July 1878, Foreign Department Proceedings, October 1878, Secret no. 4.

73. Letter of Hume to Walker, 7 September 1878, Foreign Department Proceedings, October 1878, Secret no. 7.

74. Foreign Department Proceedings, October 1878, Secret.

75. Letter of Walker, dated 18 December 1879, to the Foreign Department, enclosing a manuscript report of a journey by the Mullah made in 1878. The government responded on 8 January 1880. Foreign Department Proceedings, Secret, January 1880, nos. 69-70.

76. (Calcutta, 1880): xix-xxxvii.

77. *PRGS* n.s. 2 (1880): 434-36.

78. Walker to A.C. Lyall, Secretary to the government of India, 13 August 1879, Foreign Department Proceedings, October 1879, Secret no. 6-7.

79. Ibid. Internal memo signed "A.M.," dated 19 August 1879.

80. Ibid. Letter to Walker of 3 September 1879.

81. *GRSI, 1878-79* (Calcutta, 1880): i-iv.

82. See *PRGS* 1 (1879): 593-95; *Report of the British Association for the Advancement of Science* 49 (1879): 433-34; *PASB* (1879): 203-5.

83. Letter of Yule to the Earl of Kimberley, secretary of state for India, dated 27 June 1883, Foreign Department Proceedings, Secret 'E,' August 1883, nos. 100-106.

84. Memo of 29 July 1884, Foreign Department Proceedings, Secret, External 'A,' September 1884, nos. 233-35.

85. Letter from the secretary of state for India to the Governor-General in Council, Secret no. 16, dated 15 August 1884, L/P & S/7/329. See also Secret no. 24 of 21 November 1884. The Foreign Department was never able to ascertain the source of the unauthorized disclosure. See their letter no. 17 to Kimberley of 27 January 1885, L/P & S/7, vol. 43, no. 395.

86. Foreign Department Proceedings, Secret 'F,' September 1884, nos. 554-56.

87. Ibid. Walker formally took retirement, with the rank of general, on 12 January 1884.

88. Ibid., Letter of the Foreign Department to the Earl of Kimberly, no. 27, 29 September 1884. Also in L/P & S/7, vol. 41, no. 1617.

89. Under-Secretary at the India Office, noting receipt of no. 27 from India on 21 October 1884. L/P & S/7/329, p. 598.

90. Statistics and Commerce Despatch to India, no. 127 dated 2 October 1884, Selections from Despatches, V/6/312, pp. 283-84.

91. The original account, marked "Gen. J.T. Walker's copy," is in the possession of the RGS. It shows where the offending passages were blanked out, but not what was excised. For full citations, see ch. 4, note 97.

92. *PRGS* n.s. 7 (1885): 65-92.

93. Kimberley to the governor-general of India in Council, Political Letter no. 105, dated 4 December 1884, L/P & S/7/329, pp. 600-602. (Also in Selections from Despatches, V/6/312, p. 364.)

94. For example, the *GRSI, 1882-83* (Calcutta, 1884) had been received by the RGS with a request from the government to treat it as confidential. (See *PRGS* [1884]: 749.)

95. Cross to the governor-general of India in Council, Political Letter no. 34 of 9 June 1887, Political and Secret Despatches to India, L/P & S/7/332, vol. 13, pp. 271-288.

96. For full citations, see ch. 8, note 55.

97. For full citations, see ch. 7, note 27.

98. For full citations, see ch. 7, note 40.

99. The third expedition of Ugyen Gyatso (1883) was, however, reprinted in the *Records*. It had originally been printed only in 150 copies. (See ch. 7, note 69.) The American diplomat W.W. Rockhill edited an abridged version of the 1881-83 travels of Das and Ugyen Gyatso, published in 1902 under the title *Journey to Lhasa and Central Tibet*.

100. Cross to the governor-general of India in Council, Political Letter no. 34 of 9 June 1887, Political and Secret Despatches to India, L/P & S/7/332, vol. 13, pp. 271-288.

101. Dufferin to Cross, Secret no. 1, 3 January 1888, L/P & S/7/52. In another instance concerning sensitivity to maps, the RGS was never given permission to publish a map of W.W. McNair's journey to Kafirstan, which should have appeared in the *Proceedings* for 1884. See *PRGS* n.s. 11 (1889): 612.

102. India Office to the governor-general. Secret no. 27, 2 August 1888, L/P & S/7/334, vol. 15, 1889, pp. 147-149. India responded that the maps should no longer be considered confidential. (Secret Letter no. 135, 16 September 1889.

103. India Office to the governor-general, Public (Records) no. 53, 22 August 1889, Selections from Despatches, V/6/322.

10. Conclusion

1. See ch. 6, note 39.

2. For example, the three expeditions led by Prejevalsky (1876-77, 1879-80, 1883-85) and that of M. Pevtsov, V. Roborovsky, and P. Kozlov (1889-90).

3. Atma Ram was about twenty-four years old and had worked at Simla for the Survey of India for only six months before volunteering to join Bower. There had been time only to teach him how to use the prismatic compass and to march at a steady rate of 2,200 paces to a mile. See T.H. Holdich, "Tibet and Western China, A Report on the Route Survey executed by Atma Ram, in company with Captain Bower, in Tibet and Western China, in 1891-92," *GRSI, 1891-92* (Calcutta, 1893): lxi-lxvii. Reprinted in *Records of the Survey of India*, vol. 8, part 2, 405-11.

4. D.Dn. 594, Accounts, 1880-1890.

5. Bower, "Journey Across Tibet," 385-86.

6. Bower's confidential report is entitled *Some Notes on Tibetan Affairs*, FO 17/1167, Foreign

Office Records, Public Records Office, London. A full account of the expedition was published by the Indian government in 1893 in an edition limited to 150 copies (Calcutta: Office of the Superintendent of Government Printing). This account contained two maps, each more detailed than the single map provided with the book published one year later in London. Additional information, including an introduction by Colonel Elles, Assistant Quarter Master General Intelligence Branch, is also found in the Calcutta printing, but not in the London publication *(Diary of a Journey across Tibet)*.

7. White, "Journeys in Bhutan," 18.
8. See Wellby, *Through Unknown Tibet*. A year before the book was published, two confidential reports were issued by the Government Central Printing Office in Simla. Each contained a preface by Colonel George More-Molyneux, Assistant Quartermaster General, Intelligence Branch. The reports are: Wellby and Malcolm, *Road Report* and *Report with Map*.
9. Deasy, *In Tibet and Chinese Turkestan*.
10. Rawling, *Great Plateau*. The Indian government issued a confidential report of Rawling's activities. This report noted in its preface that "a detailed account of the road followed, and minor and military details of the forts, fords, ferries and bridges, will be found in the military report to be published by the Intelligence Branch, Quartermaster General's Department, Simla." See Rawling, *Gartok Expedition*.
11. Petech, "China and European Travellers," 221.
12. Cooper, *Travels of a Pioneer*.
13. Cooper, *Mishmee Hills*.
14. Rayfield, *Dream of Lhasa*, 78.
15. Ibid., 99 and 109.
16. Ibid., 138.
17. Petech, "China and European Travellers," 236-37. Petech (p. 230) says that this passport, together with those issued to Captain W.J. Gill and Count Bela Szechenyi, were authorized by the Separate Article of the 1876 Chefoo Convention signed between Britain and China. The Separate Article, however, provided only for a British mission to Lhasa, although it may have made it more difficult for the Chinese to refuse passports to individuals.
18. Rayfield, *Dream of Lhasa*, 156.
19. Ibid., 167.
20. Carey and Dalgleish spent two years from 1885 traveling along the borders of northern and northwestern Tibet. See A.D. Carey, "Journey round Chinese Turkistan," and "Journey of Carey and Dalgleish."
21. Rayfield, *Dream of Lhasa*, 201.
22. Petech, "China and European Travellers," 231.
23. Ibid., 233-36.
24. See Rockhill, *Land of the Lamas*.
25. See Rockhill, *Diary*.
26. Bonvalot, *Across Thibet*. The same was true of Jules Dutreuil de Rhins in 1893-94.
27. See W. Carey, *Travel and Adventure in Tibet*.
28. The book of his travels is *Through Asia*.
29. See Hedin, *Central Asia and Tibet*, vol. 2, 368-79.
30. Savage-Landor, *Everywhere*, vol. 1, ch. 19 and 20.
31. Rijnhart, *With the Tibetans*.
32. Littledale, "Journey across Tibet," 453-83. One of the maps accompanying the article indicates that they were halted about fifty-seven miles from Lhasa. However, one of the members of the audience at the RGS, Sir Henry Howorth, refers in the discussion to Littledale being "able to get within 43 miles of the Mekka of this Central Asiatic World" (p. 481).
33. Political letter 137, dated 30 October 1881, from Simla to London, L/P & S/7/30, p. 705.
34. Landon, *Lhasa*, vol. 2, 23.

Bibliography

Unpublished Sources

BRITISH LIBRARY
  Add. Mss. 33,837 f60
CAMBRIDGE UNIVERSITY LIBRARY
  Mayo Papers, Add 7490
INDIA OFFICE LIBRARY AND RECORDS
  Bailey Collection, MSS Eur F157
  General Reports on the Operations of the Great Trigonometrical Survey of India
  General Reports on the Operations of the Survey of India
  India Foreign External Proceedings
  John Lawrence Collection. MSS Eur F90
  Letters Political and Secret
  Proceedings of the Government of India Foreign Department
  Selections from Despatches to India
  Selections from the Records of the Government of India
  Selections from the Records of the Government of the Punjab
NATIONAL ARCHIVES OF INDIA
  Foreign Department Proceedings
  Survey of India Records, Dehra Dun volumes
ROYAL GEOGRAPHICAL SOCIETY ARCHIVES
  Extracts from Survey of India volumes, letters copied by R.H. Phillimore
  Correspondence files of J.T. Walker, T.G. Montgomerie, etc.
ROYAL SOCIETY
  Letters from Europe addressed to Colonel J.T. Walker, Two volumes, Extracts made by Colonel Phillimore, 1954.

Books and Articles: Selected Published Sources

Ahmad, Z. "Tibet and Ladakh. A History." *St. Anthony's Papers* 14 (1963): 23-58.
Aitchison, C.U. *A Collection of Treaties, Engagements and Sanads Relating to India and Neighbouring Countries*. Vol. 14, *Containing the Treaties, Etc., Relating to Eastern Turkistan, Tibet, Nepal, Bhutan and Siam*. Calcutta, 1929.
Alder, G.J. *British India's Northern Frontier 1865-95: A Study in Imperial Policy*. London, 1963.
Allen, Charles. *A Mountain in Tibet*. London, 1982.
Amin, Mahomed. "Route from Jellalabad to Yarkand through Chitral, Badakhshan, and Pamir Steppe . . ., with Remarks by G.S.W. Hayward." *PRGS* 13 (1869): 122-33.
Astley, Thomas. *A New General Collection of Voyages and Travels, Collected by Thomas*

Bibliography 305

Astley. London, 1745-47. 4 vols. Reprint. London, 1968. [Actually compiled by John Green, but generally known as "Astley's Voyages" or the "Astley Collection."]

Aziz, Barbara Nimri. *Tibetan Frontier Families: Reflections of Three Generations from D'ing-ri*. New Delhi, 1978.

Bailey, F.M. "Exploration on the Tsangpo or Upper Brahmaputra." *GJ* 44 (1914): 341-64.

Bailey, F.M. "Journey through a Portion of South-Eastern Tibet and the Mishmi Hills." *GJ* 39 (1912): 334-47.

Bailey, F.M. "Note on the Exploration of the Tsang-po." *GJ* 43 (1914): 184-86.

Bailey, F.M. "Note on the Falls of the Tsang-po." *Scottish Geographical Magazine* 30 (1914): 90-92.

Bailey, F.M. *Report on an Exploration on the North-East Frontier 1913*. Simla, 1914.

Bailey, F.M. "The Story of Kintup." *Geographical Magazine* 15 (1943): 426-31.

Bailey, F.M. *China-Tibet-Assam: A Journey, 1911*. London, 1945.

Bailey, F.M. *No Passport to Tibet*. London, 1957.

Ball, V. *Scientific Results of the Second Yarkand Mission: Memoir of the Life and Work of Ferdinand Stoliczka, Ph.D.* London, 1886.

Barton, Alfred. "Notes on the Yang-tsze-Kiang, etc." *JRGS* 32 (1862): 26-41.

Bell, Charles. *Tibet Past and Present*. Oxford, 1924.

Bellew, H.W. *Kashmir and Kashgar: A Narrative of the Journey of the Embassy to Kashgar in 1873-74*. London, 1875.

Bentinck, A. "The Abor Expedition: Geographical Results." *GJ* 41 (1913): 97-114.

Black, Charles E.D. *A Memoir on the Indian Surveys, 1875-1890*. London, 1891.

Blakiston, Thomas W. *Five Months on the Yang-Tsze*. London, 1862.

Bonvalot, Gabriel. *Across Thibet*. New York, 1891.

Bower, H. *Diary of a Journey across Tibet*. London, 1894.

Bower, H. "A Journey Across Tibet." *GJ* 1, no. 5 (1893): 385-408.

Buckland, C.E. *Dictionary of Indian Biography*. New York, 1968.

Burnes, Alexander. *Travels into Bokhara, etc.* 3 vols. London, 1834.

Burrard, S.G., and H.H. Hayden. *A Sketch of the Geography and Geology of the Himalaya Mountains and Tibet*. Calcutta, 1907-1908.

Cammann, S. *Trade through the Himalayas: The Early British Attempts to Open Tibet*. Princeton, N.J., 1951.

Campbell, A. "Sketch of Political Relations between the British Government and Sikkim." *The Oriental* 2, no. 7 (1874): 13-27.

Carey, A.D. "A Journey round Chinese Turkistan and along the Northern Frontier of Tibet." *PRGS* 9 (1887): 731-52, and 10 (1888): 41-44.

Carey, W. *Travel and Adventure in Tibet: Including the Diary of Miss Annie R. Taylor's Remarkable Journey from Tau-Chau to Ta-Chien-Lu through the Heart of the Forbidden Land*. London, 1902.

Chakravarty, Suhash. *From Khyber to Oxus: A Study in Imperial Expansion*. New Delhi, 1976.

Chaudhuri, K.C. *Anglo Nepalese Relations from the Earliest Times of the British Rule in India till the Gurkha War*. Calcutta, 1960.

Chen, Jack. *The Sinkiang Story*. New York, 1977.

Clubb, O.E. *China and Russia: The "Great Game."* New York, 1971.

Coelho, V.H. *Sikkim and Bhutan*. New Delhi, 1971.

Colquhoun, Archibald. "In the Heart of the Forbidden Country; or, Lhasa Revealed." *The Cornhill Magazine* n.s. 14 (Jan.-June 1903): 39-52.

Cooper, T.T. *The Mishmee Hills: An Account of a Journey Made in an Attempt to Penetrate Thibet from Assam to Open New Routes for Commerce.* London, 1873.

Cooper, T.T. *Travels of a Pioneer of Commerce in Pigtail and Petticoats: Or, an overland journey from China towards India.* London, 1871.

Curzon, George N. "The Pamirs and the Source of the Oxus." *GJ* 8 (1896): 15-54; 97-119; 239-64.

Dalal, N. "Early Indian Explorers beyond the Himalayas." *Indian and Foreign Review* 8, no. 1 (1970): 11-12.

Dalal, N. "Pandit Nain Singh." *Journal of the United Service Institution of India* 100 (1970): 301-10.

Dalal, N. "Exploits of the Pandits." *Hemisphere* 15, no. 7 (1971): 10-15.

Das, Sarat Chandra. "An Account of Travels on the Shores of Lake Yamdo-Croft." *JASB* 67, no. 1 (1898): 256-73.

———. *Autobiography: Narratives of the Incidents of My Early Life.* Calcutta, 1969.

———. *Indian Pandits in the Land of Snow.* Calcutta, 1893. Reprint. Calcutta, 1965.

———. *An Introduction to the Grammar of the Tibetan Language.* Darjeeling, 1915.

———. *Journey to Lhasa and Central Tibet.* Edited by W.W. Rockhill. London, 1902.

———. "Narrative of a Journey to Tashi-lhun-po in Tibet." *Journal of the Buddhist Text and Anthropological Society* 7, no. 3 (1904): 57-80.

———. "A Note on the Identity of the Great Tsang-po of Tibet with the Dihong." *JASB* 67, no. 1 (1898): 126-29.

———. *A Tibetan-English Dictionary, with Sanskrit Synonyms.* Revised and edited under the orders of the government of Bengal by Graham Sandberg and A. William Heyde. Calcutta, 1902.

Datta, C.L. *Ladakh and Western Himalayan Politics: 1819-1848; the Dogra Conquest of Ladakh, Baltistan and West Tibet and Reactions of Other Powers.* New Delhi, 1973.

Davies, H. *Report on the Trade and Resources of the Countries of the North-Western Boundary of British India.* 2 vols. Lahore, 1862.

Davis, H.W.C. "The Great Game in Asia (1800-1844)." *Proceedings of the British Academy* 12 (1926): 227-56.

Deasy, H.H.P. *In Tibet and Chinese Turkestan; being the record of three years' exploration.* London, 1901.

De Filippi, Filippo, ed. *An Account of Tibet: The Travels of Ippolito Desideri of Pistoia, S.J., 1712-1727.* Revised ed. London, 1937.

Deniker, Joseph. "New Light on Lhasa, The Forbidden City." *Century Illustrated Monthly Magazine* 66 (1903): 544-54.

Dozey, E.C. *A Concise History of the Darjeeling District since 1835.* Calcutta, 1922.

Dunbar, George. *Frontiers.* London, 1932.

Edgar, J. Ware. *Report on a Visit to Sikkim and the Thibetan Frontier in October, November, and December, 1873.* Calcutta, 1874. Reprint. New Delhi, 1969.

Edwardes, Michael. *Playing the Great Game: A Victorian Cold War.* London, 1975.

Elsmie, G.R. *Thirty-Five Years in the Punjab, 1858-1893.* Edinburgh, 1908.

"Exploration by A——K in Great Tibet and Mongolia." *Scottish Geographical Magazine* 1 (1885): 352-72.

"Explorations in Western Tibet, by the Trans-Himalayan Parties of the Indian Trigonometrical Survey." *PRGS* n.s. 1, no. 1 (1879): 444-52.
Field, J.A. "The History of the Exploration of the Upper Dihong." *GJ* 41 (1913): 291-93.
Fisher, Margaret W., Leo E. Rose, and Robert A. Huttenback. *Himalayan Battleground: Sino-Indian Rivalry in Ladakh*. New York, 1963.
Forbes, Andrew D.W. *Warlords and Muslims in Chinese Central Asia: A Political History of Republican Sinkiang 1911-1949*. Cambridge, 1986.
Forsyth, Ethel, ed. *Autobiography and Reminiscences of Sir Douglas Forsyth, C.B., K.C.S.I., F.R.G.S.* London, 1887.
Forsyth, T.D. "On the Buried Cities in the Shifting Sands of the Great Desert of Gobi." *JRGS* 47 (1877): 1-17.
Francke, A.H. *A History of Western Tibet, One of the Unknown Empires*. London, 1907.
Fraser-Tytler, W.K. *Afghanistan: A Study of Political Development in Central and Southern Asia*. London, 1953.
Freshfield, D.W. "The Glaciers of Kangchenjunga." *GJ* 19 (1902): 453-75.
———. *Round Kanchenjunga: A Narrative of Mountain Travel and Exploration*. London, 1903.
———. "Round Kanchinjinga." *Alpine Journal* 20, no. 149 (1900): 161-84.
Gillard, David. *The Struggle for Asia 1828-1914: A Study in British and Russian Imperialism*. London, 1977.
Godwin-Austen, H.H. "On the Lower Course of the Brahmaputra or Tsanpo." *Report of the British Association for the Advancement of Science* 47, no. 2 (1877): 144.
Gordon, Robert. "The Irawadi River." *PRGS* n.s. 7 (1885): 292-331.
———. *Report on the Irrawaddy River*. Rangoon, 1879-80.
Gordon T.E. *The Roof of the World*. Edinburgh, 1876.
———. *A Varied Life: A Record of Military and Civil Service, of Sport and of Travel in India, Central Asia, and Persia, 1849-1902*. London, 1906.
"Great Tibet: Discovery of Lake Tengri-nor." *The Geographical Magazine* 2 (1875): 41-44.
Giuseppe da Rovato. "An Account of the Kingdom of Nepal." *Asiatic Researches* 2 (1792): 169-92.
Hambly, Gavin, ed. *Central Asia*. London, 1969.
Harman, H.J. "On the Operations for Obtaining the Discharges of the Large Rivers in Upper Assam, during Season 1877-78." *JASB* 48, part 2 (1879): 4-15.
Hayward, G.W. "Journey from Leh to Yarkand and Kashgar, and Exploration of the Sources of the Yarkand River." *JRGS* 40 (1870): 33-166.
Heaney, G.F. "Rennell and the Surveyors of India." *GJ* 134 (1968): 318-27.
———. "The Story of the Survey of India." *Geographical Magazine* 30 (1957/8): 182-90.
Hedin, Sven. *Central Asia and Tibet: Towards the Holy City of Lassa*. 2 vols. London, 1903.
———. "Journeys in Tibet, 1906-1908." *GJ* 33 (1909): 353-440.
———. *Southern Tibet: Discoveries in Former Times Compared with My Own Researches in 1906-1908*. 11 vols. Stockholm, 1916-22.
———. *Through Asia*. 2 vols. London, 1898.
———. *Trans-Himalaya: Discoveries and Adventures in Tibet*. 3 vols. London, 1909-13.
Holdich, T.H. "Geographical Surveying in India." *Professional Papers of the Corps of Royal Engineers* (Occasional Papers Series) 24 (1898): paper no. 11.

———. *Tibet the Mysterious.* London, 1906.
———. "The North-Eastern Frontier of India." *Journal of the Royal Society of Arts* 60, no. 3092 (1912): 379-92.
———. "The Romance of Indian Surveys." *Journal of the Royal Society of Arts* 64, no. 3296 (1916): 173-85.
Hooker, Joseph Dalton. *Himalayan Journals; or notes of a naturalist in Bengal, the Sikkim and Nepal Himalayas, the Khasia Mountains, etc.* 2 vols. London, 1854.
Hopkirk, Peter. *Trespassers on the Roof of the World: The Race for Lhasa.* London, 1982.
Huc, E. *Travels in Tartary, Thibet, and China during the Years 1844-5-6.* 2 vols. London, 1852.
Husain, Asad. *British India's Relations with the Kingdom of Nepal, 1857-1947: A Diplomatic History of Nepal.* London, 1970.
Huttenback, Robert A. "Kashmir as an Imperial Factor during the Reign of Gulab Singh (1846-1857)." *Journal of Asian History* 2, no. 2 (1968): 77-108.
India Ministry of External Affairs. *Report of the Officials of the Governments of India and the People's Republic of China on the Boundary Question.* New Delhi, 1961.
"Journey from Peshawar to Kashghar and Yarkand in Eastern Turkestan, or Little Bokhara, through Afghanistan, Balkh, Badakhshan, Wakhan, Pamir, and Sarkol, Undertaken in Connection with the Mission of Mr. T.D. Forsyth, CB, during 1870, by F.B." *JRGS* 42 (1872).
"Journey of Carey and Dalgleish in Chinese Turkistan and Northern Tibet (Mr. Dalgleish's Itinerary)." *Royal Geographical Society, Supplementary Papers* 3 (1893): 1-86.
Karan, Pradyumna. *Bhutan: a Physical and Cultural Geography.* Lexington, Ky., 1967.
———. *The Changing Face of Tibet.* Lexington, Ky., 1976.
Kawaguchi, Ekai. *Three Years in Tibet.* Madras, 1909.
Keay, John. *The Gilgit Game: The Explorers of the Western Himalayas 1865-95.* London, 1979.
———. *When Men and Mountains Meet.* London, 1977.
Kingdon-Ward, Frank. "Botanical Exploration in Tibet, 1933." *The Gardeners Chronicle* 30, no. 92 (July-Dec. 1932): 410-11.
———. "The Himalaya East of the Tsangpo." *GJ* 84 (1934): 369-97.
———. *The Mystery Rivers of Tibet, etc.* London, 1923.
———. *The Riddle of the Tsangpo Gorges.* London, 1926.
Kirkpatrick, William. *An Account of the Kingdom of Nepaul, Being the Substance of Observations Made during a Mission to That Country, in the Year 1793.* London, 1811.
Krick, N.M. *Relation d'un voyage au Thibet en 1852 et d'un voyage chez les Abors en 1853.* Paris, 1854.
Kuropatkin, A.N. *Kashgaria: (Eastern or Chinese Turkistan. Historical and Geographical Sketch of the Country; Its Military Strength, Industries and Trade).* Calcutta, 1882.
Lake, Edward. *Sir Donald McLeod: A Record of Forty-Two Years Service in India.* London, 1875.
Lamb, Alastair. *Asian Frontiers: Studies in a Continuing Problem.* London, 1968.
———. *Britain and Chinese Central Asia: The Road to Lhasa 1767 to 1905.* London, 1960.
———. *British India and Tibet 1766-1910.* London, 1986. (A revised edition of *Britain and Chinese Central Asia*.)
———. *The McMahon Line: A Study in the Relations between India, China and Tibet, 1904 to 1914.* 2 vols. London, 1966.

———. "Tibet in Anglo-Chinese Relations: 1767-1842." *Journal of the Royal Asiatic Society* (1957): 161-176; (1958): 26-43.

Landon, Perceval. *Lhasa; An Account of the Country and People of Central Tibet and of the Progress of the Mission Sent There by the English Government in the Years 1903-4*. 2 vols. London, 1905.

———. *Nepal*. 2 vols. London, 1928.

Lattimore, Owen. *Pivot of Asia: Sinkiang and the Inner Asian Frontiers of China and Russia*. Boston, 1950.

———. *Studies in Frontier History; Collected Papers, 1928-1958*. London, 1962.

Littledale, St. George R. "A Journey Across Tibet from North to South, and West to Ladak." *GJ* 7 (1896): 453-83.

Lloyd, William. *Narrative of a Journey from Caunpoor to the Boorendo Pass in the Himalaya Mountains, etc*. Edited by G. Lloyd. 2 vols. London, 1840.

Longstaff, Thomas. *This My Voyage*. London, 1950.

Macaulay, Colman. *Report of a Mission to Sikkim and the Tibetan Frontier, with a Memorandum on our Relations with Tibet*. Calcutta, 1885.

MacGregor, John. *Tibet: A Chronicle of Exploration*. New York, 1970.

Macintyre, Donald. *Hindu-Koh: Wanderings and Wild Sport on and beyond the Himalayas*. London, 1889.

Maclagan, Sir Edward. *The Jesuits and the Great Mogul*. London, 1932.

Maclaren, Malcolm. "The Tibetan Goldfields." *The Mining Journal* 81 (1907): 825-26.

MacMunn, G. *The Romance of the Indian Frontiers*. London, 1931.

MacNair, W.W. "A Visit to Kafiristan." *PRGS* n.s. 6 (1884): 1-18.

Markham, Clements. *The Fifty Years' Work of the Royal Geographical Society*. London, 1881.

———. *A Memoir on the Indian Surveys*. 2nd ed. London, 1878.

———. *Narratives of the Mission of George Bogle to Tibet, and of the Journey of Thomas Manning to Lhasa*. London, 1876. 2nd ed., London, 1879.

———. "Travels in Great Tibet, and Trade between Tibet and Bengal." *JRGS* 45 (1875): 299-347.

Marshall, Julie G. *Britain and Tibet 1765-1947: The Background to the India-China Border Dispute. A Select Annotated Bibliography in European Languages*. Bundoora, Australia, 1977.

Mason, Kenneth. *The Abode of Snow: A History of Himalayan Exploration and Mountaineering*. London, 1955.

———. "Great Figures of Nineteenth Century Himalayan Exploration." *Journal of the Royal Central Asian Society* 43 (1956): 167-75.

———. "Himalayan Exploration." *Asian Review* 52 (1956): 191-200.

———. "A Hundred Years of Himalayan Exploration." *United Service Institution of India Journal* 58 (1928): 513-24.

———. "Kishen Singh and the Indian Explorers." *GJ* 62 (1923): 429-40.

McLeish, A. *The Frontier Peoples of India: A Missionary Survey*. London, 1931.

Michie, Alexander. *The Englishman in China during the Victorian Era, as Illustrated in the Career of Sir Rutherford Alcock, K.C.B., D.C.L*. 2 vols. Edinburgh and London, 1900.

Mill, Hugh Robert. *The Record of the Royal Geographical Society 1830-1930*. London, 1930.

Mojumdar, K. *Anglo-Nepalese Relations in the Nineteenth Century.* Calcutta, 1973.
Montgomerie, T.G. "On the Geographical Position of Yarkund, and Some Other Places in Central Asia." *JRGS* 36 (1866): 157-172.
———. "A Havildar's Journey through Chitral to Faizabad in 1870." *JRGS* 42 (1872): 180-201.
———. "Journey to Shigatze, in Tibet, and Return by Dingri-Maidan into Nepaul, in 1871, by the Native Explorer No. 9." *JRGS* 45 (1875): 330-49.
———. "Memorandum on 600 Miles of the Brahmaputra River, from its Source from the Manasarowar Lake, in Latitude 30½°, and Longitude 82°, to the Junction of the Lhasa River, in Latitude 29° 22' and Longitude 90° 40'." *JRGS* 38 (1868): 211-219.
———. "Narrative of an Exploration of the Namcho, or Tengri Nur Lake, in Great Tibet, Made by a Native Explorer, during 1871-2." *JRGS* 45 (1875): 315-30.
———. "Narrative Report of the Trans-Himalayan Explorations Made during 1868." *JASB* 39, no. 2 (1870): 47-60.
———. "Report of a Route-Survey Made by Pundit ＿ ＿ ＿, from Nepal to Lhasa, and thence through the Upper Valley of the Brahmaputra to its Source." *JRGS* (1868): 129-210.
———. "Report of The Mirza's Exploration from Caubul to Kashgar." *JRGS* 41 (1871): 132-83.
———. "Report of the Trans-Himalayan Explorations during 1867." *JRGS* 39 (1869): 146-87.
———. *Routes in the Western-Himalayas, Kashmir, etc.* Dehra Dun, 1874.
Moorcroft, William. "A Journey to Lake Manasarovara in Undes, a province of Little Tibet, with introductory note by H.T. Colebrook." *Asiatick Researches* 12 (1816): 375-534.
Moorcroft, William, and George Trebeck. *Travels in the Himalayan Provinces of Hindustan and the Panjab etc.* Edited by H.H. Wilson. 2 vols. London, 1841.
Morgan, Gerald. *Anglo-Russian Rivalry in Central Asia: 1810-1895.* London, 1981.
———. "Myth and Reality in the Great Game." *Asian Affairs* 60 (1973): 55-65.
Morison, J.L. "From Alexander Burnes to Frederick Roberts: A Study of Imperial Frontier Policy." *Proceedings of the British Academy* 22 (1936): 177-206.
Morshead, H.T. "An Exploration in South-East Tibet." *Royal Engineers' Journal* 33 (1921): 21-40.
———. *Report on an Exploration on the North East Frontier 1913.* Dehra Dun, 1914.
———. "The Topographical Results of Sir H.H. Hayden's Expedition to Tibet in 1922." *Records of the Survey of India* 18 (Dehra Dun: 1924): 113-15.
Morshead, Ian. *The Life and Murder of Henry Morshead.* Cambridge, 1982.
Narrative of Surveys Made, during 1876, by "The Mullah," in connexion with the operations of the Great Trigonometrical Survey of India. Simla, 1877.
"Narrative of the Travels of Khwajah Ahmud Shah Nukshbundee Syud Who Started from Kashmir on the 28th October, 1852, and Went through Yarkund, Kokan, Bokhara and Cabul, in Search of Mr. Wyburd—Communicated by the Government of India." *JASB* 25 (1856): 344-58.
Needham, J.F. "Excursion in the Abor Hills; from Sadiya on the Upper Assam." *PRGS* n.s. 8 (1886): 313-28.
———. "Mr. J.F. Needham's Journey along the Lohit Brahmaputra between Sadiya in

Bibliography 311

Upper Assam and Rima in South-Eastern Tibet." *Royal Geographical Society, Supplementary Papers* 2 (1887-89): 485-555.
Norins, Martin R. *Gateway to Asia: Sinkiang, Frontier of the Chinese Far West.* New York, 1944.
"Passage of the Himalaya Mountains." *Quarterly Review* 22 (1820): 417.
Pearse, H. "Moorcroft and Hearsey's Visit to Lake Manasarowar in 1812." *GJ* 26 (1905): 180-87.
Peissel, Michel. *Mustang: A Lost Tibetan Kingdom.* London, 1968.
Pelliot, Paul, ed. *Huc and Gabet: Travels in Tartary, Tibet and China 1844-1846.* 2 vols. London, 1928.
Petech, L. *China and Tibet in the Early 18th Century: History of the Establishment of Chinese Protectorate in Tibet.* Leiden, 1950.
Petech, Luciano. "China and European Travellers to Tibet, 1860-1880." *T'oung Pao* 62, nos. 4-5 (1976): 219-52.
Phillimore, R.H. *Historical Records of the Survey of India.* 5 vols. Dehra Dun, 1945-1968.
———. "Survey of Kashmir and Jammu 1855 to 1865." *Himalayan Journal* 22 (1959-60): 95-102.
Porter, Whitworth. *History of the Corps of Royal Engineers.* 2 vols. London, 1889.
Potagos, Le Docteur. *Dix Années de Voyages dans L'Asie Centrale et L'Afrique Equatoriale.* Paris, 1885.
Pranavananda, S. *Kailas-Manasarovar.* Calcutta, 1949.
———. *Exploration in Tibet.* 2nd ed. Calcutta, 1950.
Purdon, William H. "On the Trigonometric Survey and Physical Configuration of the Valley of Kashmir." *JRGS* 31 (1861): 14-30.
Rahul, R. *The Himalaya Borderland.* Delhi, 1970.
Ram, Hari. "Extracts from an Explorer's Narrative of His Journey from Pitoragarh, in Kumaon, via Jumla to Tadum and Back, along the Kali Gandak to British Territory." *JRGS* 45 (1875): 350-63.
Rawat, Indra Singh. *Indian Explorers of the 19th Century.* New Delhi, 1973.
Rawling, C.G. *The Great Plateau: Being an Account of Exploration in Central Tibet, 1903, and of the Gartok Expedition, 1904-1905.* London, 1905.
———. *Report on the Gartok Expedition Including the Brahmaputra, Sutlej and Indus Valleys, and That Portion of Tibet Which Lies to the West of Gyantse.* Calcutta, 1905.
Rawlinson, H.C. "Monograph on the Oxus." *JRGS* 42 (1872): 482-513.
Rayfield, Donald. *The Dream of Lhasa: The Life of Nikolay Przhevalsky (1839-88) Explorer of Central Asia.* London, 1976.
Reid, Sir Robert. *History of the Frontier Areas Bordering on Assam from 1883-1941.* Shillong, 1942.
Rennell, James. "An Account of the Ganges and Burrampooter Rivers." *Philosophical Transactions* 71 (1781): 87-114.
———. *Memoir of a Map of Hindoostan, etc.* London, 1783.
Report of a Mission to Yarkund in 1873, under Command of Sir T.D. Forsyth, K.C.S.I., C.B., Bengal Civil Service, with Historical and Geographical Information Regarding the Possessions of the Ameer of Yarkund. Calcutta, 1875.
Report on the Explorations in Great Tibet and Mongolia, made by A.K. in 1879-82: In Connection with the Trigonometrical Branch, Survey of India. Dehra Dun, 1884.

Report on the Explorations of Lama Serap Gyatsho, 1856-68; Explorer K — P, 1880-84; Lama U.G., 1883; Explorer R.N., 1885-86; Explorer P.A., 1885- 86; in Sikkim, Bhutan and Tibet. Prepared in the Office of the Trigonometrical Branch, Survey of India. Lieut.-Colonel G. Strahan, RE, Officiating Deputy Surveyor-General, in Charge, and published under the direction of Colonel H.R. Thuillier, RE, Surveyor-General of India. Dehra Dun, 1889.

Richardson, Hugh E. *Tibet and Its History.* 2nd ed. Boulder and London, 1984.

Rijnhart, Susie C. *With the Tibetans in Tent and Temple: Narrative of Four Years' Residence on the Tibetan Border, and of a Journey into the Far Interior.* Chicago, 1901.

Risley, H.H., ed. *The Gazeteer of Sikkim.* Calcutta, 1894.

Robertson, George. *The Kafirs of the Hindu-Kush.* London, 1896.

Robertson, George. *Chitral: The Story of a Minor Siege.* London, 1899.

Rockhill, W.W. *Diary of a Journey through Mongolia and Tibet in 1891 and 1892.* Washington, D.C., 1894.

———., ed. *The Journey of William of Rubruck to the Eastern Parts of the World, 1253-55, as Narrated by Himself.* London, 1900 (Hakluyt Society, Second Series, no. 4). Reprint. 1967.

———. *The Land of the Lamas: Notes of a Journey through China, Mongolia and Tibet.* New York, 1891.

Rose, Leo E. *Nepal: Strategy for Survival.* Berkeley, 1971.

"The Route of Ibrahim Khan from Kashmir through Yassin to Yarkand in 1870." *PRGS* 15 (1871): 387-92.

Ryder, C.H.D. "Exploration in Western China." *GJ* 21 (1903): 109-26.

Sandberg, Graham. "The Exploration of Tibet." *Calcutta Review* 98, no. 196 (1894): 327-60.

———. *The Exploration of Tibet, Its History and Particulars from 1623 to 1904.* Calcutta, 1904. Reprint. Delhi, 1976.

———. "A Journey to the Capital of Tibet." *Contemporary Review* 58 (1890): 64-82.

———. *Tibet and the Tibetans.* London, 1906.

Sandeman, J.E. "The River Irawadi and its Sources." *PRGS* n.s. 4 (1882): 257-73.

Sandes, E.W.C. *The Indian Sappers and Miners.* Chatham, 1948.

———. *The Military Engineer in India.* Chatham, 2 vols. 1933-35.

Sanwal, B.D. *Nepal and the East India Company,* London, 1965.

Sarel, Henry. "Notes on the Yang-tsze-Kiang, from Han-kow to Ping-shan." *JRGS* 32 (1862): 1-25.

Savage-Landor, A. Henry. *Everywhere: The Memoirs of an Explorer.* 2 vols. New York, 1924.

Schiern, Frederic. "The Tradition of the Gold Digging Ants." *The Indian Antiquary* 4 (1875): 225-32.

Schlagintweit, A. and R. "A Short Account of the Journey from Milum to Johar, to Gartok in the Upper Indus Valley, and of the ascent to the Ibi Gamin Peak." *JASB* 25 (1856): 125-133.

Schlagintweit, Hermann, Adolph Schlagintweit, and Robert Schlagintweit. *Results of a Scientific Mission to India and High Asia Undertaken between the Years MDCCCLIV and MDCCCLVIII, by Order of the Court of Directors of the Honourable East India Company.* 4 vols. Leipzig, 1861-1866.

Secret and Confidential Reports of Trans-Himalayan Explorations in Badakhshan and

beyond the Frontier of Sikkim: Prepared for Publication with the Annual Report for 1881-82 of the Survey of India. 1883.
Shakabpa, Tsepon W.D. *Tibet: A Political History.* New Haven, Conn., 1967.
Shaw, Robert. "A Visit to Yarkand and Kashgar." *PRGS* 14, no. 2 (1870): 124-37.
Shaw, Robert. *Visits to High Tartary, Yarkand and Kashgar.* London, 1871.
Sherring, Charles. *Western Tibet and the British Borderland: The Sacred Country of Hindus and Buddhists with an Account of the Government, Religion and Customs of Its Peoples.* London, 1906.
Singhal, D.P. *India and Afghanistan 1876-1907: A Study in Diplomatic Relations.* St. Lucia, 1963.
Skrine, C.P., and Pamela Nightingale. *Macartney at Kashgar: New Light on British, Chinese, and Russian Activities in Sikiang, 1890-1918.* London, 1973.
Smith, H.U. "A Trip to Thibet, Kylas, Source of the Sutluj, and the Mansurwar and Rakhas Lakes." *PRGS* 11, no. 3 (1866-7): 119-22.
Snellgrove, D.L., and H.E. Richardson. *The Cultural History of Tibet.* London, 1968.
Spate, O.H.K. *India and Pakistan: A General and Regional Geography.* London, 1954.
Spear, Percival. *The Oxford History of Modern India 1740-1975.* 2nd ed. Delhi, 1978.
Stein, R.A. *Tibetan Civilization.* Stanford, 1972.
Strachey, Henry. "Narrative of a Journey to Cho Lagan (Rakas Tal), Cho Mapan (Manasarowar), and the Valley of Pruang in Gnari, Hundes, in September and October 1846." *JASB* 17, part 2 (1848): 98-120; 125-82; 327-51.
———. "Physical Geography of Western Tibet." *JRGS* 23 (1853): 1-69.
Strachey, Richard. "Notice of a Trip to the Niti Pass." *JASB* 19 (1850): 79-82.
Strachey, Richard. "Narrative of a Journey to the Lakes Rakas-Tal and Manasarowar, in Western Tibet, undertaken in September, 1848." *GJ* 15 (1900): 150-70; 243-64; 394-415.
Strahan, C. "The Survey of India." *Professional Papers of the Corps of Royal Engineers* (Occasional Papers Series) 28 (1902): paper no. 8.
Styles, Showell. *The Forbidden Frontiers. The Survey of India from 1765 to 1949.* London, 1970.
Survey of India. *Exploration in Tibet and Neighbouring Regions, Part I, 1865-1879; Part II, 1879-1892.* 2 vols. Dehra Dun, 1915. (Records of the Survey of India, vol. 8.)
Swinson, Arthur. *Beyond the Frontiers: The Biography of Colonel F.M. Bailey, Explorer and Secret Agent.* London, 1971.
Sykes, Percy. *A History of Persia.* 3d ed. 2 vols. London, 1951.
———. *The Right Honourable Sir Mortimer Durand, etc.* London, 1926.
Tanner, H.C.B. "Notes on the Chugani and Neighbouring Tribes of Kafiristan." *PRGS* n.s. 3, no. 5 (1881): 278-301.
———. "Our Present Knowledge of the Himalayas." *PRGS* n.s. 12 (1891): 403-23.
Temple, Richard. *Journals Kept in Hyderabad, Kashmir, Sikkim and Nepal.* Edited by R.C. Temple. 2 vols. London, 1887.
Thuillier, H.L., and R. Smyth. *A Manual of Surveying for India.* 3d ed. Calcutta, 1875.
Trotter, H. "Account of the Pundit's Journey in Great Tibet from Leh in Ladakh to Lhasa, and of his return to India via Assam." *JRGS* 47 (1877): 86-136.
———. *Account of the Survey Operations in Connection with the Mission to Yarkand and Kashghar in 1873-74.* Calcutta, 1875.

———. "The Amir Yakoub Khan and Eastern Turkestan in Mid-Nineteenth Century." *Journal of the Central Asian Society* 4, part 4 (1917): 95-112.

———. "On the Geographical Results of the Mission to Kashgar under Sir T. Douglas Forsyth in 1873-74." *JRGS* 48 (1878): 173-234.

———. *Secret and Confidential Report of the Trans-Himalayan Explorations by Employés of the Great Trigonometrical Survey of India, during 1873-74-75*. Calcutta, 1876.

Turner, Samuel. *An Account of an Embassy to the Teshoo Lama, in Tibet; containing a narrative of a journey through Bootan, and part of Tibet. To which are added, views taken on the spot, by Lt. Samuel Davis; and observations botanical, mineralogical, and medical, by Mr. Robert Saunders.* London, 1800.

Vaurie, C. *Tibet and Its Birds.* London, 1972.

Vibart, H.M. *Addiscombe: Its Heroes and Men of Note.* London, 1894.

Waddell, L.A. *Among the Himalayas.* London, 1900.

———. *The Buddhism of Tibet or Lamaism.* Cambridge, 1939.

———. "The Falls of the Tsang-po (San-pu), and Identity of That River with the Brahmaputra." *GJ* (1895): 258-60.

———. *Lhasa and Its Mysteries: A Record of the Expedition of 1903-1904.* London, 1905.

Wade, C.M. *A Narrative of the Services, Military and Political, of Lt. Col. Sir C.M. Wade.* C.B. Ryde, Isle of Wight, n.d.

Walker, J.T. "Exploration of the Great Sanpo River of Tibet during 1877 [sic] in Connection with the Operations of the Survey of India." *PASB* (1879): 203-5.

———. "Four Years' Journeyings through Great Tibet, by One of the Trans Himalayan Explorers of the Survey of India." *PRGS* n.s. 7 (1885): 65-92.

———. "The Hydrography of South-Eastern Tibet." *PRGS* n.s. 10 (1888): 577-84.

———. "The Lu River of Tibet; Is It the Source of the Irawadi of Salwin?" *PRGS* n.s. 9 (1887): 352-77.

———. "Notes on the RGS Map of Tibet." *GJ* 4 (1894): 52-54.

———. "On the Highland Region adjacent to the Trans-Indus Frontier of British India." *JRGS* 32 (1862): 303-16.

Watson, F. *The Frontiers of China,* London: 1966.

Webber, Thomas W. *The Forests of Upper India and their Inhabitants.* London, 1902.

Wellby, M.S. *Through Unknown Tibet.* London, 1898.

Wellby, M.S., and N. Malcolm. *Report with Map upon a Journey through Northern Tibet and Northern China.* Simla, 1897.

Wellby, M.S., and N. Malcolm. *Road Report of Route across Tibet and China.* Simla, 1897.

Wessels, C. *Early Jesuit Travellers in Central Asia, 1603-1721.* The Hague, 1924.

White, John Claude. "Journeys in Bhutan." *GJ* 35 (1910): 18-42.

———. *Sikhim and Bhutan: Twenty-one Years on the North-East Frontier, 1887-1908.* London, 1909.

Wilcox, R. "Memoir of a Survey of Assam and the Neighbouring Countries executed in 1825-6-7-8." *Asiatick Researches* 17 (1832): 314-469.

Wood, John. *A Journey to the Source of the River Oxus.* Edited by Alexander Wood. London, 1872.

Woodman, Dorothy. *Himalayan Frontiers: A Political Review of British, Chinese, Indian and Russian Rivalries.* London, 1969.

Wright, Daniel. *History of Nepal.* Cambridge, 1877.

Bibliography

Wylly, H.C. "Lhassa and its Armed Rabble." *United Services Magazine* n.s. 30 (1904-05): 31-38.

Yakushi, Yoshimi. *Catalogue of the Himalayan Literature*. Tokyo, 1984.

Yapp, Malcolm. *Strategies of British India: Britain, Iran and Afghanistan, 1798-1850*. New York, 1980.

Yate, A.C. "Captain F.M. Bailey's Latest Exploration." *Scottish Geographical Magazine* 30 (1914): 191-97.

Yate, C.E. *Northern Afghanistan; or, Letters from the Afghan Boundary Commission*. Edinburgh, 1888.

Younghusband, Francis. "The Geographical Results of the Tibet Mission." *GJ* 25, no. 5 (1905): 481-98.

———. *India and Tibet, etc.* London, 1910.

Yule, Henry, ed. *Cathay and the Way Thither: Being a Collection of Medieval Notices of China*. 4 vols. London, 1913-16. New ed., revised by Henri Cordier.

———. *The Late Colonel T.G. Montgomerie*. London, 1878.

———. "Papers Connected with the Upper Oxus Regions." *JRGS* 42 (1872): 438-81.

Note on Map Sources

In most cases, the routes of the explorers were mapped in published reports of their journeys; where no source map was available, we were able to reconstruct the route from a narrative account of the journey.

Map 1. Abdul Hamid, *JRGS* 36 (1866); Nain Singh, *JRGS* 38 (1868).

Map 2. The Mirza, *JRGS* 41 (1871); The Havildar, 1870, *JRGS* 42 (1872); The Havildar, 1873-75, from narrative in Captain Henry Trotter, "The Havildar's Journey from Badakhshan to Kolab, Darwaz, and Kubadian," *Report on the Trans-Himalayan Exploration by Employees of the Great Trigonometrical Survey of India during 1873-74-75* (Calcutta: 1876).

Map 3. The Mullah, 1873-74, from narrative in Captain Henry Trotter, *Report on the Trans-Himalayan Exploration by Employees of the Great Trigonometrical Survey of India during 1873-74-75* (Calcutta: 1876); The Mullah, 1875-76, *General Report on the Operations of the Great Trigonometrical Survey of India during 1876-77* (Calcutta: 1878); The Mullah, 1878, *General Report on the Operations of the Survey of India during 1878-79* (Calcutta: 1880).

Map 4. Nain, Kalian, and Mani Singh, *JRGS* 38 (1868); Kalian Singh, from narrative in T.G. Montgomerie, *Report on the Trans-Himalayan Explorations in Connection with the Great Trigonometrical Survey of India during 1868* (Dehra Dun: 1869); Kishen Singh, *JRGS* 45 (1875); Nain Singh, *JRGS* 47 (1877).

Map 5. Kishen Singh, *PRGS* 7 (1885).

Map 6. Forsyth Mission, *JRGS* 48 (1878); Abdul Subhan, *JRGS* 48 (1878); M.S., Survey of India, Trigonometrical Branch, Trans-Himalayan Exploration Map No. 14, *Secret and Confidential Report of Trans-Himalayan Explorations in Badakshan* (N.p.: 1883).

Map 7. Hari Ram, 1871-72, *JRGS* 45 (1875); Hari Ram, 1873, *JRGS* 45 (1875); Hari Ram, 1885-86, from report compiled by Mr. C. Wood, in 1885-86, *Records of the Survey of India* 8, Part II, *Exploration in Tibet and Neighbouring Regions, 1879-1892* (Dehra Dun: 1915).

Map 8. Sarat Chandra Das and Ugyen Gyatso, *Journal of the Buddhist Text and Anthropological Society* 7, No. 1 (1900); Ugyen Gyatso, H.R. Thuillier, *Report of the Explorations . . . in Sikkim, Bhutan and Tibet* (Dehra Dun: 1889).

Map 9. Lala, *General Report on the Operations of the Survey of India during 1878-79* (Calcutta: 1880); Nem Singh and Kintup, ibid.; Kintup, *General Report on the Operations of the Survey of India during 1886-87* (Calcutta: 1888); Rinzing Namgyal and Phurba, ibid.

Index

Abor Expedition (1911-12), 224, 237, 238, 240, 244
Abor people, 215, 221, 231, 237, 238, 241, 245
Afghanistan: and Russian/British rivalry, 54, 55, 56, 57, 59, 60, 67, 77, 93, 252, 260; mapping of, 63, 266; pundit expeditions in, 81, 83, 98, 253, 267, 272; boundaries of, 147, 159, 264; mentioned, 12, 85, 87, 157. *See also* Kabul
Afghan Wars: first (1838-42), 57, 63; second, (1878-80), 57, 188, 268
Afridi people, 21
Agnew, P.A. Vans, 13, 103
Agra, 2, 3, 4, 127
A.K. *See* Singh, Kishen
Aksai Chin plateau, 113, 115, 151, 282n1
Aksu, 77, 149, 155, 156, 157, 162, 167
Aktagh, 151, 161
Aktash, 159, 160
Alaga, 225
Alcock, Sir Rutherford, 105, 125, 259
Alexander, Czar, 14, 54
Alexander the Great, 54, 86, 107
Ali, Awazi, 35, 37
Ali, Muhommad, 23
Ali, Sher, 66, 69, 70, 88, 93, 157, 158, 159
Alladand, 85, 86
Allahabad, 127, 257
Almeida, Diogo de, 2
Alphabetum Tibetanum (Giorgi), 6-7
Altyn Tagh mountains, 133, 134
Aman-i-Mulk, 87-88
Amin, Mahomed, 34, 63, 76
Amir, Saiyad, 95
Andrade, Antonio de, 2, 3, 6, 102, 107, 283n40
Anglo-Bhutanese War, 232
Anglo-Burmese War, 11
Anglo-Nepalese War, 11, 16, 38, 102, 171, 175, 185
Anglo-Russian Agreement, 58, 93
Anglo-Sikh Wars, 13, 18, 65, 101
Aral Sea, 55, 75
Armenians, 2, 4
Arun River, 169, 170, 178, 179, 182
Asiatic Society of Bengal, 24, 26, 27, 29, 64, 208, 249, 250, 295n27
Assam, 29, 46, 141, 215, 226, 268, 272; and Tibet, 7, 8; British occupation of, 11, 16, 232; and exploration of Brahmaputra, 137-38, 216, 221, 227, 238, 241, 244; mentioned, 112, 123, 127, 139, 188, 190, 214, 229, 234, 235, 237, 256, 270
Astley, Thomas: *Voyages and Travels*, 6
Ata Gang pass, 138
Atalik Ghazi. *See* Beg, Yakub
Azevedo, Father Francisco, 3

Babur, 54, 76
Back, Admiral Sir George, 208
Badakhshan, 56, 63, 72, 74, 85, 88, 89, 91; description of mir of, 72, 250; surveying of, 92, 157, 161, 165, 166, 168, 252, 267; political information on, 92, 159, 250; mentioned, 2, 57, 62, 69, 70, 71, 82, 84, 158, 263. *See also* Faizabad; Oxus River
Badrinath, 105, 110, 174
Bahadur, Jung, 176, 181
Bailey, Frederick M., 141, 222, 230, 239-47, 297n89, 299n128
Baksh, Faiz (Ghulam Rabbani), 146, 149
Baksh, Nubbi (the jemadar), 79, 80, 81, 154
Baltistan ("Little Tibet"), 19, 85
Baluchistan, 58, 112
Baroghil pass, 94, 160, 161, 165, 166, 252, 255, 257
Bashahr, 11, 13, 45, 46, 50, 102, 107, 109, 110, 112
Batang, 136, 140, 141, 239, 264, 271, 285n94
Beg, Alif, 72-73
Beg, Yakub (the Atalik Ghazi), 72-81, 144-47, 154, 157, 162, 164
Bellew, Dr., 147, 153, 156, 160
Belowti pass, 156
Bengal: British conquest of, 7, 8, 171, 172; Education Department of, 197, 206, 209; mentioned, 9, 10, 11, 12, 22, 38, 84, 108, 147, 174, 184, 188, 191, 193, 195, 215, 232, 243
Bengal Secretariat Press (Calcutta), 207
Bentinck, Lord William, 23
Bentinck, Mr. (political officer with Abor Expedition), 238, 245
Bethell, Captain, 238
Bhotia people, 38-39, 40, 42, 44, 45, 101, 102, 105, 143, 222, 232
Bhutan, 3, 266, 268, 269, 272; and Tibet, 9,

Index

173, 186, 232; mentioned, 7, 8, 49, 119, 123, 169, 185, 210, 211, 216, 231, 243, 268
Biddulph, Captain, 147, 148, 151, 153, 155, 156, 157, 159, 160, 161, 166, 188
Biet, Bishop, 136, 137
Black, C.E.D., 261
Blacker, Valentine, 16
Blakiston, Captain Thomas W., 30, 31
Bogle, George, 8, 9, 49, 108, 130, 172, 194, 199, 205
Bokhara, 55, 93, 252; pundit travel to, 23, 63, 70, 84, 88, 90, 91, 92, 165; mentioned, 12, 21, 22
Bombay, 22, 148
Bonvalot, Gabriel, 124, 271
Boury, Father, 138, 141, 298n97
Bower, Hamilton, 240, 268, 269, 271
Brahmaputra River, 29; and Tsangpo River, 2, 16, 44, 46, 51, 99, 116, 119, 123, 139, 141, 190, 214-47 passim, 267. *See also* Lohit River; Tsangpo River
Bruce, Frederick, 31
Buddhism, 28, 42, 44, 62, 71, 74, 77, 99; Tibetan, 10, 135, 195, 199, 203, 204, 208
Buddhist Text Society of India, 207
Burma, 137, 214, 215, 225, 236, 247, 268, 271; British annexation of, 187, 189, 207
Burnes, Alexander, 23, 57, 59, 62, 63
Burrard, Sir Sidney, 246

Cabral, John, 3, 170
Cacella, Stephen, 3
Calcutta, 126, 186, 193, 194, 196, 209; mentioned, 20, 24, 30, 31, 50, 64, 119, 123, 129, 148, 185, 202, 205, 208, 217, 240, 245, 252, 258, 260
Campbell, Dr. Archibald, 186
Campbell, Sir George, 191, 193, 208
Canning, Lord, 20, 24
Canton, 7, 10, 171
Capuchins, 4, 5-6, 7, 108, 170-71
Carey, A.D., 163, 270, 303n20
Caspian Sea, 54, 55
Changchenmo road, 119, 120, 151
Chang Tang (northern plain), 43, 44, 99, 112, 113-14, 121, 132, 133, 135, 163, 207, 268
Chapman, Captain, 147, 148, 156
Chefoo Convention (1876), 184, 186, 195, 207, 303n17
Chetang, 211, 219-20, 223, 224, 243; and Nain Singh, 123, 130, 139, 216, 219, 222-23, 267; Chandra Das in, 204, 235; Kintup in, 228, 234, 245
Chichiklik-Davan pass, 76
China, 2, 6, 77, 78; and Tibet, 1, 5, 10, 31-32, 108, 136, 171, 172-73, 179, 186, 187, 207, 239, 242, 252; trade with, 7-9, 136, 171, 172;

expeditions to Tibet from, 30, 31, 239, 251, 270-71; Great Wall of, 112, 113, 115, 117; exploration in, 129, 133-35, 268. *See also* Turkestan, Chinese
Chitral, 64, 69, 84, 85, 86, 88, 89, 94, 159, 257, 260, 267; survey of, 22, 267; siege of, 87; description of, 87, 90
Chittagong, 193, 204
Choki (Ugyen Gyatso's wife), 213, 294n71
Christianity, 2, 10, 127. *See also* Jesuits; Missionaries
Chulalonkorn, King (Siam): Tushiti Mala Decorations of, 208
Chulikattas, 240
Chumbel, 119, 129, 131, 132, 133, 134, 135, 136, 137, 138
Chumbi valley, 185, 186, 187, 211, 212, 220, 223, 239
Churchill, Lord Randolph, 207
Clarke, C. B., 193
Clive, Robert, 7, 171
Colebrook, Robert, 174
Cooper, T.T., 251-52, 270
Cornwallis, Lord, 9-10, 173
Crawford, Charles, 174
Croft, Sir Alfred, 191, 193, 195-96, 197, 200, 201, 203, 204, 209
Cross, Viscount, 265, 266
Cunningham, Captain Alexander, 13, 103

da Fano, Domenico, 5
Dafla people, 221
Dalai Lama, 5, 8, 32, 49-50, 202, 203
Dalbuing (Tarpin), 245
Dalgleish, Douglas, 270, 303n20
d'Anville, Jean-Baptiste, 6, 8, 214, 215
Daphla Expedition (1874-75), 188
Darjeeling (Dorjé-ling), 185-86, 187, 188, 189, 207, 208, 213; expeditions to Tibet from, 127, 133, 140, 178, 179, 197, 199, 200, 201, 204, 206, 209, 211, 217, 220, 222, 223; Bhutia Boarding School in, 187, 193-94, 195, 208, 292n7; mentioned, 49, 136, 139, 226, 227, 230, 231, 232, 235, 246
Darkoth pass, 166
da Rovato, Father Giuseppe, 171
Darwaz, 165, 166
Das, Babu Sarat Chandra (S.C.D), 124, 184, 193-208, 212, 265, 294n63; as headmaster of Bhutia Boarding School, 187, 209; first expedition of, 188, 191, 266; second expedition of, 210, 211, 219, 235, 266
Davies, Major, 237, 239
Deasy, H.H.P., 269
Dege Gonchen monastery, 136
Dehra Dun: as Survey of India headquarters, 16, 19, 20, 45, 51, 60, 67, 81, 89, 117, 148, 179,

183; training of pundits in, 39, 41, 44, 115, 164-65, 194; mentioned, 40, 166, 175, 217, 221
De Lesseps, Ferdinand, 142
Delhi, 2, 240
della Penna, Orazio, 5, 6, 170
Demchok, 110, 111, 112, 115, 283n32
Dera Ghazi Khan, 69
Desgodins, Abbé, 136, 270, 297n87
Desideri, Ippolito, 4-5, 7, 43, 47, 102, 170, 179, 223
Diaz, Father Manuel, 3
Dibong River, 214, 221, 222
Dihang River, 214, 215, 216, 221-22, 224, 227, 234, 235, 236, 237, 238, 240, 244, 298n98
Dingri, 179, 182, 183, 184
Dingri Maidan, 178, 181
Dir, 85, 87, 94
Doaba valley, 165
Dogra people, 101, 103, 108
Dongtse, 199, 201, 202, 203, 204, 206
Donkya pass, 200, 209, 226, 227, 230
Dorah pass, 89
Dora Imam valley, 165
d'Orville, Albert, 3-4, 6, 170, 179
Drepung monastery, 211, 228
Drew, Frederick, 61-62
Drummond, Robert, 102
Dudh Kosi River, 182, 183, 184
du Halde, Jean Baptiste, 6, 140
Dunbar, George, 244-45
Durand, Henry, 264
Durand, Sir Mortimer, 56
Durand Line, 56, 58
Dzungaria, 5, 14

East India Company, 7, 8-9, 10, 11, 18, 22, 108, 171, 172, 173, 174, 251
Eden, Sir Ashley, 196, 232, 269
Edgar, John Ware, 186, 193, 194, 195, 208, 212
Elias, Ney, 163
Elphinstone, Mountstuart, 56, 63, 86
Everest, George, 16-18, 176

Faizabad, 72, 82, 83, 85, 88, 89, 91, 92, 158, 165
Fedchenko, Alexis, 256
Forsyth, Sir Douglas, 34, 125, 145, 147, 149, 150, 164; expedition to Yarkand, 145, 151, 153, 160-61; expedition to Kashgar, 148, 154-64, 259; and pundits, 154, 158; Treaty of Commerce with emir of Kashgar, 155, 156, 161
Forsyth missions, 82, 94, 118, 129, 144-68, 181, 217, 259, 267
Foxcroft, Mr., 172
Freshfield, Douglas, 190-91, 289n18

Freyre, Father Manuel, 4-5, 43, 102, 170

Gabet, Joseph, 10, 31, 49, 50, 52, 117, 129, 201, 205, 271
Gandak River, 169, 181, 182, 183, 184, 190
Ganden monastery, 228
Gangaram, 130, 131, 133, 135
Ganges River, 44, 105, 110, 169, 174, 241
Gardiner, Alexander, 14
Gardner, Edward, 175
Garhwal, 5, 11, 13, 51, 59, 102, 104, 105, 174, 188
Gartang River, 110
Gartok, 12, 104, 107, 108, 114-15, 117; as trading center, 11, 43, 44; description of, 100-101; survey of, 111, 177, 249, 283n33; mentioned, 5, 13, 31, 51, 102, 110, 113
Gartok-Lhasa Road, 45, 46, 47, 50-51
Genghis Khan, 54, 71
Geographical Exhibition and Congress (Venice, 1881), 142
Geographical Society of Italy, 142
Geographical Society of Paris, 142
Gerard, Alexander, James, and Patrick, 12
Gerard, Lieutenant John, 173
Giachuraf, 107, 109, 110
Gia pass, 139
Gi La Pass, 136, 137
Gilgit, 61, 62, 66, 87, 95, 97, 146, 165, 166, 188, 261
Giling monastery, 229
Gill, Captain William, 137, 139, 140, 141, 271
Goa, 2, 3
Gobi Desert, 14, 104, 129, 145, 150
Godwin-Austen, Henry, 103, 111, 113, 120, 221, 232, 284n65
Goes, Benedict, 2, 14, 62, 74, 83, 91, 129, 134, 150, 162
Gogra, 151, 153
Gora pass, 237
Gorchakof-Granville Agreement, 58, 159
Gordon, Robert, 225, 226, 235-36
Gordon, T.E., 82, 147, 155, 156, 157, 158, 159, 160
Great Britain: and Tibet, 7-13, 111, 172, 185-86, 187, 189, 193, 207, 272; and Chinese Central Asia, 14-21, 24-32, 33, 63, 78, 272; and China, 25, 164, 171, 186-87, 276n74; and Russia, 54-59, 77-78, 81, 93, 248, 252, 255; and Persia, 57; and Nepal, 171, 185; annexation of Upper Burma, 187; and Sikkim, 185-87. See also East India Company
Great Trigonometrical Survey (GTS), 1, 6, 15-21; and pundits, 40, 43, 44, 69, 84, 124, 126, 127, 140, 142, 168, 184; and political intelligence, 53, 59-60, 63, 67; training of pundits for, 65, 66, 67, 164, 167, 209; and

northward exploration, 90, 91, 94, 97, 98, 140, 178, 179, 182, 188, 217, 248; and exploration of Tibet, 117, 118, 184, 187, 196-97, 210, 212; annual reports of, 181, 233, 251, 252, 257, 262, 265-66; Darjeeling (Himalayan) party of, 188, 189, 190; and Tsangpo-Brahmaputra controversy, 216, 219, 220, 226, 235-36, 245, 246; reorganization of, 226; and British government of India, 248-49, 252, 255, 258, 264; secret reports of, 252-54; focus of, 267. *See also* Dehra Dun; Forsyth missions; Pundits
Grueber, John, 3-4, 6, 170, 179
GTS. *See* Great Trigonometrical Survey
Guge, 3, 101
Gurkhas, 11, 173, 175, 179, 183, 234, 237; in Nepal, 7, 8, 108, 172, 289n2; invasion of Tibet, 9-10; in Sikkim, 174, 185. *See also* Anglo-Nepalese War
Gurkha War. *See* Anglo-Nepalese War
Gurla Mandhata mountains, 99
Gyala Peri, 223
Gyala Sindong, 232, 242, 246; Nem Singh at, 223, 224, 228, 231, 234; Kintup at, 227, 228, 229, 231, 233, 237, 242, 243, 246
Gyantse, 49, 206, 228; British trade agency in, 239, 272; mentioned, 8, 43, 130, 133, 139, 170, 199, 202, 203, 209, 220
Gyatso, Serap, 212
Gyatso, Thupten (13th Dalai Lama), 203-04
Gyatso, Ugyen (U.G.), 187, 190, 196, 197, 208-13, 222, 224, 232, 233, 246, 265, 294n72; first expedition, 191, 197, 199, 200, 266, 296n39; as teacher of Tibetan at Bhutia Boarding School, 194, 195; second expedition, 201, 202, 204, 219, 235, 266
Gyunsar monastery, 197

Hamid, Abdul (Mohamed-i-Hameed), 1, 33-37, 38, 42, 66, 67, 82, 145, 153, 249, 252, 267
Hamilton, Alexander (East India Company physician), 8
Hardinge, Lord, 13
Hargreaves, Lieutenant, 269
Harman, Captain Henry John, 188, 196, 226-27, 232, 233, 297n90; and Tsangpo River controversy, 220-21, 224, 225, 234, 235; and Nem Singh, 222, 263; and Kintup, 223, 227, 229, 230
Hastings, Warren, 8, 9, 172, 173
Hati pass, 170
Havildar, The. *See* Shah, Hyder
Hayward, George, 61-62, 82, 90, 150, 160; murder of, 61, 64, 80, 87-88, 97, 165; expedition to Kashgar, 76, 81, 83, 144
Hearsey, Hyder Young, 11, 12, 39, 102, 174, 175
Hedin, Sven, 107, 110, 114, 271, 272, 284n66, 288n78, 295n27

Henderson, Dr., 145, 146
Hennessey, J.B.N., 236, 265, 285n94
Herat, 56, 57, 63, 65, 84
Herodotus, 108, 109
Himalayas: geography of, 1, 35, 60, 83, 100, 117, 215; passes over, 2, 46, 51, 101, 123, 138, 139, 169-70; first expeditions across, 9, 102; as shield, 10, 50, 144; mapping of, 12, 18, 19, 150, 177, 179, 188; and exploration of Tibet, 21, 31, 107, 110, 130; pundits' view of, 47-48, 140; mentioned, 7, 11, 16, 23, 25, 43, 52, 59, 69, 115
Hinduism, 7, 44, 50, 70, 99, 105, 108, 178, 183
Hindu Kush: pundit explorations in, 22, 59, 71, 94; and Great Britain, 54, 56, 60; passes over, 58, 69, 70, 84, 86, 88, 91, 92, 160, 161; geography of, 85, 89, 90
Hindustan-Tibet road, 11, 14, 18
Hodgson, Brian, 175, 177
Hodgson, John, 22
Holdich, Sir Thomas, 209, 212, 238, 245-46, 299n128
Hong Kong, 13, 30, 171
Hooker, Sir Joseph, 177, 178, 186, 188, 189, 217, 220
Huang Ho (Yellow River), 135
Huc, Evariste, 10, 31, 49, 50, 52, 117, 129, 139, 201, 205, 271
Hume, A. O., 256-57, 261-62
Hundes. *See* Tibet: Western
Hunza, 159, 160

Ibrahim Khan, 146, 149, 157
Ilchi, 161-62
Ili valley, 78, 146, 287n16
Imperial Russian Archaeological Society, 208
India: British rule in, 7-8, 54-59, 251; mapping of, 15-21; boundaries of, 54-56; and Chinese Turkestan, 144-45, 164; trade with Tibet, 163, 172; trade with Nepal, 172. *See also* China; Great Britain; Russia
Indian Mutiny, 15, 19, 20, 55, 176, 251
India Office: Geographical Department of, 251-52, 265
Indus River: source of, 2, 44, 100; surveying of, 18, 19, 83, 85, 94, 95, 97, 103, 104, 109-10, 111, 113; mentioned, 23, 69, 101, 107, 112, 261, 262
Irrawaddy River, 137; and Tsangpo River, 2, 141, 190, 214, 215, 216, 222, 225, 226, 235, 236
Ishkashim, 71, 72, 92, 158, 159, 165, 166

Jacquemont, Victor, 13
Jalalabad, 91, 94
Jammu, 13, 18, 19, 20, 101, 102
Jaxartes (Sir Darya) River, 55
Jelap pass, 186, 212

Jesuits: in China, 2, 6, 24, 33, 134, 214; in Tibet, 3, 4, 5, 7, 43, 102, 108, 117, 136, 139, 170; in Turkestan, 62, 83; in Nepal, 170
Johnson, William, 19, 21-22, 37, 103-4, 119, 150, 162, 163
Jongjuk Jong, 228, 242, 244
Jongka, 182, 183, 184
Jonsong pass, 191, 197
Jumla, 181, 183
Jyekundo (Yushu), 135, 136

Kabul, 69, 81, 82, 83, 88, 90, 91, 92, 93; British occupation of, 55, 57; Elphinstone mission to, 56, 63, 86; description of, 70; and Forsyth mission, 157, 158, 159, 160; mentioned, 2, 22, 24, 29, 59, 62, 65, 66, 112. *See also* Afghanistan
Kabul River, 85
Kadir Khan, Abdul, 173
Kafir brigands, 86, 88
Kafiristan, 62, 85, 86-87, 89, 90
Kailas mountains, 43, 44, 99, 110, 113
Kalimpong, 213, 220
Kali River, 169, 174, 185, 181
Kandahar, 55, 56, 69, 70, 83
Kangra pass, 217
Kangxi, Emperor, 5, 6
Kansu Province, 144, 164
Kantze monastery, 136
Karakash river, 35, 151, 153, 162
Karakorum mountains: geography of, 11, 14, 16, 19, 43, 54, 60, 100, 112; trade routes over, 34, 113, 144; expeditions over, 95, 118, 150, 151, 153, 160, 161, 286n11
Karakorum pass, 21, 22, 25, 29, 35, 37, 58, 81
Karatagh pass, 151
Karkang pass, 123
Karnali River, 44, 169, 181, 188, 284n51
Karo pass, 49, 203
Kashgar, 14, 21, 22, 60, 78, 84, 113, 271; expeditions to, 59, 67, 80, 82, 83, 177; description of, 77, 78-79; Chinese conquest of, 78, 164; trade between India and, 144, 164; Forsyth mission to, 148, 149, 154-64, 181, 259; British commercial treaty with, 155, 156, 161. *See also* Beg, Yakub
Kashmir, 37, 101, 119, 136, 165; trade with Lhasa, 9, 47, 49, 199; ceding of, to British, 13, 101-2; surveying of, 18-21, 25, 26, 27, 29, 34, 38, 65, 103; tariffs in, 144, 145, 163; mentioned, 50, 61, 81, 85, 146, 159, 247. *See also* Ladakh; Srinagar
Kashyapa Buddha, 203
Kathmandu, 169, 171, 181; British in, 11, 173, 175, 176, 185; expeditions through, 45, 50, 170, 182; surveying of, 51, 174, 177, 184; mentioned, 4, 179, 183. *See also* Nepal
Kawaguchi, Ekai, 206, 208

Kazul River, 78
Kebong, 237, 238
Kemball, Sir Arnold, 259
Kham, 49, 120, 139
Khamba Jong, 200, 201, 202, 204, 209, 217, 220, 224
Khampa people, 270
Khiva, 55, 57, 147, 252
Khojah Saleh (Khwaja Sahar), 58, 59
Khotan, 14, 21-22, 104, 150, 153, 161-63, 164, 288n75; mentioned, 77, 118, 119, 123, 259
Khumbu, 183, 184
Khyber pass, 56
Kila Punja, 71, 73, 157, 165, 166
Kila Wamur, 158, 165
Kimberley, Lord, 265
Kingdon-Ward, Frank, 140
Kinlock, Captain, 171
Kintup (K.P.), 212, 223, 227-31, 233, 237, 238, 241, 246, 265, 298n99; and Tsangpo controversy, 141, 234, 235, 236, 239, 242-43, 244-45, 267
Kipling, Rudyard: pundit in *Kim*, 193, 292n2
Kircher, Athanasius, 4
Kirghiz, 25, 60, 72, 75, 76, 156, 157, 166
Kirkpatick, Captain William, 10, 173, 174
Kirong, 45, 46, 50, 182, 183, 184
Kirong pass, 170, 179
Klaproth, Heinrich, 215
Knox, Captain William, 11, 174
Kohistan, 63, 95, 97
Kokand, 24, 55, 67, 69, 78, 79, 82, 88, 149, 161
Koko Nor ("blue lake"), 4, 5, 133
Kolab (Kulyab), 93, 158, 164, 165
Kosi River, 169, 179
Krick, Father, 138, 141, 298n97
Kublai Khan, 62
Kulm-Tashkurgan, 71, 75, 92
Kumaon, 12, 41, 108, 174, 179, 189, 251; British annexation of, 11, 38, 102, 171; and expeditions to Tibet, 30-31, 40, 44, 175, 183; survey of, 59, 104, 105, 176, 188, 217; mentioned, 51, 115, 143, 169, 178, 182, 272
Kumbum monastery, 272
Kunar (Chitral) River, 94
Kunlun mountains, 34, 129, 131, 132, 140, 161-62; geography of, 14, 43, 60, 100, 112, 133, 286n11; passes over, 58, 118, 135, 163
Kuti pass, 170, 179

Ladakh, 2, 13, 19, 21, 58, 102, 108, 119; and Tibet, 7, 43, 49, 51; expeditions to, 22, 40, 80, 81, 118, 146; surveys of, 25, 110, 111, 112, 161; boundary with Tibet, 99, 100, 103, 109; mentioned, 11, 14, 31, 46, 48, 95, 101, 112, 114, 129, 271. *See also* Leh

Index

Lahore, 23, 62
Lahul, 101, 102, 103
Lake Bul (Borax), 116, 118
Lake Chadyr Kul, 155
Lake Dumo, 210, 212
Lake Ghazkol, 166
Lake Issyk Kul, 55, 270
Lake Karatagh, 153
Lake Kurlyk, 133
Lake Manasarowar, 11, 12, 99, 102-3, 112, 114, 174, 272; in 1840s, 13, 282n9; and pundit explorations, 43, 44, 51, 104, 115, 116, 177; and Indus River, 95, 100
Lake Namtso. *See* Tengri Nor
Lake Palgutso, 182, 183
Lake Pamir Kul, 73, 74
Lake Pangong, 31, 99, 101, 103, 120, 121, 123, 146, 150, 151, 163
Lake Pho Mo Chang Tang, 210
Lake Rakas Tal, 11, 13, 282n9, 284n51
Lake Tosun, 130, 133, 135
Lake Victoria (Lake Zorkul; Wood's Lake), 59, 62, 73, 157, 159
Lake Yamdok, 49, 203, 204, 210, 211, 212, 219, 223
Lala, 216-20, 221, 223, 267, 295n12
lamas, 3, 5, 6, 32, 133, 134-35, 187, 193, 197, 201
Lambton, William, 15, 16
Landon, Perceval, 139, 273, 292n2
language: Tibetan, 41, 194, 195, 201, 205, 207, 208, 222, 239; Pushtu, 64, 65; Persian, 64, 65, 71; Arabic, 94; Mongolian, 131; dialects of Sikkim, 195; Hindi, 196, 199; Sanskrit, 199, 201, 205; English, 202; Tibetan-English dictionary (1902), 205, 212
Lani La pass, 132
Lawrence, Sir John, 67, 144
Leh, 3, 4, 12, 23, 80, 102, 108, 145; and pundit explorations, 21, 23, 34, 35, 37, 81, 113, 118, 119, 120, 121, 122, 123, 146, 252; and Forsyth mission, 150, 151, 153, 157, 160, 161, 163
Lewin, Major Herbert, 195
Lhasa, 2-13 passim, 29-31 passim; expeditions to (in 1860s and 1870s), 38-44 passim, 59, 104, 112-22 passim; 177, 195, 196, 200, 223, 252, 260, 267, 270; description of, 49, 52, 130-31, 137; British in, 80, 186, 272; expeditions to (in 1840s), 117, 271; geographical position of, 124; missionaries in, 129, 170, 214; trade between Kathmandu and, 170, 179, 181; expeditions to (in 1880s), 201-03, 205, 209-11, 212, 228, 230; smallpox epidemic in 203, 204; mentioned, 102, 109, 113, 127, 139, 140, 150, 217, 234, 237, 238, 270. *See also* Gartok-Lhasa Road; Tibet
Lhobra River, 210
Lipu Lek pass, 188

Littledale, St. George R., 272, 303n32
Lobsang, 192
Lockhart, Colonel, 58, 86
Logan, James, 172
Lohit River, 141, 214, 215, 221, 222, 236, 237, 240, 241, 298nn97, 101
Longstaff, Thomas, 104, 143
Lopchak mission, 119, 122
Lop Nor, 133, 134, 150, 156, 270, 271
Lytton, Lord, 61, 126, 196, 258-59, 261, 263

Macaulay, Colman, 184, 186-87, 193, 195, 206, 207, 209, 212
Macaulay mission, 184, 187, 232, 233
MacDonnell, Anthony, 213
Ma Chu River, 135
Mackenzie, Captain Colin, 65
Macleod, Sir Donald, 67, 69
McMahon, Sir Henry, 240, 241, 244, 245
McMahon Line, 244
MacNair, William, 86-87, 89, 281n63
Madras, 15, 16
Mahomed, Ata (the Mullah), 85, 91, 94-98, 161, 165, 252, 255, 257, 260, 261, 262, 267, 301nn70, 75
Mahomed-i-Hameed, *see* Hamid, Abdul
Malakand Agency, 86
Malakand pass, 85
Malcolm, Lieutenant, 269, 272
Mana pass, 2, 102, 104, 105, 107
Manning, Thomas, 9, 10, 49, 130, 194, 205
Marco Polo, 14, 21, 60, 62, 74, 76, 77, 79, 82, 83, 129, 134, 155, 162
Markham, Clements, 9, 10, 126, 194, 256, 257, 259, 261
Marpung, 229, 231, 245
Marques, Manuel, 2, 3
Marquess of Dufferin and Ava's Silver Medal, 208
Mason, Kenneth, 91, 140, 149, 164, 178, 224
Maunsell, Lieutenant-Colonel Frederick, 84
Mayo, Lord, 57, 61, 144, 145, 146
Meadows, Thomas Taylor, 30
Mechi River, 175
Mejid, Abdul, 24, 62, 67, 85, 92
Mekong River, 43, 137, 214, 239
Milam, 39, 40, 41, 43, 44, 46, 51, 105, 115, 127, 143, 284n51
Mirza, the. *See* Shuja, Mirza
Mishmi people, 138, 141, 215, 235, 236, 237, 240, 298n97
missionaries, 2-6, 7, 31-32, 33, 101, 107, 108, 136, 138, 170, 214, 223, 243
Moghuls, 2, 7, 54
Mohammad, Dost, 66
Molesworth, Captain E.H., 141, 236
Mongolia, 127, 130, 134, 254

INDEX   323

Mongols, 2, 5, 14, 31, 54, 131, 132
Montgomerie, Captain Thomas George, 18-21, 51, 112; and use of pundits, 22, 24, 25, 26, 29; and expeditions to Tibet, 30, 39, 52-53, 101, 103, 112-13, 117, 177-78, 179, 181, 182; and expedition to Yarkand, 32, 33, 34, 35, 67, 267; and the Singhs, 42, 43, 44, 45, 46, 104, 105, 108, 109, 110, 111, 114, 115, 116, 118, 124, 283n17; on Nain Singh's audience with the Dalai Lama, 50; and the Mirza, 59, 60, 65, 66-67, 69, 73, 76, 79, 80, 82, 83, 84; put in charge of trans-Himalayan exploring, 59, 273; and northward exploration, 61, 63-65, 70, 94, 98, 145, 148, 149, 153, 188, 217; and the Mirza, 67, 84; on the Atalik Ghazi, 80; and the Havildar, 84-85, 88, 89, 90, 91, 92; departure from India, 118, 129, 147, 179; and British government, 125, 249, 260, 261; death of, 129, 164; and RGS, 248, 249-50, 251, 285n86
Montgomery, Sir Robert, 26, 33, 67
Moorcroft, William, 11-12, 21, 22-23, 39, 40, 71, 102, 175
Morrison, M.C., 52, 283n17
Morshead, Captain Henry, 141, 241, 242, 243, 244, 245, 246, 247, 298n120
Moslems, 4, 35, 50, 74, 78, 79, 81, 86, 133, 146; as pundits, 24, 27, 64, 84, 149, 164, 249; insurrections of, 33, 77, 144; and Kafirs, 87. *See also* Pathans
Mount Annapurna, 169
Mount Dhaulagiri, 169, 170, 174
Mount Everest, 169, 176, 178, 179, 183, 184, 185, 251
Mount Godwin-Austen, 185
Mount Gosainthan (Shisha Pangma), 169
Mount Kailas, 5
Mount Kamet, 105
Mount Kanchenjunga, 169, 170, 176, 185, 187, 189, 190, 191, 197, 201, 230, 289n18
Mount Makalu, 169
M.S. *See* Shah, Muktar
Muir, Sir William, 67
Muktinath, 115, 170, 181, 182
Mula pass, 69
Mullah, the. *See* Mahomed, Ata
Munphool, Pundit, 63, 70, 85
Munshi, the. *See* Subhan, Abdul
munshis (native secretaries), 22, 33, 34, 35, 37, 38, 65, 149, 249
Murchison, Sir Roderick, 20, 52, 76, 249
Murghab River, 166, 167
Mussoorie, 84, 105, 221
Mustagh mountains, 76
Mustang, 170, 181

Naib Muhmamad Alum Khan, 253

Nain Singh Range, 121
Namcha Barwa, 223, 224
Namchi monastery, 231
Namgyal, Rinzing (R.N.), 185-92, 194, 201, 207, 294n71; and Tsangpo controversy, 231-32, 233, 237, 267; visit to Bhutan, 269
Namohon pass, 135
Nanda Devi, 39, 169, 170, 176
Nanga Parbat, 95, 97
Nangpa La pass, 170
Nan Shan, 112, 134
Napier, Lord, 255
Napoleon, 14, 54, 56
Narayan, Prithvi, 172, 174
Narratives of the Mission of George Bogle to Tibet, and of the Journey of Thomas Manning to Lhasa, 9, 10
Needham, J.F., 141, 234, 236, 237, 238, 240, 245, 298nn99, 101
Nepal, 18, 26, 38, 171, 197; travels through, 3, 44, 201, 271; and Tibet, 7-8, 9, 49, 169, 172-73, 189; surveys of, 46, 51, 175-76, 184, 185, 189, 190, 269; boundaries of, 99, 169, 175, 189, 190; conquest by Gurkhas, 108, 172-73; mentioned, 4, 11, 17, 30, 45, 115, 247, 249, 267, 268, 272. *See also* Anglo-Nepalese War; Kathmandu; Treaty of Segauli
Nevill, Captain G. A., 241
Newar kingdom, 7, 8, 171
Ngagong Chu River, 239
Nganglaring Tso, 114, 118
Ngari-korsum. *See* Tibet: Western
Niti pass, 16, 102
Noh, 121, 123, 163
No La pass, 46
Norpu, 233, 246
Northbrook, Lord, 146, 147, 194, 252-53, 263
North-West Frontier Province, formation of (1901), 56
Nuksan pass, 88, 89
Nyen Chen Tanglha Range, 132

Ochterlony, Sir David, 175
Odoric of Pordenone, Friar, 2
Onlet (Olon), 231, 244, 245
Orleans, Prince Henri of, 124, 271
Ottoman Empire, 78
Oxus River, 60, 98, 112, 149, 161, 267; and Russian-British rivalry, 57, 58-59; search for source of, 59, 61 62; the Mirza's exploration of, 63, 67, 71, 72, 73, 74, 81, 83, 89, 255; the Havildar's exploration of, 85, 88, 89, 91, 92, 93, 252, 255; the Munshi's exploration of, 158-59, 254, 259; M.S.'s exploration of, 164-67

Pakistan, 18

Index

Pamir, the, 43, 54, 57, 60-62, 63, 144, 146, 147; explorations across, 2, 24, 59, 67, 72, 73, 74, 76, 80, 81, 112, 149, 157, 158, 159, 160, 166, 267, 272; geography of, 14, 58, 60, 83
Panchen (Tashi) Lama, 8-9, 48, 172, 195, 196, 199, 200, 202, 204
Pangu pass, 183
Panjkora River, 86
Paris Geographical Society, 125, 126
pashm (shawl wool) trade, 11, 12, 39, 101, 102, 103, 107, 108
Pathans, 56, 57, 60-61, 64, 84, 85, 86, 90, 91, 94, 97, 126
Paul, A.W., 231
Peking, 3, 6, 13, 31, 105, 122, 184, 186, 239, 271; expeditions to, 118, 119, 123, 201, 207. *See also* China
Pemakochung, 228, 231, 234, 242, 243, 246
Pemberton, Captain Robert, 216, 232, 269
Pemberton mission, 232, 269
Pemionchi monastery, 193, 194, 195, 197, 208, 211, 222, 293n36
Persia, 54, 55, 56, 57, 65, 67, 77
Peshawar, 29, 54, 57, 89, 91, 92, 98; pundits from, 64, 65; mentioned, 19, 21, 24, 62, 66, 69, 84, 85, 95, 97, 146
Petermann, August, 256
Phari, 130, 139, 186, 208, 211, 217, 220, 223
Phurba (P.A.), 232, 269
Phurching, 197, 201, 202, 204
Pir Panjal Range, 19
Pithoragarth, 179, 181
Plassey, battle of, 7, 171
Poba people, 242
Pollock, Major, 66, 84
Pome, 237, 242
Portuguese, 2, 3, 4
Potala palace (Lhasa), 4, 6, 49, 131
Pottinger, Eldred, 63, 65
Prejevalsky, Nikolai, 129, 134, 139, 140, 156, 201, 205, 254, 270, 271
pundits (native explorers), 1, 21-32, 267-68; training of, 41-42, 193; salaries of, 43, 182, 189, 201, 209, 231; explorations by, in 1867, 104-12; and Forsyth mission, 147-64; and need for secrecy, 177, 248-66; extent of explorations, 269-70, 272-73. *See also* Montgomerie, Captain Thomas George; *individual explorers*
Punjab, 23, 30, 61, 69, 86, 101; annexation of, 18, 56; British government of, 25, 33, 34, 63, 67, 144, 145, 249, 252. *See also* Sikhs

Qian Long, Emperor, 10
Qing (Manchu) dynasty, 5

Ram, Atma, 268, 302n3

Ram, Hari (M.H.; No.9), 177-84, 211, 251, 267, 269, 279n5, 284n55, 290n39
Rampur, 102; Nawab's College in, 94
Ramsay, Colonel, 30, 44-45
Rangit River, 185
Rangoon, 214, 225, 226
Rawling, C. G., 107, 239, 269, 303n10
Rawlinson, Sir Henry, 38, 84, 90, 125, 126, 142, 249, 258
Réclus, Elisée, 215
Rennell, James, 15, 141, 214, 215, 226
Reynolds, Charles, 22
RGS. *See* Royal Geographical Society
Rijnhart, Dr. Susie, 272
Rima, 138, 140, 141, 236
Robert, William, 188, 190
Robertson, Sir George, 87
Rockhill, William Woodville, 142, 205, 271
Roorkee, engineering college at, 39, 44, 67
Roshan, 93, 158, 159
Royal Geographical Society (RGS), 22, 24, 26, 38, 52, 59, 61, 112; medals of, 20, 38, 240, 245, 246, 247; and the Mirza, 64, 76, 84; and the Havildar, 90; and Kishen Singh, 142-43; and Nain Singh, 124-26, 143; and Forsyth mission, 155, 164; and Sarat Chandra Das, 207-08; and Tsangpo-Brahmaputra controversy, 225, 234, 235, 238, 239, 246; and Survey of India, 248, 249-50, 251, 252, 257, 258, 262, 264, 265, 266
Royal United Service Institute of India, 240
Rudok, 3, 100, 101, 112, 113, 120, 163, 284n65, 288n84
Russia: expansion of, 14, 24, 54-60, 77, 111, 158, 161, 187, 252, 260, 268; and Chinese Turkestan, 22, 73, 144, 146, 155, 164, 280n40; treaties in Central Asia, 78, 93; explorations by, 98, 167, 254, 255, 267; and Tibet, 232
Russian Geographical Society, 255, 270
Russo-Afghan Boundary Commission, 57-58
Russo-Persian War, 55
Ryder, Colonel, 140, 234, 237, 239

Sacken, Baron Frederick Osten, 256
Sadiya, 141, 215, 221, 234, 236, 237, 238, 240
Sakya monastery, 178, 204
Salisbury, Lord, 259, 260, 261
Salween River, 43, 137, 214
Samarkand, 55, 77
Samding monastery, 203
Samti, 92, 165
Samye monastery, 122, 204, 211, 219
Sandberg, Graham: *The Exploration of Tibet*, 191
Sandeman, Captain J. E., 225, 226
Sanju, 153, 160

Santucci, Father, 170
Sarel, Lieutenant-Colonel H. A., 30, 31
Sarel expedition, 30
Sarhadd, 94, 165, 166
Sarikol, 60, 72, 75, 160
Sarolang pass, 91, 92
Saunders, Trelawney, 260
Savage-Landor, A. Henry, 272
Schlagintweit, Adolph, 13, 14, 21, 34, 40, 63, 77, 177
Schlagintweit, Hermann, 177
Schlagintweit brothers, 13, 27, 33, 37, 40, 83, 282n9
Selipuk, 112, 114
Sera monastery, 49, 228
Shadee, Mirza, 145-46
Shah, Hyder (the Havildar), 84-94, 116, 158, 159, 164, 165, 167, 251, 252, 253, 255, 257, 259, 260, 271n74
Shah, Muktar (M.S.), 164-68, 267
Shahidula, 150, 151, 153, 154, 160
Shakdarah River, 159, 166
Shaw, Robert, 80-81, 82, 83, 144, 145, 146, 150, 161, 280n43, 286n11
Shensi Province, 144
Shigatse, 3, 43, 116, 219; capture of, by Gurkhas, 10, 172; description of, 48; mentioned, 8, 49, 112, 114, 115, 170, 178, 195, 199, 200, 204, 209, 210, 217, 220, 224
Shignan, 92, 93, 158, 159, 165
Shipki, 11, 102, 110
Shugden monastery, 141, 239
Shuja, Mirza (Sajjad; the Mirza), 59-60, 61, 62, 63-84, 85, 116, 252, 260; trip to Kashgar, 67-81, 144, 145, 154, 157, 250, 252; survey of Oxus River, 72, 88-89, 91, 92, 158, 255
Shyok River, 151
Sikhs, 13, 18, 23, 30, 56, 57, 79, 101
Sikkim, 172, 174, 175, 193, 226, 266, 269, 272; and Tibet, 7, 187, 190, 196, 217; and Great Britain, 11, 173, 186, 188, 269; geography of, 169, 185; travel through, 195, 197, 201, 204, 206, 268, 271; expedition of 1888, 212; mentioned, 49, 176, 177, 178, 208, 211, 231, 232, 237, 247
Sikkim-Tibet Convention (1890), 187
Siliguri, 186, 237
Silk Road, 77, 162
Simla, 11, 102, 148, 193, 221, 240, 241, 245, 246, 258, 261
Sind, 56, 58, 112
Singh, Gulab, 13, 18, 19, 101, 102, 103
Singh, Kalian (G.K.), 104, 107-8, 109, 110, 111, 120, 130; expedition to Tibet in 1868, 112-17, 250, 256; on Forsyth mission, 118, 149, 151, 160
Singh, Kishen (A.K.), 40, 115-17, 127-43, 182, 204, 205, 211, 284nn50,51, 285n94, 292n2; journey to Tengri Nor, 116, 118, 121, 124, 181, 251; on Forsyth mission, 118, 149, 151, 153, 154, 155, 157, 161, 163-64; journey to Khotan, 123, 259; journey through Tibet, 129-32, 263, 264, 265; and Tsangpo-Brahmaputra controversy, 235-36, 239
Singh, Mani ("the Patwar;" GM), 39-46, 48, 51, 104, 105, 107, 110, 111, 115, 117, 127, 182
Singh, Nain ("Chief Pundit"), 39-52, 63, 64, 85, 94, 104, 115, 130, 136, 139, 140, 177, 181, 211, 216, 251, 259; first expedition of, 43-52, 59, 116, 182, 203, 205, 220, 249, 250, 252, 260, 267, 283n17; recognition by RGS, 52, 124-26; expedition to goldfields of Tibet, 105, 107-8, 109, 110, 111, 112, 121, 250, 256; last exploration of, 117-27, 129, 217, 219, 220, 222-23, 232, 268, 284n66; and British government, 126-27; and Forsyth mission, 145-46, 149, 151, 154, 160, 164; training of pundits by, 164, 196, 224; and Tsangpo River controversy, 216, 220, 223, 243
Singh, Nem (N.M.G. or G.M.N.; Nyima Tsering), 222-25, 227, 228, 230, 231, 234, 263, 267, 293n36, 295n27, 296n39
Singh, Rambir, 19
Singh, Ranjit, 18, 56, 101
Singh, Sukh Darshan (G.S.S.), 182
Singh, Zorawar, 101
Sining, 4, 117, 131, 135, 270, 271
Sinji-Chogyal (Shingche Chogye), 242, 243, 246
Smyth, Major Edmund, 30-31, 38, 39, 40, 41, 126, 127
Sorghak goldfields, 162
Spiti, 101, 102, 103, 112
Srinagar, 4, 19, 165, 166
Stein, Aurel, 135
Stewart, Sir Donald, 266
Stoliczka, Dr., 147, 151, 153, 155, 156, 157, 159, 160
Strachey, Henry, 13, 40, 113, 282n9
Strachey, Richard, 13, 40, 282n9
Strangford, Lord, 24
Subansiri River, 214, 215, 221, 222, 223, 224
Suchow (Jiayuguan), 113
Suget pass, 153
Suhan, Abdul (the Munshi), 93, 255, 257, 258, 260, 288n65; and Forsyth mission, 149, 151, 153, 154, 155, 157, 158, 159, 164, 165, 166, 259
surveying instruments, 27-29, 34, 41-42, 150, 154-55, 197, 209; concealment of, 34, 42, 45, 50, 75, 142, 154, 158, 163, 167, 183, 217, 228, 249, 250, 256
Survey of India, establishment of, 226. *See also* Great Trigonometrical Survey
Sutlej River, 44, 54, 100, 101, 102, 104, 107, 110, 111, 174, 250

Swat, 54, 66, 85, 86, 90, 94, 97, 98
Szechenyi, Count Bela, 129, 134, 137, 140-41, 201, 205, 270, 271
Szechuan, 130, 136

Tachienlu (Darchendo; Kangting), 130, 135, 136, 137, 139, 140, 239, 268
Tadzhikistan, Soviet, 93
Takla Makan desert, 14, 60, 150, 161-62, 271
Takla pass, 170
Talung valley, 188
Tamerlane, 54
Tankse, 119, 120, 151
Tanner, Henry Charles Baskerville, 97, 167, 188, 189, 190, 196, 209, 231, 232, 233, 236, 237
Tashi Lama. *See* Panchen Lama
Tashilhunpo monastery, 3, 49, 195, 196, 209; and Panchen Lama, 8, 9, 48; Gurkha attacks on, 10, 172; Chandra Das at, 199, 200, 201, 202, 203, 204, 206, 207
Tashkent, 24, 55, 80, 252
Tashkurgan, 75, 157, 158
Tawang, 123, 124, 219, 243, 244
Taylor, Annie, 271
Temple, Sir Richard, 176, 194
Tengri Nor, 112, 116, 118, 120, 121, 123, 124, 132, 181, 251, 268, 271, 272
Tengyur, 208
Terek passes, 149
Terekty pass, 155
Thok Daurakpa gold mines, 121
Thok Jalung gold mines, 108-09, 111, 112, 114, 115, 116, 120, 121
Thomson, Dr. Thomas, 13
Thubden monastery, 134, 135
Thuillier, Henry, 20, 26, 59, 149, 213, 256, 258, 261
Thun Tsung, 228
Tian Shan ("heavenly mountains"), 14, 38, 77, 78, 149, 155
Tibet: and China, 1, 5, 10, 31-32, 45, 48, 49, 77, 108, 136, 171, 172-73, 179, 186, 187, 207, 239, 242, 252; and Nepal, 7-8, 9, 49, 169, 172-73, 189; as goal of Survey of India, 25, 98, 164, 249, 267, 268; Western (Hundes; Ngari-korsum), 99-112; goldfields in, 107-9, 112, 114, 115, 121, 124, 250, 256; trade with India, 163, 172; and Sikkim, 185-87. *See also* Jesuits: in Tibet; Lhasa; Tsangpo River; *individual explorers*
Tipta La pass, 170, 178
Tista River, 185, 190
Toling (Totling), 101, 102, 107, 110, 111
Tradom monastery, 46, 47, 50, 51, 112, 114, 170, 181

Traill, G. W., 12
Trans-Alai mountains, 149
Treaty of Amritsar, 102
Treaty of Lahore, 101-2
Treaty of Peking, 14
Treaty of St. Petersburg, 287n16
Treaty of Segauli, 11, 175, 176
Treaty of Tientsin, 30, 32
Treaty of Titalia, 185
Treaty of Yandabo, 215
Trotter, Henry, 83, 91-92, 93, 94, 129; and Nain Singh, 118, 119, 121, 122, 123, 124, 216; recognition from RGS, 125, 126; departure for Diplomatic Service, 129, 187; and Forsyth mission, 147, 148, 149, 150-51, 153, 154-55, 156, 157, 159, 160, 161, 163, 164, 165, 166, 181; and GTS, 147-48, 252; and British government, 253, 254-55, 256, 257, 258, 259, 260, 261
Tsaidam ("salt marsh"), 114, 133, 135, 140
Tsangpo River: and Brahmaputra River, 2, 16, 44, 119, 139, 214-47, 267; and Gartok-Lhasa Road, 43, 47, 49, 113, 114, 122, 177; and pundit explorations, 46, 51, 111, 116, 130, 181, 200, 203, 209, 211; geography of, 99, 109, 112, 117, 170; mapping of, 118, 123, 124, 141, 190, 212, 265, 267; mentioned, 199, 204, 272. *See also* Brahmaputra River
Tsaparang, 2, 3, 4, 5, 101, 102, 107
Tsinghai Province (China), 130, 133
Tungani Moslem uprising (1862), 77, 146
Tunhuang (Saitu), 134-35, 140
Turgat pass, 155
Turkestan, Chinese, 1, 14-21, 25, 77, 100, 129, 134, 263; Jesuits in, 2, 62; trade with India, 25, 144-45; pundits in, 26, 40, 72, 75, 83, 119, 164, 272; mapping of, 37, 38, 150, 153, 161, 249, 267; Russia in, 54, 77, 78, 81, 269. *See also* Forsyth missions
Turkestan, Russian, 55, 60, 71, 252, 256
Turkey, 146-47, 161
Turner, Samuel, 9, 43, 48, 49, 51, 108, 130, 205, 206, 220

Udalguri, 123, 217
Uighurs, 77
Ullah, Mir Izzet, 14, 22, 71
Ural River, 54

Van der Putte, Samuel, 6, 140
Vanj River, 167
Venice International Geographical Congress, 168
Venioukoff, Colonel, 255, 257
Victoria, Queen, 191

Waddell, L. Austine, 206, 227, 237

Wade, Claude, 23
Wakhan, 57, 62; and British-Russian rivalry, 58, 73; pundit explorations in, 71, 72, 75, 94, 95, 252; and Forsyth mission, 151, 158, 159, 161, 165
Walker, James T., 21, 64, 85-86, 97, 148, 226; as superintendent of GTS, 25, 26, 27, 37, 51, 59, 84; and training of pundits, 39, 41, 65-66; and RGS, 52, 126, 235-36, 250-51, 285n94; and Mongomerie, 60, 147, 249, 256; and British government, 67, 69, 252-53, 255-57, 258-59, 260, 261-62, 263-64, 265; and the Havildar, 90, 91, 93, 94; and explorations in Tibet, 118, 122, 124, 181; tribute of British secretary of state, 125, 262; and Kishen Singh, 127, 129, 136, 139, 142, 285n94; and pundit M.S., 164, 165, 166, 167, 168; as surveyor-general of India, 188, 196, 226, 233; and exploration of Brahmaputra, 216, 221, 222, 225, 226; and Russian Geographical Society, 255-56, 279n7
Walli, Mir, 87, 89
Waugh, Sir Andrew Scott, 17-18, 19, 20, 24, 26, 38, 65, 84, 176, 185, 249
Webb, William, 12, 174
Wellby, Captain, 269, 272
White, John Claude, 191, 192, 269
Wilcox, Captain, 141, 215-16
William of Rubruck, Friar, 2
Williamson, Noel, 238, 240
Winterbottom, J.E., 13
Wood, Captain Henry, 177
Wood, John, 59, 62, 63, 73, 82, 91, 158
Woodthorpe, Captain, 222
wool trade. See *pashm* trade

Wright, Daniel, 177

Xinjiang Province, 14, 78

Yakub Khan, Syud, 70, 147, 154
Yalung River, 137
Yangang, 208, 209, 212, 213
Yangi Hissar, 77, 159, 160
Yangi pass, 160
Yangtse River, 30, 31, 43, 137, 214, 239
Yarkand, 1, 65, 72, 75, 77, 79, 80, 81, 108, 119, 120, 134; and Russian-British rivalry, 14; expeditions to, 22, 32, 33-34, 62, 67, 94, 95, 146, 148, 150, 151, 249, 252, 267; surveying of, 25, 29, 76, 286n11; Forsyth mission to, 118, 154, 157, 158, 160, 161, 164; trade between India and, 144-45, 164. See also Hamid, Abdul; Singh, Nain
Yarkand River, 151
Yarlung River, 123, 210-11, 243
Yasin, 85, 87, 90, 97, 146, 165, 166, 261
Yembi, 133, 134
Younghusband, Francis, 80, 297n89
Younghusband military expedition, 10, 139, 187, 206, 234, 237, 238, 239, 272, 273
Yule, Sir Henry, 38, 82-83, 125, 126, 127, 260, 261, 263, 264, 266
Yunnan Province, 237, 271
Yurungkash River, 162, 164
Yusufzai tribe, 85

Zayul River (Lohit Brahmaputra), 137-38, 140, 236, 239
Zebak, 88, 89

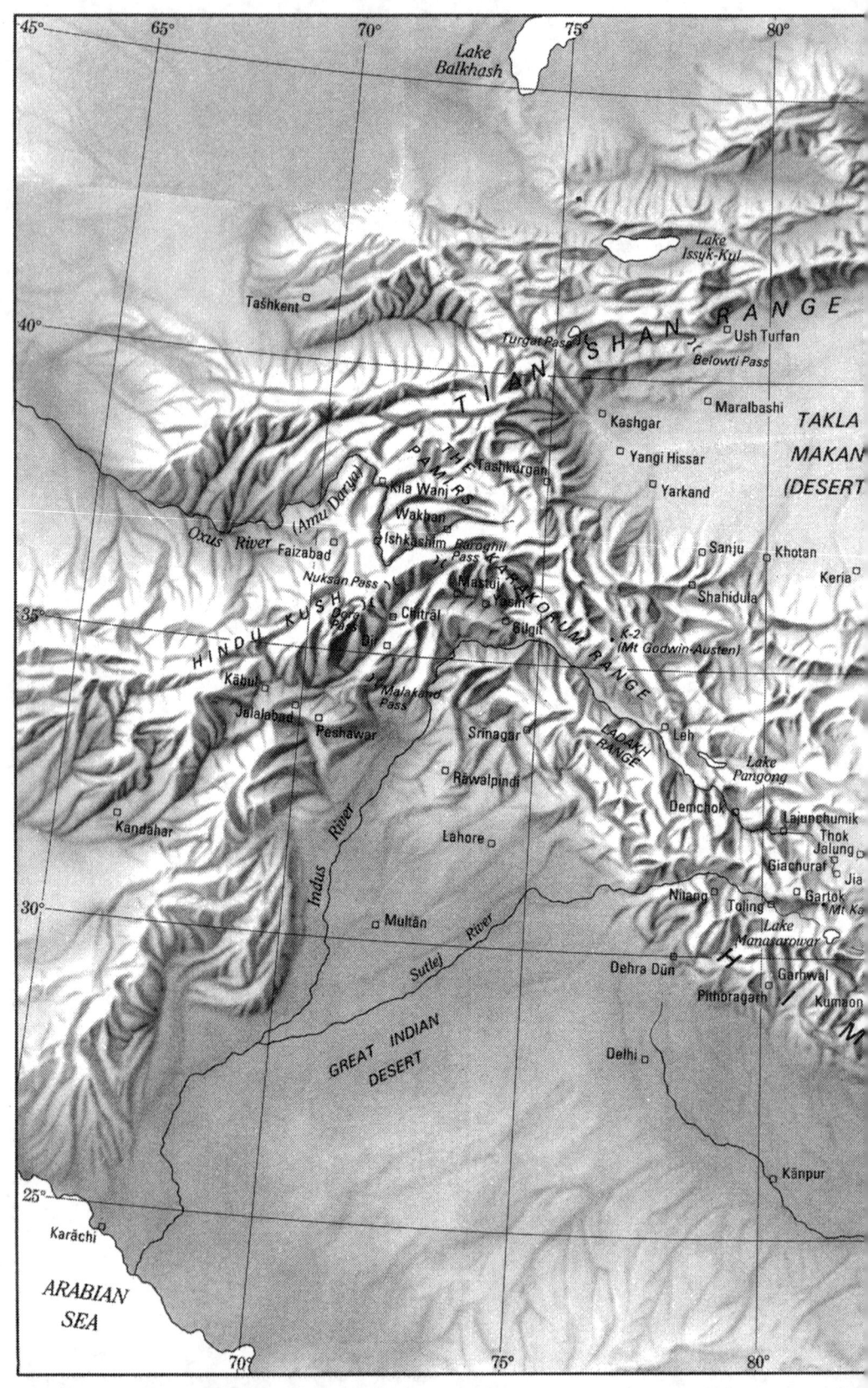

www.ingramcontent.com/pod-product-compliance
Lightning Source LLC
Chambersburg PA
CBHW070335240426
43665CB00045B/2019